Celebrating First Nations Languages and Language Learning in Australian Schools

This book introduces key underlying principles for teaching First Nations languages and language learners in schools across a range of contexts. It takes a comprehensive approach covering traditional languages, new languages, and English.

At a critical time for Indigenous languages across the globe, the United Nations Decade of Indigenous Languages (2022–2032) draws attention to the endangerment of these languages and advocates for the role of education to preserve and revitalise Indigenous languages. At the same time, many new language varieties spoken by Indigenous peoples often remain unrecognised in education systems, and their English language learning needs are left unaddressed. This book provides crucial information to enhance the reader's knowledge of these critical issues in language and education with a view to promote future action. The chapters showcase the advocacy, activism, and allyship for First Nations languages and language learners undertaken by educators, education systems, and researchers in Australia. With a practical focus, this book illustrates innovative and contemporary approaches to language learning for First Nations students; educators can use this text to guide and develop language-learning approaches in their respective contexts.

This is a foundational resource for both Indigenous and non-Indigenous teachers and aspiring teachers alike, and all education professionals who appreciate the fundamental importance of language in education.

Carly Steele is a non-Indigenous applied linguist and qualified teacher with experience in diverse educational contexts. She holds the position of Senior Lecturer and Master of Education course coordinator in the School of Education at Curtin University, Perth. Her research focuses on culturally and linguistically responsive pedagogies.

Robyn Ober is a Mamu/Djirribal woman from North Queensland. She is the Indigenous research practice leader at Batchelor Institute. Her research focus and expertise is on both-ways pedagogy, working to combine Indigenous and non-Indigenous ways of knowing, being, and learning in teaching practice and research.

Rhonda Oliver has researched extensively in the areas of second language and dialect acquisition, and task-based language learning. Her recent work includes studies within Australian Aboriginal education settings. She co-edited the award-winning textbook *Indigenous Education in Australia: Learning and Teaching for Deadly Futures*.

Celebrating First Nations Languages and Language Learning in Australian Schools

Stories Across Generations of Language Activism, Advocacy and Allyship

Edited by Carly Steele, Robyn Ober, and Rhonda Oliver

LONDON AND NEW YORK

Designed cover image: Jacqueline Hunter

First published 2025
by Routledge
4 Park Square, Milton Park, Abingdon, Oxon OX14 4RN

and by Routledge
605 Third Avenue, New York, NY 10158

Routledge is an imprint of the Taylor & Francis Group, an informa business

© 2025 selection and editorial matter, Carly Steele, Robyn Ober and Rhonda Oliver; individual chapters, the contributors

The right of Carly Steele, Robyn Ober and Rhonda Oliver to be identified as the authors of the editorial material, and of the authors for their individual chapters, has been asserted in accordance with sections 77 and 78 of the Copyright, Designs and Patents Act 1988.

All rights reserved. No part of this book may be reprinted or reproduced or utilised in any form or by any electronic, mechanical, or other means, now known or hereafter invented, including photocopying and recording, or in any information storage or retrieval system, without permission in writing from the publishers.

The designs, concepts and language used in Chapter 3 embed cultural concepts and law that are owned by the Warlpiri people of Yuendumu, Lajamanu, Willowra and Nyirrpi, and Yolŋu people of Milingimbi and Yirrkala in the Northern Territory, Australia under Indigenous Cultural Intellectual Property (ICIP). The creation of this chapter has followed the cultural protocols of informed consent, cultural integrity, and attribution to Warlpiri and Yolŋu people of Yuendumu, Nyirrpi, Milingimbi and Yirrkala. Using this knowledge (words, content, concepts) for any purpose without consultation with Warlpiri or Yolŋu people may breach the customary laws, as well as copyright and moral rights under the *Copyright Act 1968* (Australian Commonwealth). All requests for reproduction or communication should be made to Routledge Publishers.

Trademark notice: Product or corporate names may be trademarks or registered trademarks, and are used only for identification and explanation without intent to infringe.

British Library Cataloguing-in-Publication Data
A catalogue record for this book is available from the British Library

ISBN: 9781032577975 (hbk)
ISBN: 9781032577968 (pbk)
ISBN: 9781003441021 (ebk)

DOI: 10.4324/9781003441021

Typeset in Times New Roman
by KnowledgeWorks Global Ltd.

Dedication

To the authors of this volume, thank you for your generosity in sharing your stories of activism for First Nations languages and language learning in Australian schools. Your work is impacting the lives of many children and shaping the future of education. Without you and your exceptional contributions, this book would not be possible.—Carly

I dedicate this book to the late Dr. Jeanie Bell, a Jagera and Dulingbara linguist who introduced me to the world of Indigenous Australian Languages through her passion and commitment to strengthen, sustain, and maintain Aboriginal and Torres Islander languages through education and research.—Robyn

For the staff and students of Wongutha CAPS and especially 'our Kimberley son', Kostya Daylight. Thank you for your generosity and for sharing your language and culture. You have impacted my life, and that of my family, in so many ways. I have learnt so much along the way and I will remain forever grateful.—Rhonda

Contents

List of Contributors	*x*
Acknowledgement to Country	*xvii*
About the Cover Artwork	*xviii*

Introduction   1
CARLY STEELE, ROBYN OBER, AND RHONDA OLIVER

PART I
Contexts, Theories, Principles, Practices, and Protocols for Language Learning and Teaching in Schools   9

1 **Language Learning in Schools: Contexts, Theories, and Practice**   11
RHONDA OLIVER, CARLY STEELE, ROBYN OBER, AND LYNETTE GORDON

2 **Consent, Copyright, Consultation, Collaboration, and Co-design: Principles and Protocols for Developing School Language Programs**   27
VINCENT BACKHAUS, MIKE EXELL, AND GRAEME GOWER

PART II
Learning and Teaching Traditional Aboriginal and Torres Strait Islander Languages in Schools   39

3 **Teaching Aboriginal Languages as First Languages in the Northern Territory: Reflections of Educators in the Warlpiri Triangle and Yolŋu Communities**   41
ELIZABETH MILMILANY, BARBARA MARTIN NAPANANGKA, MERRKIYAWUY GANAMBARR, FIONA GIBSON NAPALJARRI, EMMA BROWNE, AND MELANIE WILKINSON

4 Teaching First Nations Languages in Queensland Schools   66
   DES CRUMP, LARENA THOMPSON, NAOMI FILLMORE,
   AND SAMANTHA DISBRAY

5 Western Australia Department of Education, Aboriginal
   Languages Teaching Training Course   81
   LOLA JONES, COLEEN SHERRATT, DEBBIE O'HARA, COCO YU,
   AND JUDITH BIRCHALL

6 The Journey to the Opening of Gumbaynggirr Giingana
   Freedom School   96
   CLARK WEBB

PART III
Aboriginal and Torres Strait Islander Contact
Languages in Education   107

7 The Diverse Indigenous Creole Languages and First
   Nations Language Repertoires in Queensland,
   with Information for Educators   109
   DENISE ANGELO, CARLY STEELE, BERNADINE YEATMAN,
   AND ALLAN YEATMAN

8 Kriol in the Northern Territory   136
   RIKKE L. BUNDGAARD-NIELSEN, BRETT J. BAKER,
   AND JOCELYN E. UIBO

9 Aboriginal English in Education   152
   IAN MALCOLM, PATRICIA KÖNIGSBERG, AND GLENYS COLLARD

PART IV
Learning and Teaching the Curriculum through
Aboriginal and Torres Strait Islander Languages   171

10 Gija Curriculum at Purnululu School   173
   SOPHIA MUNG, LIBBY LEE-HAMMOND, AND RHONDA OLIVER

11 Content Language Integrated Learning (CLIL) for Learning
   Aboriginal and Torres Strait Islander Languages   184
   HELEN CD MCCARTHY, JACQUELINE HUNTER, RUSSELL CROSS,
   AND RHONDA OLIVER

PART V
Learning, Teaching, and Assessing Learning in Standard Australian English for Speakers of Aboriginal and Torres Strait Islander Languages   197

12 **Aboriginal and Torres Strait Islander Students' Language and Learning through a Both Ways Approach**   199
   ROBYN OBER

13 **Aboriginal and Torres Strait Islander Students' Language Learning for Literacy Development**   212
   DEBRA HANNAGAN AND GRACE LEWIS

14 **Understanding the EAL/D Extra: Assessing English as an Additional Language or Dialect in First Nations Contexts**   228
   DENISE ANGELO, CATHERINE HUDSON, AND SUBERIA BOWIE

   Conclusion   248
   CARLY STEELE, ROBYN OBER, AND RHONDA OLIVER

   Index   *252*

List of Contributors

Denise Angelo is a non-Indigenous researcher and teacher based at the Australian National University. She works with diverse First Nations communities and peoples and with schools on the many facets of contemporary Aboriginal and Torres Strait Islander language contexts, including teaching and learning traditional languages, recognising creole languages and Indigenised Englishes, and supporting English as an Additional Language/Dialect.

Vincent Backhaus is a Kalkadoon, Kiwai, and Malaita man with familial connections to Gimuy region. He is a Research Fellow in the Cairns Institute, James Cook University. He is also Manager Research Training and Ethics for the Centre of Excellence (COE) for Indigenous and Environmental Histories and Futures (CIEHF). Vincent's work covers Reef Traditional Owner research across Sea Country, Learning, and Traditional Knowledge. His research interests encompass Learning, Knowledge Translation, and Theory of Knowledge.

Brett J. Baker is an Associate Professor in Linguistics at The University of Melbourne, with around 30 years of experience working closely with Indigenous people in the Roper River region and Numbulwar. He has published books and articles on grammatical topics in Australian languages and engaged in grassroots maintenance and revival efforts in regional Aboriginal language centres.

Judith Birchall is a Yamatji woman who is born and raised in Boorloo (Perth). She enrolled in the Aboriginal Languages Teacher Training (ALTT) course in 2012 and graduated as a Noongar language specialist in 2014. Judith currently works 3 days teaching Noongar language in primary school and works 2 days as Senior Consultant for Aboriginal Languages with the Department of Education, WA.

Suberia Bowie is a Maluilgal, Badhu women from the Torres Strait Region in far north Queensland. She also has connections to the Wuthathi tribe on Cape York Peninsula area. Suberia has worked in schools as a teacher and leadership positions for over 20 years mainly in the Torres Strait and Cairns region. Her key current role is to lead the Traditional Language and Culture curriculum and Cultural Capability within Tagai State College. Suberia has always been very passionate about improving teaching and learning within schools through utilising English as an Additional Language practices so students can access the curriculum.

List of Contributors xi

Emma Browne is a non-Indigenous researcher and language worker who has worked with educators teaching Aboriginal languages in schools in Central Australia and the Barkly region since 2013.

Rikke L. Bundgaard-Nielsen is a Danish psycholinguist and Senior Lecturer at The University of Melbourne. She studies first and second language acquisition and has worked with speakers of a range of traditional and new Indigenous Australian languages. She is interested in how sharing knowledge about the shape and acquisition of Indigenous languages can improve educational outcomes for Indigenous students.

Glenys Collard is a Nyungar woman from the South-West of Western Australia and matriarch within her nuclear family of over 400 people. She is an educator, writer, and Honorary Research Fellow in Linguistics at the University of Western Australia. Glenys has pioneered the original Nyungar Language Project and plays a key part in continuing to develop understandings in Aboriginal English through the West Australian linguistic research. She has held a range of government positions, including in the West Australian Aboriginal Legal Service and Department of Education.

Russell Cross is based in the Melbourne Graduate School of Education at the University of Melbourne and is coordinator of the Master of Education (Content and Language Integrated Learning) program. His background is in bilingual education and immersion, with his research focusing on the social, cultural, historical, and political nature of the knowledge base that informs second language teacher education.

Des Crump is a Gamilaroi man from South-West Queensland with a teaching background of 22 years in QED. He was in the first intake of Masters of Indigenous Languages Education (MILE) at University of Sydney in 2006. He has worked with language revitalisation in schools for over 20 years and was on the Advisory Committee for the Australian Curriculum, Assessment and Reporting Authority's (ACARA) Framework for Aboriginal and Torres Strait Islander Languages and the earlier Queensland P-10 Aboriginal and Torres Strait Islander Languages Syllabus. Since 2002, Des has worked with the Gunggari language community at Mitchell, built on his relationships with community Elders established at QED. Des has a great-great-grandfather from the Maranoa region, who was born near Mitchell in 1850s; however, his matrilineal line is Gamilaroi and considers Gunggari as a neighbouring language. Bearing this in mind, he has always been respectful and mindful that Gunggari language belongs to the Gunggari community, and his role is one of support.

Samantha Disbray is a non-Indigenous linguist. She lived for many years in Alice Springs, learning from and working together with Warumungu language activists, Warlpiri educators and Pintupi-Luritja people at Papunya, with whom she continues to document and celebrate their bilingual illustrated literature. Now at the University of Queensland, Samantha works closely with Des Crump and other Indigenous colleagues, in particular Robert McLellan, to develop and deliver a Graduate Certificate in Indigenous Language Revitalisation.

Mike Exell has worked with Aboriginal students for many years, as a research assistant, youth mentor, and teacher across Western Australia in the Goldfields, Kimberley, and Pilbara regions. Mike has published about language and language programs inclusive of Aboriginal English in educational and community settings.

Naomi Fillmore is a non-Indigenous applied linguist and education specialist, interested in the role of languages in early education policy and practice. She researches culturally and linguistically sustaining education policy and pedagogies for multilingual children at the University of Queensland, and has a background working with government and non-government education organisations in Australia and abroad.

Merrkiyawuy Ganambarr is a Yolŋu woman and the co-principal of Yirrkala School. She has played an important role in the bilingual education movement in Arnhem Land working with Yolŋu Elders to develop both-ways learning and is a member of an Indigenous-academic collective that works with Macquarie University. Her vision is that every child is appreciated, and that every child knows that dreams are possible.

Lynette Gordon is a proud Gooniyandi and Jaru woman and she teaches a traditional language (Gooniyandi) to mostly Aboriginal students in a remote K–12 school in Western Australia. Lynette has been teaching Gooniyandi at this school for more than 7 years and working at the school for 13 years. She has strong cultural, familial, and ancestral relationships with the community in which she resides and teaches. In fact, the longevity of the Gooniyandi program can be attributed to her commitment to stay 'On Country' – her place of belonging.

Graeme Gower (PhD) is from Yawuru Country (Broome). He is an Associate Professor at Curtin University and is Project Lead of the On Country Teacher Education Training Program. Graeme has been actively involved in teaching and research in Aboriginal education for many years. His work includes ethical practices in Aboriginal research, developing and maintaining relationships with Aboriginal families and communities, implementing culturally responsive practices, and more recently, the On Country Teacher Education Program, and the transitioning of Aboriginal students from Year 12 to university, and post university in Western Australia.

Debra Hannagan is a non-Indigenous educator and applied linguist living on Djugun and Yawuru Country. She has over 20 years' experience working in the Kimberley and Goldfields regions of Western Australia as an early years teacher, a curriculum leader, and a language and literacy specialist and consultant. Debra is passionate about recognising, valuing, and promoting awareness of the linguistic strengths Aboriginal students bring to school.

Catherine Hudson is a non-Indigenous researcher and EAL/D specialist teacher based at the Australian National University. She researches EAL/D proficiency assessment which is inclusive of the language and learning needs of the full cohort of EAL/D learners, inclusive of Aboriginal and Torres Strait Islander EAL/D learners in their diverse language-learning contexts.

Jacqueline Hunter is a proud Bardi woman. She lives in the community of Ardiyooloon (One Arm Point) in the far north of Western Australia (WA). She has worked at the local school in her community for many years and is currently completing her Bachelor of Education.

Lola Jones is from Yinggarda Country (Carnarvon) and lived in Yawuru Country (Broome) for many years. She is now located in Noongar Baladong Country (Toodyay/Northam). She is a teacher-linguist and has worked with Aboriginal language speakers and teachers in communities across Western Australia. She is the Principal Consultant Aboriginal Languages and since 1995 has led the Aboriginal languages initiative for the Department of Education, WA.

Patricia Königsberg works in the Department of Education, across Western Australia. She is a linguist, educator, and leading advocate for students who are learning in a language that is not their own. Since 1996, Patricia has worked closely with esteemed UWA Honorary Research Fellow Glenys Collard and Professor Ian Malcolm to initiate an English as an Additional Language or Dialect (EALD) practice, empowering Aboriginal and non-Aboriginal students and educators to value and recognise Aboriginal English as an essential linguistic resource to educational success through two-way learning.

Libby Lee-Hammond has been principal of Boornoolooloo (Purnululu) Aboriginal Independent Community School for four years. She has worked closely with Sophia, Gija Educators – Aboriginal Teaching Assistants (ATAs), curriculum consultants, linguists, and teachers at the school, as well as the local community to develop a curriculum and pedagogy that is most appropriate for the students at this school.

Grace Lewis (nee Doyle) is a proud Bardi woman. She was born and raised on Yamtaji Country in the Geraldton area. Grace is a qualified teacher who has worked in many schools throughout the Kimberley for 30 years. She started her teaching career on her mother's country on the Dampier Peninsula at Christ the King Catholic School in Djarindjin/Lombadina in 1993. Grace recently returned to the school in 2021 where she met Debra; together they embarked on an amazing two-way learning journey with the Bardi Baawa (Bardi Children) in the classroom and On Booroo-Country.

Ian Malcolm, Emeritus Professor of Applied Linguistics at Edith Cowan University Western Australia, is widely recognised for his longstanding collaborative contributions to research into Aboriginal English. He has been influential in bringing Aboriginal English research to international attention and, in association with Glenys Collard and Patricia Konigsberg, in developing policies and resources for two-way bidialectal education.

Helen C.D. McCarthy has worked with and learned from the Warnindilyakwa, Yolngu, Nyungar, and Wongi – First Nations peoples of Australia – across primary, secondary, and tertiary settings. For over 40 years, her interest has been in bidialectal approaches for the development of holistic, emergent curriculum frameworks that venerate Indigenous epistemological traditions and ways of knowing.

Elizabeth Milmilany is a Wangurri woman and qualified teacher who retired after working for 40 years in the Bilingual program at Milingimbi school, including 11 years as the Teacher-linguist. She then returned to work part-time for almost another decade as a senior advisor to support the ongoing successful delivery of bilingual, bicultural education at the school.

Sophia Mung is a Jarlaloo woman from Gija Country where Boornoolooloo school is located. In close collaboration with Libby, she is part of the leadership team at the school and, in particular, she leads the Gija language and culture program.

Fiona Gibson Napaljarri is a Warlpiri educator from Nyirrpi community. She is passionate about bilingual and bicultural education and campaigned to establish Nyirrpi's first school in the 1980s. Studying through the Remote Aboriginal Teacher Education Program (RATE), Fiona is a fully qualified teacher and member of Nyirrpi school's Local Engagement and Decision-making (LEaD) committee. Fiona is a founding member of the Warlpiri Education Training Trust and continues in her role as a WETT Advisory Committee member.

Barbara Martin Napanangka is a Warlpiri teacher and mentor, who began her career in 1981 and has worked in schools in both Lajamanu and Yuendumu as a literacy worker and teacher. She graduated from the Batchelor Institute Remote Aboriginal Teacher Education Program (RATE) and became a senior teacher and cultural advisor for Yuendumu School. Barbara has championed Warlpiri language and culture education for over 40 years and was instrumental in developing the Warlpiri Theme Cycle, a local curriculum for Warlpiri schools. She is a founding member and chairperson of the Warlpiri Education Training Trust (WETT) which advises on and funds educational projects in the Warlpiri communities and works as the Cultural Advisor to the Community Development Unit at the Central Land Council, teaching Warlpiri language to non-Indigenous staff.

Robyn Ober is a Mamu/Djirribal woman from North Queensland and a Lead Researcher at Batchelor Institute, Northern Territory. She has worked at Batchelor Institute for over three decades developing both-ways pedagogy which combines Indigenous and non-Indigenous ways of knowing, being, and learning in teaching practice and in research. She also works in the fields of Indigenous educational leadership and Indigenous research methodologies.

List of Contributors xv

Debbie O'Hara is a descendant of the Meriam people from the island of Mer in the Torres Strait, North Queensland, and now resides on Wadjak Noongar Country (Perth). She holds a Bachelor of Education and has worked with the Department of Education for nearly 30 years, serving in various roles including Aboriginal and Islander Education Officer (AIEO), Primary School Teacher, Aboriginal Education Consultant, and currently, Senior Consultant for Aboriginal Languages. Since joining the Aboriginal Languages team, Debbie has developed a keen interest in linguistics, particularly to support her learning of her ancestral language, Meriam Mir.

Rhonda Oliver has researched extensively and is widely published in the areas of second language and dialect acquisition, age differences, and task-based language learning. Over the years, many of the participants in her research have been children and adolescents learning a second language or dialect, a heritage language, and in CLIL and TBLT contexts, particularly within Australian Aboriginal education settings. Her extensive publication record includes her award-winning textbook *Indigenous Education in Australia Learning and Teaching for Deadly Futures*.

Coleen Sherratt is a Noongar Wadjak woman from Boorloo (Perth area). She enrolled in the Aboriginal Languages Teacher Training (ALTT) course in 2001 and graduated as a Noongar language teacher in 2002. She is currently the Principal Education Officer for Aboriginal Languages with the Department of Education, WA.

Carly Steele is a non-Indigenous applied linguist and a qualified teacher with over 12 years' experience in diverse educational contexts across Australia including urban cities, and rural and remote communities. She holds the position of Senior Lecturer and Master of Education course coordinator in the School of Education at Curtin University, Perth. Her research aims to promote culturally and linguistically responsive teaching and assessment practices.

Larena Thompson and her brother Henry Thompson teach Yagara language in schools and Community learning settings in the Ipswich region of greater Brisbane, their traditional Country of Yagara people. Larena's daughters have also joined the growing teaching team and will support school programs as they develop.

Jocelyn E. Uibo is a Nunggubuyu/Estonian early childhood educator who has taught in early primary school and preschools in both remote and urban contexts in the Northern Territory. She grew up in Numbulwar, Batchelor, and Darwin, where she currently lives with her family.

Clark Webb is a Gumbaynggirr and Bundjalung man living in the heart of Gumbaynggirr country. As an adult learner of Gumbaynggirr who has become a fluent speaker, language is the main driver in establishing Bularri Muurlay Nyanggan Aboriginal Corporation (BMNAC) and the Gumbaynggirr Giingana Freedom School (GGFS).

Melanie Wilkinson is a linguist who began working with Yolŋu and their languages in 1980. She recently retired, after 32 years, from the NT Department of Education where she worked supporting school programs, regional language networks, and professional learning in East Arnhem Schools. She supported the gathering, transcribing, and translation of the Milingimbi material and introductory notes on the Yolŋu language ecology.

Allan Yeatman is a Yidinji man from the Yarrabah Aboriginal Community in far north Queensland. He also has connections to the Kuku-Njunkul, Kuku-Djangan, and Kuku-Yalanji tribes. Allan has long-term experience working at the local school. He has also been involved in researching the local language situation, especially the local creole language – Yarrie Lingo/Yarrabah Creole, and was part of the team that developed the famous At Da Crick community vernacular language poster.

Bernadine Yeatman is a Yidinji woman from the Yarrabah Aboriginal Community in far north Queensland. She is a fully trained and practising teacher and has been working in the field of education for over 20 years. Bernadine also conducts key language research for her community as well as raising awareness and achieving recognition for Yarrie Lingo/Yarrabah Creole – the local creole language of the Yarrabah speech community.

Acknowledgement to Country

This book has been collectively written on the unceded lands of many First Nations, and we acknowledge that it always was, and always will be, the lands belonging to the First Peoples of Australia. We pay our respects to their ancestors, current and future generations, and walk alongside you in the fight for educational justice. We thank you for sharing your languages with us, and with children, youth, and adults across the nation through education.

About the Cover Artwork

Our Country Library by Jacqueline Hunter

Jacqueline Hunter is a proud Bardi woman. She lives in the community of Ardiyooloon (One Arm Point) in the far north of Western Australia (WA). She has worked at the local school in her community for many years and is currently completing her Bachelor of Education at Curtin University.

Jacqueline Hunter's explanation about her artwork, *Our Country Library*:

Our Country Library is a painting of a landscape representing the origins of Aboriginal languages. It symbolises the connection between Aboriginal languages, culture, and the land. The landscape depicted is of the Dampier Peninsula. This place is not my Country but is a place significant for language and cultural learning that is next to my Country. It is a peaceful place where language meetings are held with the surrounding language groups. The lines and border around the edges symbolise the boundaries of the Country and the different tribes and clans. The fire in the painting represents the communal gatherings where language and culture are shared and taught. The painting includes symbols like spears, boomerangs, and footprints which signify cultural and linguistic connections to land. I choose this because getting back on Country is crucial for language preservation and revitalisation.

Introduction

Carly Steele, Robyn Ober, and Rhonda Oliver

Introduction

It has been an honour, a privilege, and a deeply humbling experience to edit this crucially important book, in the current United Nations International Decade of Indigenous Languages (2022–2032). Through this decade, the UN seeks to draw global attention to the critical endangerment of Indigenous languages globally and promote preservation and revitalisation efforts for these languages (UNESCO, n.d.). It highlights and advocates for the critical role that education and schools must play in meeting these goals. To this end, this book showcases the important work that education systems, schools, and educators have been collectively undertaking in their efforts to support First Nations languages and language learners in Australia. Their stories of advocacy, activism, and allyship for First Nations languages and language learners in education have inspired us, and on occasion, brought tears to our eyes as we recognise the depth of the courage and strength required to undertake this work and to dedicate their lives to improving the quality of education in Australia, as those in this book have done.

Historical context

Before British invasion, it was predicted there were more than 300 languages and over 700 dialects of these languages spoken by the traditional owners and custodians of Australia (Dixon, 2019). Moreover, the number of First Nations languages being recognised is constantly increasing as our knowledge grows (Tudor-Smith et al., 2024). However, as a direct consequence of the ongoing process of colonialisation since 1788, these languages have been before forcibly silenced as an intentional strategy of colonial powers for the assimilation of First Nations peoples and even, as argued by Patrick Wolfe (2006), for their eradication. Now sadly only about 12 Aboriginal and Torres Strait Islander languages in Australia continue to be learnt as a child's first language (DoITRDC, AIATSIS, & ANU, 2020). The work that the authors of this book have been doing in schools over many years, and decades, seeks to redress this for the future generations by not only ensuring the continuation of Aboriginal and Torres Strait Islander languages, but also through recognising the language varieties that do exist, highlighting the ways that educators can respond with culturally and linguistically proactive educational practices. In this section of the introduction, we provide a brief overview of the historical context to make clear the need for this work, and the key role that languages play in education and how educators can support First Nations languages and language learning.

As described in Chapters 7 and 8, there has been a long history of linguistic change in Australia; however, the deleterious policy and practices that have been followed since the beginning of colonisation have had the greatest impact on Aboriginal and Torres Strait Islander languages. Moreover, schools have played an instrumental role by banning the use of Aboriginal and Torres Strait Islander languages, which have in some cases continued to be actively discouraged even up until the present day. There have, however, been pockets of progress that have positively shaped the future.

In the 1970s, the progressive politics of the Whitlam government advocated for Indigenous self-determination, and bilingual education was established initially in five schools in the Northern Territory (Oldfield & Lo Bianco, 2019), which was expanded until the hugely damaging first four hours in English was implemented in 2008 (Devlin, 2017). Yet, in spite of these policies that sought to subjugate First Nations languages and language learners, through the activism of Aboriginal educators and their communities, the learning and teaching of traditional languages has continued. This is described by the Warlpiri and Yolŋu educators in Chapter 3.

Progress did continue through the 1980s and 1990s. First this occurred with the introduction of the Australian Languages Policy (Lo Bianco, 1987) and next through the recognition of Aboriginal English as an official dialect in 1990. The National Policy on Languages represented 'the first multilingual declaration and Australia's first formal Commonwealth policy on language' (Oldfield & Lo Bianco, 2019, p. 170) and an 'unprecedented recognition' for First Nations languages (McKay, 2011, p. 88).

However, this period was followed by a sharp turn towards English-literacy and an almost sole focus on English to the exclusion of other languages. This was in spite of the importance of language for cultural identity, academic success, and general wellbeing clearly understood at this time (Angelo et al., 2019). From the 2000s onwards in what has been referred to as the 'English as literacy' period (Lo Bianco, 2016), national testing regimes have strongly shaped both the content of schooling and how students are taught (Steele et al., 2022).

Yet the resilience of First Nations peoples and their languages prevail. Supported by global Indigenous political movements and language advocacy, as well as changing societal attitudes and growing awareness of past injustices, language revitalisation efforts have grown in strength and gained traction in education as well as in mainstream society (Steele & Oliver, 2024). In Australia, this has been reflected in the establishment of the Framework for Aboriginal Languages and Torres Strait Islander languages (ACARA, 2015); the 2017 NAIDOC theme 'Our Languages Matter' – a precursor to the UN International Year of Indigenous Languages in 2019; and now, the International Decade of Indigenous Languages (2022–2032). It also can be tied to the United Nations Declaration on the Rights of Indigenous

Peoples (2007) that states the 'right to establish and control education systems in their own language... in their own culture' (Article 14). Although passed in 2007, Australia did not become a signatory until 2009 (Oldfield & Lo Bianco, 2019, p. 168).

Increasingly, education systems, educators, parents, and children are recognising the importance of Aboriginal languages and there is a desire to learn about the languages, cultures, and histories of the First peoples of this country. For example, in Western Australia, over 10,000 students currently learn an Aboriginal language at school, which is an increase of 4,000 students in just two years (Bourke, 2022). This growth has been driven by Department of Education programs to train Aboriginal language teachers and help to develop resources for language teaching described in Chapter 5. Such initiatives are supported nation-wide, and upon election the Albanese government pledged $14 million to introduce more First Nations teachers into schools (Dhanji, 2022).

There has been further support for the teaching of First Nations languages through curriculum initiatives. In May 2022, in response to the first significant curriculum review undertaken, Version 9.0 of the Australian Curriculum was released. Whilst much of the review focused on 'decluttering' the curriculum, the Aboriginal and Torres Strait Islander histories and cultures cross-curriculum priorities were significantly enhanced, reflecting the increased desire to learn about the languages, cultures, and histories of the First peoples of this country. And very recently, a new Framework for Aboriginal Languages and Torres Strait Islander Languages has been released.

Yet, this recent progress is clouded by the outcome of the failed referendum that sought to recognise First Nations peoples in the Australian constitution and constitutionally enshrine a First Nations voice to parliament. Thus, the present time represents a significant juncture in our nation's history. Clearly there is a need to continue our advocacy, activism, and allyship that brought the country to a point where constitutional reform was a possibility. It is a time to renew our courage, conviction, and commitment to the future of Australia that we would like to see for our children and for generations to come. As indicated by the 2024 NAIDOC theme, it is time to 'Keep the fire burning!' (NAIDOC, 2024).

Key terminology

In this book, we embrace the learning and teaching of traditional languages (e.g., Warlpiri, Gija, Bardi Jawi, Yagara, Gunggari, and Gumbaynggirr), contact languages – such as creoles (e.g., Kriol and other varieties of Indigenous creoles) and dialects (e.g., Aboriginal English), and standard Australian English. This diversity is reflected in the terminology we use. You may have noticed that in this introduction we have used the term First Nations peoples to describe Aboriginal and Torres Strait Islander peoples. This is our preference, but at other times, we also use the terms 'First Peoples', 'Aboriginal peoples', and 'Aboriginal and Torres Strait Islander peoples'. These terms are sometimes used to promote the readability of the text, or at times, they may reflect the source of the information. We recognise that there are a variety of preferences across the nation. These preferences can be personal or may reflect the histories connected to peoples and places. Throughout the book, the reader will encounter a range of terms used which will reflect the choices made by the authors and the history of the languages, peoples, and places that they write about. Most commonly, it is preferred to use the language name and/or nation specific to the peoples being referred to. For example, Warlpiri, Yolŋu, Gija, Bardi Jawi, Yagara, Gunggari, and Gumbaynggirr.

We also use the plural 'peoples' or 'First Nations' to indicate that Aboriginal and Torres Strait Islander peoples are not one, but are many peoples each with their own languages, histories, and cultural practices. In this way, we recognise the diversity that exists across the country. Knowledge about First Nations languages helps to make this diversity evident to non-Indigenous Australians; the linguistic differences between two neighbouring First Nations languages are similar to the differences between German and French, whilst the differences between Aboriginal languages in the north of Australia (non-Pama-Nyungan languages) and those in the south (Pama-Nyungan languages) can be as great as Chinese and English (Dixon, 2019).

In this book we give due respect to the languages of the First Nations peoples and use the full names of these languages, avoiding the use of acronyms. Once more, however, we understand the different views and are respectful of the language use of our contributors.

Outline of the book

This book focuses on the learning and teaching of First Nations languages in Australian schools for the benefit of Indigenous and non-Indigenous children and is also about teaching First Nations children for whom standardised Australian English (SAE) is not their first language or dialect. There are five sections, and in the following we provide a brief overview of each section.

The first section provides key underlying principles for teaching First Nations languages and language learners in Australian schools. The first chapter introduces diverse language learning contexts, theories of language learning, and the different models for language learning and teaching in schools, whilst the second focuses specifically on the principles and protocols for developing school language programs for First Nations languages.

These principles and protocols are reinforced through the illustrations of practice presented in section two. There are four chapters in this section covering the Northern Territory (NT), Queensland (Qld), Western Australia (WA), and New South Wales (NSW). The educators in this section showcase their ways of learning and teaching traditional Aboriginal languages across a range of different learner pathways.

Section three shifts from a focus on traditional language contexts to exploring the learning and teaching of Indigenous contact languages. Again, with a focus on the varieties of contact languages that exist across Qld, the NT, and WA, the first two chapters describe the development of Indigenous creole languages in Qld and

Kriol in the NT, whilst the third chapter describes Aboriginal English in WA. All three chapters address ways education systems, schools, and educators can respond effectively when teaching SAE.

Section four focuses on traditional languages and demonstrates the ways First Nations languages can be learned through integrated curriculum approaches, such as cross-curricular programs (Chapter 10) and Content Language Integrated Learning (CLIL) (Chapter 11).

Lastly, section five is comprised of three chapters that describe ways to teach and assess speakers of Aboriginal and Torres Strait Islander languages who are learning SAE. The first chapter offers a broad introduction to children's social, cultural, and linguistic backgrounds, whilst the second delves more deeply into the how and why of literacy instruction before the last chapter presents ways of assessing EAL/D learning for speakers of First Nations languages.

The authors of this book

This book demonstrates the highly collaborative and multidisciplinary nature of the work that is undertaken in the field of language learning and teaching. The authors of this book represent language teachers, linguists, applied linguists, educational leaders at the school level, and those who are employed by various departments of education to lead language learning and teaching at a system level. Without this important collaboration across all levels of education, change would not be possible.

Sadly, however, for those of us who work in this space and who continue to advocate for meaningful educational progress for First Nations languages, language teaching, and for learners, we still find our voices silenced in the dominant educational discourses that represent monolingual policies and practices. This book, therefore, represents an opportunity to hear the 'on the ground' experiences of educators, to better understand the diverse contexts and the situational complexities, and to see what decades of hard work has achieved in Australian schools – with the aim to ensure that this progress is not only continued, but expanded upon.

Not only is the book a testament to the collaboration across disciplinary fields and educational hierarchies, but it is also the product of the relationships built between First Nations and non-Indigenous educators, researchers, and authors. There are 40 authors in the edited volume. Of these authors, 23 authors identify as Aboriginal and/or Torres Strait Islander people, representing slightly over half of the authorship. Likewise, half of the 14 chapters are led by First Nations authors. Significantly, there are three chapters that are authored only by First Nations peoples. Chapter 5 is authored by the team at the Department of Education WA, who lead the Aboriginal Languages Teaching Training Course, whilst Chapter 6 and Chapter 12 are solo-authored by Clark Webb and Robyn Ober, respectively. We hope this is just the beginning, and that the issues of representation that Aileen Moreton-Robinson (2004), amongst others, speak of can be increasingly addressed in academic knowledge and educational contexts.

References

Angelo, D., O'Shannessy, C., Simpson, J., Kral, I., Smith, H., & Browne, E. (2019). *Well-being and Indigenous Language Ecologies (WILE): A strengths-based approach: Literature review, National Indigenous Languages Report, Pillar 2*. https://dspace-prod.anu.edu.au/server/api/core/bitstreams/7e3ec65b-58a2-4e1f-a3e5-e779039469a8/content

Australian Curriculum Assessment and Reporting Authority (ACARA). (2015). *Framework for Aboriginal languages and Torres Strait Islander languages*.

Bourke, K. (2022, July 4). *Indigenous languages being taught to 10,000 West Australian school kids*. ABC Online. https://www.abc.net.au/news/2022-07-04/wa-students-learn-indigenous-languages-at-record-rate/101194088

Dhanji, K. (2022, March 29). *Labor's $14 million plan to expand Indigenous languages education in schools*. SBS News. https://www.sbs.com.au/news/article/labors-14-million-plan-to-expand-indigenous-languages-education-in-schools/yx2nwmfux

Department of Infrastructure, Transport, Regional Development and Communications (DoITRDC), Australian Institute for Aboriginal and Torres Strait Islander Studies (AIATSIS), & Australian National University (ANU). (2020). *National Indigenous Languages Report (NILR)*. Australian Government. Available from https://www.arts.gov.au/sites/default/files/documents/1national-indigenous-languages-report-pdf-introduction.pdf

Devlin, B. C. (2017). Policy change in 2008: Evidence-based or a knee-jerk response? In B. C. Devlin, S. Disbray, & N. R. Friedman Devlin (Eds.), *History of bilingual education in the Northern Territory* (pp. 203–218). Springer.

Dixon, R. M. (2019). *Australia's original languages: An introduction*. Allen and Unwin.

Lo Bianco, J. (1987). *National policy on languages*. Australian Government Publishing Service.

Lo Bianco, J. (2016). Multicultural education in the Australian context: An historical Overview. In J. Lo Bianco & A. Bal (Eds.), *Learning from difference: Comparative accounts of multicultural education* (pp. 15–33). Multilingual Education 16, Springer International Publishing. https://doi.org/10.1007/978-3-319-26880-4_2

McKay, G. (2011). Policy and Indigenous languages in Australia. *Australian Review of Applied Linguistics, 34*(3), 297–319. https://doi.org/10.1075/aral.34.3.03mck

Moreton-Robinson, A. (2004). Whiteness, epistemology and Indigenous representation. In A. Moreton-Robinson (Ed.), *Whitening race: Essays in social and cultural criticism* (pp. 75–88). Aboriginal Studies Press.

NAIDOC. (2024). *2024 NAIDOC week them – 'Keep the fire burning! Blak, loud and proud'*. https://www.naidoc.org.au/news/2024-naidoc-week-theme-keep-fire-burning-blak-loud-and-proud

Oldfield, J., & Lo Bianco, J. (2019). A long unfinished struggle: Literacy and Indigenous cultural and language rights. In J. Rennie & H. Harper (Eds.), *Literacy education and Indigenous Australians* (pp. 165–184). Springer. https://doi.org/10.1007/978-981-13-8629-9_10

Steele, C., Dovchin, S., & Oliver, R. (2022). 'Stop measuring black kids with a white stick': Translanguaging for classroom assessment. *RELC Journal, 53*(2), 400–415. https://doi.org/10.1177/00336882221086307

Steele, C., & Oliver, R. (2024). Distraction in Australian language education policy: A call to re-centre language rights. *Current Issues in Language Planning*, 1–26. https://doi.org/10.1080/14664208.2024.2358273

Tudor-Smith, G., Williams, P., & Meakins, F. (2024). *Bina: First Nations languages, old and new*. Black Inc.

UNESCO. (n.d.). *Indigenous Languages Decade (2022-2032)*. https://www.unesco.org/en/decades/indigenous-languages

United Nations. (2007). *United Nations Declaration on the Rights of Indigenous Peoples*. https://www.un.org/esa/socdev/unpfii/documents/DRIPS_en.pdf

Wolfe, P. (2006). Settler colonialism and the elimination of the native. *Journal of Genocide Research, 8*(4), 387–409. https://doi.org/10.1080/14623520601056240

Part I
Contexts, Theories, Principles, Practices, and Protocols for Language Learning and Teaching in Schools

1 Language Learning in Schools
Contexts, Theories, and Practice

*Rhonda Oliver, Carly Steele, Robyn Ober,
and Lynette Gordon*

Who we are

The first three authors of this chapter are the editors of this book.

Rhonda Oliver's family have been in Australia since at least colonisation. She originally trained as a primary school teacher and then quickly moved into ESL teaching and worked in schools for more than a decade, before becoming an academic. She now works at Curtin University in the School of Education as a research professor.

Carly Steele is a non-Indigenous academic in the School of Education at Curtin University. Prior to joining academia, she worked as a teacher for 12 years in NSW, WA, NT, and Qld. Much of her teaching experience is in regional and remote parts of Australia serving First Nations communities.

Robyn Ober is a Mamu/Djirribal woman from North Queensland and a Lead Researcher at Batchelor Institute, Northern Territory. She has worked at Batchelor Institute for over three decades developing both-ways pedagogy which combines Indigenous and non-Indigenous ways of knowing, being and learning in teaching practice and in research. She also works in the fields of Indigenous educational leadership and Indigenous research methodologies.

Lynette Gordon is a proud Gooniyandi and Jaru woman and she teaches a traditional language (Gooniyandi) to mostly Aboriginal students in a remote K-12 school in Western Australia. Lynette has been teaching Gooniyandi at this school for more than 7 years and working at the school for 13 years. She has strong cultural, familial, and ancestral relationships with the community in which she resides and teaches. In fact, the longevity of the Gooniyandi program can be attributed to her commitment to stay 'On Country' – her place of belonging.

Language learning contexts

In Australia, First Nations peoples have diverse language and cultural backgrounds. They may speak Standard Australian English (SAE) – the language spoken by many non-Aboriginal people across the nation. Many also speak another dialect of English, namely Australian Aboriginal English (AAE). It is also a variety of English that differs from SAE phonetically, syntactically, semantically, and pragmatically. It is often spoken by Aboriginal and Torres Strait Islander peoples as a first language/dialect or what is often referred to as their 'mother tongue' or 'home language'. AAE is used to convey Aboriginal identity and cultural understandings and often serves as the lingua franca (i.e., the common language) for communicating with other Australian First Nations people. Others, especially those living in the north of Australia, may also speak a creole language, spelt 'Kriol' with localised varieties spoken. This language originated as a pidgin – a type of hybrid language that was used for communication during early contact between non-Aboriginal and Aboriginal peoples at the beginning of colonisation – but then evolved to become an important language, including a home language for many (also see Chapter 7, this volume). It contains both English and traditional language words and is structured grammatically in different ways to the English language (e.g., in English 'ed' is often used to mark past tense, but in Kriol 'bin' before the verb serves the same function). In addition to these languages and dialects, there are traditional languages such as Arrernte, Boon Wurrung, Wurendjeri, Gooniyandi, and Gija. At the beginning of colonisation, it is estimated that over 250 traditional languages were spoken across Australia. However, now only about 12 continue to be learnt as children's first languages.

Because of this diversity in language backgrounds, when First Nations children enter school there are various ways in which they may learn traditional Aboriginal and Torres Strait Islander languages which is described in the Australian curriculum (Australian Curriculum, Assessment and Reporting Authority [ACARA], n.d.-a). These contexts include:

- First Language Learner Pathway (L1)
- Language Revival Learner Pathway (LR)
- Second Language Learner Pathway (L2)

Whilst First Nations students may be learning traditional languages in any of these three pathways, non-Indigenous students will only learn in the language revival or second language learner pathways. In addition, there is also a significant proportion of Aboriginal and Torres Strait Islander students who are learning:

- English as an Additional Language/Dialect (EAL/D)

These pathways are outlined below:

First Language Learner Pathway (L1)

The locations for this teaching pathway are more likely to be remote communities with the students living 'On Country'. That is, the students are learning their first or home language on the traditional lands where it has been spoken for millennia. The students are taught this home language along with other curriculum (e.g., mathematics, science, health). It is akin to non-Aboriginal English background students being taught from the English curriculum at school. When First Nations students are learning in this way, they have the opportunity to interact with Elders and other speakers of this language, but the curriculum also encourages using L1 beyond the type of communication this language is normally used for (i.e., more than just within the family and home community). Learning L1 in this way serves to strengthen students' cultural identity, sense of self and belonging within their community, and provides a connection to place (Angelo et al., 2019). Taken together, learning in this way enhances students' well-being. Such a pathway is also facilitative of the cognitive development of the learners. Importantly, supporting students to be strong in their home language supports them as they learn other languages, including English and the associated literacy skills (Wigglesworth et al., 2021).

The Language Revival Learner Pathway (LR)

Language Revival Learner Pathway (LR) includes language revitalisation, language renewal, and language reclamation, and the curriculum for these are informed by the Australian Indigenous Languages Framework (AILF). Unlike the pathway described above, the languages taught are not the first language of the students. In this context, the languages being taught are spoken only by a small number of people or no longer spoken at all. In most cases, however, like the L1 pathway, the language being taught is geographically connected to the place and to the culture of the traditional custodians of the land. These locations may be regional and remote areas, but also larger towns and even cities. The students who are learning the language may have a close relationship to it because of their family connections, but there may be some who have no connection at all such as non-Aboriginal, English only speaking background students.

Language Revitalisation occurs in contexts where the language is spoken only by older generations and, for various reasons such as the impact of stolen generations, the language has not been passed on. According to the Australian curriculum documents, Meriam in the Torres Strait and Walmajarri in the Kimberley region are examples of such languages. We suggest that the way Lynette – one of the authors of this chapter – teaches Gooniyandi is also an instance of language revitalisation. Later in this chapter we provide a case study – an account of what she does in her Gooniyandi program.

Language Renewal, on the other hand, may have speakers in the community who know some of the language, but not fully and teachers and curriculum writers have to rely on historic recordings and descriptions of the language to supplement these speakers' knowledge in order to teach the language. In this case, the curriculum uses examples including Noongar in south-west Western Australia and Ngarrindjeri on the Lower Murray Lakes in South Australia.

Finally, within this LR pathway there is *Language Reclamation*. In this case historical resources are the only sources of language knowledge as there are no full language speakers. Here the curriculum cites examples including Awabakal from the Newcastle area in New South Wales and Narungga from the Yorke Peninsula.

Second Language Learner Pathway (L2)

Second Language Learner Pathway (L2) involves teaching an additional language to students that is not traditionally connected to the land on which it is being learnt – that is, off-Country. The students are unlikely to have a cultural or linguistic connection to the target language – although some may, and it gives these students who may not have grown up speaking the language of their ancestors the chance to reconnect to their cultural identity.

The Second Language Learning Pathway provides students with an opportunity to study a language that is structurally very different from English and one from a culture quite distant from the English-speaking mainstream. This develops a deeper appreciation of the nature and diversity of languages and cultures, and it also supports the acquisition of knowledge and skills necessary to learn and understand an Aboriginal or Torres Strait Islander language and its cultural context.

EAL/D

Related to the L2 pathway are those First Nations students who may have a home language other than English and, therefore, who will be learning English as an additional language or dialect (EAL/D). For some this is because they speak a traditional language or Kriol as their first language, for others it will be because they have AAE as their first dialect and main form of communication outside of school. Therefore, once at school they need to not only learn SAE but learn through and about it.

For EAL/D students, school often represents a context where they are required to use a language/dialect with forms and meaning quite different from how they usually communicate. Schools also reflect the dominant culture and are based on understandings and knowledge that echo the social and cultural 'everyday' contexts of non-Aboriginal people, including the teachers. This means educators need to be conscious of their own perceptions, bias, and beliefs and be aware that these may vary from their students' understanding and experiences (Rahman, 2013). As the curriculum documents (ACARA, n.d.-b) indicate, in an EAL/D context teachers need to work to support students to develop the English language needed to *access the curriculum*, but also the language needed to *demonstrate achievement*.

Fortunately for teachers, there are a number of online curriculum documents and resources that can help teachers navigate the needs of these learners. For instance, the ACARA (n.d.-b) provides a host of useful material. In addition, many of the state and territories within Australia also offer helpful materials (e.g., *Tracks to two-way learning,* Department of Education (DoE), Western Australia (WA) [n.d.]).

Opportunities and challenges

Undertaking the journey of learning a traditional Indigenous language or learning SAE as a second language/dialect provides learners with the opportunity to better understand how languages work. This is achieved because learning another language helps them to reflect on language, thinking about it 'metalinguistically' (i.e., considering language as object, rather than just using language without being consciously aware of its form and meaning). The process of language learning also helps students develop an appreciation or at least an understanding about the perspectives of others – their languages and culture, and in doing so it helps build empathy with others. It also serves to enhance the appreciation of diversity, but also the commonalities of humankind.

However, teaching traditional languages and EAL/D does present a number of challenges including practical considerations about the availability of appropriate teaching resources such as print and digital material. A sizeable set of various media resources, such as local documentaries, bilingual narrative, and descriptive texts, is also an asset. Consideration also needs to be given to the availability of human resources such as teachers to be able to support the language learning and, also, with respect to traditional languages, those who can offer related language and cultural experiences as well. For example, in a community where more than one traditional language is spoken, if it is only possible to employ one teacher, there is a need to select that language where there exists an opportunity for students to interact with Elders, family, and other community speakers because this enriches and authenticates the learning. The availability for the students to have 'On Country' visits to the land connected to the language being taught is another important factor. As we will see in the case study presented later in this chapter, these factors – especially family input –were important in Lynette's choice of Gooniyandi as the target language.

Alongside these important considerations, when beginning the journey of teaching a traditional language it is important to consult with community members and, in particular, the Elders who are owners of the language. Specifically, there is need to seek permission about the teaching of the language and how this should be done. It is crucial that they are appropriately and respectfully consulted and involved in the decision-making process about the teaching of their language. The importance of this step cannot be understated – but it is also acknowledged that this adds another layer of complexity and time to the task, particularly with regard to preparing a record of the language to be taught (see also Chapters 2 and 5 for further details about these processes). As noted above, for some 'sleeping' languages there are only few or no full language speakers and so this requires teachers and curriculum writers to rely on historical documentation. However, even in this situation it is vital to consult with community Elders who traditionally own the language.

A further challenge for teachers and curriculum writers is that Indigenous languages traditionally exist only in an oral form so they will need to consult with those who have the expertise in speaking the language, and also those who have the ability to convert this spoken language into a written form – that is to translate the spoken word into written orthography. This, too, is a complex task with different perspectives about such things as the pronunciation and subsequent spelling of different words, what different words mean, and how they are most appropriately used. This is another reason the consultation process requires time and respectful interactions. This is coupled with a more general challenge concerning the lack of language teaching materials, especially those catering for the specific languages and again this requires considerable effort and time on the teachers' behalf to work with expert speakers of the language to develop the resources.

Resource availability and development is also a challenge in EAL/D context. Materials need to cater for the specific needs of the learners which in the case of second dialect learners can be problematic because the distinction of the two forms of language (i.e., SAE and AAE) can be less transparent (see Siegel, 2010; Steele, 2020). Materials that are developed need to make the difference between the two dialectal forms very explicit. Furthermore, as with the teaching of traditional languages, resources for the EAL/D contexts need to be culturally inclusive, but also appropriate and so once again there is a need to consult with Elders, community members, or Aboriginal teaching support staff so that material development or selection is well considered.

Time is also an issue when it comes to actually teaching language. Whilst school timetables are congested, it needs to be recognised that it takes time to develop language skills (Cummins, 1981). Further, in some of the pathways and contexts outlined above there are limited opportunities to speak and practice the target language. Later in this chapter (and throughout this book) we describe some ways that can be used to overcome these challenges, but even with potential solutions comes a further need to consult with Elders and speakers of the language to ensure these are undertaken in appropriate ways.

Related to this is a much broader issue around the importance of language. It is vital that educators understand language learning is not just another subject in a busy timetable and do not allow it to be marginalised or to become an 'optional extra'. Learning language offers an important opportunity for all students to develop skills and understandings important for our society. Beyond this, it is essential for the wellbeing and success of First Nations students (Angelo et al., 2019). Understanding and celebrating the language and culture of all our students is fundamental to academic achievement (Cummins et al., 2005). Finally, with respect to the learning of traditional languages, it provides a way to address some of the past injustices where languages were not 'lost' (as they are often referred to) but actively 'stamped out' by past policies and practices.

Second language and dialect acquisition

Although learning a first language (L1) is distinct from learning a second (L2), there is much about the process that is valuable in helping our understanding of what occurs and what we can do as educators to facilitate second language acquisition (see Lightbown & Spada, 2021 for a full description). From the time we are born caregivers interact with us in meaningful ways, talking about what they and what we are doing, feeling, seeing, touching, eating, and so on. In this way we are receiving abundant input about the world and about language – its sounds, words, and the way these come together. That is, we are learning language and at the same time learning through language. Caregivers rarely stop to explicitly teach us words, though they might do incidentally and if they do, in ways strongly connected to who we are, where we are, and what we are doing. And what they talk about with us is closely bound to the cultural customs and behaviours that our speech community value. As we grow and develop, we interact with them and then those others we come into contact with, producing and practising our language, and again in meaningful ways. We talk about things we need and want and, as we grow, how we feel, what is of interest to us, what we know and want to learn, our opinions, and on it goes until we have full L1 proficiency. If we receive feedback about how we talk, it is most often about whether we are being truthful or saying something that is correct or not, rather than the form of what we produce (i.e., whether it is grammatical). And if parents do correct their children, it is done in context and often incidentally. For example,

Child: And then, we goed to the park ...
Caregiver: Oh, you went to the park? How nice, and what did you do there?
Child: Yes, we went to the park and played on the slide.

Many of these aspects contributing to L1 learning – meaningful input, output and practice, interaction and feedback, and contextualised language use – are also important for L2 learning. The difference is that L2 learners, unless they are learning bilingually, have already learned a language and, therefore, have an understanding of how language works and what can be done with language. Furthermore, even young learners will have developed a level of metalinguistic awareness and communicative competence. In the first instance, they will understand that language has structure – words can be changed just by changing one sound, the words can carry different meanings, and that the structure of language (e.g., morphology and grammar) can change the meaning of what is expressed. They will also understand that they may need to adjust how they speak to different people and in different contexts (e.g., talking to grandparents vs talking with siblings, talking to their parents vs to their teacher). By middle childhood, they will start to understand such things as humour, irony, and sarcasm. And, of particular relevance to this book, they will understand how culture and language come together in different ways when they interact with other people. These understandings can also impact their learning of another language.

A number of factors will influence how individuals learn a language; however, with very few exceptions, everyone is capable of learning a second language although their ultimate attainment (how successful they are) will vary. Personal characteristics such as age, intelligence, personality (e.g., willingness to take risks, 'have a go', and to communicate), and aptitude will make a difference (Philp, 2003). For example, some people have an acuity for learning languages – just as some people are good at playing sport or learning a musical instrument. Some other characteristics that will influence outcome include motivation to learn and the attitude towards the language (Norton, 2016). For example, if experiences with English speakers are negative, then learners may have a poor attitude to learning that language. The environment and how the language is being learnt will also make a difference, as will the need to learn the language, relevance of the language to personal circumstance, and opportunity to hear and use the language (Steele, 2020; Steele & Wigglesworth, 2023). The target language to be learnt will also make a difference. For instance, languages that are some distance from the target language are harder to learn than those closer. An example of this – English speakers often find learning German easier to learn than Mandarin because German is more like English. However, the reverse can also be true.

The closeness of languages or dialects also inhibits learners from acquiring full proficiency because it is hard to recognise the distinction between them, and in some cases, there may be 'false friends'; words that look or sound the same but are not, causing confusion. This is often the case for second dialect learners (e.g., who are engaged in an EAL/D curriculum). In this learning situation, many of the words may be the same in the two languages or dialects, giving speakers a natural communicative advantage. Speakers, generally, will be able to communicate across the two languages or dialects. However, the initial gains in communicative ability may result in slower rates of language learning in the long term (see Winer, 1989, 2006). This is because of the closeness of the two languages or dialects makes it difficult to notice the differences. Moreover, because the speakers are generally understood by others, it can make these differences, communicatively redundant (Long, 2007); that is, not necessary to learn for the purposes of basic communication. Academic performance in the target language where adherence is standardised language forms is required is, therefore, likely to be impacted. One example is speakers of Aboriginal Englishes (AAE) who are learning SAE through schooling, as described in Chapters 9 and 12.

Approaches to language learning and teaching in schools

Given the complexity and impact context and individual characteristics have, one key question asked by educators is 'how best to teach and to learn languages?' The simple answer is – there is no right way because these same factors will also influence how this is best done. In the following section, we present some options and explore how these can be implemented and some of the advantages and challenges. Further illustrations of these appear in the chapters that follow.

Language as stand-alone subjects

LR and L2 pathways are commonly taught as separate non-integrated subjects in schools, and most often using traditional approaches for teaching language. It includes the use of such methods as PPP (i.e., presentation, production, and practice), grammar-translation, and audio-lingual methods. Whilst such methods may be effective at the beginning stages, they are often based on behaviourist methodologies, and a considerable body of research shows this is not how languages are best learned – especially for acquiring higher levels of proficiency (Mitchell et al., 2019). The other issue is learning language in isolation restricts its applicability and usefulness outside the context in which it is taught. A communicative language teaching approach and more contemporaneously task-based language learning goes some way to addressing the short-comings of traditional methods and makes the language being taught more authentic with greater real-world application (see, for example, Oliver, 2020, 2021; Oliver & Sato, 2021). In reality, many language teachers in the LR and L2 pathways use an eclectic approach that combines different methods because of the issues they encounter with respect to resource availability (as described above).

Content Language Integrated Learning (CLIL)

CLIL is an approach, a little like immersion (see below) when students learn a new language whilst simultaneously learning a new subject. For example, Australian English-speaking students may learn maths and science using Mandarin as the language of instruction (see Oliver & Sato, 2021; Oliver et al., 2019). The content of the subject being taught provides the context for target language learning. This enables the language to be meaningful, authentic, and contextualised, as shown in Chapter 11. It does require a different way of approaching L2 learning that many teachers may not be familiar with, and they will also need skills and knowledge both about subject as well as language. However, this does create an opportunity for collaboration between language teachers and subject specialists.

Immersion programs

Immersion programs are similar to CLIL, but extend to the use of the L2 into almost all the curriculum areas. It is an approach that has been in place around the world since at least the middle of last century. For example, French immersion programs were introduced in Canada in the 1960s. In that context, English-speaking background students were taught almost all their subjects, apart from English curriculum, in French. In Australia, for newly arrived migrant students who enter schools where such learners are in small numbers, their experience in the classroom is similar as is that of First Nations EAL/D students who attend schools where only English is used. Whilst the Canadian immersion program has been very successful, the context is very different from these Australian examples. In Canada, the students belong the dominant language and cultural group, often residing in middle class areas with the advantages that such a background brings (e.g., books at home, highly literate parents, etc). For immersion programs to be beneficial for the diverse learners in Australian contexts, there is often a need to scaffold the learning in the L2, such as by using EAL/D approaches, so that linguistic and cultural differences can be made transparent – which in turn supports the learners' acquisition.

Bilingual programs

As the name suggests, language is taught bilingually in such programs. School subjects are taught using more than just one language – sometimes using two staff to co-teach, sometimes with one teacher using two languages to teach the subject. Beginning in the 1970s, bilingual education was a common approach for supporting Aboriginal and Torres Strait Islander students, particularly in the Northern Territory (NT). It allowed students to maintain and to be strong in their own language and to develop English at the same time. Internationally it is an approach recognised as one that contributes in positive ways to linguistic and cognitive development and the overall academic achievement of students. Unfortunately, in Australia it fell victim to political precarity, and in 2009 'First four hours in English' was introduced NT, effectively leading to the demise of many bilingual programs. However, even under these conditions and often without funding, some schools continued to operate as bilingual schools (see Morales et al., 2018) relying instead on the advocacy and investment from the school community to continue with bilingual education. Chapter 3 describes the experiences of four Aboriginal language educators who have played a strong advocacy role for their languages and have implemented bilingual education programs in their community schools over many years and through this period.

EAL/D approaches

EAL/D learners may enter school speaking a language other than English at home such as a traditional language or Kriol or they may speak a different dialect other than SAE at home, such as AAE. Some will have exposure to English at home and/or in their community, but others such as those in remote communities may not come into contact with English very often if at all. In these setting, learning EAL/D is more like learning English as a Foreign Language (Wigglesworth et al., 2011). It is important to realise that under these conditions, English language learning may be slower because, as mentioned earlier, exposure to the target language and opportunities to practice the target language is crucial to language learning (Steele & Wigglesworth, 2023). This is particularly true when it comes to learning academic content in a language that you are learning at the same time (Cummins, 1981). To promote English language learning, EAL/D approaches focus on developing students' knowledge of the English language at all levels of language – semantic, grammatical through to discourse. But how this is done may differ according to the language backgrounds of students. For example, learning and teaching approaches for students who speak a traditional language with little exposure to SAE will differ to an AE speaker who has regular exposure to SAE, as described in the model of Indigenous language ecologies presented in Chapter 7.

To account for these contextual differences, teaching approaches need to be modified appropriately for the cohorts being taught. Teachers may include an eclectic range of methods and materials to best cater for their students' needs and the context in which they learn. In the following case study, we illustrate how one teacher has carefully considered different ways of teaching her traditional language to students at her school in a remote area of northern Australia.

Teaching Gooniyandi in a remote school – A case study

Gooniyandi is the language of Lynette's father's family and it is spoken by some people in the town in which she lives and others living not too far away. It should be noted, however, that it is not the most common language of the town, but instead Jaru and Kija are more often spoken by local people. However, she chose to teach Gooniyandi because of her family connection and because this meant that the resources she would need to access to develop teaching materials were more readily available. Despite not teaching the most common language within her community, she described that during her time teaching this language in town she has 'never ever had any negative feedback' and that she has received considerable support from the larger community. In fact, she feels it has contributed positively to the town during what have been challenging times before, during, and after Covid-19.

Lynette describes how teaching students Gooniyandi now will mean that future generations 'will know' (their language and culture) and she is already looking to the next generation to continue her teaching work. She further describes that: 'Our languages are dying and this is how we can revive them …. When old people (who are the last speakers of the language) pass away, it's like a library burning down'. She believes, as do many others (e.g., Comajoan-Colomé & Coronel-Molina, 2021), that there is a need for a long-term vision or languages will continue to be taken. She wants to continue to teach her family's language, and beyond that to expand her teaching for the other language groups in town (i.e., Kija and Jaru).

She has worked hard to build a strong Gooniyandi language learning community – within her classroom, but more generally – and the results and support she has received has in her words been 'really awesome'. All students at the school are engaged with the program regardless of whether they are Aboriginal or not and whether they have ties to Gooniyandi, Jaru or Kija. It has given the students something to connect them to their place and their ways of 'being and doing' within their community.

Lynette feels that teaching and learning Gooniyandi empowers not only herself as a teacher, but her people by supporting and promoting their language and culture. It also supports students and their 'mainstream' class teachers to work in linguistically and culturally appropriate ways – ways that are both inclusive and respectful. She says that everyone is welcome to learn the language and this includes 'non-Indigenous kids even – lots of kids in the community'. Her learning environment is positive and intentionally created to be 'fun' so that the students at the school enjoy the experience of learning Gooniyandi together. And even visiting adults want to join in.

When you see her in action in class, it is evident that she is enthusiastic and there is no doubt that she is passionate about her teaching. As she says herself: 'I love what I'm doing – I look forward to it. Hopefully I will teach language until I retire'. Of course, many language teachers feel the same way, but in challenging times and in such a remote location – where she travels long distances for the sake of her teaching – such positivity is laudable.

To ensure her students are engaged, both with the language and with learning collaboratively, when teaching she uses all sorts of activities and games, such as playing cards and she uses key word cards taken from a Gooniyandi dictionary for this purpose. She also has the students play a game called 'hot board' which is a race to spell the words correctly. She also uses lots of movement, especially with younger children. As a consequence, she describes how the students think they are playing with each other rather than learning. However, her eye remains on the curriculum pathway, so she makes sure she always 'scaffolds' all the students' learning ensuring they are successful language learners who are willing to work together in collaborative ways. To do this, she has developed and made a lot of resources for use in her classroom.

In her teaching, Lynette plans for successful language teaching and learning by using the 'Aboriginal language revival pathway' – the curriculum supported by the Education Department of Western Australia (described in Chapter 5). This is a data-driven resource, developed by a linguist and language consultant who not only wrote the curriculum, but also continue to provide professional mentorship to teachers such as Lynette. The consultant is located in the town of Broome, in the Kimberly region – a 7-hour drive from Lynette's school (which for most people is a long drive, but not uncommon in the Kimberly region where Lynette's school is located). She also uses her family as a valuable linguistic resource, consulting with her 'aunty and dad' who reside 20 kms away and another 'aunty' who is located an hour and a half away to ensure that what she is teaching is linguistically correct and authentic. In particular, she will consult with them to double check the form and meaning of the language she is teaching her students.

The curriculum she is using is organised in a sequential way, but within her teaching she also breaks this down further so that she can carefully develop her lesson plans and then make her own teaching resources. Her lessons are closely tied to the assessment criteria, and she uses an achievement standards checklist for this purpose. She collects data on each child and 'uses spreadsheets for reporting – noting individuals that are coming along – whether this is forward or neutral' (i.e., when students plateau) – and enters this onto her assessment spreadsheet as an ongoing record of what students are achieving. In turn, she uses this to further refine and recalibrate her teaching to match where her students are at in a cyclic manner.

Aboriginal language checklist and report

Language: Gooniyandi Year 3   Term 3

✓✓✓ Achieved regularly ✓✓ Developing/sometimes +● Developing with guidance
● Not yet developed

Year 3 Listening and Responding and Speaking	Student Names					Comments
Socialising						
Use familiar language and sentence patterns to share information and join conversations						
Respond to and use routine classroom language and instructions.						

Figure 1.1 Example of assessment rubric

To encourage the students to take risks she constantly scaffolds their learning – ensuring that they can achieve at each stage so that it seems 'easy'. In fact, she reflected that she has found that sometimes the tasks and activities are actually too easy and that she needs to carefully consider what she asks the students to do to challenge them further. (Figure 1.1)

Lynette's teaching demonstrates a real success because Aboriginal student engagement across the nation, particularly in regional and remote areas, continues to be at a considerably lower level than for non-Aboriginal students. It is likely that her teaching success and ability to challenge her students to take risks is tied to the rapport she has with them and the pedagogical practices that she employs. Specifically, regardless of how easy or difficult the learning experience is, she always attempts to provide abundant encouragement and it appears that such positive reinforcement encourages her students to take risks.

With her students, she is very explicit about the need to take risks in order to be successful learners: 'I say to my students – I'm still learning – I have to take risks'. She also does this in recognition of the cultural background of many of her students – encouraging them to take risks in ways so 'they don't feel shame'. It should be noted here that the word 'shame' is used by Aboriginal people in a way dissimilar to how non-Aboriginal people understand the word: It is beyond embarrassment and can be not only disempowering, but also physiologically overwhelming (Oliver & Exell, 2020). In the classroom context, it often leads to diminished engagement or even refusal to participate at all. By taking this into account and adjusting her teaching practices accordingly, Lynette has a classroom where risk taking is an everyday occurrence.

Lynette's comments and actions also reflect the hard work she has personally engaged in to increase her own proficiency in this language. Her initial low level of proficiency is not uncommon amongst Aboriginal people who may culturally identify as belonging to a particular language group, despite not being able to speak that language. However, through various sources and experiences, she has 'become a fluent speaker'. She described how at the beginning of her journey she aimed at: 'Getting myself fluent – keeping in contact with language speakers', but not satisfied with that, her aim is now to 'keep on learning'. In this way, therefore, she is leading by example. She is able to show her students, the staff at the school, and her wider community that she is a successful language learner – one who keeps working at learning her family's language.

Overall, Lynette brings to her role as a teacher of a traditional language a clear understanding of the task at hand, but she also shows awareness and willingness to seek help and support as required – in this way demonstrating both openness and maturity as a language educator. She continues to strive to improve her own language proficiency, taking risks along the way and sharing this in explicit ways with her students. She also works diligently to continue to improve and provide effective language teaching – experimenting with what she does in terms of activities and language learning tasks, but also following the advice of an expert mentor. At all times, she works to set her students up for success, providing encouragement and positive reinforcement, and at the same time taking into account the cultural context of her students' ways of learning, 'being and doing'. She is able to support other educators to overcome deficit views about her students and encourage positive identity amongst her students. She also provides support within the wider community and demonstrates a commitment and vision for her people into the future. In this way she is able to act as a strong advocate for language maintenance and teaching, not only of her own traditional language, but all such languages.

Conclusion

Australian First Nations' languages are diverse as are the learners and the contexts in which they are learnt. In response, the Australian curriculum provides a number of pathways teachers may follow to support their students and to support the learning of the various languages. We have provided a case study of how one teacher has approached this task, and in the chapters that follow there are descriptions of other contexts and different ways other educators have undertaken this. In these chapters, we will also read about some of the challenges and opportunities that language learning and teaching presents in schools and some considerations that need to be taken into account.

References

Angelo, D., O'Shannessy, C., Simpson, J., Kral, I., Smith, H., & Browne, E. (2019). *Wellbeing and Indigenous Language Ecologies (WILE): A strengths-based approach: Literature review*, National Indigenous Languages Report, Pillar 2. https://dspace-prod.anu.edu.au/server/api/core/bitstreams/7e3ec65b-58a2-4e1f-a3e5-e779039469a8/content

Australian Curriculum, Assessment and Reporting Authority (ACARA). (n.d.-a). *Framework for Aboriginal languages and Torres Strait Islander Languages—Structure*. https://www.australiancurriculum.edu.au/f-10-curriculum/languages/framework-for-aboriginal-languages-and-torres-strait-islander-languages/structure/

Australian Curriculum, Assessment and reporting Authority (ACARA). (n.d.-b). *Framework for Aboriginal Languages and Torres Strait Islander Languages*. https://www.australiancurriculum.edu.au/f-10-curriculum/languages/framework-for-aboriginal-languages-and-torres-strait-islander-languages/

Australian Curriculum, Assessment and reporting Authority (ACARA). (n.d.-c). *Meeting the needs of students for whom English is an additional language or dialect*. https://www.australiancurriculum.edu.au/resources/student-diversity/meeting-the-needs-of-students-for-whom-english-is-an-additional-language-or-dialect/

Comajoan-Colomé, L., & Coronel-Molina, S. M. (2021). What does language revitalisation in the twenty-first century look like? New trends and frameworks. *Journal of Multilingual and Multicultural Development*, *42*(10), 897–904. https://doi.org/10.1080/01434632.2020.1827643

Cummins, J. (1981). Age on arrival and immigrant second language learning in Canada: A reassessment. *Applied Linguistics*, *2*(2), 132–149. https://doi.org/10.1093/applin/2.2.132

Cummins, J., Bismilla, V., Chow, P., Cohen, S., Giampapa, F., Leoni, L., Sandhu, P., & Sastri, P. (2005). Affirming identity in multilingual classrooms. *Educational Leadership*, *63*(1), 38–43.

Department of Education (DoE), Western Australia (WA). (n.d.). *Tracks to two-way learning*. https://myresources.education.wa.edu.au/programs/tracks-to-two-way-learning

Lightbown, P., & Spada, N. (2021). *How languages are learned* (5th ed.). OUP.

Long, M. H. (2007). *Problems in SLA*. Erlbaum.

Mitchell, R., Myles, F., & Marsden, E. (2019). *Second language learning theories*. Routledge.

Morales, G., Vaughan, J., & Ganambarr-Stubbs, M. (2018). From home to school in multilingual Arnhem Land: The development of Yirrkala School's bilingual curriculum. In G. Wigglesworth, J. Simpson, & J. Vaughan (Eds.), *Language practices of Indigenous children and youth: The transition from home to school* (pp. 69–98). (Palgrave Studies in Minority Languages and Communities). Palgrave Macmillan.

Norton, B. (2016). Identity and language learning: Back to the future. *TESOL Quarterly*, *50*(2), 475–479. https://doi.org/10.1002/tesq.293

Oliver, R. (2020). Developing authentic tasks for the workplace using needs analysis: A case study of Australian Aboriginal vocational students. In C. Lambert & R. Oliver (Eds.), *Using tasks in diverse contexts* (pp. 146–161). Multilingual Matters.

Oliver, R. (2021). Developing a task-based approach: A case study of Australian Aboriginal VET students. In M. J. Ahmadian & M. H. Long (Eds.), *The Cambridge handbook of TBLT* (pp. 99–108). CUP.

Oliver, R., & Exell, M. (2020). Identity, translanguaging, linguicism and racism: The experience of Aboriginal people living in a remote community. *International Journal of Bilingual Education and Bilingualism*, *23*, 819–832. https://doi.org/10.1080/13670050.2020.1713722

Oliver, R., & Sato, M. S. (2021). Tasks for children: Using mainstream content to learn a language. In M. J. Ahmadian & M. H. Long (Eds.), *The Cambridge handbook of TBLT* (pp. 416–431). CUP.

Oliver, R., Sato, M., Ballinger, S., & Pan, L. (2019). Content and language integrated learning classes for child Mandarin L2 learners: A longitudinal observational study. In M. Sato & S. Loewen (Eds.), *Evidence-based second language pedagogy* (pp. 81–102). Routledge.

Philp, J. (2003). Constraints on 'noticing the gap': Nonnative speakers' noticing of recasts in NS-NNS interaction. *SSLA, 25*, 99–126. https://doi.org/10.1017/S0272263103000044

Rahman, K. (2013). Belonging and learning to belong in school: The implications of the hidden curriculum for indigenous students. *Discourse: Studies in the Cultural Politics of Education, 34*(5), 660–672. https://doi.org/10.1080/01596306.2013.728362

Siegel, J. (2010). *Second dialect acquisition*. Cambridge University Press.

Steele, C. (2020). *Teaching Standard Australian English as a second dialect to Australian Indigenous children in primary school classrooms* [Doctoral dissertation]. University of Melbourne.

Steele, C., & Wigglesworth, G. (2023). Recognising the SAE language learning needs of Indigenous primary school students who speak contact languages. *Language and Education, 37*(3), 346–363. https://doi.org/10.1080/09500782.2021.2020811

Wigglesworth, G., Simpson, J., & Loakes, D. (2011). Naplan language assessments for Indigenous children in remote communities: Issues and problems. *Australian Review of Applied Linguistics, 34*(3), 320–343. https://doi.org/10.1075/aral.34.3.04wig

Wigglesworth, G., Wilkinson, M., Yunupingu, Y., Beecham, R., & Stockley, J. (2021). Interdisciplinary and intercultural development of an early literacy app in Dhuwaya. *Languages, 6*(2), 106. https://doi.org/10.3390/languages6020106

Winer, L. (1989). Variation and transfer in English creole—Standard English language learning. In M. R. Eisenstein (Ed.), *The dynamic interlanguage. Topics in language and linguistics* (pp. 155–173). Springer.

Winer, L. (2006). Teaching English to Caribbean English creole-speaking students in the Caribbean and North America. In S. J. Nero (Ed.), *Dialects, Englishes, creoles, and education* (pp. 105–118). Lawrence Erlbaum Associates, Publishers.

2 Consent, Copyright, Consultation, Collaboration, and Co-design

Principles and Protocols for Developing School Language Programs

Vincent Backhaus, Mike Exell, and Graeme Gower

> **Who we are**
>
> The three authors come together with a diverse range of experiences and qualifications that have led to a focus on education and the impact upon learning for Aboriginal and Torres Strait Islander students in regional, rural, remote, and urban settings. Vincent is a university academic and engages with community-led co-design research focused on the environment, learning, and Sea Country management. Mike has had extensive experience working with Aboriginal communities and youth as a mentor, researcher, and educator. Graeme has a long and distinguished level of commitment and engagement with Aboriginal education and supporting the next generation of educators entering Indigenous educational contexts. We three come together to write as guides sharing the space with those that wish to enter in respectful ways the Aboriginal communities our work serves. Our chapter wishes to highlight the importance of working with language and the communities who connect with and maintain the knowledge of Country through language.

Introduction

The development of a successful school language program is underpinned by a respectful relationship between the education professionals who design such programs and the community for whom it is designed. When designing language programs, educational professionals must marry their pedagogical knowledge with the target community's expertise in their language, understanding how they want it taught recognising their needs and aspirations for the future generations of their community. At the same time, there is a need to understand that educational professionals can often be viewed as 'outsiders', so when undertaking program development, they need to follow recommended protocols in order to build trust and to be welcomed into the community.

All educators need to be cognizant of the strong connection between language and culture, and how together these are tied closely to the identity of Aboriginal people. They also need to understand how self-identity is in turn connected to well-being and how culture involves being part of something 'bigger than yourself' (Eades, 1988; Jackson-Barrett & Lee-Hammond, 2018; Kickett-Tucker, 2008; Zubrick et al., 2004). This is described in *Languages ideologies and practice from the land and the classroom* (Disbray et al., 2020, p. 2), and highlighted by Martin who explains 'I don't 'speak' Warlpiri, I 'am' Warlpiri'.

The close connection between Aboriginal language and culture was also described by a recently graduated high-school student this way:

> I think it's important to keep the language alive because it's our language, if you grow up and don't know it, then that's a part of your culture you can't have.
> (Oliver & Exell, 2019, p. 37)

And another:

> Black fellas that grew up (only) in Eastland Town don't have a close connection (to culture) because they don't speak language. They speak more English.
> (Oliver & Exell, 2019, p. 37)

Hence, developing a program is not just about outlining the language to be taught – it also involves including culture, building upon students' connection to land, and helping them form a positive cultural identity (Department of Education, 2019).

Seeking consent for the inclusion of such language and cultural knowledge is the critical first step to designing a successful program. The Aboriginal and Torres Strait Islander Corporation of Languages (2004) developed the five C protocols for community language projects. The five C protocols – consent, copyright, consultation, collaboration, and co-design – provide a valuable framework to follow when building relationships, particularly when developing your own understanding of the community's cultural practices, customs, and norms. This five C framework informs the current chapter. We provide an analysis and examples of how each can be applied when designing and implementing a successful language program (Oliver and Excell, 2020).

Consent

Consent is a fundamentally important concept for establishing the scope of the project and the tone of the relationship between the community and the educators. The Aboriginal and Torres Strait Islander Corporation of Languages (2004, p. 6) explains that a formal written agreement 'provides clarity' on what the project is trying to achieve and how and what it will be used. In some Indigenous communities, oral consent may be considered sufficient; however, the educators designing the language program should look to get agreements in writing and done in collaboration with appropriate community representatives, such as members of the local Indigenous corporation.

In whatever way this is approached, the strength of this agreement is underpinned by a respectful, reciprocal relationship between the community and the educators. In fact, it is important to enact this approach in all interactions, as noted in the introduction of this chapter. Educators and researchers, including linguists, may be viewed as outsiders and Aboriginal communities can have a sceptical view of such people, who like other visitors 'leave behind ... unfinished projects, misunderstandings and misplaced good intentions' (Mahood, 2012, p. 43). As such, they must approach the community knowing that Aboriginal and Torres Strait Islander people are the custodians of the cultural and linguistic heritage (Aboriginal and Torres Strait Islander Corporation of Languages, 2004). Any projects that are undertaken or programs that are implemented, including language programs, cannot be successfully achieved without due respect given to their knowledge and their input.

Aboriginal and Torres Strait Islander Corporation of Languages (2004) recommend educators who wish to implement a language program with a community need to first make contact with the local area representative organisations. These groups are in the best position to advise about the local protocols that need to be followed. They can also facilitate further introductions and act as advocates for the educators. Importantly, they are able to identify the most appropriate community members who can work to develop the program or project. While representative groups can be an important resource, it also needs to be recognised that there may be division within the community. While consent may seem a daunting task, it is not insurmountable and can be as simple as making time to develop respectful mutual relationships.

The importance of making time is highlighted in the following examples which are based on personal experiences encountered in research and school settings across metropolitan, rural, and remote communities. Community agencies and participants who are approached for their involvement in research activities and/or the development of educational resources, such as school language programs, may be reluctant to engage with 'outsiders' due to several reasons, including previous negative experiences with educational professionals. Some notable examples include:

- not being involved in the early planning stages of the program and, therefore, not clearly understanding the purpose, benefits, and ultimate ownership of the proposed activity;
- a lack of consultation on who should be involved;
- the feeling of not being able to voice concerns and/or issues as an equal partner;
- the notion of being 'over researched' or consistently 'picked on' by educational professionals.

If these factors are not taken into consideration, this may inhibit the granting of consent by community members, and this will likely impact on the level of participation.

First impressions are long lasting, so it is also of crucial importance that mutual and respectful relationships are developed from the outset of any proposed activity, such as designing a language program. It is important to first identify who are the main contacts within the community who should be approached and be involved in the first instance. This may mean at least two – if not more – initial visits to a community to meet with Elders, community agencies, and community members over morning tea or lunch. These meetings provide the opportunity to exchange introductions, explore shared experiences (e.g., hobbies, interests, previous work with other Aboriginal people), and, thereafter, to explain in detail the proposed program that is earmarked for the school or community. The issue of consent to participate or not to participate or the option to withdraw at any time can then be discussed and confirmed. It is also important to continue to have these informal meetings with Elders and community members during the period of the program development or to ensure that understandings of the project can be reinforced, that ongoing consent can be acknowledged, and to allow for opportunities to provide on-going feedback and respond to any questions that may be raised.

All long-term relationships take time and effort to come to fruition; however, if it is done with genuine intentions right from the start, community Elders and other participants will be willing to collaborate and share their knowledge with you. In addition, you would have developed a lasting friendship with community members that you have met.

Copyright

Copyright and intellectual property rights are some of the most difficult areas to navigate when developing a language program. This is due to the complex relationship which exists between Indigenous Cultural and Intellectual Property (ICIP) and Australian copyright law.

Aboriginal and Torres Strait Islander people are recognised as having one of the oldest continuous cultures in the world – one that has existed for more than 60,000 years (Referendum Council, 2017). This culture, which has a living history, has survived due to traditional knowledge, practices, language, beliefs, and arts being handed down through the generations (Janke, 2005, p. 95; National Copyright Unit, n.d.). The Australian Copyright Act 1968 outlines that works must be written down or recorded, with general copyright limits tied to the life of the artist plus 70 years. However, this Act does not protect information or knowledge, or oral songs or stories (Aboriginal Land Trust, n.d. p. 5; Queensland Government, 2022). In this way, the Act, as it currently exists, sits in direct opposition to how Aboriginal cultural heritage has been retained and owned.

So what exactly are ICIP rights and how does it apply to designing a language program? A simple explanation is that it is steeped in the principle of Aboriginal self-determination and exists to ensure ICIP is owned, controlled, and protected by the primary guardians of the culture (Janke, 2005, p. 97). ICIP recognises Indigenous knowledge and practices and provides cultural guidelines and protocols to protect the language and culture and so needs to be appropriately applied to any program. Because language is intrinsic to cultural identity, knowledge, skills, and the teaching of the culture, language and how it is taught and passed on to the next generation is an intricate part of ICIP (Janke, 2005, p. 97).

Language program designers need to be knowledgeable both about ICIP and how it interacts with current Australian copyright laws. In particular, the Aboriginal Land Trust (n.d.) explains the close collaboration program designers should have with Aboriginal people and how their knowledge should be recorded and appropriately acknowledged and attributed. This ensures the work done by the program designers is recognised, but copyright ownership is retained by Aboriginal language custodians. Entering into suitable copyright license agreements with Indigenous collaborators ensures the designers still have access to their work and ICIP rights are respected and retained.

Copyright and ownership are important elements to discuss and confirm with community Elders and members at the earliest possible stage of planning. This will usually take place after initial introductory meetings have taken place and ideally when participants themselves are involved in the planning stages. Although these interactions and the sharing of knowledge are built on strong foundations of mutual benefit, the knowledge that is shared by participants is, and will always be, owned by the community language group whom you are working with.

Non-Aboriginal and Aboriginal educational professionals who have the expertise in appropriate language teaching pedagogy and developing language resources play a role in the development of school language programs. Elders and local community language speakers, however, are the key players in providing local language examples that are required to produce teaching and learning resources.

The following example is based on the development of a resource for a school language program in a remote Aboriginal community school in Western Australia. The major aim of a teaching and learning project was to develop a school language program using iPads. Elders and community language speakers were shown examples of how iPads could be used to teach the local language and the Standard English equivalent, using words and sentences. The iPad template's design provided a means for photos or student drawings to be included to illustrate a word and/or capture the meaning of the word in a sentence. Audio was also a feature of the iPad language program with both the local and English languages spoken, using local community and student voices.

After a workshop about the iPad template conducted with Elders and local language teachers from the school, some adjustments were made to the functions of the template to incorporate ideas that were suggested by them. The iPad language program was developed over three visits to the community, with each visit involving Elders and community members. During these visits, the issue of ownership and copyright was confirmed. The language program developed for the school continues to be owned by the community and not the developers. In fact, the template developer gifted the language template to school community. This confirmation led to the increased local participation and interest in the school language program.

Collaboration

Collaboration between educational professionals and Indigenous communities is critical to the success of any language program. These collaborative relationships, underpinned by trust, respect, and reciprocity, must exist throughout the entirety of the program in order for it to become established and accepted within the community and school where it will be taught (Lowe & Ash, 2006). As outlined in the introduction, language programs teach students about their culture and, in turn, relate to developing positive identities, so there must be appropriate care in design and implementation. Genuine partnerships between education and the Indigenous community can lead to better educational outcomes for Aboriginal students such as increased school attendance, deeper engagement, and better learning outcomes (New South Wales Aboriginal Education Consultative Group & New South Wales Department of Education & Training, 2004).

Successful language programs benefit communities and empower them to development resources, and revitalise and maintain the languages themselves (Aboriginal and Torres Strait Islander Corporation of Languages, 2004). Educational professionals involved with this process need to collaborate with the whole community, so that they feel heard and so that their goals and aspirations are duly recognised. Community members are the ones who hold the knowledge of the language, so the more involved they are, the richer the program will be in content and delivery. This can be achieved throughout every stage, such as facilitating introductions to important members of the community, collecting language data using technology and documenting the language, to final decisions on the formatting, design, and layout (Aboriginal and Torres Strait Islander Corporation of Languages, 2004). Non-community people working on the language project must remember its success will be measured in how the community engages with it.

Education professionals also must recognise that engaging Indigenous communities in teaching programs and especially in research projects have a tumultuous history which cannot be ignored. As covered in the consent section, how professionals approach and first engage with the community sets the tone for all future engagement. However, it cannot be ignored that many community members may have had negative experiences with outsiders, including previous research practices which exploited Indigenous people in disrespectful ways (Humphery, 2000). To overcome this, there is a need to use the culturally appropriate methodology – for instance, when collecting language data to develop a program. For example, an approach known as 'yarning', or Aboriginal storytelling, enables the collection of authentic data in respectful ways (Ober, 2017). This traditional practice is integral to the Indigenous way of learning, particularly for developing cultural understanding (Barker, 2008; Geia et al., 2013). It is a 'formal process of sharing knowledges that is reliant upon relationships, expected outcomes, responsibility and accountability between the participants, country and culture' (Barlo, 2017, p. 21). Engaging in this practice will allow the community to be engaged, and language data to be collected, in a culturally appropriate way.

Collaboration is not just limited to the development of the language program, but also its implementation within the classroom. In addition, during the development of a language program, there are likely to be opportunities for further collaboration on related matters. However, this is again dependent on building respectful relationships prior to formal involvement of participants. For example, the development of school language programs can extend to other community activities such as the Aboriginal Ranger Program, which operate in many remote communities in Western Australia. Note: This program is funded by the state government and is led by Aboriginal people who manage and protect 'Country' and the environment, but educators can use the knowledge that is shared in their classrooms and involve using the rangers themselves as teaching resources (see for example, Chapter 11 this volume).

Co-design

Co-design raises important questions of the people who are involved in the process of knowledge co-creation: What is the impact of the co-design process on relationships, the engagement, and how does the process of co-design help to effect change on those most affected by its impact? Importantly, co-design, where Aboriginal and Torres Strait Islander people are involved, raises questions about what is produced by who and for what purpose (Shay et al., 2023). Briefly, co-design with Indigenous people has highlighted non-Indigenous perspectives about experiences on Country with Indigenous peoples, to consider how better engagement between western and Indigenous forms of knowing can work across shared values meaningfully (e.g., St John & Akama, 2022). Additionally, recent signalling from Indigenous policy development and Indigenous education has intimated the potential strength of co-design through participatory empowered design (Mark & Hagen, 2020; Shay et al., 2023). Participatory empowered design describes the importance of shared decision making, co-production of outcomes, and the contribution of diverse Indigenous voices to outcomes like education policy, practice, and knowledge production (Shay et al., 2023). While the novel aspirations of co-design are potentially transformational for education projects and communities, limited empirical and Indigenous evidence in the testing of co-design exists and highlights the risk of new initiatives perpetuating previous legacies of knowledge production about Indigenous peoples rather than working *with* Indigenous communities and the priority of local needs.

This limited but emerging research at least helps to support the development of co-design processes when it comes to considering school language program development. For instance, previous research studies have echoed the tenets of co-design such as the *Centring Anangu Voices* project which talks about 'both ways capital' in the co-creation of understanding *Anangu* language priorities and educator-researcher agendas (Osborne et al., 2020). Underpinning the project was the incorporation of Anangu voices, languages, aspirations, epistemologies, and ontologies and ensuring researchers were competent in both Anangu and western contexts while also acknowledging the involvement of Anangu in the research process. Another example is the Kuku Yalanji language program which began in 2019 and focused on sentence structure and vocabulary. It involved an extensive consultation process of over 18 months with Elders to support the continual revitalisation and everyday use of Kuku Yalanji into the future (O'Brien & Bobongie-Harris, 2023). The various chapters in this book also contribute to a broader understanding of co-design.

What these examples highlight is that co-design can mean different things to different people, and our understanding and definitions of 'co' in co-design continues to be developed. However, generally it is a term that describes the opportunity to widen participation for groups of people as they share in a co-creation of outcomes from various activities and tasks across the life of a program or project. The foundations of this emerge from participatory approaches and social policy development where design thinking is supported (Blomkamp, 2018). These activities could be variously considered as part of planning, delivery, and evaluation, and in this way contributions can be realised as part of a co-production of outcomes through shared social values (Raiden & King, 2021). In thinking about co-production and co-design in First Nations contexts, we can at least start with thinking about (i) power sharing opportunities, (ii) capacity development, (iii) thinking about the relationships of course between people and processes, and (iv) ensuring everyone can think through how they wish to participate in the co-design process (Shay et al., 2023).

The Australian Institute of Aboriginal and Torres Strait Islander Studies (AIATSIS, 2012) ethical guidelines are a useful code for thinking through co-creation of program or project based on the knowledges of Indigenous peoples. The guideline document supports individuals and organisations to understand their accountability towards the collective rights and interests of Indigenous peoples in relation to their lands, waters, cultures, and histories. In this chapter, we can draw on their guiding principles of (i) informing, (ii) consulting, (iii) involving, (iv) elaborating, and (v) empowering Indigenous participants as co-producers of outcomes. Specifically,

I informing helps us to understand that all involved need to be informed from the start to the finish,
II consulting is part of an ongoing and negotiated continuous process,
III involving means involving Indigenous people,
IV elaborating means to ensure knowledge translation occurs so everyone can be aware of what a program project attempts to achieve and why, and
V empowering Indigenous peoples ensures that through the previous five stages Indigenous participants can realise the longevity, outcomes, and relationships of a program or project.

Together these principles can draw upon outcomes and relationships for future development and/or to address other community priorities. They also allow for the skills and resources of those who have collaborated to be called upon in different and unique ways.

'If you can't do it properly, don't begin'

In the following section, Vincent shares his own personal perceptions and experiences of implementing various programs and projects based on co-design:

The process of co-design is interrelated, interconnected, ongoing, iterative, and responsive. In co-design you never reach an end-point – you never really arrive at an outcome or impact space. That's why it's a process not a product. It moves in different directions, it is non-linear.

When co-designing a program, there are various elements that contribute to it, before, during, and after. It is not necessarily about the impact. Co-design is about the innovations or new knowledges that emerge as part of the relationship-building process. So, it is not about the final product, but rather the innovations that happen along the way.

The first steps include the assembly of partners, identifying capacities and dispositions for working in shared spaces, the scope of the program or project and its parameters. In this stage of the timeline, it is essential all the people that need to be in room for these discussions are there. Part of the challenge, especially for those not familiar with the local context or Indigenous community they are working in, is knowing who those people are!

Once those elements are in place, the relationship-building process continues to develop. The strengths of the team need to be identified, as well as how to further build team capacity. This includes developing the capacity of the educators to work with Indigenous peoples, as well as opportunities for mentoring less experienced Indigenous educators.

From here, you can then move into a longer-term relational space where there's an exploration of community goals, values, and aspirations. It's an entry point, but it's an important entry point for establishing the context of your program or project – one that you should revisit over and over again to provide the opportunities to engage and connect with community. Initially it may be brief and a surface level engagement. This is normal and natural – engagement takes time. Time is vital for relationship building – the key thing you need for co-design is time. It takes a long time to build relationships, and remember, you're not only building relationship with people, but with communities, community partners, and so on.

Throughout the process of co-design, you are continually going back to the community to build both ways understanding (also see Chapter 12, this volume). By building understanding both ways, you create transformation within the relational space because you're really grounded within community aspirations and community thinking. This also shapes what you do in meaningful and transformative ways. Often it is the case that opportunities are created that you may not have been aware of as an outside researcher. Communities are aware of how innovation informs meaningful projects, and they take time to teach you as an outsider to help you to think outside the box.

The process in co-design continues, it is never final. The project might end, in terms of a timeline, but the process of co-design continues. This is because you've built up a connection with the community. The community is wanting you to think differently about other projects that may or may not be within your initial design brief. This makes it deeply rewarding work, but it is not without its challenges.

The challenges lie in not fully realising the opportunities and value of co-design from both an institutional perspective and community perspectives. There is a tension between these two perspectives in terms of the time commitment. While co-design is an ongoing process, funding and the requirement to produce educational outcomes are not and tend, instead, to be short-lived – often with non-negotiable expiration dates.

Co-design is also about sharing – and sharing equally. Power sharing is a big challenge, educational institutions tend to have a lot of impact compared to communities. There needs to be opportunities for communities to exercise their agency to seek out programs that align with their goals, values, and aspirations.

In terms of how people engage in co-design and the knowledges needed, it is important to be prepared not to know, not to be the expert, and to be open to learning. Acknowledge your own ignorance in different spaces and be willing to listen and to learn. This means, not assuming what community needs and what the priorities are. It is also useful to understand that your program or project does not exist outside the historical contexts that have built the present day. Furthermore, accountability is needed now, in the future, and in relation to past events. I suggest there should be no saying that 'it wasn't me', instead the past needs to be acknowledged and written into the future in terms of actions needed to remedy previous injustices.

A big learning curve for me was learning how to navigate the governance structures across Indigenous communities. Some communities are connected to a native title process and then there are those that are run independently. So, there can be a tension between the individual community and the broader governance frameworks. I learned to be aware of these structures and to respond sensitively to all traditional owners. This goes back to the original message about getting all the people in the room that need to be there from the start. Ultimately, it needs to be understood that co-design can't be done lightly and if you can't do it properly – don't do it and especially don't do it until you have developed good relationships.

Co-design while broad in its understanding at its heart is about relationships. This helps us to then think about how we form genuine partnerships with Aboriginal and Torres Strait Islander contributors and the ways potential projects help to focus outcomes on building programs with outcomes that work towards self-determination for Aboriginal and Torres Strait Islander Peoples.

Conclusion

This chapter reinforces the significant importance of building and maintaining strong relationships with Aboriginal community members who are approached to be involved in program or project development. As these activities are usually carried out by education professionals who are often considered to be 'outsiders' or non-community members, it is vital that these relationships are built on foundations of trust, respect, and mutual benefit. These elements are fundamental in achieving successful outcomes for the planned and for future projects.

Many Aboriginal communities and participants have encountered negative experiences in being involved in previous projects and, therefore, may be reluctant to offer their consent and a willingness to participate. This chapter provides some insights and offers several key guidelines for developing and maintaining relationships with Aboriginal Elders and community members.

References

Aboriginal and Torres Strait Islander Corporation of Languages. (2004). *Community protocols for indigenous language projects*. FATSIL. https://www.wipo.int/tk/en/databases/creative_heritage/indigenous/link0014.html

Aboriginal Land Trust. (n.d.). *Working with Aboriginal language custodians: Guidelines for ethical and respectful collaborations*. https://www.alt.nsw.gov.au/assets/Uploads/downloads/files/ACIP-Working-with-Aboriginal-Language-Custodians-Guidelines-for-ethical-and-respectful-collaborations.pdf

Australian Institute of Aboriginal and Torres Strait Islander Studies. (2012). *Guidelines for ethical research in Indigenous studies*. AIATSIS. Available at the AIATSIS website. https://aiatsis.gov.au/sites/default/files/2020-09/gerais.pdf

Barker, L. (2008). 'Hangin' out' and 'yarnin': Reflecting on the experience of collecting oral histories. *History Australia, 5*(1), 9.1–9.10.

Barlo, S. (2017). Lessons from the participants in decolonising research. *Learning Communities: International Journal of Learning in Social Contexts [Special Issue: Decolonising Research Practices], 22,* 16–25, https://doi.org/10.18793/LCJ2017.22.03

Blomkamp, E. (2018). The promise of co-design for public policy. *Australian Journal of Public Administration, 77*(4), 729–743. https://doi.org/10.1111/1467-8500.12310

Council, R. (2017). Final report of the Referendum Council. Department of the Prime Minister and Cabinet (Australia).

Department of Education. (2019). *Keeping Indigenous languages and cultures strong, a plan for the teaching and learning of Indigenous languages and cultures in Northern Territory schools*. Northern Territory Government.

Disbray, S., Plummer, R., & Martin, B. (2020). Languages ideologies and practice from the land and the classroom. *The Modern Language Journal, 104*(2), 519–525. https://doi.org/10.1111/modl.12658

Eades, D. (1988). They don't speak an Aboriginal language, or do they? In I. Keen (Ed.), *Being Black: Aboriginal cultures in 'settled' Australia* (pp. 97–115). Aboriginal Studies Press.

Geia, L. K., Hayes, B., & Usher, K. (2013). Yarning/Aboriginal storytelling: Towards an understanding of an Indigenous perspective and its implications for research practice. *Contemporary Nurse, 46*(1), 13–17.

Humphery, K. (2000). *Indigenous health and 'western research': Discussion paper*. VicHealth Koori Health Research and Community Development Unit.

Jackson-Barrett, E. M., & Lee-Hammond, L. (2018). Strengthening identities and involvement of Aboriginal children through learning On Country. *Australian Journal of Teacher Education, 43*(6), 86–104.

Janke, T. (2005). Managing Indigenous knowledge and Indigenous cultural and intellectual property. *Australian Academic & Research Libraries, 36*(2), 95–107. 10.1080/00048623.2005.10721251

Kickett-Tucker, C. (2008). Exploring the racial identity of Australian Aboriginal children and youth. *Health Sociology Review, 18*(1), 119–136.

Lowe, K., & Ash, A. (2006). *Talking each other's lingo: the Aboriginal languages K–10 Syllabus and its role in language revival in NSW* [Online]. Available: https://citeseerx.ist.psu.edu/document?repid=rep1&type=pdf&doi=089a8b1b98fae6d53af290873969fbc1693266cf

Mahood, K. (2012). Kartiya are like Toyotas: White workers on Australia's cultural frontier. *Griffith Review*, (36), 43–59.

Mark, S., & Hagen, P. (2020). *Co-design in Aotearoa New Zealand: A snapshot of the literature*. Auckland Co-design Lab.

National Copyright Unit. (n.d.). *Indigenous cultural and intellectual property rights*. Retrieved 20th June 2024 from https://smartcopying.edu.au/guidelines/copyright-basics/indigenous-cultural-and-intellectual-property-rights/

New South Wales Aboriginal Education Consultative Group & New South Wales Department of Education & Training. (2004). *The report of the review of Aboriginal education: Yanigurra muya: Ganggurrinyma yarri guurulaw yirringin.gurray. Freeing the spirit: Dreaming an equal future*. New South Wales Department of Education & Training.

Ober, R. (2017). Kapati time: Storytelling as a data collection method in Indigenous research. *International Journal of Learning in Social Contexts, 22*, 8–16.

O'Brien, G. M., & Bobongie-Harris, F. (2023). Revitalization of First Nations languages: A Queensland perspective. *Australian Journal of Language and Literacy, 46*(2), 183–193. https://doi.org/10.1007/s44020-023-00036-4

Oliver, R., & Exell, M. (2019). Promoting positive self-identity in Aboriginal students: Case studies of Clontarf academy youth living a rural community. *Australian and International Journal of Rural Education, 29*(1), 30–44.

Oliver, R., & Exell, M. (2020). Identity, translanguaging, linguicism and racism: The experience of Australian Aboriginal people living in a remote community. *International Journal of Bilingual Education and Bilingualism, 23*(7), 819–832.

Osborne, S., Lester, K., Tjitayi, K., Burton, R., & Minutjukur, M. (2020). Red Dirt Thinking on first language and culturally responsive pedagogies in Anangu schools. *Rural Society, 29*(3), 204–218. https://doi.org/10.1080/10371656.2020.1842597

Queensland Government. (2022). *Indigenous cultural and intellectual property protocol for the teaching of Aboriginal languages and Torres Strait Islander languages in Queensland State Schools*. State of Queensland. https://education.qld.gov.au/student/Documents/icip-protocol.pdf

Raiden, A., & King, A. (2021). Social value: Co-creation, challenges, and assessment. In W. Leal Filho, A. M. Azul, L. Brandli, A. Lange Salvia, P. G. Özuyar, & T. Wall (Eds.), *No poverty* (pp. 995–1004). Springer International Publishing. https://doi.org/10.1007/978-3-319-95714-2_105

Shay, M., Sarra, G., & Lampert, J. (2023). Indigenous education policy, practice and research: Unravelling the tangled web. *The Australian Educational Researcher, 50*(1), 73–88. https://doi.org/10.1007/s13384-022-00581-w

St John, N., & Akama, Y. (2022). Reimagining co-design on Country as a relational and transformational practice. *CoDesign, 18*(1), 16–31. https://doi.org/10.1080/15710882.2021.2001536

Zubrick, S. R., Lawrence, D. M., Silburn, S. R., Blair, E., Milroy, H., Wilkes, T., Eades, S., D'Antoine, H., Read, A., Ishiguchi, P., & Doyle, S. (2004). *The Western Australian Aboriginal child health survey: The health of Aboriginal children and young people*. Telethon Institute for Child Health Research.

Part II
Learning and Teaching Traditional Aboriginal and Torres Strait Islander Languages in Schools

3 Teaching Aboriginal Languages as First Languages in the Northern Territory

Reflections of Educators in the Warlpiri Triangle and Yolŋu Communities

Elizabeth Milmilany, Barbara Martin Napanangka, Merrkiyawuy Ganambarr, Fiona Gibson Napaljarri, Emma Browne, and Melanie Wilkinson

Foreword

Graphics, ideas, and text in this chapter include cultural and intellectual property of Warlpiri people and Yolŋu people of Yirrkala and Milingimbi in the Northern Territory. Use of this knowledge should respect Indigenous Cultural Intellectual Property (ICIP) as recognised in Australia. Copyright law and ICIP work together. Refer to the imprint page for more details.

The authors of this chapter are:

Merrkiyawuy Ganambarr is a Yolŋu woman and the co-principal of Yirrkala School. She has played an important role in the bilingual education movement in Arnhem Land working with Yolŋu Elders to develop both-ways learning and is a member of an Indigenous academic collective that works with Macquarie University. Her vision is that every child is appreciated, and that every child knows that dreams are possible.

Elizabeth Milmilany is a Wangurri woman and qualified teacher who retired after working for 40 years in the Bilingual program at Milingimbi school, including 11 years as the teacher linguist. She then returned to work part-time for almost another decade as a senior adviser to support the ongoing successful delivery of bilingual, bicultural education at the school.

Barbara Martin Napanangka is a Warlpiri teacher and mentor, who began her career in 1981 and has worked in schools in both Lajamanu and Yuendumu as a literacy worker and teacher. She graduated from the Batchelor Institute Remote Aboriginal Teacher Education Program (RATE) and became a senior teacher and cultural adviser for Yuendumu School. Barbara has championed Warlpiri language and culture education for over 40 years and was instrumental in the Warlpiri Theme Cycle project. She is a founding member and chairperson of the Warlpiri Education Training Trust (WETT) which advises on and funds educational projects in the Warlpiri communities. She currently works as the Cultural Adviser to the Community Development Unit at the Central Land Council, teaching Warlpiri language to non-Indigenous staff.

DOI: 10.4324/9781003441021-6

Fiona Gibson Napaljarri is a Warlpiri educator from Nyirrpi community. She is passionate about bilingual and bicultural education and campaigned to establish Nyirrpi's first school in the 1980s. Studying through the Remote Aboriginal Teacher Education Program (RATE), Fiona is a fully qualified teacher and member of Nyirrpi school's Local Engagement and Decision-making (LEaD) committee. Fiona is a founding member of WETT and continues in her role as a WETT Advisory Committee member.

Emma Browne is a linguist who has worked with educators teaching first languages in Central Australia for the past decade and coordinated the compilation of this chapter from contributions of all the authors. She worked with Barbara and Fiona on the Warlpiri reflections and with Melanie on setting the context for this chapter.

Melanie Wilkinson is a linguist who began working with Yolŋu and their languages in 1980. She recently retired, after 32 years, from the NT Department of Education where she worked supporting school programs, regional language networks, and professional learning in East Arnhem Schools. She supported the gathering, transcribing, and translation of the Milingimbi material and introductory notes on the Yolŋu language ecology.

Milmilany's family members who worked on the original transcription, translation, and editing of Milmilany's text are: Lorraine Yurranydjil, Rhoda Goluŋ, Fiona Dhawunymurruwuy, and Gwen Boyukarrpi. Dr. Michael Cooke recorded Milmilany. Dr. Rebecca Green, Jenny Robins, and Dr. Carmel O'Shannessy offered editing support to the chapter.

In the next section (Context), Emma and Melanie give an overview of the four communities, their language ecologies, and then a background to the types of programs on offer in the NT to provide context to the reflections of first language educators in this chapter.

Context: Northern Territory communities and their language ecologies

The Northern Territory (NT) covers a vast and sparsely populated area of 1.35 million square kilometres, sharing its borders with Western Australia to the west, South Australia to the south, and Queensland to the east. Over half of the 250,000 population live in remote communities (some of which are covered in this chapter, see Figure 3.1), which for many are located on traditional lands. There are 153 schools in the NT, three quarters of these are located in remote and very remote areas, with 44 per cent of the NT's total student population attending those remote schools. Students in remote localities speak a range of traditional languages and contact languages including creoles and varieties of English (Wigglesworth et al., 2017, p. 8). They also communicate through hand signs and gestures, body language, dance and symbols, patterns, paintings, oral stories, and songs (Burarrwanga et al., 2019). Multilingualism in Aboriginal languages in the NT is significantly higher than elsewhere in Australia due to the remoteness and relatively late European settlement (Devlin et al., 2017, p. 6). Many First Nations people in the NT also have links to traditional country and languages of other parts of Australia. All but one of the twelve First Nations languages considered 'strong' or still spoken by all generations are used in the NT (Department of Infrastructure, Transport, Regional Development and Communications, Australian Institute of Aboriginal and Torres Strait Islander Studies et al., 2020). There are also many other NT languages that are less strong – some with few living speakers, and some with none.

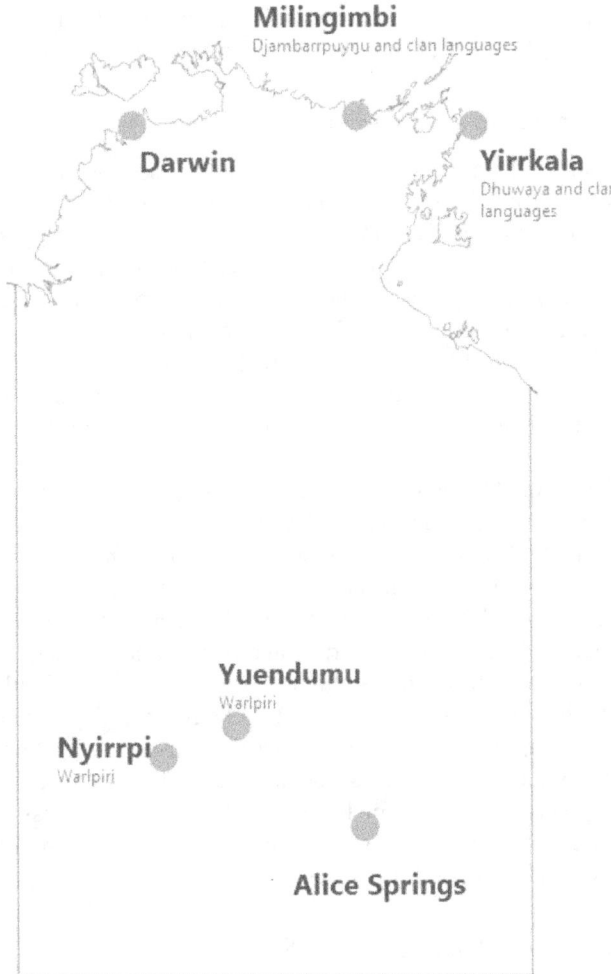

Figure 3.1 Map of the communities in this chapter: Yuendumu, Nyirrpi, Milingimbi, Yirrkala

Yuendumu and Nyirrpi in the Warlpiri Triangle

Warlpiri country lies to the east of the Northern Territory-Western Australia border and northwest of the regional town of Alice Springs, in and around the Tanami Desert of Central Australia. The four Warlpiri communities of Yuendumu, Nyirrpi, Lajamanu, and Willowra comprise what is known as the Warlpiri Triangle. Warlpiri is the dominant community language; English is learned as an additional language, and other Aboriginal languages such as Pintupi-Luritja and Anmatyerr are also spoken by some community members. Several dialects of Warlpiri have been documented, and differences across the four communities have been identified in terms of pronunciation and vocabulary, usually influenced by neighbouring languages (Browne, 2019). Light Warlpiri, a contact language spoken in Lajamanu community, systematically draws on elements of Warlpiri, Kriol, and Aboriginal Englishes (O'Shannessy, 2020).

Two Yolŋu communities in north-east Arnhem Land

Milingimbi and Yirrkala are two of five communities established as Methodist Missions in north-east Arnhem Land, Milingimbi in 1922 and Yirrkala in 1935. The people and languages of this region are now commonly referred to, by themselves and others, as Yolŋu, the word for 'person, Aboriginal person' in many, but not all, of the languages. The label Yolŋu Matha was engineered at the School of Australian Linguistics (SAL) as a cover term for all Yolŋu languages (Amery, 1985: Footnote 18, p. 21). There are 40–50 Yolŋu clans, each claiming their language is distinct, even if sometimes they are recognised as being close to each other. The languages are important markers of identity for members of each clan.

The missions brought together members of a number of clan groups, and over time use of a common language has developed. The mixture of clans was different for each community. Milingimbi, the western-most community, and Yirrkala, the furthest east, have distinct combinations of clan groups. Djambarrpuyŋu or Dhuwal is the language most widely used today at Milingimbi, and Dhuwaya the language most widely used at Yirrkala. Djambarrpuyŋu has arisen through the extended use of a traditional language by members of other clans (Tamisari & Milmilany, 2003). Dhuwaya has arisen as a new Yolŋu language, a koine emerging from contact between different Yolŋu clan languages at Yirrkala (Amery, 1985; Morales et al., 2018; Wigglesworth et al., 2021). Both communities include speakers of traditional clan languages, most of which are no longer widely transferred across generations. Elders in both communities have indicated that children should be supported in learning their own clan languages at school.

Teaching First Nations languages in the NT

Aboriginal languages have been taught in government schools in the NT since 1973, when the bilingual education program was established. Before this, a few mission schools had taught literacy in the children's Aboriginal first language (Carew et al., forthcoming; Devlin et al., 2017). The accreditation of these first bilingual programs 50 years ago demanded development of language curriculum and teaching materials in Aboriginal languages, as well as the training of Aboriginal teachers (Disbray, 2014). To meet these needs, a bilingual unit was established in the Department of Education, and Literature Production Centres were set up in schools to produce language resources in several communities, including Yuendumu, Milingimbi, and Yirrkala (Devlin et al., 2017). A method of bilingual team teaching was developed and widely promoted with three key elements: learning together, planning together, and teaching together (Devlin & Gapany, 2017; Graham, 2017).

The School of Australian Languages (SAL) was set up at Batchelor, near Darwin, in 1974, to provide linguistics training for Aboriginal and Torres Strait Islander people that would enable them to carry out linguistic analysis and sociolinguistic research, and to develop literacy materials in over 20 different languages (Black & Breen, 2001; Carew et al., forthcoming; Disbray & Devlin, 2017). Batchelor College (later Batchelor Institute of Indigenous Tertiary Education) was established in 1976 (Reaburn et al., 2015) to provide teacher education for remote Aboriginal students. Batchelor's Remote Area Teacher Education (RATE) program offered a combination of Batchelor-based and community-based training and teaching. Graduates received an Associate Diploma of Teaching (Aboriginal Schools) with authority to teach in their 32 home communities (Bat et al., 2014; Lee et al., 2014). In the 1980s, a partnership between Deakin University and Batchelor College offered a three-year Bachelor of Arts (Education) degree through what was known as the Deakin-Batchelor-Aboriginal Teacher-Education (D-BATE) program (Street et al., 2017). In recent decades there have been VET courses in Education Support and an upgrade to a full Batchelor of Education; however, community-based teacher education has not been sustained.

> These Aboriginal teacher training programs fostered professional reflection and triggered sophisticated discussions, which contributed to innovations in Aboriginal pedagogy and curriculum.
> (Disbray & Devlin, 2017, p. 110)

They provided a 'powerful forum to create curriculum that had Aboriginal languages and knowledge at its centre' (McMahon & Maymuru, 2023). Among the local frameworks which developed during these years were the:

- Arrernte Curriculum Intelyape-lyape Akaltye (Hartman, 1994),
- Papunya School Curriculum,
- Yirrkala School's Garma Maths and Galtha Rom (Marika-Mununggiritj & Christie 1995; Marika-Mununggiritj et al., 1990; Marika et al., 1992),
- Gattjirrk at Milingimbi (Tamisari & Milmilany, 2003),
- the Warlpiri Curriculum Framework (also known as the Warlpiri Theme Cycle) (Disbray & Martin, 2018),
- the Wubuy Curriculum, and the Tiwi Language Curriculum (NT Department of Education, 2017a, p. 30).

In 2002, the NT Department of Education published the Northern Territory Curriculum Framework (NTCF), which identified learning outcomes for all curriculum areas from the Transition year to Year 10 (NT Department of Education, 2002). It included an Indigenous Languages and Cultures (ILC) component, developed in consultation with Aboriginal educators across the NT, and drew heavily on developments within the bilingual programs. During 2012–2013 a national Australian Curriculum was developed, which included a Framework for Aboriginal Languages and Torres Strait Islander Languages (Australian Curriculum Assessment and Reporting Authority [ACARA], 2023). The NT responded to this by developing its own framework drawing and expanding on the NTCF from 2002 as well as the national framework. It was developed by reference groups led by Indigenous Elders, educators, and linguists from across the Northern Territory, including some authors of this chapter.

There are two components of this framework. The first is a plan for the teaching of Indigenous languages in the NT today: *Keeping Indigenous Languages and Cultures Strong – A Plan for the Teaching and Learning of Indigenous Languages and Cultures in Northern Territory Schools* (NT DoE, 2017a), accompanied by a set of guidelines for the implementation of ILC programs in schools (NT DoE, 2017b). The second component is curricula to implement the teaching of the language pathways and cultural content and knowledge identified in the guidelines. These are collectively referred to as the Northern Territory Indigenous Languages and Cultures (NTILC).

The guidelines outline five key principles, underpinned by a foundation of strong ownership by Indigenous Elders, the custodians and owners of the languages and cultures. These are interconnected and show the roles and responsibilities of schools, communities, and stakeholders as depicted in this water lily metaphor in Figure 3.2.

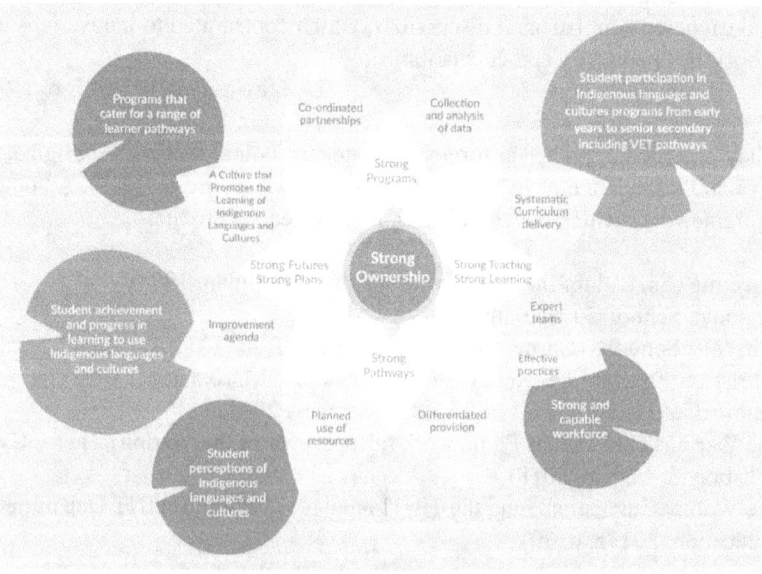

Figure 3.2 Representation of the principles, goals, and strategies for teaching and learning Indigenous Languages and Cultures, based on the water lily as a metaphor, suggested by Lorraine Bennett (NT DoE, 2017a, p. 8)

Teaching Aboriginal Languages as First Languages in the NT 47

The Northern Territory Indigenous Languages and Cultures (NTILC) offers flexible options to cater for the local language ecologies and program goals. There are seven separate curriculum documents. One to frame cultural content and knowledge and six to meet the needs of different language programs:

- A Bilingual (L1B) curriculum and a First Language Maintenance (L1M) curriculum in the First Language Pathways (top circle in Figure 3.3) (NT DoE, 2018b; NT DoE, 2018c).
- A Language Revitalisation (LRV) curriculum and a Language Renewal (LRN) curriculum in the Language Revival (LR) Pathways (shown in right hand circle in Figure 3.3) (NT DoE, 2018d; NT DoE, 2018e).
- A curriculum for Second Language Learning (L2) (bottom circle in Figure 3.3) (NT DoE, 2018f).
- A curriculum for Language and Cultural Awareness (shown on left hand circle in Figure 3.3) (NT DoE, 2018g).

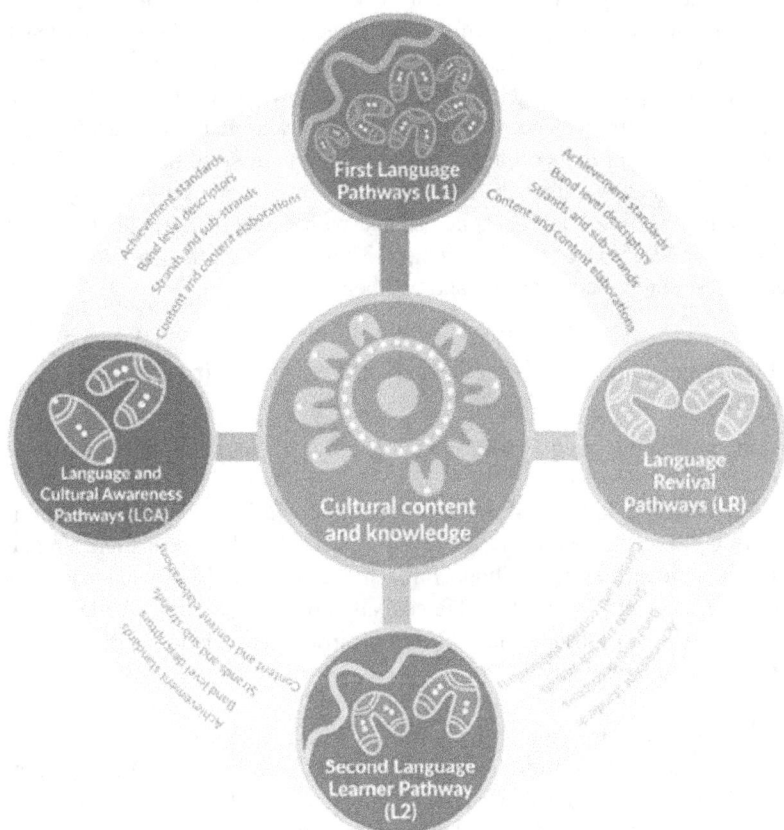

Figure 3.3 A model for the NT Curriculum for Indigenous Languages and Cultures (NTILC) (NT Department of Education, 2017a, p. 46)

At present, over 40 schools teach Indigenous Languages and Cultures programs across all language pathways in the NT. Of these, there are fewer than 15 schools delivering bilingual programs. Each of these language pathways is underpinned by the Cultural Content and Knowledge curriculum (the circle at the centre of Figure 3.3) which outlines the key ideas that teachers can work with in all the language pathways. This guides appropriate cultural knowledge that can be taught in schools and a series of learning progressions for developing knowledge, understandings, and skills for using language. According to the document, 'The language is the skill being used, and cultural knowledge is the medium through which that skill is learnt and practised' (NT DoE, 2018a, p. 3). The content, ideas, and ways the learning develop across the different Band Levels are informed by local curricula which are continually evolving, and being developed and expanded through intra- and inter-community workshops. It is noteworthy that the development of local curricula is strongest in schools with sustained bilingual programs and associated resourcing for learning in first languages across the curriculum.

Yuendumu, Nyirrpi, Milingimbi, and Yirrkala schools follow the First Language (L1) Bilingual curriculum (part of the top circle in Figure 3.3) whereby teaching and learning happens in first languages across the curriculum and alongside English as an additional language (McMahon & Murray, 2000). In the next sections, four educators from those communities provide a rich picture of teaching and assessing languages in their bilingual programs; they describe the role of Elders in integrating local knowledges in schools and growing local teachers. They also talk about the power of collaboration across and within schools, and their aspirations for the future teaching of their languages. They reflect on the important implications of these for student learning and wellbeing.

First language educators' reflections about teaching their languages in NT schools

The first question these educators reflect upon is: 'Why is it important to teach our languages in our schools?'

Throughout the history of formal education, Warlpiri and Yolŋu communities have continued to advocate for recognition and inclusion of their languages, cultures, and identities to maintain linguistic and cultural knowledges and as a means for taking an active role in the education of their children (Anderson et al., 2018; Warlpiri-patu-kurlangu-jaru, 2011). Merrkiyawuy Ganambarr co-principal of Yirrkala school explains:

> For almost 50 years Yolŋu people here in Yirrkala have insisted on having a say in how their children are educated often defying shifting government policies. In our school vision statement (see Figure 3.4), there are guidelines our Elders visualised that the school goes by and Yolŋu children grow up with two laws, Dhuwa and Yirritja. This foundational knowledge

moulds who a person is, where that person comes from, what their vision is, how they think, how they will be able to deal with contemporary life and whether they will be able to sort out and analyse the new ideas they encounter in their lives in a balanced way. As teachers we must be prepared for operating in the contemporary world in a strong and balanced way so that we will be able to achieve the visions and aspirations of our Elders. We see Yambirrpa Schools [Yirrkala School and Laynhapuy Homelands School] as an important part of the community development process which has the goal of achieving a self-determining, self-managing community. Our school programs will encourage our students to develop skills, hope, and vision for their future.

Yambirrpa Schools need to develop strong Yolŋu and Ngäpaki (formerly known as Balanda [non-Indigenous]) curriculum so that students can develop all the skills they will require in the future. This includes the ability to use new technologies to access the knowledge that is required for a self-determining community.

Yambirrpa Schools need to assist students to develop the skills required to understand political power and how this fits into community development.

Yambirrpa Schools value the heritage, culture, and knowledge that the students bring with them and use these as a starting point for the students' life-long education journey.

Yambirrpa Schools believe the students are capable of learning high level knowledge and responding to the challenges required for employment and participation in local community life and in the wider national and international community.

Yambirrpa Schools recognise and value the importance of developing a strong identity and self-concept in the students. This will lead to confident, self-motivated, responsible students and will assist them to become *ralpa*, strong adults.

Yambirrpa Schools will help students achieve unity within the community by opening up issues related to difference, leadership and the skills needed to work collaboratively. Racism, sexism, bigotry, and the devaluing of students with special needs will be dealt with openly and in a constructive manner. The culture of Yambirrpa schools seeks to maintain a *bala ga lili* reciprocal philosophy where community involvement plays an integral part. Within this school culture all participants in the education enterprise will be valued and respected and feel that their ideas and views are important.

YAMBIRRPA SCHOOLS VISION STATEMENT
Nhäŋa Ŋathil'yurra

Yambirrpa goḻ yukurra djingaryun Community-ŋura ŋapuŋga'. Dhuwala goḻ gumurr'yun-marrtji yukurra ga märrama rom wukirriwu yolŋuwalana goṉlili. Märr yurru rom dhiyala goḻŋura ganydjarrmirriyama yothu'nha buluŋuwu marŋgithinyarawu, ga gatjpu' nhänhara nhanukuŋu yothu'wuŋu ŋathil'yunara yurru rumbalthirrina.

Yambirrpa goḻyu yurru ŋamaŋamayun dhukarr ga rom ḏälkuma marŋgithinyaramirri, märr yurru yothu' maŋgithirri wirrki ŋurukuna bala ŋäthil'yun yalalaŋuwuna. Balanyara bitjan ŋayi yothu' yurru marŋgithirri yuṯawu girri'wu mulkuruwu malanyŋuwu, märr ŋayi yolŋu yurru djingaryun nhanukalay ŋayi ḻukuyu ga goŋdhu mulka djäma yalalaŋumirri wuṉḏaŋarrkuma.

Dhiyala Yambirrpa goḻŋura yurru gunga'yun yothu'nha marŋgikuma ga gaḏamanguma wirrki ḻiya, nhaltjan ŋayi yurru nhanukalay ŋayi ganda'yu ga gakal'yu djäma ga marŋgithirri ṉiṉ'thun yuṯawu ga mulkuruwu romgu, märr yurru dharaŋan nhäma.

Dhiyala goḻŋura yukurra dharaŋan nhäma nhanŋuway yothu'wu ḻuku-rom, nhä ŋayi bäpurru' ga mala, yol ŋayi, wanhaŋuru ŋayi, ga bukmak nhä ŋayi yukurra yothu'yu ŋunhi mulka ga gäma. Ŋayi ŋurrunydja dhiyala goḻŋura yothu yurru ŋurru-yirr'yun marŋgithirri, ga djunamana wala yukurra marrtji ŋunha gumurr'yun ga nhäma ŋathil'yun marŋgithinyarawu mulkuruwu ga yuṯawu romgu.

Yurru yothunydja nhina märr-yuwalkmirri ga ḻiya nhanŋu yurru barrku guyaŋinyarawu. Marŋgithirri ŋayi yurru bulu nhaltjan ŋayi yurru nhina ga djäma yalalaŋumirri. Ŋayi yurru marŋgithirri gakal'wu mulkurwu romgu dhiyala bäyma wäŋaŋura, dhiyaku bäymawu nhinanharawu romgu ga djämawu. Bulu ŋuriki bala wäŋawu yindiwu mulkuruwu, dhiyaku ŋayi yurru gaḏamandhirrinydja dharaŋanarawu.

Goḻŋura rom yurru dharaŋan nhäma nhä yothu'yu yukurra ŋayaŋuyu-ḏälkuma, ga märryu-ḏapmarama, ga nhaltjan ŋayi yukurra ŋir'yun. Gunga'yurra ŋanya, ŋayi yurru ŋayaŋuyu latjuyu marrtji, rom-dhunupayu, ŋoyyu ḏälyu ga ḏukṯuk-waŋa buluŋuwu marŋgithinyarawu.

Dhiyaŋu goḻyu yurru gunga'yun yothu'nha nhänharawu barrku-ḏakthunarawu ga nhinanharawu manapanminyarawu bäpurruwu ga djäma ga marŋgithirri rrambaŋi bala ga lili. Ga balanyara ŋunhi mala nyamir'yunaramirri, ḻikandhu-ḏupthunaramirri, bäpurru-nyamir'yunaramirri miny'tji-nyamir'yunaramirri, ŋunhiyinydja rom yurru ḏupthuna. Yäna nhina waŋganyŋura ga guŋga'yun yothu'nha märr yurru nhänharamirri latjukunharamirri ga märryu-ḏapthunmaranhamirri bala ga lili. Dhiyaŋu romdhu yurru gunga'yun yothu'nha ŋayi yurru ŋayaŋu-lapthun bukmakku yolŋuwu. Melyu manymakthu nhänharamirri ga birrimbirryu ga ŋayaŋuyu waŋganydhu nhina.

Rom ga dhukarr Yambirrpa'wu goḻwu, nhänharana ḻiŋguwuynha djarr'yunarana yukurra djingaryun, gumurr-wekanharamirri bala ga lili rom. Dhiyala goḻŋura yurru marr-manapanmirri ga waŋayu-märrama, märr-ḏapthunaramirri rom, märr yurru ḻiya ga dhäruk-manapanmirri ga ŋamaŋamayun waŋany rom ga dhukarr.

Figure 3.4 The original Vision Statement by Elders and Yolŋu educators in Gumatj (Yirrkala School, 2024)

Barbara Napanangka, former senior teacher at Yuendumu school, explains why learning traditional languages as well as English is important for Warlpiri children:

Ngurrju jaru jirrama-ju. Kurdu-kurdu kuja kalu pina-jarrimi Warlpiri yungulu milya-pinyi English-i. Englishirlalku yangka yungulu nyanu-ngurlulku yirarrnirra manu wangkamirra Warlpiri-jangka. Yuwayi kuja-ku ka karrimi Warlpiri-ji kamparruju jaruju. Kurdu yungulu pina-jarrimi Warlpiri-wiyi yungulu milya-pinyi Englishi. Bilingual-u-ju kujalku yungu karrimi tarnnga-juku, ngulalujana pina-mani milya-pinjaku yungulu mardarni tarnnga-juku. Kajili yangka wiri-wiri jarrimi-lki manu yungulu tarnnga-juku mardarni jaru jirrama nyanungu yungulu pina-pina-mani and nyanurra-nyangu kurdu-kurdu. Kajili next generationili milya-pinyilki nyanu-ngula-lku yungulu milya-pinyi and pina-pina-mani kurdu-kurdu nyanurra-nyangulku. Wita-wita-jangka wiri-wiri-kirra. Yuwayi tarrnga-juku nyampu-ju nati ka jirrama jaru lawa-jarri. Lawa, tarnnga-juku.

It's good to have two languages. If kids learn Warlpiri, then they can understand English. They learn English after learning to write and speak Warlpiri. Warlpiri is our first language. If kids learn in Warlpiri, then they can learn English. And they will remain bilingual forever, and they will understand and be able to work with two languages. They'll have two languages. And their children will have two languages and they'll teach their children those languages and the next generation will know too. They'll learn from young children into adulthood. Yes, and their two languages won't be lost. They'll keep them forever.

Next, the educators reflect on the question: How do we teach and assess through first languages in Warlpiri and Yolŋu schools today?

Teaching through Australian Aboriginal first languages requires a skilled workforce of language educators enacting strong languages curricula and pedagogies, diverse teaching resources in these languages, mentoring from Elders and formal professional development, collaboration within regions and between cross-linguistic teaching teams, and, ideally, strong institutional support. These elements are discussed below.

Local knowledge systems and the important role of community Elders

Maps of local knowledge systems, developed during the later years of remote teacher education work with the NTILC to guide the delivery of teaching first languages in remote schools. Milmilany retired teacher-linguist at Milingimbi school, explains the process of developing the Gaṯjirrk cycle (Milmilany, 2023, pp. 3–6):

Ga napurr gan ŋunhi marŋgi-gurrupar walalany djamarrkuḻiny' ga bulu ga napurr nhawi balanya Workshop napurr gan running ŋalapaḻmirriw adults-ku wulma'-wulmangu ga wulgu'-wulgumangu. Walal gan marrtjin beŋur, räli school-lil. Ga lakaraŋal walal gan bitjarr 'Dhuwal, dhuwal, dhuwal. Dhiyak napurr djäl nhuma dhu ga marŋgi-gurrupan djamarrkuḻiny' dhiyal school-ŋur'. Bitjarr walal gan waŋan.

Ga napurr gan ŋunhi wukirri, djorra'lil mala. Wukirri napurr gan. Ga napurr gan ditja' mala waŋanhamin ga bulu napurr gan walalany waŋan dhä-birrka'yurr napurr gan walalany ŋalapalmirriny yolŋu'-yulŋuny nhä ŋunhi ŋayi dhukarr ŋalapalmirriw ŋathiliŋuw ga bala ga marŋgi-gurrupan ŋunha djamarrkuḻiny' yuṯany, ŋunhi ŋayi ga dhiyaŋ bala ŋuthan.

Ga djämany napurr ŋunhi, ga nhäŋal napurr gan ŋunhiyi dhukarr, märrma' pathway napurr gan nhäŋal Balanda ga Yolŋu dhukarr, märr ga napurr gan ŋunhi djämany Bilingualnydja dhuwandja ŋayi dhäruk märrma', märrma'yaka yan waŋgany, yaka nhe dhu waŋgany dhäruk djäma, märrma' dharuk, märr ga ŋayi dhu ga djäma waŋganyŋur ga guŋga'yunmirr manḏa dhu. Ga wanhal ŋayi dhu nhakun ŋunhi djamarrkuḻiny' napurruŋ marŋgi-gurrupan ga wanhal year-ŋur ga wanhal nhakun djamarrkuḻi' ŋayi dhu ŋunhi dhawar'yun.

Ga nhäŋal napurr gan ŋunhi nhakun everytime napurr gäŋal walalany out, napurr marŋgi gurrupan walalany djamarrkuḻiny' nhakun napurr barpuru program djäma, Gaṯtjirrk dhuwal yäku program. Dhuwal napurr gan djamarrkuḻiny' gäŋal out, dhawaṯmaraŋal wäŋalil wirpuŋulil wiripuŋulil, nhä napurr gan nhäŋal ga nhä napurr dhu marŋgikum walalany djamarrkuḻiny' nhakun dhuwal ya-dhuwal calendar ŋunha nhe ga nhäma yellow-one-ŋur (Figure 3.5-ŋur).

We were teaching the children and, also, we were running workshops with Elders and adults, old men and old women. They came to the school here. And they spoke in this way, 'This, this, and this. This is what we want you to teach the children here at the school.'

And we were writing everything down. And us teachers were talking about this and we were also finding out about ways of learning from the Elders so as to use these to teach the new children who are now growing up.

And we kept on working on this until we could see the pathway, in fact, two pathways, Balanda and Yolŋu, so that we were doing Bilingual. This word is about two, two ways, not only one pathway. You don't just work on one. We work on both and the two help each other. We worked out at what level our students are taught, and what we will teach at what year level and where the students will finish. We created the Gaṯtjirrk Program where we would take the children out to different places, and we were seeing and teaching those children. For example, this calendar here – can you see the yellow one (Milmilany points to a seasons calendar which informed the Gaṯtjirrk cycle in Figure 3.5).

Teaching Aboriginal Languages as First Languages in the NT 53

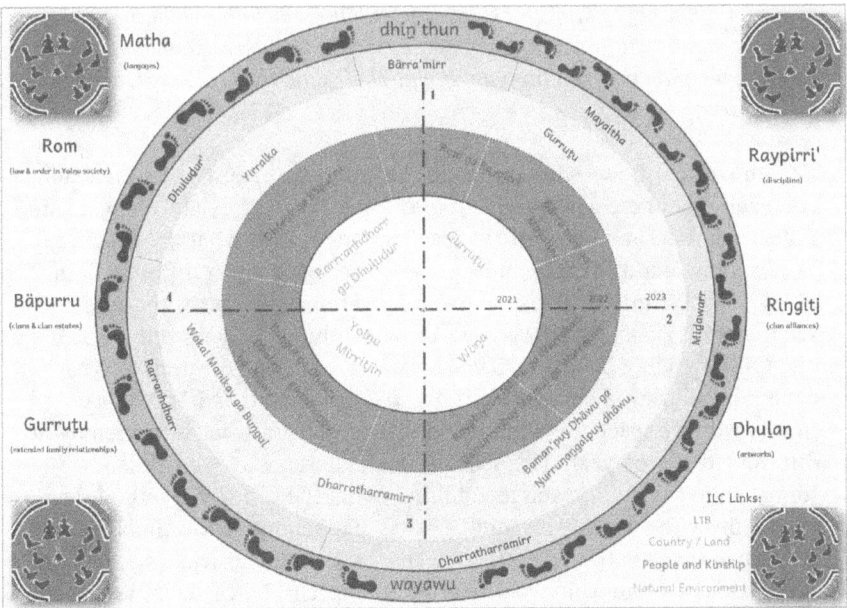

Figure 3.5 Gaṯjirrk cycle – the footprints show the learning of the children (Milingimbi School, 2024)

Yo ŋuruŋuny ga maŋutji-ḻakaram barrkuwatj nhä mala marŋgithinyawuy djamarrkuḻiw' ŋunhi dhu ga ditjay' marŋgikum dhiyal school-ŋur.

Yurr djämany walal dhu ga ŋunhi ga as long as ŋayi dhu ŋaḻapaḻ yolŋu marrtji guŋga'yunaraw ya-bitjan märr ga ŋayi ga ditjiŋdja ŋunhi, ga through ŋayi ga ŋaḻapaḻyu yolŋuy nhäma nhä ŋayi ŋunhi djamarrkuḻiw' marŋgithinyaraw.

Ga wiripu napurr walalany gan marŋgikuŋalnydja every year ga bitjarr napurr gan rulwaŋdhurr, 'Ma' dhuwandja limurr dhu nhäma dhiyaŋuny bala Dhärratharran,' bitjarr napurr gan. Ga nhä ŋayi ga happening Dhärratharramirriynydja? Wäŋany ga nhaltjana ŋayi? Guyiŋarrthirra ŋayi ga mirithirra. Ya-bitjana dhu ga djamarrkuḻi'nhany marŋgi-gurrupan märr ga ŋayi dhu ga marŋgi nhaliy dhuŋgarray ŋayi dhu yothu be aware ŋurikiyi. Ya-balanya. Season mala dhuwal, Season mala barrkuwatj. Nhumalaŋ Balandaw gäna ga napurruŋ Yolŋuw gäna, napurr dhu marŋgikum djamarrkuḻiny' yurr ŋuriŋiyi dhu ga wäŋay ḻakaram ga watay, wanhaŋur ŋayi dhu ga biw'yun ga nhä mala ŋayi dhu ga happening balanyamirriy. Dhuwal ŋayi bilingualtja nhawi rom ŋunhi ŋayi dhu ga balancing learning märrma' yan. Balanda Yolŋu. Märr ŋayi dhu ga marrtji yothu ŋuthan ga nhäma ŋayi dhu beŋur nhanukal, dhuwandja ŋayi balanya nhakun yuṯa ḏukitj ŋuthan ŋayi marrtji. Bala ŋayi dhu yothuynydja nhäma ŋayi dhu ḏukitj dhawaṯthun, bala ŋayi dhu guyaŋan nhän ŋayi ŋunhi nhakun walu. Nhän ŋayiny dhu yothu marrtji ga märram, ŋunha ḏiltjiŋur, ŋunha gapuŋur, ŋunha wäŋaŋur ga nhä ŋayatham, wanha gali' ŋayi ga wata biw'yun djamarrkuḻiw' nhakun rälimirriyam walalany, märr ga walal marŋgi.

Yes, this chart shows what things the children will learn when the teachers teach them here at school. But that work can only exist as long as the Elders come to help, so that the teachers only teach what the Elders see as the knowledge for the students. And we teach them different things every year. We might choose to teach *Dhärratharra* (one of the seasons - see Figure 3.5). And then we work out what things they need to be aware of. 'Ok now we will look at *Dhärratharra*, and we will think - What is happening during *Dhärratharra*? How is the country? It's really cold.' In this way we teach the children so that they learn what is happening at different times of year. The seasons are different, for you Balanda and for us Yolŋu. We will teach the children what the country is telling them, where the wind is blowing and what is happening at the time. This is Bilingual *rom*, that is, the practice that is balancing, learning for both ways, Balanda and Yolŋu. So that the young child will see a new shoot come out and think about what season it is, what places they can go and hunt or gather such as in the bush, in the sea, water, whatever the land holds, what side the wind is blowing so that children get the knowledge expected of them.

Ga napurr golḻil märram ŋaḻapaḻmirriny yolŋuny märr ga ŋayi dhu ga ḻakaram dhäwu, ŋunhiliyi, ŋaḻapaḻyu ga bulu ditjay' mala waŋganyŋur waŋgany-manapanmirr. Ga wukirri program waŋganyŋur. Yolŋu Matha Program ga English program. Balandaw dhärukku ga Yolŋuw dhärukku. Ga bitjan napurr li, 'Ma'. Limurr dhuwal djäma ga bukmak nhämunha' limurr dhuwal class mala, limurr dhu barrkuwatjkum walalany, nhakun age-lil malaŋulil'. Balanya gäna'-gana ŋunhi ŋayi djamarrkuḻi' märr ḏilkurr.

And we bring Elders to school so they will teach the children. The Elders and the teachers working with one purpose together. And writing a program for one purpose - a Yolŋu language program and an English program. For English and for Yolŋu language. And we are talking, 'OK, we will work with all the classes, we will separate them, for example by age.' So, we work out both programs for each class.

Ŋunhiyi napurr ga malthun ŋurukiyin, nhaltjan napurr dhu marŋgikum. Learning pathway ŋunhany djamarrkuḻiw', yolŋukurr. Yo. Ga napurr ga ŋunhi waŋanhamin ŋaḻapaḻmirr napurr gan meet together waŋganyŋur, ga waŋanhamin dharrwamirr, märr ga ŋayi ŋunhidhi learning gärrin napurruŋgal ga bulu passing ŋunhidhi djamarrkuḻi'wal, ya-balanya. Ga djäma napurr gan ŋunhi Gaṯtjirrk Document napurr djäma djorra'. Ga ŋunhiliyi dhiyaŋ yäkuy Gaṯtjirrk Document-thu galkar napurr gan warrpam', galkar napurr marrtji nhä mala learnings mala balayi djorra'lilil.

[...] Yo, curriculum muka ŋayi ŋunhi nhakun nhuma dhu ḻakaram curriculum napurr dhu ḻakaram yolŋuw nhawi marŋgithinyawuy dhukarr nhänhawuy ŋuriki djamarrkuḻiw' nhakun curriculum ŋayi Gaṯtjirrk Document-ŋur gan ŋorran nhä mala marŋgithinyawuy, ŋunhi ŋayi gan gurrupar napurruny ŋaḻapaḻmirriy mala. Yaka napurr gan gäna djäma without Elders. Ŋunhiyiny napurr gan elders-kal walalaŋgal under djäma. Walal gan napurruny gurrupar ga ḻakaraŋal. Ga ŋayiny ŋunha Bilingual-nydja djäma napurr marrtji.i.i. cover ŋayi ŋuriŋi nhawiyu Gaṯtjirrkthu dhuwal school mala, ga wiripu mala school mala walal waŋgany manapar ŋunhiwili idea nhaltjarr napurr gan djäma dhiyal. Manymak.

We follow that for how we will teach, that is the learning pathway for the children in Yolŋu language. And we were talking with the Elders when we all met together, we talked many times so we got the knowledge, and we could then pass it on to the children.

We wrote all these ideas about what the children will learn in the Gaṯtjirrk document. We all worked together on this.

[...] Curriculum is what you call it, we Yolŋu call it the learning pathway for the children. The Gaṯtjirrk Document is like a curriculum describing what the Elders told us was to be the children's learning. We never work without the Elders. We do our work 'under' the Elders. They were directing us. And that Bilingual work is covered by the Gaṯtjirrk at this school. Other schools joined with us in the idea that we are working on here.

In the Warlpiri communities, Elders also played an important role in the development of the Warlpiri Theme Cycle (also known as the Warlpiri curriculum cycle) which has been expanded over four decades of educator workshops (Disbray & Martin, 2018). A Warlpiri teacher from Willowra community, Maisie Kitson, described the intergenerational knowledge transmission and patterns of articulating, restating, and systematising knowledge:

Old people told us what to put in the Warlpiri. We worked every time with Elders, about what we should teach the kids, in different parts of the school. *Jukurrpa* [traditional law], *jurnarrpa* [introduced items], what food, everything, also literacy and Warlpiri maths. In SACE [South Australian Certificate of Education] workshops, on country visits in the 80s and at Warlpiri Triangle [workshops] and sometimes *Jinta Jarrimi* ['Becoming One' workshops] they help us so they can help us teach our kids.

(Disbray & Martin, 2018, p. 31)

The three-year cycle includes 12 themes relating to land, language, and law with associated lists of key concepts, vocabulary, stories, places, dances, etc. that Warlpiri speakers agreed that Warlpiri children need to know. These are continually developed and are expanded upon during Warlpiri Triangle professional learning workshops. It is intended to be taught over the students' school life with deepening learning as the students progress from early years to senior classes according to the recursive model reflective of ceremonial cycles of knowledge transfer.

Barbara explains the interface between the NTILC and Warlpiri Theme Cycle:

Nyurru-wiyiji kalarnalu Northern Territory Indigenous Languages and Cultures framework-kirli warrki-jarrija, curriculum framework book-kurluju. Kalarnalu program plani-manu classroom-rlalku teach-i-maninjaku. Day program kalarnalu plani-manu yapa-watirli manu kalarnalu idea nyangu framework-jangka, ILC framework-jangka. Kajirnalu Warlpiri Theme Cycle mardarni, theme marda ngapa-kurlu. Ngapa-kurlu kajili yinya idea-ju mardarni jirrama-kurlu NTILC framework-kirli manu Warlpiri Theme Cycle-kurlu.

In the past we used to work with the Northern Territory Indigenous Languages Curriculum Framework (NTCF), with that document. We planned our classroom program and taught according to that. Us Warlpiri teachers planned our day programs and got ideas from that, from the ILC framework. When we had our Warlpiri theme cycle, for example a theme is water. We'd get ideas about water from both the NTILC framework and the Warlpiri Theme Cycle.

Yungurnalu yangka plani-mani program panu-jarlurlu yapa teachersurlu. Nyampu theme ngulaju ngapa-kurlu-ju. Kalarnalu panujuku ngapa-kurlu book-u mardarnu. Ngapa-kurlu, nyarrpararla ka ngunami: karru, warnirri, mulju. Kuja-rra-piya-rlu kalalu yirdi-manu ngapa-kurlangu theme-jangka. Kalarnalu yangka karrungka pangurnu, tap-i-kirli kalu manyu-karrimi, manu muljungkarlangu kujarra-piyakurlu

When are planning our program, all teachers. For example, the theme might be water. We would look up all the ideas related to water in the books. For example, different types of bodies of water such as rivers, lakes, soakages, and the like and we would name them connected to the theme. We'd take the kids to dig in the river, they'd play with the tap, and in the soakage and such like.

Theme nganayi nati jinta ngapa-kurlu: 12 themes karlipa mardarni. Ngulajangkaju kalarnalu jalangu-jalanguju jinta-kari-lki new curriculum nganayi NTILC framework manu NTILC bilingual pathway. Jalangu-jalangu kalarnalu use-mani jirrama. Theme cycle project manu curriculum kirli jintamani warrki-jirrama yungurnalu kardu-mani warrki NTILC-jangka manu Warlpiri Theme Cycle-jangka

There isn't just one theme, we have 12 themes. Then later the Theme Cycle project helped us to gather our ideas and to plan our lessons. For planning today, we have a new curriculum framework the NTILC [2018], and we use the NTILC Bilingual pathway (L1B Curriculum). We use both. We create work units from both the NTILC and the Warlpiri theme cycle.

Training first language teachers

In the above section, we described the important guiding and mentoring role of Elders in establishing learning goals in the school and in training the educators who speak and know the language and the students (Anderson et al., 2018). Merrkiyawuy calls these educators 'the most valuable in our school environment'. Barbara reflects on the important role of formal teacher education, and especially 'growing up our own':

Nyurru-wiyi four years-rnalu study-jarrija nganimpajuu. Manu kalarnalu TRB warrki-jarrija kuurlurlaju. Manu kujarnalu nyampurra finishi-manu study-wati nganimpa-nyangu ngulaju yijardurlurnalu do-manu. Kalarnalu ngampurrpa nyayirni warrki-jarrija. Batchelor-rla, CDU-rla manu kuurlu-rla warrki-jarrija. Teach-i-mani kalarnalu 2 weeks kuurlu-rla manu kalarnalu nganimpa-nyangu warrki kangu Batchelor College-kurra. Manu upgradernalu do-manu. Kujarnalu finish-jarrijalku, warrki-jarrijarnalu classroom-rla nganimpa-nyangurla warlaljarla class-rla.

And back in the day we studied for four years. And then we got teacher registration with the TRB [Teacher Registration Board] to work in the school. We finished our study properly and were really prepared and ready to work. We worked at Batchelor Institute, CDU [Charles Darwin University] and school. We taught at the school for two weeks and then we took our work to Batchelor College. We did an extra year upgrade [ITUP - Indigenous Teacher Upgrade Program] to finish our study. Once we had finished, then we worked in our very own classroom.

Teaching resources in Aboriginal languages

Across the NT, educators, linguists, and specialist staff in Bilingual schools have had to produce their own teaching resources, reference materials, stories, readers, games, and posters in local languages. Merrkiyawuy explains:

The heart of our school is the Literature Production Centre; this heartbeat produces the resources of all our goals and what we want to achieve. At this very moment we are scanning, cataloguing, and archiving our work.

Barbara described the role of the Bilingual Resource Development Unit (BRDU), as the Literature Production Centre at Yuendumu is known, in supplying four communities with shared and specialised resources:

Kujarnalu Warlpiri booku-pinki kardu-manu BRDU-rlaju. Manu kalarnalu-jana yilyaja Willowra-kurra, Nyirrpi-kirra manu Lajamanu-kurra. Ngurrju-nyayirni-kirli karlipa panujarlu nyinaja BRDU-rla, helpi-maninjaku Warlpiri-kiji manu Theme Cycle project-rlangu-rnalu do manu.

The BRDU is where we created books and resources in Warlpiri. We sent them to Willowra, Nyirrpi, Lajamanu. We all worked well together in the BRDU and helped with *Warlpiri* [lessons and resources] and also on the [*Warlpiri*] Theme cycle project.

Collaboration across and within schools

Working together among networks of language educators and in cross-cultural teams is an important process for teaching Aboriginal languages. From the very first bilingual programs, schools across the same and different language regions worked together as a community of practice (Browne & Gibson, 2021). Bilingual schools from across the NT have also regularly met in workshops to discuss curriculum, pedagogies, instructional models, and assessment. Milmilany explains (Milmilany, 2003, p. 6):

Bilingual dhuwal ŋayi, ŋunhi ga gan ŋayi ŋorran, 5 schools-thu mala. Pilot school ŋunhi ŋayi ŋurru-yirr'yurr dhiyal, Yurrwi. Märrma' ḏilttjiŋur ga guḻpurr'tja dhuwalaŋupuy bala napurr East-puy mala.

Yurr most napurr gan maḻŋ'maraŋal important-tja napurr gan waŋanhamin. Ya-bitjan. Ŋunhi mala school mala napurr gan waŋanhamin yolŋu mala yol in-charge yolŋu ŋunhili school-ŋur, napurr gan riŋimap ga bitjarr, 'Dhuwal, dhuwal, dhuwal. Nhaltjan nhumany ga djäma dhuwandja?' Ya-bitjana napurr asking question mala balanyaraw.

Ga ŋuriŋi ŋayi nhakun napurruny guŋga'yurr mirithin, ŋunhi napurr gan team teaching ga teamwork napurr gan staff-thu mala not only dhiyal but other schools mala. Yo. Ga idea gurrupanmin balanya nhakun napurr gan dhiyal djäma ga napurr gan marrtjin Bilingual Conference-lil ga ŋunhili presenting ŋunhidhi mala ga napurr gan bitjarr, 'Yo, manymak napurr dhu idea dhuwal nhumalaŋ märram balanya nhakun napurr dhu bitjan napurr dhu nhawi Yuendumuŋur nhumalaŋ school-ŋur dhuwal märram idea limurr dhu work together?' Nhakun waŋgany-manapanmirr limurr dhu ga djamarrkuḻiw' learninggu, yalalaŋuwmirr future-w walalaŋ djamarrkuḻiw'. Yaka yan dhiyak bala, but yalalan märr ga ŋayi dhu yaka dhuwal Bilingual bakthun. Dhärra ŋayi dhu ga. Ḻuku ŋayi dhuwal. Ḻuku napurruŋ.

Bilingual began in five pilot schools, Milingimbi, two in the Centre and three of us in the East (including Shepherdson College [on Elcho Island] and

Yirrkala). What we found most important was talking with each other. Us Yolŋu in those schools were talking with each other.

The Yolŋu in charge in those schools were ringing up each other and asking about how we were doing things. Asking 'How are you doing this, this and this?' And that really helped us, when we were team teaching and working as a staff team, not just here but with other schools. We shared ideas that were working from here and we went to the Bilingual workshops and presented ideas. And we would hear other ideas from other Bilingual schools we liked and bring them back. We were all working together. We were united for the children's learning, for their future. Not just for now, but for later so that Bilingual was not broken. It will continue. It is a foundation. It is a foundation for us.

(...) (Milmilany, 2003, p. 10–11)

Ŋarra dhu marrtji dhunupa yan. Ŋarra dhu ḻukuw malthun, ḻukuw. Bala napurr djorra' djäma yäku nhawi Dhiṉ'thun Wayawu yäku, ŋunhi napurr get together warrpam' nhämunha schools mala.

Ga bitjarr napurr, 'Nhä dhuwal mayali' Dhiṉ'thun Wayawu?' Dhuwandja Dhiṉ'thun Wayawuny mayali' – ŋunhi nhe ga djäma in both schools-ŋur Balanda Yolŋu you have to follow the footstep of your forefathers and so on. Ŋaḻapaḻmirriw ḻukuw malthurr, yaka nhokiyingal nhe gäna wapthurr. Nhe dhu galkirri gapulil. Ŋunhi nhe dhu gänany marrtji, ŋunhiny nhe buku-gänany yolŋu. Nhe dhu nhäman, nhä ŋayi yuwalk djamarrkuḻiw' learning-gu yalalaŋumirriw märr ga ŋayi dhu in future limurrŋydja bäyŋun, ŋayiny dhu djamarrkuḻi'nha carry on ŋunhidhi. Ŋayi dhu djamarrkuḻiy' knowledge thinking-nha ŋayi dhu ga, nhä ŋayi ŋunhi. Nhä ŋayi dhuwal bilingual mayali'? Wanhal ŋayi ga dhuwal Bilingual ŋorra? Yolku ŋayi dhuwal Bilingual yuwalktja? Ŋe?

I will proceed in the right way only. I will follow the foundation. I wrote an article called Dhiṉ'thun Wayawu, (see Figure 3.5; Tamisari & Milmilany, 2003) when a group of schools got together. And we asked, 'What is the meaning of *Dhiṉ'thun Wayawu?*' This *Dhiṉ'thun Wayawu* meaning – when you work in schools, both Balanda and Yolŋu, you have to follow the footstep of your forefathers and so on. Follow the foundation of the Elders, not jump out on your own.

If you work on your own you will fail - when you go on your own, when you are a person with your own mindset. Instead, you need to look to get to know what the real learning for the children's future is. So that in the future, when we are gone we know the children will carry it on. They will be thinking about, 'What is Bilingual? Where does it come from? Who is it for really?'

Märr ga limurr dhu Balanda Yolŋu work together waŋgandhu heart-thu, waŋganydhu guyaŋanawuyyu, waŋganydhu nhänharay. Nhä ŋayi ga future ŋorra dhiyak? Ŋunhany bala. Nhä ŋali dhu yalalaŋumirr meet goal-nydja ŋunhili. For litjalaŋguwuy djamarrkuḻiw' ŋunha ŋayi ga ŋuthar goḻŋur, ŋunha bala visitors mala, marrtji ga räli. Walal ga nhäma, mel walal ga gäma, mel. Walal ga nhäma mel wa<u>n</u>dirr walal ga. 'Go muka dhuwal latju! Dhuwal manymak mirithirr nhawi walal ga marŋgithirr, mak ŋarra dhu idea rrakuwuyŋbitjan djäma? nhaltjan ŋarra ga guyaŋa märr ga ŋarra dhu wukirri for yalalaŋumirriw?' Ya-bitjana dhu ŋayi yalalany.

So that both Balanda and Yolŋu work together with one heart, one mind and, one vision (see also Marika et al., 2009). What is the future for this? It's there. What goals will be met for it to be there in the future. For our own children that grow up in the schools. When visitors come, they will look and see what we have been teaching them and they will say 'Look at this – it's fantastic! This is really good, they are learning. Maybe I will take this idea for myself. I will do the same so as to be like this in the future'.

The Yuendumu School Language Policy (BRDU, 2015, p. 1) articulates the role of Warlpiri and non-Indigenous teachers as follows:

Jirrama jaru-jarra ngulaju jirrama-wana Warlpiri manu English wana kalu kurdu pina jarrimi jirrama yimi, jirrama jaru, jirrama tija-jarra yapa manu kardiya.

Two way = two languages, two cultures, two teachers in each class. *Kardiya* (non-Indigenous) and *Yapa* (Indigenous) working together as equals.

On reflecting the importance of collaboration among cross-linguistic, cross-cultural teams in Warlpiri schools, Barbara described the division of responsibilities in team teaching using the metaphor of complementary roles of two groups of people involved in Warlpiri ceremonies: *kirda* [custodial owner] and *kurdungurlu* [managing custodian or worker]. In Warlpiri ceremony, people in the role of kirda have the overall responsibility, and people in the role of *kurdungurlu* perform essential tasks on behalf of the owner. Each has a different but equally important role to play. In applying these concepts to school, Barbara explained that when an educator is leading instruction, they are the *kirda* and when they are supporting, they are the *kurdungurlu*. So, during Warlpiri instruction, the Warlpiri teachers are the *kirda*, the custodial owners of the lesson. The non-Warlpiri teachers are the *kurdungurlu* and their job is to support and work alongside the Warlpiri teachers.

Classroom practices: local pedagogy

Fiona Gibson, a senior educator from Nyirrpi, describes a Warlpiri classroom and how learning occurs when the students go on bush trips with elders and in the community:

Yani karnalu yupuju-kurra manu yungulu karlipa pina yanirni kuurlu-kurra, payirni karnalu-jana kurdu-kurdu, 'Nyarrpara-kurranpa yanu wirlinyi?'

Manu kurdu-kurdu kalu wangkami, 'Ah yaparla yanurna karrku-kurra, yujuku-rna nganturnu. Manu pirlingkarna warrkarnurna. Manurna yulpa'

Wangkami karnalu-jana jinta-kariki jinta-kariki, 'Yangka nyiyanpa manu? Nyarrpa jarrijanpa? Putungka mayinpa yukaja jilkarla-kujaku manu pirli yiri-kijaku?'

We go out bush and when we come back to the school we ask the kids, 'Where did you go hunting?' And the kids say, 'Oh grandma I went to Karrku, I built a humpie, we climbed the rocks and got ochre.' We ask each one of them, 'What did you get? What did you do? Did you wear shoes because of prickles and sharp rocks?'

Draw-mani kalu pija, recount yirrani kalu pipangka. Ngula-jangkaju kurdu-kurdukalu warrki- jarrimi jinta-kari jinta-kari pipa-ngka, manu manyu-kar-rimi kalu walyangka syllable-kurlu. Jintangka karnalu readi-mani Warlpiri puku. Payirni karnalujana, 'Nyiya nyampuju?'

They draw a picture and write a recount on paper. Then the kids work individually on worksheets and play with syllables on the floor. We read Warlpiri books together and I ask them, 'what is this?'

Warlpiri Theme Cycle-jangka karnalu purranjayani yangka every term. For example, theme watiya-kurlu, kuyu-kurlu manu purlapa, yawulyu-kurlu. Jirrama karnalujana mardarni kurdu-kurdu: pinangalpa manu murnma-juku, ngula kalu pina- jarrinjarni yangka for example, one to one reading puku-kurlu, syllables manu worksheets. Ngaju karnajana pina-mani yangka puku-readi-maninjaku Warlpiri puku manu kamina-kamina manu wirriya-wirriyarlu new-wani kardiyarlu manu yapangku watchi mani kajulu. Ngula-jangkaju wangkami karnajana, 'Yinyi karnanyarra puku-wati nyurrurlalku manu jintangkalku karlipa readi-mani panungku- juku.

We follow the Warlpiri Theme Cycle every term. For example, themes about trees, animals/meat and ceremony. We make two groups, kids who work very well and those that are still learning and they do for example one to one reading, syllables and worksheets. I teach by reading a Warlpiri book and girls, boys as well as new non-Indigenous classroom teachers and Warlpiri teachers watch me. Then I say to them, 'I'm giving out the books so we can read all together.'

Pina-mani karlipa-jana kurdu-kurdu Warlpiri pirrjirdi, nyurru-wiyi ngu-lalpalu wangkaja. Manu kalu wangkami muturna manu purlka-purlka yangka stili karnalujana pina-pina-mani kuurlurla. Yirrarni karlipa yirdi pipangka pija-kurlu, flashcard-rla wangkami karnalu kurdu-kurduku. Manu manyu-karrimi karnalu bingo manu matching games. Yirrarni karnalu Learning Centrerla, Clinic-rla, japu-ngka yirdi-wati pirrjirdi Warlpiri-wati. Yapa patu wiri-wiri-rli ngula kalu nyina ngurrangka kula kalu milya-pinyi, pina-jarrimi kalu nyanungurra-rlangu.

We teach the kids strong Warlpiri that they used to speak a long time ago. It's the language the old women and men speak, we teach it at the school. We write the words on a paper with a picture, a flashcard, and we talk about it to the kids. We play bingo and matching games. We put those flashcards with the strong Warlpiri words up around the community in the Learning Centre, the clinic and the shop. The adults who are at home don't know those words and they can also learn them.

Looking to the future

As speakers and custodians of their languages, Barbara, Fiona, Milmilany, and Merrkiyawuy share a vision where their children, and their children's children, can continue to learn in the languages that they speak and that connect them to country, kinship, and local knowledge systems. Barbara reflects that despite the challenges, she is hopeful for the future:

The good story is we haven't lost everything – it's all there altogether for people to see it and make it fresh again. We need lots of support so that we can teach our kids what we want through to their children and the next generation. This is a really good story for our kids. They will remember it for a very long time when we are all gone. Our dream is for kids to walk in two worlds, to be strong in their first language and in English.

And we conclude this chapter on teaching first languages with Merrkiyawuy's powerful words:

We will strive to teach the children here and now and those that are yet to come. Our vision is coming into reality. We will carry the legacy of our Elders into the future. Let the Indigenous languages of our world rise up again. Let them flourish, grow, and develop in a healthy and vigorous way. So that the environment, the habitats, the countries, the lands know that we are still here.

References

Amery, R. M.. (1985). *A new diglossia: Contemporary speech varieties at Yirrkala in North East Arnhem Land* [MA thesis]. Australian National University.

Anderson, L., Andrews, T., Gibson, F., Kantawara, M., Martin, B., Oldfield, Y. N., Windy, C., & Hall, L. (2018). *We always stay: Stories from seven remarkable Aboriginal teachers in remote Australia*. Batchelor Institute Press.

Australian Curriculum Assessment and Reporting Authority (ACARA). (2023). *Australian curriculum*. Sydney. https://www.australiancurriculum.edu.au

Bat, M., Kilgariff, C., & Doe, T. (2014). Indigenous tertiary education – We are all learning: Both-ways pedagogy in the Northern Territory of Australia. *Higher Education Research & Development, 33*(5), 871–886.

Bilingual Resource Development Unit (BRDU). (2015). *Yuendumu School Language Policy (Draft)*. Yuendumu School, Yuendumu, NT.

Black, P., & Breen, G. (2001). The school of Australian linguistics. In J. Simpson, D. Nash, M. Laughren, P. Austin, & B. Alpher (Eds.), *Forty years on: Ken Hale and Australian languages* (pp. 161–178). Pacific Linguistics.

Browne, E. (2019). Multimodal tools for exploring communicative practices among multilingual students in remote central Australia. *Babel, 54*(1/2), 28–33. https://afmlta.asn.au/babel/

Browne, E., & Gibson, F. N. (2021). Communities of practice in the Warlpiri Triangle: Four decades of crafting ideological and implementational spaces for teaching in and of Warlpiri language. *Languages, 6*(2), 68. https://www.mdpi.com/2226-471X/6/2/68

Burarrwanga, L., Ganambarr, R., Ganambarr-Stubbs, M., Ganambarr, B., Maymuru, D., Wright, S., & Lloyd, K. (2019). *Songspirals: Sharing women's wisdom of country through songlines*. Allen & Unwin.

Carew, M., Green, R., & Lynch, C. (forthcoming). Learning to read and write Aboriginal languages through phonics in the Northern Territory.

Department of Infrastructure, Transport, Regional Development and Communications, Australian Institute of Aboriginal and Torres Strait Islander Studies; Battin, J., Lee, J., Marmion, D., Smith, R., Wang, T., Dinku, Y., Hunt, J., Markham, F., Angelo, D., Browne, E., Kral, I., O'Shannessy, C., Simpson, J., and Smith, H. (2020). National Indigenous Languages Report (NILR), Department of Infrastructure, Transport, Regional Development and Communications. https://www.arts.gov.au/what-we-do/indigenous-arts-and-languages/indigenous-languages-and-arts-program/national-indigenous-languages-report

Devlin, B., Disbray, S., & Devlin, N. (2017). *History of bilingual education in the Northern Territory*. Springer.

Devlin, N. R., & Gapany, D. (2017). Reminiscences: Working together in a bilingual classroom. *History of bilingual education in the Northern Territory: People, programs and policies* (pp. 325–330).

Disbray, S. (2014). Evaluating bilingual education in Warlpiri schools. In R. Pensalfini, M. Turpin, & D. Guillemin (Eds.), *Language description informed by theory* (pp. 25–46). John Benjamins.

Disbray, S., & Devlin, B. (2017). Consolidation, power through leadership and pedagogy, and the rise of accountability, 1980–1998. *History of bilingual education in the Northern Territory: People, programs, policies* (pp. 101–112). Springer.

Disbray, S., & Martin, B. (2018). Curriculum as knowledge system: The Warlpiri theme cycle. In G. Wigglesworth, J. Simpson, & J. Vaughan (Eds.), *Language practices of Indigenous children and youth: The transition from home to school* (pp. 23–48). Palgrave Macmillan UK.

Graham, B. (2017). Reflecting on team teaching. In B. Devlin, S. Disbray, & N. Devlin (Eds.), *History of bilingual education in the Northern Territory: People, programs, policies* (pp. 27–33). Springer.

Hartman, D. (1994). The Intelyape-Iyape Akaltye Project: Arrernte curriculum development. In D. Hartman & J. Henderson (Eds.), *Aboriginal languages in education*. IAD Press, Alice Springs (pp. 17–24).

Lee, P., Fasoli, L., Ford, L., Stephenson, P., & McInerney, D. (2014). *Indigenous kids and schooling in the Northern Territory: An introductory overview and brief history of Aboriginal education in the Northern Territory*. Batchelor Press.

Marika, R., Ngurruwutthun, D., & White, L. (1992). Always together, yaka gäna: Participatory research at Yirrkala as part of the development of a Yolŋu education. *Convergence*, *25*(1), 23.

Marika, R., Yunupingu, Y., Marika-Mununggiritj, R., & Muller, S. (2009). Leaching the poison–the importance of process and partnership in working with Yolŋu. *Journal of Rural Studies*, *25*(4), 404–413.

Marika-Mununggiritj, R., & Christie, M. (1995). Yolŋu metaphors for learning. *International Journal of the Sociology of Language*, *1995*(113), 59–62.

Marika-Mununggiritj, R., Maymuru, B., Mununggurr, M., Munyarryun, B., Ngurruwutthun, G., & Yunupingu, Y. (1990). The history of the Yirrkala community school: Yolŋu thinking about education in the Laynha and Yirrkala area. *Ngoonjook* (3), 32–52.

McMahon, K., & Maymuru, D. (2023). Garma maths: Our journey 1986-2023. Presentation at the 2023 bilingual workshop, Northern Territory Department of Education.

McMahon, K., & Murray, F. (2000). Bilingual education: Looking for the big picture. *TESOL in Context*, *10*(2), 37–44.

Milingimbi School. (2024). Gaṯjirrk Unpublished document.

Milmilany, E. (2023). Reflections on 50 years of Bilingual Education (Djambarrpuyŋu with English translation) handout for presentation at the PULiiMA conference in August 2023 in Darwin.

Morales, G., Vaughan, J., & Ganambarr-Stubbs, M. (2018). From home to school in multilingual Arnhem land: The development of Yirrkala School's bilingual curriculum. In G. Wigglesworth, J. Simpson, & J. Vaughan (Eds.), *Language practices of Indigenous children and youth: The transition from home to school* (pp. 69–98). (Palgrave Studies in Minority Languages and Communities). Palgrave Macmillan.

Northern Territory Department of Education. (2002). *Northern Territory Curriculum Framework (NTCF)*. Northern Territory Government.

Northern Territory Department of Education. (2017a). *Keeping Indigenous Languages and Cultures strong: A plan for the teaching and learning of indigenous languages and cultures in northern territory schools*. Northern Territory Government. https://education.nt.gov.au/__data/assets/pdf_file/0012/413202/Policy_Keeping-Indigenous-Languages-and-Cultures-Strong-Document_web_updated.pdf

Northern Territory Department of Education. (2017b). *Guidelines for the implementation of Indigenous Language and Cultures programs in schools*. https://education.nt.gov.au/__data/assets/pdf_file/0004/471712/indigenous-languages-and-cultures-guidelines.pdf

Northern Territory Department of Education. (2018a). Culture: Cultural knowledge and content: *NT Indigenous Languages and Cultures (ILC)*. Northern Territory Government. https://education.nt.gov.au/__data/assets/pdf_file/0018/715230/ntilc-cultural-knowledge-nov18-02.pdf

Northern Territory Department of Education. (2018b). *First language bilingual (L1B) - First language pathways: NT Indigenous Languages and Cultures (ILC)*. Northern Territory Government. https://education.nt.gov.au/__data/assets/pdf_file/0019/715231/ilc-curriculum-first-language-bilingual-pathway-l1b.pdf

Northern Territory Department of Education. (2018c). *First language maintenance (L1M) - First language pathways: NT Indigenous Languages and Cultures (ILC)*. https://education.nt.gov.au/__data/assets/pdf_file/0020/715232/ntilc-l1m-nov18-03.pdf

Northern Territory Department of Education. (2018d). *Language Revival: Revitalisation Pathway (LR). NT Indigenous Languages and Cultures (ILC)*. https://education.nt.gov.au/__data/assets/pdf_file/0006/715236/ntilc-lr-nov18-03.pdf

Northern Territory Department of Education. (2018e). *Language Revival: Renewal Pathway (LRN). NT Indigenous Languages and Cultures (ILC)*. https://education.nt.gov.au/__data/assets/pdf_file/0005/715235/ntilc-lrn-nov18-03.pdf

Northern Territory Department of Education. (2018f). *Second Language Learning Pathway (L2): NT Indigenous Languages and Cultures (ILC)*. https://education.nt.gov.au/__data/assets/pdf_file/0003/715233/ntilc-l2-nov18-03.pdf

Northern Territory Department of Education. (2018g). *Language and Culture Awareness Pathway (LCA): NT Indigenous Languages and Cultures (ILC)*. https://education.nt.gov.au/__data/assets/pdf_file/0004/715234/ntilc-lca-nov18-03.pdf

O'Shannessy, C. (2020). Language contact in Warlpiri and light Warlpiri. In A. P. Grant (Ed.), *The Oxford handbook of language contact*. Oxford University Press.

Reaburn, S., Bat, M., & Kilgariff, C. (2015). Looking for a new common ground: A reflection on Batchelor Institute's teacher education training programs for remote Aboriginal education professionals in the Northern Territory. Finding the *common ground: Narratives, provocations and reflections from the 40 year celebration of* Batchelor Institute (Vol. 40, pp. 31–42). Batchelor Press.

Street, C., Guenther, J., Smith, J. A., Robertson, K., Motlap, S., Ludwig, W., & Ober, R. (2017). The evolution of Indigenous higher education in Northern Territory, Australia: A chronological review of policy. *Access: Critical Explorations of Equity in Higher Education, 4*(2), 32–51.

Tamisari, F., & Milmilany, E. (2003). Dhinthun Wayawu-looking for a pathway to knowledge: Towards a vision of Yolŋu education in Milingimbi. *The Australian Journal of Indigenous Education, 32*, 1–10.

Warlpiri-patu-kurlangu-jaru. (2011). *Submission 121 to the House of Representatives Standing Committee on Aboriginal and Torres Strait Islander Affairs: National Inquiry 'Language Learning in Indigenous Communities'*. https://www.aph.gov.au/parliamentary_business/committees/house_of_representatives_committees?url=atsia/languages2/subs/sub121.pdf

Wigglesworth, G., Simpson, J., & Vaughan, J. (Eds.). (2017). *Language practices of Indigenous children and youth: The transition from home to school*. Springer.

Wigglesworth, G., Wilkinson, M., Yunupingu, Y., Beecham, R., & Stockley, J. (2021). Interdisciplinary and Intercultural Development of an Early Literacy App in Dhuwaya Languages 6: 106. https://doi.org/10.3390/languages6020106

Yirrkala School. (2024). *The original Vision Statement by Elders and Yolŋu educators in Gumatj*. Unpublished document.

4 Teaching First Nations Languages in Queensland Schools

Des Crump, Larena Thompson, Naomi Fillmore, and Samantha Disbray

Introduction

The continent now known as Australia has, since time immemorial, been home to rich and diverse First Nations languages, with evidence that 490 unique languages and many more dialects were spoken in Australia (Bowern, 2023). The north-east corner of this vast continent, now known as Queensland, contributes strongly to the multilingual landscape, with over 100 traditional Aboriginal and Torres Strait Islander languages recognised in Queensland (Queensland Department of Education [QED], 2018) and many more newer Indigenous languages that have developed since colonisation. These Queensland contact languages are both related to the array of varieties spoken across Australia, and locally distinct (Angelo, 2023).

As in other states and territories, First Nations languages in Queensland are in various states of vitality and revitalisation, the result of a long-standing national language reclamation movement (Hobson et al., 2010). Some traditional languages, such as Wik Mungkan in the Western Cape and Kala Lagaw Ya in the north-west Torres Strait, continue to be spoken across all generations, including by children. Many more, such as Yugambeh in the Southeast corner and Kuku Yalanji on the far north coast, are in active states of revival and revitalisation with recent increases in speakers reported (AIATSIS, 2020). Newer creoles and contact languages that emerged from the convergence of traditional Indigenous languages, Englishes, Asian and Pacific Island languages, including Yumplatok in the Torres Strait, Kriol in the Cape, Gulf and far west, and Yarrie Lingo in Yarrabah outside of Cairns, are all now widely spoken by children and their families (Angelo & McIntosh, 2014). Varieties of Aboriginal Englishes are also widely used in Queensland and across the country, with varying levels of resemblance to SAE (Butcher, 2008; Eades, 1988).

This diversity is naturally reflected in the state's classrooms, as First Nations students in Queensland are a significant and diverse cohort. In 2023, First Nations students represented 11.1% of all Queensland school students, well above the national average of 6% (ACARA, 2022). Most of these students are enrolled in state schools in the northern part of the state, with 42.8% of First Nations students located in the Far North and North Queensland administrative regions

DOI: 10.4324/9781003441021-7

(QED, 2023a). While only 20% of Queensland First Nations students are formally identified as using a language other than Standard Australian English (SAE) at home and requiring support to learn SAE as an additional language or dialect (EAL/D), its widely acknowledged that this is a significant underrepresentation of the state's rich multilingual landscape (Dixon & Angelo, 2014; Sellwood & Angelo, 2013). Contributing to this underestimation is the fact that Indigenous contact languages in Queensland, as elsewhere, often face additional challenges of recognition and visibility, due to their perceived similarity with SAE (see Dixon & Angelo, 2014; Sellwood & Angelo, 2013). Recent efforts by the QED aim to raise awareness of these varieties (e.g., Angelo et al., 2019), with a 'three ways strong' approach promoted with the goal to equally recognise Aboriginal and Torres Strait Islander students' rights to learn and extend their traditional languages, contemporary home languages (creoles and varieties of Indigenous English), and SAE (QED, 2018).

Given this diverse linguistic landscape, it is clear that all Aboriginal and Torres Strait Islander students in Queensland bring rich linguistic repertoires to school (as they do across Australia). As more Queensland schools embrace this diversity, there's a growing movement to not just acknowledge, but to actively extend and enrich these repertoires through the integration of First Nations language learning into schools. Self-reported departmental data shows that 26 different languages are currently and actively being taught in 44 schools and Outdoor and Environmental Education Centres (O&EECs) across Queensland, serving around 6,788 Indigenous and non-Indigenous students (personal communication, 2024). Demand is growing, with an additional 107 schools and O&EECs either developing or investigating new programs in 29 languages in 2022. These figures are an increase from earlier estimates in 2018 which reported only 55 Queensland schools implementing or exploring such programs at the time (First Languages Australia, 2018). This increase in school-based First Nations language programs has been supported by recent policy and funding initiatives. Contemporary initiatives are built on earlier work and advocacy by many First Nations educators, linguists, and communities (see e.g., Bell, 1995; Kretschmann, 1988; Schrieber in Angelo & Poetsch, 2019). We acknowledge this history, but due to space constraints, do not detail it here.

Critical approaches to Language Policy and Planning (LPP) has drawn attention to the 'intertwining dynamic between on-the-ground LPP practices and top-down language policies [which] can both open and close spaces favourable for minoritized languages and multilingualism' (Hornberger et al., 2018, p. 161). In this chapter, we explore some current initiatives that are opening spaces for First Nations languages in Queensland. Many of the initiatives enacted as well as the issues faced by First Nations languages here are emblematic of broader challenges and opportunities experienced by First Nations communities across Australia, and so links will be drawn to national policies and initiatives where appropriate. The discussion of policy achievements and barriers will then set a stage for the two case-studies by co-authors and Queensland language educators Des Crump and Larena

Thompson, who share their practice and experience in two different teaching contexts. In our discussion, we attend to the elements that allow these programs and languages to thrive and be sustained.

Who we are

Des Crump is a Gamilaroi man from South-West Queensland with a teaching background of 22 years in QED. He was in the first intake of Masters of Indigenous Languages Education (MILE) at University of Sydney in 2006. He has worked with language revitalisation in schools for over 20 years and was on the Advisory Committee for the Australian Curriculum, Assessment and Reporting Authority's (ACARA) Framework for Aboriginal and Torres Strait Islander Languages and the earlier Queensland P-10 Aboriginal and Torres Strait Islander Languages Syllabus. Since 2002, Des has worked with the Gunggari language community at Mitchell, which built on his relationships with community Elders established at QED. Des has a great-great grandfather from the Maranoa region, who was born near Mitchell in 1850s; however, his matrilineal line is Gamilaroi which considers Gunggari as a neighbouring language. Bearing this in mind, he has always been respectful and mindful that Gunggari language belongs to the Gunggari community, and his role is one of support.

Larena Thompson and her brother Henry Thompson teach Yagara language in schools and Community learning settings in the Ipswich region of greater Brisbane, their traditional Country of Yagara people. Larena's daughters have also joined the growing teaching team and will support school programs as they develop.

Naomi Fillmore is a non-Indigenous applied linguist and educationalist, interested in the role of languages in early education policy and practice. She researches culturally and linguistically sustaining education policy and pedagogies for multilingual children at the University of Queensland. She also has a background working with QED for First Nations languages and cultures, as well as on language and education initiatives with non-government organisations in Australia and abroad. As a descendent of settlers, Naomi has benefited and learnt from the generous teachings of First Nations and language-minoritised mentors, colleagues, and friends, over many years.

Samantha Disbray is a non-Indigenous linguist. She lived for many years in Alice Springs, learning from and working together with Warumungu language activists, Warlpiri educators, and Pintupi-Luritja people at Papunya, with whom she continues to document and celebrate their bilingual illustrated literature. Now at the University of Queensland, Samantha works closely with Des Crump and other Indigenous colleagues, and in particular, Robert McLellan, to develop and deliver a Graduate Certificate in Indigenous Language Revitalisation.

Contemporary context

Notable state-level policy initiatives in Queensland include the 'Many Voices: Indigenous Languages Policy' (QLD Government, 2019), a whole-of-government commitment to promoting Aboriginal and Torres Strait Islander languages. A central tenet of this policy is the aspiration that 'all Queensland children can learn First Nations languages in school' (p. 11), an aspiration echoed in QED's 'Aboriginal and Torres Strait Islander Languages Statement' (QED, 2018). These documents explicitly acknowledge the pivotal role of language in the academic success of Aboriginal and Torres Strait Islander students, underlining the importance of First Nations languages in the broader educational experience. They do not mandate schools to offer First Nations languages nor directly attach funding or resources to language programs, but they do represent an important opening up of 'ideological and implementational space' (Hornberger, 2005) by affirming the importance of First Nations languages in education and providing schools the flexibility to integrate language programs in response to the unique needs and aspirations of their students and communities with the backing of policy.

The Many Voices policy and other state-level documents tend to focus on aspirational and supportive declarations, rather than curricular or programmatic detail. This gap is in part filled by the national 'Framework for Aboriginal Languages and Torres Strait Islander Languages' (the Framework) within the Australian Curriculum (ACARA, 2015). The Framework, launched in 2015, sets out pathways for learning Indigenous languages as a first language, revival language, or second languages as part of the Languages learning areas of the Australian Curriculum, thus opening space and time for First Nations languages inside an otherwise busy curriculum. In Queensland, state schools are required to teach Languages for at least 90 minutes per week in Years 5 and 6 and at least 160 hours per band in years 7 and 8, and it is 'encouraged' schools offer languages from Prep to Year 12 (QED, 2024). Schools may now elect to offer an Aboriginal or Torres Strait Islander language as their Language learning area and dedicate these mandated learning hours to the subject. While this a promising and growing approach, self-reported QED data shows that only 36 schools currently align their language program with the Australian Curriculum framework, with only 31 schools teaching the recommended number of hours for languages under the Queensland curriculum frameworks (personal communication, 2024).

The availability of formally qualified First Nations language teachers is one impediment to greater adoption of Australian Curriculum aligned programs. There is a widespread shortage of teachers of all languages nationally and in Queensland (Department of Education, 2022); however, this is particularly acute for First Nations languages. Significant systemic barriers prevent Aboriginal and Torres Strait Islander graduates, particularly from remote areas, from continuing onto the higher education programs to become fully qualified language teachers (Guenther et al., 2017). Other barriers include unequal compensation structures, legal and systemic requirements such as Blue Card (Working With Children Checks) restrictions, limited professional development and mentoring support for new teachers, the difficult nature of teaching in a language revival context, and the isolation and lack of cultural safety that comes with being the only First Nations language teacher in a school. Not unique to Queensland, these issues have been reported across other jurisdictions and systems in Australia (First Languages Australia, 2023).

In response, new approaches to increasing the number of First Nations language teachers and educators in Queensland through non-traditional qualification and training pathways have been adopted. For example, the QED is engaging an Indigenous Registered Training Organisation to scope and deliver certificate level programs in learning and teaching First Nation's languages, as part of a wider strategy to improve First Nations' languages paraprofessionals training pathways (QLD Government, 2021). Similarly, internal initiatives like the Language Upskilling Program (QED, 2022b) sponsors current teachers to add a language specialisation to their professional qualifications through a 24-week online training course. This program is open to in-service teachers who are proficient in an Australian Curriculum language (including Aboriginal languages and Torres Strait Islander languages) and focuses on pedagogy for teaching languages in classroom settings (QED, 2022b).

In many cases, Aboriginal and Torres Strait Islander people are already teaching their language, but without formal qualifications must do so under the supervision of a qualified teacher (who is often non-Indigenous) and at a lower salary bracket (First Languages Australia, 2023). In these scenarios, seeking a Permission to Teach, a process which grants special approval as a teacher based on equivalent skills or experience (QCT, 2023), may be appropriate. Usually reserved for teachers of subjects such as music and manual arts, in 2023 QED granted what is believed to be the first Permission to Teach to a First Nations language teacher, Wakka Wakka teacher Corey Appo, recognising his cultural background and experience as equivalent to traditional teaching qualifications (Heagney, 2023). This is a promising development, and it is likely that more permissions will be sought in coming years.

The university sector also forms part of the First Nations language teacher training ecosystem. The University of Queensland offers courses in Language Revitalisation, aimed at participants involved in language reclamation activities, including language teaching and learning (The University of Queensland, 2023a, 2023b). The short-form credentials equip participants with the skills to create sustainable and responsive Indigenous languages teaching, learning, and research programs (The University of Queensland, 2023b). A Graduate Certificate in Indigenous Language Revitalisation, with specialist courses aimed at teaching, learning, and resource and language development, is in development. At the University of Sydney, the one-year MILE program at the University of Sydney targets Indigenous teachers and equips them with knowledge of Indigenous languages to then apply this knowledge in their teaching (The University of Sydney, n.d.). Queensland teachers have completed this qualification (The University of Sydney, 2019), many with QED support. These initiatives, and others, collectively aim to overcome the barriers to qualification and expand the pool of qualified teachers for Aboriginal and Torres Strait Islander languages programs in Queensland schools. However, this is a long-term undertaking with outcomes yet to fully materialise. Currently, only a modest proportion of schools report having a dedicated First Nations language teacher position as part of their program (personal communication, 2024). Much remains to be done to improve the recognition and status of First Nations language teachers in Queensland, as in other jurisdictions.

Establishing new or continuing existing language programs requires financial resources. Many language programs in Queensland schools are new, recent, or have punctuated histories – few (if any) resources, and small speaker and community bases. Many rely on archival or general linguistic resources (which may or may not exist depending on the language), requiring substantial revisions to create new teaching-focused materials. This, along with crucial activities, such as engaging with language owners, holding community events, providing salaries for staff and advisors, and conducting professional development, requires adequate budgeting (First Languages Australia, 2021). To support schools who are currently teaching or planning to teach First Nations languages, the QED offers a First Nations Languages Grant funding stream. In 2024, the total available funding was $200,000, with grants of either $7,500 or $15,000 per school for a range of activities (QED, 2023c). Community-based language programs, including those implemented by Parents and Citizens Associations, can also apply for funding through the Department of Treaty, Aboriginal and Torres Strait Islander Partnerships, Communities and the Arts (DSDATSIP) (QLD Government, 2023).

Another area that represents both a challenge and an area of promising development in Queensland is respecting and upholding Indigenous Cultural and Intellectual Property in school-based languages programs (also see Chapter 2, this volume). Indigenous Cultural and Intellectual Property (ICIP) refers to the rights that Indigenous people have in relation to all aspects of their cultural heritage. As First Nations languages programs inherently involve the collection and sharing of Indigenous cultural heritage (in the form of language elements, stories, songs, artwork, and cultural knowledge), consideration of ICIP is crucial from the outset of developing ethical, sustainable First Nations language programs. Furthermore, histories of dispossession and exclusion, including within education settings, have justifiably eroded many Aboriginal peoples' and Torres Strait Islander peoples' trust towards schools and governments and, therefore, their willingness to engage in school-based language programs (QED, 2022a). Recognising this, Queensland has become the first state with departmental ICIP protocols to guide schools in the respectful engagement with language owners and in upholding the rights of Indigenous people to control and protect their cultural heritage (QED, 2022d). Developed through extensive consultation with Aboriginal and Torres Strait Islander language leaders, Elders, community members, school staff, families, and others involved in the provision of language programs, with input from the leading international ICIP authority and Wuthathi and Meriam lawyer Terri Janke (QED, 2022a), the protocols provide a framework for the effective and respectful engagement of language owners, the use and sharing of ICIP, the collection and recording of language and cultural knowledge, and the adaptation of materials into new language resources. It includes templates such as a Statement of Intent, Terms of Reference,

Copyright Consent, and others, to assist schools in navigating ethical and legal considerations (QED, 2022d). Having only been introduced in late 2022, it is yet too early to evaluate the uptake and outcomes of the new protocols; however, anecdotally they been well received by communities and schools alike.

Desmond Crump and the Gunggari case study

Gunggari historically was spoken across the Maranoa region, centred in the Present-day town of Mitchell. Due to early settlement of the region and the impact of colonisation – notably Native Police, later the Protection Act of forced removals, like many others in Queensland – this language is now considered highly endangered with minimal speakers and knowledge holders (Mushin et al., 2016). In the early 2000s, several Elders who had some knowledge were actively involved in school-community language activities; however, there were no fluent speakers, nor a structured revitalisation program in place. Historical materials dating back to 1840s and recent linguistic material and recordings by Gavan Breen, Nils Holmer, and others from the 1960–80s, including recordings of Des's Great Aunt, have been significant in the revitalisation of Gunggari language, alongside the traditional knowledge retained by the main Elders. This case study details the work undertaken since 2002 to revive and revitalise Gunggari language and culture. It highlights the gradual evolution of this work, the role schools play in giving a context for language development, teaching and learning, and future needs to expand and extend the revival of Gunggari.

Work on the ground

In November 2002 and January 2003, Des worked with community Elders and a large school in the region to develop a curriculum program for teaching Gunggari language. It was implemented in February 2003 for students in years 4–8, then expanded in 2004 to include all year levels at the school. This school-based work was complemented by community language workshops run by Des during his visits to Mitchell. This was also supported by the Yugambeh Museum (a language research and heritage centre located in Beenleigh), which served as the Indigenous Languages Centre for Southern Queensland. For lack of fluent speakers and suitable teachers, Des was invited by Elders and the Gunggari Native Title Prescribed Body Corporate (GNTPBC) to teach their language and support the revitalisation work. Although this work continues to present time, it has been impacted by a range of events including floods, drought, families leaving Mitchell for work and health reasons, changes of school staff and, of course, the passing of community Elders.

Since 2021, Des has worked alongside Tennille Bainbridge. Tennille is a qualified teacher and a Gunggari descendant, who lives off country and recently completed the MILE program at University of Sydney. Tennille's involvement created a dramatic impact on Gunggari language in schools and the community – having a Gunggari teacher with language knowledge and skills added credibility and authority to Gunggari language revitalisation, alleviating delays Des faced previously, waiting for directions from Elders and GNTPBC.

Currently, Des and Tennille work across five state and one non-government schools in the Gunggari Nation. Some are small country schools with less than 12 students, so activities are adapted to suit multi-level age ranges (from Prep to Year 6). The programs are largely language awareness programs, incorporating language perspectives into the curriculum. However, one has a part-time Gunggari teacher aide and teaches language in one 45-minute lesson for the year 3–6 class each week, and incidental learning in Prep to Year 2. At this school, language is incorporated into language use in everyday settings through greetings, marking the roll, signage, and classroom instructions, as well as sharing and promoting Gunggari language through a word or phrase of the week on Facebook. The remaining schools rely on term-wise visits from Des and Tennille, who also provide resources and other materials to the schools so that the teachers can continue working on languages as part of their curriculum. Incidental learning of everyday words also takes place in most of the schools. Copies of lessons, units of work, community wordlists, and support materials are left with each school. In addition to the schools, Des and Tennille also undertake language activities at local kindergartens during their visits.

A typical teaching week for Des and Tennille entails visits to all schools, negotiated beforehand with the teachers to incorporate topics relevant to current curriculum programming. Language programs that orient to the Australian Curriculum are embedded through a language perspectives approach – for example a school may be undertaking a unit on weather/climate, hence the teaching focus is on Gunggari words and phrases relating to the weather and elements. As well as leading revision and guided practice with students, Des and Tennille support school staff with basic professional development and resource materials. They may support school planning to maintain continuity and develop a scope and sequence of language learning. School-community events allow for sharing student learning and Gunggari promoting Gunggari language. Gunggari has been used in ANZAC Day events, school concerts, and speech nights. Translations of mainstream texts have supported this sharing, with songs such as the National Anthem, Silent Night, and We Are Australian translated, along with localised school signage and through Welcome to Country undertaken in this language. This has instilled a sense of pride in the Mitchell and Gunggari community.

Adult language learning is important for Gunggari Language and Culture revival, and has been delivered through community workshops by Des, and more recently co-facilitated with Tennille. Workshops focus on equipping adults to speak Gunggari in everyday contexts, such as greetings and self-introductions, and recording and developing of resources for community use. GNTPBC recently initiated the development of the first community dictionary, collating published materials and community knowledge from the three main Elders. This work was supported by DSDATSIP and First Languages Australia. Des and Tennille provided input into this document and are actively seeking funding to develop a Gunggari Learner's Guide.

Another recent initiative was the implementation of 'off-country' workshops to support language skills of Gunggari community members living away from Mitchell – these were held in Toowoomba, Logan, Brisbane, Woorabinda, and Townsville, with a further Sydney workshop held early in 2024. The use of social media platforms allows further sharing of cultural knowledge and language use. These strategies have proved very effective, with requests for follow-up learning and the need expressed by community members for some sort of structured or accredited learning, such as a Certificate I in Speaking Gunggari.

Creating a Gunggari archive has also been a recent priority, with GNTPBC's Cultural Heritage Officer working with Des and Tennille to access Language material from the Australian Institute of Aboriginal and Torres Strait Islander Studies, the University of Queensland, the State Library of Queensland, and other collections to collate in the archive. Resources developed by Des and Tennille are also deposited in these archives. Print and electronic material is held at the local *Yumba* (Gunggari word for camp or home) and a site of significance to the local Gunggari community, who were removed from stations to the Yumba on the outskirts of Mitchell and later to Cherbourg, Taroom, or Woorabinda. The site is used for community events and school groups from Mitchell undertaking cultural learning, supported by Gunggari community members.

Wrapping up

The elements discussed here – community and organisational involvement, schools, adult learning, Des and Tennille as visiting teachers/linguists, historic materials, and modern technologies – are all crucial to the revitalisation of Gunggari language and culture in the Mitchell community and with Gunggari community members living off-country. Future work will be dependent on ongoing support from agencies such as DSDATSIP and the QED to build upon the language in schools and communities. There is also a need for skilling and training community members to play a more active role in community language revitalisation and to upscale school programs. The GNTPBC's 10-year strategic plan guides and shapes the direction of the Gunggari language revitalisation program. Its governance structures and processes allow the Gunggari group to manage their language, though at times processes can be lengthy and a challenge to the urgency of language reclamation and documentation of remaining knowledge.

Outcomes have fluctuated over the long history and gains tend to be small, but rewarding. In the school settings, students are enthusiastic learners who acquire language readily. They self-report that Gunggari lessons are their favourite activity at school and revel in the opportunity to share their learning with visitors to the school. However, school is the main, if not only, space where Gunggari language is used currently, and learning time is limited. The school programs are based on the Australian Curriculum Framework's Language Revival Pathway, but at present, the Gunggari curriculum brings Gunggari language perspectives into the classroom. Further, there is a lack of opportunities to use and practice language at home or in the community. But these can be grown. Finally, it is acknowledged that Gunggari language use and fluency may never return to historical levels, and realistic outcomes are now framed in terms of pride, self-identity, and a sense of belonging and connection to Gunggari Country. These are the rewards for teaching Gunggari language.

Larena Thompson and the Yagara case study

Yagara Community members, like many in Queensland, are reviving their language after their older generations were forbidden by white authorities to use it. The process of reclaiming language has been long. Around seven years ago, a group of family and Community members took part in a series of Language camps. The group recorded Elders and brought together Community Language knowledge with archival materials. They learned language and culture together and made plans for reclaiming their Language. An important outcome of the Language camps was a draft learner's dictionary. The growth in knowledge, expertise, and confidence, along with the dictionary, has formed the foundation for the next steps, and one of those is the teaching and learning program they have been progressing since the camps.

Work on the ground

Yagara language teaching in schools in the region is growing. In 2023, Larena, Henry, and Larena's daughters taught grade 5 and 6 classes at two state schools the area, and an alternative education program in Ipswich City. They started to deliver four-week units of work for the program, focusing on one topic for three weeks, then a review class in the fourth week, which worked well. Often the units of work lead to some real-world learning, such as learning about animals and animal names ahead of an excursion to Queens Park animal sanctuary in Ipswich. They also teach about place names and names of the suburbs by looking at these place names, learning the right pronunciation, the history of places and how places came to be named. Language words and names are placed all over the local map. In another unit, they look at the names for plants, and the uses of different plants ahead of a visit to a council conservation site for hands-on-learning. Sharing language on Country has a special power – a real-world power. For Larena, it is 'something spiritual, and something you can feel. It's like the Country is hearing its language again, and it responds'.

At one school, there are a lot of Yagara *jarjum* (children), including two of Larena's own, plus nieces and nephews. And while they use the school's curriculum, the first lesson is the Yagara children's lesson so it is important to acknowledge that the class is learning their language. They focus on pronunciation, and the jarjums are becoming confident that they are speaking correctly. Their weekly class isn't all about language either. Many children are still learning about their extended families, who they are and how they are related. This is important for jarjums to understand about who belongs to what Country, and to start to learn about borders. Teaching about why Yagara people are having to relearn their language is part of the national and local history. This knowledge is interconnected in truth telling and healing, and these are all part of the reclamation and sharing journey.

Larena and her family are also involved with the early childhood centre near one of the schools, where children learn some songs with language words, giving little jarjums access to language learning from a young age. The daycare centre takes part in NAIDOC week events, which the Yagara team help to run each year.

Spreading language further, in 2024 Larena and the other family members began teaching at the high school so that as students from the primary schools transition, they can continue to learn Language and Culture. Building strong programs across a set of schools is important for providing on-going language learning so that jarjums in the region really can learn deeply and so they can also share their knowledge with others. In fact, Larena notes that Yagara jarjums are teaching their parents and grandparents, and the non-Indigenous children are teaching linguistic and cultural knowledge to their parents. She says, 'They'll go past a suburb and say, 'oh mum, this is 'Deebing Heights', '*deebing*' is 'mosquito''.

Larena and her family find the feedback they receive from the schools is overwhelmingly positive, and they observe how engaged students are in their classes. Teachers report to them that many of the children with additional needs or with challenging behaviours particularly enjoy learning Language and Culture. They comment positively on the teaching style, which is gentle and respectful. This is intentional, as Larena and her family actively connect teaching and learning to healing for everyone. Although there are families in the schools that they are not related to, no one has ever asked for their child not to learn Yagara. The support is strong, and this motivates Larena and her team to keep going, to keep teaching and learning themselves. Like others around the world, Larena and Henry are 'Indigenous language learners [who] must stand up and become teachers' (Johnson, 2017, p. 512), roles they take very seriously. At a recent grade 6 graduation ceremony, a speech by a Murrie student in Yagara touched Larena's father heart. He was proud to hear Yagara spoken, and this sums up a key goal: to hear Yagara language being spoken on country, by countrymen, and others, in respect to this Country, it is Language and Culture.

Yet, a common challenge that can hold school language programs back is the local political and family situation, particularly when Native Title claims come into play; and this has been true of Yagara Country. Larena recognises that schools are fearful of who to approach and advise that it is wise to tread lightly. One school was determined to overcome a previously difficult attempt at offering a Yagara language program and drew on the strength and Community relationships of the Aboriginal Liaison Officer to try again. For Larena, watching schools work through this and 'give it a go' is pleasing because, over time, building new relationships brings success in terms of student learning and well-being.

Like many Indigenous language teachers across Australia, Larena and her brother go into different schools to deliver classes. Their experience of the commitment and support from the schools has been positive. They have found that the schools' staff want to behave respectfully, and support language teachers, keeping the language teachers and the traditional owners front and centre of the initiative. They have found that leadership and commitment from the principal makes a lot of difference. For instance, at one school the principal makes sure that there is funding to pay language teachers and supports the cost of printing the teaching resources they create. However, there is clear agreement and understanding that intellectual copyright does not belong to the school; the resources belong to Larena, Henry, and their family. For one of principals, it appears that her positive support to the language program is her own background as a refugee. Larena has noticed that deep within herself, this principal understands that as a people, Yagara need to reclaim and keep their own language.

However, it is also important to note that teachers that come into schools to deliver language programs are generally not involved in broader professional development and school-wide learning or in teacher and education networks across regions or states. They sit outside of renumeration arrangements for teachers, often creating curriculum and resources in their own time and using their own equipment. While this may suit some language teachers, it does raise crucial questions about how to ensure sustainability and equity in the teaching force.

Looking forward

As Yagara language programs grow more popular, more schools are sending requests. While this is good news, there is a lack of capacity to meet the growing demand, not only in Yagara Country, but nation-wide. As discussed earlier this is because of the lack of language teaching training opportunities. Larena did take part in the University of Queensland Indigenous Language Revitalisation Summer Intensive program in 2023, which gave her access to new networks, skills, and resources, and moving her journey along.

Another limitation is the lack of language speakers: As in many First Nations contexts, Yagara-speaking adults stopped speaking Yagara language in front of children and young people for fear of punishment if children were heard speaking in language by white people. Larena's father recalls, 'my Grannie would tell us to go out of the room if she started talking language'. Like many others, Larena and her father before her grew up hearing just a few words here and there. Her Dad now speaks some words to her and other family members that they hadn't previously heard, as he remembers more.

However, like many communities across Australia, Larena and her family are committed to learning more language and to teaching others. In 2023, with a grant from First Languages Australia, Larena and her family set up an adult language learning group, which met once a week. The focus of the group was to give those who have done some language learning the opportunity to do some deeper learning, including learning the spelling system so as to be able to read and write Yagara language. This not only assists their learning, but it also helps them to share their knowledge with beginners. As they increase the number of knowledgeable people, hopefully there will be more language teachers as time goes on. This is particularly important across the generations. However, the classes can raise difficult emotions, as language learning can be difficult and older people recall not being allowed to learn or speak their language and who remember earlier times of cultural and linguistic suppression. In Larena's reflections, the reclamation efforts she and her family have undertaken have taken her along a new and different pathway related to, but different from her work in land management. It is a pathway that her whole family has joined, and one that fills them with self-esteem and pride.

Concluding remarks

A review of current government initiatives and the two case studies reveal the complex, multi-faceted and long-term nature of developing and teaching First Nations languages programs in Queensland. Points of overlap are found in the top-down moves and Des and Larena's on-the-ground practice. These include protocols, due attention to language ownership, recognition of the need for (adequate) budgetary resourcing, ideological and practical support for the program by school leadership and staff, and language teacher training, mentorship, and fair renumeration. These are all necessary elements to ensure thriving and sustainable school language programs. However, they are not enough. Des' and Larena's accounts draw our attention to the teams they work in, the relationships they build, and the language and community development that occurs generally outside of schools which are a necessary part of the broader program of revival and revitalisation of languages. Such work includes archival research, review and repurposing, documentation of existing community knowledge, reference material creation and consensus building, adult language teaching and learning, and, critical to the community journey of revival, revitalisation, and healing. These tasks are difficult and contextual factors, both top-down and local, pose challenges; however, our chapter shows that First Nations languages and their speakers can no longer be suppressed – the rewards are too great.

References

ACARA. (2015). *Australian curriculum framework for Aboriginal Languages and Torres Strait Islander Languages*. Australian Curriculum, Assessment and Reporting Authority (ACARA). https://www.australiancurriculum.edu.au/f-10 curriculum/languages/framework-for-aboriginal-languages-and-torres-strait-islander-languages/

ACARA. (2022). *Student numbers* [dataset]. Australian Curriculum Assessment and Reporting Authority (ACARA). https://www.acara.edu.au/reporting/national-report-on-schooling-in-australia/student-numbers

AIATSIS. (2020). *National Indigenous Languages Report* (p. 108). Australian Government Department of Infrastructure, Transport, Regional Development and Communications, the Australian Institute of Aboriginal and Torres Strait Islander Studies (AIATSIS), and the Australian National University. https://www.arts.gov.au/what-we-do/indigenous-arts-and-languages/national-indigenous-languages-report

Angelo, D. (2023). Language contact. In C. Bowern (Ed.), *The Oxford guide to Australian languages* (pp. 56–64). Oxford University Press. https://doi.org/10.1093/oso/9780198824978.001.0001

Angelo, D., Fraser, H., & Yeatman, B. (2019). The art of recognition: Visualising contact languages with community vernacular language posters. *Babel, 54*(1 & 2), 34–40.

Angelo, D., & McIntosh, S. (2014). Anomalous data about Aboriginal and Torres Strait Islander language ecologies. In E. Stracke (Ed.), *Intersections: Applied linguistics as a meeting place* (pp. 270–293). Cambridge Scholars Publishing. https://ro.uow.edu.au/sspapers/1487

Angelo, D., & Poetsch, S. (2019). From the ground up: How Aboriginal languages teachers design school-based programs in their local language ecology, with Carmel Ryan, Marmingee Hand, Nathan Schrieber and Michael Jarrett. *Babel, 54*(1 & 2), 11–20.

Bell, J. (1995). Working on a dictionary for Murri languages. In *Paper and talk: A manual for reconstituting materials in Australian Indigenous languages from historical sources* (pp. 1–7). Aboriginal Studies Press.

Bowern, C. (2023). How many languages are and were spoken in Australia? In C. Bowern (Ed.), *The Oxford guide to Australian languages* (pp. 56–64). Oxford University Press. https://doi.org/10.1093/oso/9780198824978.001.0001

Butcher, A. (2008). Linguistic aspects of Australian Aboriginal English. *Clinical Linguistics & Phonetics*, 22(8), 625–642. https://doi.org/10.1080/02699200802223535

Department of Education. (2022). *Issues paper: Teacher workforce shortages* (p. 14). Australian Government. https://ministers.education.gov.au/sites/default/files/documents/Teacher%20Workforce%20Shortages%20-%20Issues%20paper.pdf

Dixon, S., & Angelo, D. (2014). Dodgy data, language invisibility and the implications for social inclusion: A critical analysis of Indigenous student language data in Queensland schools. *Australian Review of Applied Linguistics*, 37(3), 213–233. https://doi.org/10.1075/aral.37.3.02dix

Eades, D. (1988). They don't speak an Aboriginal language, or do they? In *Being black: Aboriginal cultures in 'Settled' Australia* (pp. 97–115). Aboriginal Studies Press. http://search.informit.org/doi/10.3316/informit.393266898588734

First Languages Australia. (2018). *Nintiringanyi: National Aboriginal and Torres Strait Islander language teaching and employment strategy* (p. 90). First Languages Australia. https://www.firstlanguages.org.au/images/Nintiringanyi_language_strategy_WEB_3.pdf

First Languages Australia. (2021). *Report on best practice implementation of the Framework for Aboriginal Languages and Torres Strait Islander Languages* (p. 50). First Languages Australia. https://www.firstlanguages.org.au/yalbilinya

First Languages Australia. (2023). *Yalbilinya: Indigenous Language Education Workforce Strategy* (p. 98). First Languages Australia. https://www.firstlanguages.org.au/yalbilinya

Guenther, J., Disbray, S., Benveniste, T., & Osborne, S. (2017). 'Red Dirt' schools and pathways into higher education. In J. Frawley, S. Larkin, & J. A. Smith (Eds.), *Indigenous pathways, transitions and participation in higher education: From policy to practice* (pp. 251–270). Springer. https://doi.org/10.1007/978-981-10-4062-7_15

Heagney, P. (2023, June 22). *Indigenous educator now Queensland's first allowed to teach his language without qualifications*. ABC News. https://www.abc.net.au/news/2023-06-23/indigenous-teacher-to-teach-ald-wakka-wakka-language-to-save/102504462

Hobson, J., Lowe, K., Poetsch, S., & Walsh, M. (Eds.). (2010). *Re-awakening languages: Theory and practice in the revitalisation of Australia's Indigenous languages*. Sydney University Press. https://ses.library.usyd.edu.au/handle/2123/6647

Hornberger, N. H. (2005). Frameworks and models in language policy and planning. In T. Ricento (Ed.), *An introduction to language policy: Theory and method* (pp. 24–41). John Wiley & Sons.

Hornberger, N. H., Tapia, A. A., Hanks, D. H., Dueñas, F. K., & Lee, S. (2018). Ethnography of language planning and policy. *Language Teaching*, 51(2), 152–186. https://doi.org/10.1017/S0261444817000428

Johnson, S. M. K. (2017). Syilx language house: How and why we are delivering 2,000 decolonizing hours in Nsyilxcn. *Canadian Modern Language Review*, 73(4), 509–37.

Kretschmann, G. C. (1988). Bilingual program—The Aurukun experience where from? Where to? *Aboriginal Child at School*, 16(4), 21–28.

Mushin, I., Angelo, D., & Munro, J. M. (2016). Same but different: Understanding language contact in Queensland Indigenous settlements. In J.-C. Verstraete & D. Hafner (Eds.), *Culture and language use* (Vol. 18, pp. 383–408). John Benjamins Publishing Company. https://doi.org/10.1075/clu.18.18mus

QCT. (2023). *Permission to teach QLD*. Queensland College of Teachers. https://www.qct.edu.au/registration/other-approval-permission-to-teach

QED. (2018). *Aboriginal and Torres Strait Islander Languages Statement* (p. 6). Queensland (QLD) Government. https://education.qld.gov.au/student/Documents/aboriginal-torres-strait-islander-languages-statement.pdf

QED. (2022a). *Indigenous Cultural and Intellectual Property Protocol for the teaching of Aboriginal languages and Torres Strait Islander languages in Queensland State Schools* (p. 37). https://education.qld.gov.au/student/Documents/icip-protocol.pdf

QED. (2022b). *Languages Upskilling program*.

QED. (2023a). *State school enrolments: August 2019-23*. https://qed.qld.gov.au/our-publications/reports/statistics/Documents/enrolments-summary.pdf

QED. (2022d, October 10). *Indigenous Cultural and Intellectual Property Protocol for the teaching of Aboriginal languages and Torres Strait Islander languages* [Text]. Education. https://education.qld.gov.au/students/aboriginal-torres-strait-islander-education/indigenous-cultural-and-intellectual-property

QED. (2023c, November 14). *First Nations Languages Program (FNLP)* [Text]. Education.

QED. (2024). *K–12 Curriculum, assessment and reporting framework* (p. 50). Queensland (QLD) Government. https://education.qld.gov.au/curriculums/Documents/k-12-curriculum-assessment-reporting-framework.pdf

QLD Government. (2019). *Many Voices: Indigenous Languages Policy* (p. 16). Queensland (QLD) Government.

QLD Government. (2021, November 2). *QED109515—Provision of Development and Delivery of Australian First Nations' Languages Teacher Training Pathway Courses*. QTenders. https://qtenders.epw.qld.gov.au/qtenders/tender/display/tender-details.do?CSRFNONCE=653233FE7F34E9164DF48D18B71F8477&id=34599

QLD Government. (2023, October 23). *Indigenous Languages Grants* [Text]. https://www.qld.gov.au/firstnations/grants-funding/languages

Sellwood, J., & Angelo, D. (2013). Everywhere and nowhere: Invisibility of Aboriginal and Torres Strait Islander contact languages in education and Indigenous language contexts. *Australian Review of Applied Linguistics*, *36*(3), 250–266. https://doi.org/10.1075/aral.36.3.02sel

The University of Queensland. (2023a). *Shorter form credentials in language revitalisation*. School of Languages and Cultures. https://languages-cultures.uq.edu.au/shorter-form-credentials

The University of Queensland. (2023b, March 15). *Revitalising Indigenous languages at UQ*. School of Languages and Cultures. https://languages-cultures.uq.edu.au/article/2023/03/revitalising-indigenous-languages-uq

The University of Sydney. (n.d.). *Master of Indigenous languages education*. The University of Sydney. Retrieved 29 November 2023, from https://www.sydney.edu.au/courses/courses/pc/master-of-indigenous-languages-education.html

The University of Sydney. (2019, April 3). *A man of his word: Revitalising Indigenous languages*. News. https://www.sydney.edu.au/news-opinion/news/2019/04/03/protecting-aboriginal-languages-from-extinction.html

5 Western Australia Department of Education, Aboriginal Languages Teaching Training Course

Lola Jones, Coleen Sherratt, Debbie O'Hara, Coco Yu, and Judith Birchall

> **Who we are and where we come from**
>
> Lola Jones is from Yinggarda Country (Carnarvon). As a teacher-linguist she has worked with Aboriginal language speakers and teachers in communities across Western Australia. She is the Principal Consultant Aboriginal Languages and since 1995 has led the Aboriginal languages initiative for the Department of Education, WA.
>
> Coleen Sherratt is a Noongar Wadjak woman from Boorloo (Perth area). She enrolled in the Aboriginal Languages Teacher Training (ALTT) course in 2001 and graduated as a Noongar language teacher in 2002. She is currently the Principal Education Officer for Aboriginal Languages with the Department of Education, WA.
>
> Debbie O'Hara is from Townsville, North Queensland and she is a descendant of the Meriam people of the island of Mer in the Torres Strait. She now resides on Wadjak Noongar Country (Perth). Debbie has worked in education for 29 years as an Aboriginal and Islander Education Officer (AIEO), Primary School Teacher, Aboriginal Education Consultant and now as a Senior Consultant with Aboriginal Languages.

Introduction

Aboriginal languages are part of Australia's rich linguistic and cultural heritage. They have been carried through stories, song, art, and dance and have been passed from generation to generation. They encompass scientific knowledge including astronomy, agriculture, engineering, and ecology (First Languages Australia, 2017).

In Australia, the teaching of traditional Aboriginal languages in schools has been ad hoc at best. In Western Australia, prior to 1990 the teaching of Aboriginal languages was often determined by school principals with programs often ceasing when new principals were appointed to the school. Some languages were taught at one-off events like NAIDOC or when a guest speaker was available. In the late 1990s, Aboriginal languages came under the umbrella of Languages Other Than English (LOTE), with all students in the classes learning the same language. However, there were only a few schools teaching an Aboriginal language on a regular basis.

In Western Australia, Aboriginal languages have been taught in public schools since 1992 and are embedded within the Languages Learning area of the Western Australian curriculum. Initially, language teaching was in response to requests from language speakers to have their language taught in schools. Aboriginal languages were included in the LOTE 2000 strategy which was aimed at increasing the teaching of all languages in primary schools. Since 2008, LOTE has been known as the Languages Learning area.

The number of schools teaching an Aboriginal language has increased dramatically since 1996 when there were just four schools teaching an Aboriginal language. There have been noticeable increases in 2018, 2021, and 2023 (see Table 5.1). In 2023, Department census data report that 97 public schools were teaching one of 24 Aboriginal languages to 14,857 Kindergarten to Year 12 students (Department of Education, Western Australian, 2023). The increases may be attributed to the implementation of the Languages policy in 2000 and 2018 and schools' increased cultural responsiveness (DoE W.A., 2015).

Table 5.1 Number of students learning an Aboriginal language in 2006–2023 (Data source: Department of Education System Performance Semester 2, 2023).

Year	Number of schools	Number of students primary	Number of students secondary	Total number K–12
2006	29	1,410	45	1,455
2018	61	5,540	438	5,978
2021	67	8,793	824	9,617
2023	97	11,962	2895	14,857

Background

In the 1990s, the Department of Education (the Department) responded to the swell of interest from schools, communities, and Elders wanting their traditional Aboriginal languages to be taught in schools. The Department engaged a consultant to write the Framework for Teaching Aboriginal Languages in Primary Schools. The Framework promoted a team-teaching model with community language speakers working with teachers and an Aboriginal and Islander Education Officer (AIEO). The Framework provided guidance on protocols for engaging speakers and teaching an Aboriginal language to students in mainstream classrooms. The Framework also detailed the roles of the language team and suggested topics with related teaching and learning activities.

Professional learning for working together and implementing the Framework was provided for team members. This co-teaching model was used from the early 1990s until 1998. However, the diminishing number of language specialists, who were often Elders, and the continued change of class teachers meant the model was not sustainable. A more sustainable model that built the capacity of younger Aboriginal staff to work with language speakers was sought.

Following consultation with stakeholders, an 'in school' traineeship was developed based on language teaching methodology courses facilitated by The Education Department and the University of WA which was taught from 1995 to 1997. The traineeship model of language teaching was designed to build the skills of younger speakers to work with Elders and other language speakers from their local community, enabling them to teach the language with their support. Since 1998, the ALTT course has been provided by the Education Department. Course content has been regularly reviewed and updated to cater for the changing ecology of languages and to stay abreast of curriculum development and other changes.

Curriculum content in the course utilised the West Australian Outcomes and Standards Framework until 2016, until the national Framework for Teaching Aboriginal Languages was introduced in 2017. These frameworks have guided the development of locally produced scope and sequences for the teaching of Aboriginal languages.

One area of significant change has been the development of teaching resources. Language-specific teaching resources are generally not available for Aboriginal languages. In the 1990s, teaching resources were handwritten, and pictures were hand drawn. To support the need for culturally appropriate images, the Aboriginal Languages Resources File (Figure 5.1) was developed in 1996, providing a bank of black line images (Department of Education, WA, 1996).

Figure 5.1 The Aboriginal Languages Resources File (Department of Education, WA, 1996)

These images were photocopied and then used for resource development. Later with the availability and access to computers, images were scanned and stored digitally. This began the era of digital resource development and teaching digital literacy in the ALTT course.

The changing ecology of languages and decline in the number of full language speakers has also led to other changes. In 2015, Lola Jones undertook research into Canadian language revitalisation initiatives including language teaching in schools, language teacher training and community projects in four communities. She visited education offices, language centres, and schools, an immersion kindergarten class, attended cultural events, and met with language teachers.

A key finding from the community language initiatives was the concept of focussing on 'rebuilding the adult speaker base'. Despite the best efforts of language teachers and considerable funding over many years, research and observations suggest that school language programs do not produce language users. In response, several individuals and community organisations changed their focus of language revitalisation to rebuilding the adult speaker base and re-establishing intergenerational language transmission.

As part of this, the approaches included:

- Assess the resource pool of available language speakers
- Prioritise the best use of language speakers
- Focus on building adult speakers
- Establish immersion early childhood education and enable parents to attend
- Use in community and 'On Country' learning and participation in regular cultural events
- Establish school programs that support and build adult learning through:
  - Participation in regular cultural events
  - Immersion teaching in schools
  - On Country learning though regular camps and excursions
  - Kindergarten immersion – on Country every afternoon

Adult First Nations learners often encounter emotional, psychological, and identity blockers that hinder their ability to learn and progress. These need to be identified and strategies developed (individually and as a group) to overcome them.

Based on knowledge gained from visiting Canada, an additional component was developed for the ALTT course which allows for a focus on language revitalisation strategies and the building of language skills. Participants work closely with a language speaker to increase their language knowledge and skills and importantly their language use. These practical skills in language revitalisation involve:

- learning to use the orthography or spelling system for the language
- using recording devices to record a speaker
- recording and transcribing texts, and
- strategies to learn and use language every day.

The success of the course is demonstrated by the increasing number of students learning an Aboriginal language in WA public schools. The course was awarded the Education Department Western Australia (EDWA) Equal Employment Opportunity Diversity Award in 1999 in the category of Aboriginal and Torres Strait Islander People. Over 20 years later in 2021, it was awarded Best Practice in Corporate Social Values by the Institute Public Administration Australia.

Since 2008, the training model has also been recognised nationally and recommended as a strategy for training Indigenous language teachers (see Purdie et al., 2008). The course also has been commended as a training model for Aboriginal language teachers in 2017 and in 2023 by First Languages Australia (see Nintiringanyi: National Aboriginal and Torres Strait Islander Language Teaching and Employment Strategy [First Languages Australia, 2017], and Yalybilinya the National First Languages Education Workforce Strategy [First Languages Australia, 2023]). The Department has committed to continuing to provide the ALTT course and support to meet the continued growth of, and demand for, Aboriginal languages teachers.

Establishing an Aboriginal language program in a school

Knowing that many languages are critically endangered, the Department supports community language revival/revitalisation through teaching language in schools. However, the decision to teach an Aboriginal language in a school should be made in consultation with language speakers and local Aboriginal community members. Therefore, as part of this course, guidelines are provided for schools to establish an Aboriginal language program, beginning with understanding the importance of Aboriginal languages.

Implementing an Aboriginal language program gives all students access to engage with and learn the language. The program promotes building staff and student respect for Aboriginal histories, cultures, people, knowledge, and experiences while strengthening Aboriginal students' wellbeing, sense of identity, pride, and self-esteem.

Aboriginal language programs support the Department of Education's strategic directions 2020–2024 (DoE, W.A., 2019) namely to:

- create culturally responsive classrooms that build on the strengths of Aboriginal students;
- engage Aboriginal students in learning and enable them to thrive academically and socially;
- make sure the educational opportunities provided match the aspirations of families and communities.

Collaborating with members of the local Aboriginal community is a vital part of the process as it has the potential to create positive connections and relationships with Elders, parents, families, and local language centres (see also Chapter 2 Exell et al., this volume). To establish a respectful and reciprocal relationships with community, it is suggested that educators learn about the language backgrounds (the heritage language/s) of the students and families at the school. The local Aboriginal community members discuss and decide if they want language taught in schools and if so, what local language or languages should be taught. Language is connected to 'Country', to people, and the geographical location of the school and local historical events.

Once the language or languages to be taught have been established, a language advisory group should be formed to represent the community and ensure that the language program maintains cultural integrity and provides support to the language teacher. The group then provides advice and guidance on the language program being taught. A language agreement or statement of intent is created with the school that articulates their shared vision for language revitalisation.

The advisory group may include Aboriginal people who identify with the local language such as: Elders, Aboriginal community members, Aboriginal parents, school staff, young people and emerging speakers, members from Aboriginal community agencies, and the language teacher or trainee, if the school has one. The group can assist in identifying language speakers and resources to support the program and can identify possible staff or community members to teach language.

Interested Aboriginal staff submit an Expression of Interest to enrol in the ALTT training. To be eligible to apply the applicant must be an Aboriginal person with some oral language skills and be working at a school. Applicants are required to demonstrate their language proficiency through an oral exercise conducted by an Aboriginal languages' consultant or local language speaker. During this exercise, applicants need to demonstrate some knowledge of the language and have access to language speakers to improve their language skills. Successful applicants progress to attending Block 1 of the training. Before endorsing an applicant to enrol in the course, the school's principal must consider the school's capacity to provide classroom placement and support for the trainee for the duration of the course.

Overview of the Aboriginal Languages Teacher Training course

The course incorporates language revival and maintenance strategies, language teaching methodology, and digital literacy for the development of language-specific resources for teaching (See Table 5.2). Trainees to attend five block releases of five days spread over 2 ¼ years. Content is cumulative to enable participants to apply and practice knowledge and skills gained within each teaching block.

Table 5.2 Overview of the Aboriginal Teacher Training course (Department of Education, 2022).

Block 1 Language revitalisation	Block 2 Introduction to teaching	Block 3 Teaching	Block 4 Teaching student focus	Block 5 Teaching student focus
Language revitalisation strategies	2nd language teaching methodology explicit teaching steps	Practice 2nd language teaching methodology explicit teaching steps	Consolidate 2nd language teaching practice	Consolidate 2nd language teaching practice

(Continued)

Table 5.2 (Continued)

Block 1 Language revitalisation	Block 2 Introduction to teaching	Block 3 Teaching	Block 4 Teaching student focus	Block 5 Teaching student focus
Use a device to record language	Plan the language to teach	Curriculum plan the language to teach	Plan for language using curriculum and achievement standards	Plan for language using curriculum and achievement standards
Work with a speaker	Plan language lessons – Level 1 template	Plan language lessons – Level 2 template	Consolidate planning – Level 3 template	Independently plan – Level 3 template
Spelling systems	Process to produce teaching resources	Process to produce teaching resources	Produce multimodal teaching resources	Produce and critique multimodal teaching resources
Process to transcribe	Language for common class instructions and activity-specific instructions	Language for class routines and activity-specific instructions	Task instructional language 1 Language grammar 1	Task instructional language 2 Language grammar 2
		Classroom management 1	Classroom management 2	Management instructional language
			Monitoring achievement using checklists	Assessment and monitoring achievement

Block 1 is five days of professional learning building knowledge and practical skills in language revitalisation. Participants identify and build upon their existing language knowledge and use. Increasingly, more participants start the course with limited oral language capacity, so working with a language speaker is imperative. For some who are first language speakers, the focus is on improving literacy in their first language. All participants use a Language Use Rubric to identify their current skills and set goals for improving language learning and use.

Block 2 is the start of the teacher training. It is a five-day introduction to teaching using language immersion. Trainees use language they have recorded with their language mentor to plan and make basic-language-specific teaching and learning resources. Lessons are planned using templates, and participants learn about and practice using explicit teaching steps for learning activities. They learn to plan and apply language to the classroom domain, identifying general and activity-specific language instructions.

After block 2, participants use the *ALTT In-school Practicum Logbook*, which details weekly tasks to be completed by the trainee. The logbook is used until the completion of the training.

After blocks 2–5, participants teach a minimum of one language class per week (supervised) as a trainee language teacher and then a year as a probationary language teacher. As part of their commitment, schools provide a mentor-teacher to assist with planning and a supervising teacher. Lesson observations are conducted by trainers and participants are assessed on their skills in planning, resource development, and teaching, including language proficiency and use in lessons. Feedback is provided to the trainee and their mentors.

Block 3 increases the level required for lesson planning, teaching, and for the production of language-specific teaching resources. It is also an introduction to behaviour management for the classroom, planning, and using curriculum documents. Trainees use a Teaching Competency Rubric to identify their current skill levels and set goals for improving their teaching and language skills for the classroom.

After completion of block 3, trainees (who do not hold a teaching degree) are eligible to be registered with the Teachers Registration Board of Western Australia for Limited Teacher Registration.

In block 4, the focus shifts from building the trainees' capacity in language and teaching, to the trainee developing the skills of their students. This includes more detailed planning, teaching, and assessment. Resource-making focuses on multi-modal resources, and there is a wider application and use of instructional language in teaching, and an introduction to planning using the Achievement standards for Aboriginal Languages, and monitoring student achievement using checklists.

The focus of block 5 is planning for and using on-Country learning to provide connection to Country and an opportunity to involve other language speakers in the school program. Trainees are independently able to create a range of digital, printed, and multi-media teaching and learning resources. They engage in peer critique to provide feedback to each other on the resources they have produced. They share their experiences monitoring and assessing students' achievement against the achievement standards and gain more information about reporting to parents.

Figure 5.2 Wangkatja language teacher, Felicity Harris, Leonora District High School, WA (Department of Education, WA, 2021)

For example, Felicity Harris (personal comment 2024) provided the following comment:

> Students love learning about language and culture, they are so eager and hungry to learn as much as they can. Bringing in animals like the joey or other tools to grab student interest is always good.

Each cohort or intake in the ALTT course is different with participants bringing a range of life experiences and language skills. In a group of 20–25 participants there are usually five or more language groups, for some languages there may be only one participant, for others there may be a couple or a group of people from the same language. A few participants may be full language speakers who use their language every day, a few may have some proficiency, and many know only common words and phrases. Participants' language use varies widely from those who use language every day to those who rarely use their language. Many have little or no experience in reading and writing in their language. Some participants are long-term staff at their schools, others are relatively new staff. Some are qualified teachers; many are staff who work in support roles in a school.

The uniting factor in the diversity is that everyone is there to learn, to strengthen their language skills and possess the desire to become a language teacher. Everyone has something to offer. Language is the link to identity, to Country, to family, it comes from the heart.

As Lola comments from her experience

> The ALTT course does not teach people their language, rather it provides strategies and processes to enable participants to revitalise and strengthen their language skills, and then how to teach language in a school context. Many participants in the course are learning their language, while learning how to teach language.

The course has used a strength-based approach since its inception focussing on building individual and group capacity. From 2008, this approach was consolidated by incorporating a range of processes from the Stronger Smarter Leadership (SSL) program developed by Professor Chris Sarra, an internationally recognised Indigenous education specialist (Stronger Smarter, n.d.).

The course invests time in people sharing their stories and experiences and making connections. Participants learn with and from their peers, mentors, and trainers. It creates cultural safety and a supportive learning environment that values diversity and builds mutually respectful relationships between trainers, mentors, and participants.

The course content and explanations are mostly in English, supplemented with language examples. A range of language demonstrations, supported practice, and individual or partner practice scaffold participants' learning through the application of content, practical planning, and teaching strategies. Participants are supported and mentored with high expectations throughout the course. This strength-based approach builds stronger, smarter, and more resilient trainees, and ultimately highly skilled language teachers.

The reality of language revitalisation and language teaching, particularly the time and commitment required, can be very different to what some people expect. As a result, there can be a 25–40% drop-out rate between blocks 1 to 3. Those who complete the five block releases and graduate as an Aboriginal language teacher become part of the language family. Some past graduates return as speakers and mentors for participants in successive intakes. The sense of cohesion and being part of the language family helps maintain group capacity and unity beyond the training.

In 2021, the Department invested in the development of a proposal for nationally recognised training course based on the ALTT course. In September 2022, the West Australian Training and Accreditation Council approved the accreditation of two qualifications, the first being the WA Certificate III in Teaching Aboriginal and Torres Strait Islander Languages and, the second, the WA Certificate IV in Teaching Aboriginal and Torres Strait Islander Languages (Australian Government, n.d.-a, n.d.-b). The anticipated timeline to commence delivery is 2025.

The Education Department of WA is working with the School of Isolated and Distance Education (SIDE) Registered Training Organisation to develop Learner resources and Assessment materials as well as Recognition of Prior Learning materials, for the two courses. These resources will be central to delivery of the course into the future.

The success of trainees has been considerable. The following account comes from one of the graduates of the program – Coco Yu. She describes her journey:

Coco Yu – Yawuru language teacher, Broome

I enrolled in the ALTT course in 2012, after listening to our Elders speak about language and land being interconnected and warning us that our language was in dire need of revitalisation and reclamation.

I was working in a school administration role and was approached to see if I was interested in becoming a Language Teacher. I was but was also terrified – 'can I actually do it, I'm too old, I might say the wrong thing, can I manage a classroom, what will other people say, do I have a right to learn and teach my language, who's going to teach me how to speak and how to teach.'

The ALTT course was straight forward, with basic step by step instructions on how to teach language and understand the requirements of the Education Department. But most importantly, my observation was that each participant in the course, regardless of age or knowledge of language, was supported and guided all the way through the course. This support was continued when needed after graduating the course.

Since graduating, I have encouraged other younger people to enrol into the ALTT course and assisted in mentoring their language reclamation. The skills taught during this course have allowed me to be more courageous in searching for lost words, phrases, sentences reclaiming them and reincorporating them into common everyday language for everyone to speak. My language journey is now to recover and share as much language as possible with the younger generations until one day English will be their second language.

Coco is now Walalangga Yawuru Co-facilitator at Mabu Yawuru Ngan-ga (Yawuru Language Centre), working with adults to rebuild the Yawuru adult speaker base. She is part of the Yawuru language team and the go-to person for questions about the Yawuru thesis (Meanings in Yawuru, Hosokawa, 1994).

Resources to support the teaching of Aboriginal languages

As described above, numerous resources have been developed as part of the ALTT course. The following description outlines how resources were developed for the Noongar language program.

Noongar and Wajarri Languages Curriculum

The Language Revival P-10 Scope and Sequence for Noongar and Wajarri are available on the WA School Curriculum and Standards Authority (SCSA) website. The curriculum aligns to the Australian Curriculum Framework for Teaching Aboriginal Languages and Torres Strait Islander Languages. A Language Revival P-10 Scope and Sequence template is also available to support the development of language-specific curriculums for other Western Australian Aboriginal languages.

The Noongar language curriculum was the first language-specific curriculum written for Aboriginal languages in Western Australia. The Noongar curriculum is supported by the Yikan Noongar language program and resources.

Yikan Noongar

The Department has committed to supporting the teaching and learning of Aboriginal languages with the provision of the ALTT course and supporting resources for Aboriginal languages teachers.

Over 90% of public schools in Western Australia are located on Noongar Country, and Yikan Noongar (awakening Noongar) was developed to support the increased demand for Noongar language to be taught and learned in the Southwest of Western Australia. This demand has seen added pressure on the Aboriginal Languages Teacher training program as schools attempt to address the interest to teach the language of the land.

Yikan Noongar is a language program to engage students who attend a school on Noongar Country in learning one of the oldest living languages in the world. Starting in Year 3, the program builds respect and understanding for Noongar language, histories, cultures, people, knowledge, and experiences. It supports students to understand the importance of sustainability and caring for Country.

Implementing Yikan Noongar in schools supports students to learn the language of the Country on which they live and supports schools to deliver the mandated languages curriculum.

A rigorous, culturally responsive process was used to develop the Yikan Noongar language program including direct and ongoing engagement with Noongar community members and language teachers. The program has been developed to include the three main dialectal regions of the language: Diraly, Kongal-Marawar and Kongal-boya.

Yikan Noongar language program can be taught by a Noongar language teacher or Noongar person (with the classroom teacher becoming a co-learner with students). Program guidelines explain who can teach and how it can be taught in the classroom.

Each term includes:

- 2 × 45 minute lessons each week, for 9 weeks of each term.
- 1 × 2 ½ hour extended learning experience celebrating language, Country, and community.
- classroom resources, including videos, key word cards, language texts, and a Noongar picture dictionary.
- classroom resources for each of three dialectal regions with capacity for further adaptation to include local dialects.

Many Noongar language teachers that have graduated from the Aboriginal Languages Teacher Training course contributed to the development of this resource.

Below, Coleen Sherratt shares her journey to becoming a Noongar language teacher and then progressing to a Principal Education Officer Aboriginal languages. Coleen is the lead Noongar consultant in the development of the Yikan Noongar program.

Coleen said,

> The skills I gained whilst attending the ALTT course were invaluable. I learnt more about my language and culture as there was always an Elder present to help us with understanding and passing on their knowledge. The course was two years and I learnt so much and now after more than 20 years I am still learning more about my language and culture, which I can now pass it on.
>
> The journey to becoming a Noongar language teacher started as a job opportunity but has turned into a lifelong journey. Along the way I have been a primary school teacher, and then Aboriginal Languages Project Officer with the Department of Education, WA. I've also completed a Masters in Indigenous Languages Education.
>
> In 2002, I worked as both an AIEO and trainee Noongar language teacher at one primary school. After I completed the ALTT course, I worked at two

primary schools teaching Noongar language. I also mentored an AIEO at the second school as well as being the language teacher. This was very rewarding, and it improved my language speaking and listening skills because I was teaching Noongar every day and having conversations with the trainee I was mentoring.

My teaching excelled because I was teaching and using Noongar every day. I decided to gain a full teaching qualification as I found teaching so rewarding. I enrolled in the Bachelor of Education Conversation Course (BECC) for AIEOs and started university to become a classroom teacher. I felt confident in my studies because I already knew how to plan lessons and prepare for classes as well as being quite skilled with behaviour management. This was all due to the knowledge and skills gained and support from the ALTT course.

I have come full circle, now I am the Principal Education Officer and one of the course trainers and have been for 14 years. I now teach others how to teach their language in schools, which is very rewarding and an honour.

Support Coordinators

The Department provides funding for experienced Aboriginal language teachers to lead and support other Aboriginal language teachers by becoming language coordinators for their region. Coordinators respond to individual and group needs and facilitate network meetings and professional learning for teachers to share and learn more about teaching, learning and assessing, and producing language-specific texts.

Below, Judith Birchall shares her journey to becoming a Noongar language teacher, and then progressing to become an Aboriginal Languages Support Coordinator.

Judith Birchall – Noongar language teacher

I enrolled in the Aboriginal language teacher training course in 2012, graduating in 2014. I originally enrolled to try and connect with my identity. I am adopted from birth and raised by non-Aboriginal parents. Although I am not Noongar, I was born and raised in Noongar Country, so I was looking for a connection to mob. Working as an AIEO (Aboriginal Islander Education Officer) I was involved in the Noongar community and saw this as an opportunity to help them connect with their identity.

The ALTT course gave me a pathway from being an AIEO, it has enabled me to become a teacher. I have gone from working part-time in three schools as an AIEO to a permanent full-time teaching position in one school, teaching K-6. I have become passionate about teaching Noongar language and teaching our kids how to connect with Country through language. Most of the students I teach are first generation Australians and are still forming their identity and how they fit into Noongar Country. A bit like me in a way, we are learning together, and I feel that learning Noongar language gives them a positive outlook on Country, Noongar people and helps them build a solid foundation for their futures.

Over the years I have taught language classes voluntarily in my local Aboriginal community, it has been away to build relationships with mob in my local area and we have become a support network for each other. I also volunteer as a mentor for trainees completing the course and support Noongar language teachers currently working in schools. Teaching language has impacted my sense of identity, well-being and has given me opportunities to learn culture from my peers, Elders, and members of the community. I am incredibly grateful to have been given this opportunity and feel a deep sense of obligation to the Noongar people. Boordawan.

Judith has now been a Noongar language coordinator for several years and encourages other Aboriginal staff to learn their language so they too can become language teachers.

Conclusion

Since the inception of the Aboriginal Languages Teacher Training, approximately 160 graduates have completed the course and become language teachers. This, for some, is an achievement they never thought would be possible with many challenges and obstacles in life with family, work, and cultural commitments. As we have shown in the case studies of three graduates, their experience from trainee to Aboriginal Language Teacher has been challenging but rewarding. Graduates are language warriors making a difference and teaching all students to develop language knowledge and skills, and an understanding of Aboriginal and Torres Strait Islander histories, cultures, and experiences. For Aboriginal students, it enhances wellbeing and strengthens culture, identity, and self-esteem.

References

Australian Government. (n.d.-a). Training. Australian Government. training.gov.au—52897WA: Certificate III in Teaching Aboriginal and Torres Strait Islander languages.
Australian Government. (n.d.-b). Training. Australian Government. training.gov.au - 52898WA: Certificate IV in teaching Aboriginal and Torres Strait Islander languages.
Department of Education (DoE), W.A. (1996). *Aboriginal language resource file*.
Department of Education (DoE), W.A. (2015). *Aboriginal cultural standards framework*. DoE, W.A. https://www.education.wa.edu.au/dl/jjpzned
Department of Education (DoE), W.A. (2019). *Building on strength: Future directions for the Western Australian public school system 2020–2024*. https://www.education.wa.edu.au/dl/oelpev
Department of Education, (DoE), W.A. (2021). Wangkatja language teacher, Goldfields.

Department of Education (DoE), W.A. (2023). *Overview Aboriginal languages.*

First Languages Australia. (2017). Nintirringanyi: National Aboriginal and Torres Strait Islander Languages Teaching and Employment Strategy. National Aboriginal and Torres Strait Islander Languages Education Strategy — First Languages Australia.

First Languages Australia. (2023). *Yalbilinya: National first languages education workforce strategy.* https://static1.squarespace.com/static/603c934c25c28820314562e0/t/64f69a9c0006d220add76f81/1693883051876/Education+report+Yalbilinya+SCREEN.pdf

Hosokawa, K. (1994). Meanings in Yawuru—A semantically oriented description of an indigenous language of Kimberley, Western Australia submitted to Pacific Linguistics for publication September 1994.

Purdie, N., Frigo, T., Ozolins, C., Noblett, G., Thieberger, N., & Sharp, J. (2008). *Indigenous language programmes in Australian schools: A way forward.* Department of Education, Employment and Workplace Relations (DEEWR), Australian Government. https://research.acer.edu.au/cgi/viewcontent.cgi?article=1017&context=indigenous_education

Stronger Smarter. (n.d.). Home page. Stronger Smarter. Home – Stronger Smarter https://strongersmarter.com.au/

6 The Journey to the Opening of Gumbaynggirr Giingana Freedom School

Clark Webb

> **Who Am I?**
>
> My name is Clark Webb and I am Gumbaynggirr man. I am also the founder and CEO of BMNAC, and throughout this chapter I detail the journey of establishing the Gumbaynggirr Giingana Freedom School.

Gaduyi – Introduction

The process of revitalising language and culture is not for the faint hearted. It is a momentous task that requires a lot of hard work, teamwork, courage, and a thick skin. Through our years of working and progressing to the point of being able to open a school, we have heard the criticisms that our language and culture will apparently hold our children back, leave them illiterate, and unable to participate in mainstream society. Even from the beginning, it was evident that such work can be frustrating, emotional, and sometimes even thankless. In addition to the frustration caused by the nay sayers, within the cultural space the more you learn, the more you realise what you don't know. Therefore, since undertaking my first ever Gumbaynggirr language lessons as a 22-year old in 2007, I have found myself in a constant state of learning and unlearning, which has resulted in both confusion and absolute light-bulb moments that have significantly contributed to my identity enhancement and overall well-being. Language learning is a process of claiming our cultural being and this shapes and changes our worldview.

To me, learning language and culture is our most important work. It is so central to the happiness and well-being of our communities. As First Nations people, we must collectively elevate this work as our number one priority. As a young person, I grappled with the idea of education and whether or not higher education meant greater success. I questioned: What is education? And what is success? Now it appears it all depends on the cultural lens we are viewing it through.

Given that western ideas of success revolve around getting highly educated in order to attend university and then gain a job that pays well, my grappling centred

DOI: 10.4324/9781003441021-9

around a concern that education can be used as a tool to assimilate our communities and take us further away from our languages and cultures. Clearly there is a need for compromise.

When it comes to language and cultural revitalisation, however, there is simply no compromise. Our community felt that through our process of learning we could add value to our happiness and well-being. We could also add to the cognitive development of our young and begin to Indigenise notions of success. For example, we see that, through language and culture, many of our young people gain a desire to positively contribute to country and community, hence highlighting a measure of success from a Goori perspective. As one adult learner commented: 'I used to be just an Aboriginal man, but now that I'm learning culture, I'm a Gumbaynggirr man'.

It must also be remembered that Aboriginal communities have been educating children since time immemorial. Therefore, our ways of education have the potential to provide a much deeper holistic learning experience than the mainstream monocultural system.

When I first started my journey of learning Gumbaynggirr in 2007, I made the decision that I'd one day speak Gumbaynggirr as well as I do English. Sixteen years later I still haven't reached this goal, but the more I share and the more other learners improve in their speaking ability, the more my ability improves too. This highlights that sharing and teamwork are absolute vital ingredients in the revitalisation of language and culture. As Uncle Max Duluumum would say constantly, 'we've gotta share it to keep it'.

The opening of our seven-week pilot school in 2020 and Gumbaynggirr Giingana Freedom School in 2022 marked significant milestones in the development of our language journey. The eagerness and ability of our children has pushed us adult speakers into creating immersive environments that, four years ago, I wouldn't have thought possible. Therefore, I'm continually edging closer to my personal goal and I estimate that within the next few years, due to having more people to converse with, my Gumbaynggirr ability will match my English.

There are questions that one must continually ask when embarking on language and cultural work: What is best for the culture and language? What is best for our children? The importance of these questions is highlighted by the fact that, of the once 250–300 distinct languages that existed on the continent prior to colonisation, only 12 are considered strong today (DoITRDC, AIATSIS, & ANU, 2020). The further impact of colonisation can be seen in the following startling figures: less than 10% of the Aboriginal and Torres Strait Islander population speak their language, and our young people are more likely to go to jail than attend university.

Although there is no *bad* language work, not all language work is of equal value. Therefore, it is critical that languages are not just add-on programs that only skim the surface. In order to bring our languages back into everyday use, we need to set high expectations and live and breathe our language and cultural revitalisation. This can be done by creating our own schools with which to educate our children our way provides a key avenue for this to occur.

Furthermore, and despite what can be described as the arrogance of colonialist perspectives, English is not a prerequisite for successful learning in science, geography, mathematics, and other subjects. Nor is it necessary for creating a 'whole person'. Therefore, there is a need to consider the danger of resting only on the idea of bilingual schools, and instead there is a need to shift toward a First Nations education system, such as that proposed by *Children's Ground,* and a move toward immersion schools.

This chapter describes how the passion of our community over multiple generations to keep our culture intact led to the foundations for us younger generation to build our own bilingual school *Gumbaynggirr Giingana Freedom School.* It is our goal to transition this into a full immersion school by 2027.

Garla-Daarimba Gumbaynggirr – Make Gumbaynggirr strong again

Gumbaynggirr is officially listed as a *critically endangered language* due to having no person in our community who speaks Gumbaynggirr as their first language, and there are approximately only 30 people who speak Gumbaynggirr at a proficient or highly proficient level. However, despite this seemingly low number, we are seeing an increase in the number of speakers in our community. In mid-2022, it was estimated that we had 20 proficient and highly proficient speakers, so in the space of a year our school has facilitated an improvement not only in our language, but also in our ability to teach this language.

To put this into context, our highly proficient speakers have the ability to tell a minimum of six stories completely in Gumbaynggirr and participate in fully immersive environments and conversations. They have also acquired no less than ten songs. In mid-September 2023, having demonstrated an ability to tell their sixth story, six GGFS students also moved into the highly proficient category. This sixth story they have learnt is a traditional Gumbaynggirr story that is quite challenging and long – taking approximately 4.5 minutes to tell in its entirety. As with all stories they learn, the children have learnt this story without scaffolding in English; it has been taught to them through the medium of only Gumbaynggirr. It is noteworthy that they have acquired the ability to tell the story after less than one hour of instruction.

There also has been a butterfly effect related to our student's rapid acquisition of their traditional language in that it has also sped up the language acquisition of all the teachers. This equates to nine teachers as each of the four classes is staffed by both a classroom teacher and a language teacher to ensure language is implemented throughout all learning.

Our school's five language teachers facilitate and lead much of the learning throughout the day, and they are disciplined in using Gumbaynggirr wherever possible. The ability of our students means that our language teachers are always working hard to stay ahead – for instance, working hard to be able to share the aforementioned stories fluently for their students to learn.

Furthermore, our four classroom teaching staff, three of whom had no prior language learning, are able to function in immersive environments. They intentionally also write Gumbaynggirr into their lesson planning and provide students instruction in Gumbaynggirr (having acquired the ability to tell at least one story). Additionally, in all the classes there is a Student Learning Support Officer (SLSO), who is there to help the teachers and students navigate the classroom learning – doing so wherever possible in Gumbaynggirr. These staff continue to work to acquire language as evidenced by their ability to tell at least one Gumbaynggirr story.

The desire among all our staff to strive toward immersion is evidenced by their commitment to engaging in their own language learning every afternoon after school. Highly proficient language teachers impart their knowledge to our classroom teachers and support staff, all of whom engage and consider that their language learning is key to their professional development.

Our school community understands that professional development among staff is paramount to the future of our school. For instance, in addition to undertaking their full-time working duties our language teachers, as part of their professional development, are studying university teaching degrees with the long-term strategy that every classroom teacher will be a highly proficient Gumbaynggirr speaker. They are supported in their university work by our classroom teachers who have prior experience of study.

Jalumgal Girrwaadu Maaning – Our Elders held on for us

Despite the colonial pressures placed on the Gumbaynggirr language through dehumanising racism that endangered it and its related culture, many of our Elders maintained their conviction and belief that our language is of the utmost importance. They had amazing foresight to record their language in different eras; early 1900s with explorers (written material); 1930s/40s (written material); and with the introduction of voice recording technology, recordings from the 1960s. Together these are proving to be invaluable resources today.

In 1929, a Gumbaynggirr Elder, Uncle Phillip Shannon audio recorded, in Gumbaynggirr, 20 stories and the names of more than 100 sacred places with the German-American linguist, Gehardt Laves. Approximately 30 years later, a number of Gumbaynggirr Elders began to record their language with linguists. Informants such as my great-great-grandfather, Poppy Clarence Skinner; Granny Florence Ballangarry; Uncle Frank Archibold; Uncle Les Nixon; Uncle Len De Silva; and Uncle Harry 'Tiger' Buchanan had the foresight to recognise that their voices would someday breathe life into our community.

With increasing distress at the decline of their language, in the 1980s a group of Gumbaynggirr Elders took action and steps toward reclaiming their language for the benefit of their children, grandchildren, and future generations. Their foresight led to the opening of Muurrbay Aboriginal Language and Culture Centre in 1986, which has and continues to inform the core of our language and culture work.

Uncle Cecil 'Bing' Laurie, was our last Elder to speak Gumbaynggirr as his first language. He was crucial to our cultural revitalisation efforts and to the opening of our school, and his importance cannot be overstated. Sadly, he passed away in 2019 and, therefore, did not get to witness the opening of our school, but his love of language continues to inspire us and I know he would be thrilled to hear our children speaking Gumbaynggirr today.

Drawing on the wisdom of our Elders is a vital foundation to the work at our school. At GGFS, we employ two Elders in Residence who are supported by the GGFS parent entity, Bularri Muurlay Nyanggan Aboriginal Corporation's (BM-NAC) 13 member Elders Advisory Council. Our children thrive when they are able to connect with Elders both at school and on-country.

Accelerated Second Language Acquisition (ASLA)

In 2014, Neyooxet Greymorning an Arapaho Language Teacher and the developer of Accelerated Second Language Acquisition (ASLA), visited, unannounced, a language conference we were facilitating in Coffs Harbour (note: the Arapaho language is a First Nations language of the United States of America with Arapaho people whose traditional lands are the plains of Colorado and Wyoming). His feedback was brutely honest, saying that, as teachers, we did not really know what we were doing, but that he saw potential in our work given the obvious passion of our community. He offered to work with us and since 2015 has regularly visited us from the USA in order to conduct workshops on the teaching method that he has developed (i.e., ASLA).

Put simply, ASLA has worked for us. And we have found that it works fast. By undertaking Greymorning's training and staying disciplined to the method, teachers can very rapidly move their students along their language learning continuum from simple through to complex language. As the purpose of this book is designed for language practitioners, I strongly suggest that readers do some further research into ASLA (see for example: https://www.nccie.ca/story/asla-of-the-cree-language).

We have been able to utilise the resources provided by our Elders and combine this knowledge with Greymorning's ASLA framework to create proficient and highly proficient speakers of our language and to do so within a short space of time. On this basis, we have the goal of having babies speaking Gumbaynggirr as their first language in the coming years. ASLA has and continues to be an important cog in our wheel of language revitalisation and provides a way for the continued quality improvement of our school.

Ngiyaala bayi ngiyambandi junuybin wagin – We proper love our children

> Children who are going to mainstream schools are being forced to leave their identity, culture and language at the door.

A factor that sets GGFS apart from other schools is that we have a deep respect and love for *our* children. Because they are part of our extended families, we want what is best for them. Our children know that all the feedback we provide them, whether it be positive or negative, comes from a place of love. Therefore, they know that our positive reinforcement is heartfelt and genuine, and that negative feedback reinforces our effort to ensure they become the best possible versions of themselves. In turn, our children feel safe in the knowledge that, at GGFS, their culture is not only respected, but also celebrated every day. For many, if not most, mainstream schools this claim could not be made. Despite their multicultural student populations, the education systems in mainstream schools remain monolingual and monocultural reflecting their English dominant Anglo values and standards. Consequently, staff at these school may lack the cultural and linguistic understanding and/or are bound by external curriculum and assessment protocols that prevent them from providing a supportive and culturally appropriate educational experience – one where students' home culture is honoured. In fact, we believe we have intentionally addressed the colonial 'concern' for the welfare of our students by immersing them in culture. I continually respond to comments expressing concern with a couple of simple questions: 'How are our children doing in mainstream schools?' Noting here that our young people are more likely to go to jail than attend university. And then, I ask 'What is the mono-cultural education system doing to change this alarming statistic?'

Recently, *Children's Ground* released the M. K. Turner Report (Turner and Children's Ground, 2023) which provides the recommendation that a First Nations Education System, developed and governed by First Nations communities, needs to be created. Throughout the report, highlighted is the love that Aboriginal communities have for their children and that communities are best placed to ensure that all children receive an education that is holistic and holds culture at the core. BMNAC and GGFS align fully with this philosophy. We support this recommendation and, in fact, call on governments to invest in the First Nations Education System. Such an education system would be one founded on love for First Nations' children and the belief of learning in ways that foster 'whole person' development. We strive for GGFS to become a full Gumbaynggirr immersion school by 2027 and, in doing so, continue to work in ways that align with this philosophy.

Dangers of bilingualism

It should be noted here that the aspiration is for GGFS to be an immersion school, not a bilingual school. This is because of the language context of the students who are learning an endangered language as their second. Greymorning (personal communication) asserts that bilingual environments do not revitalise endangered languages. The reason for this failure, he suggests, is that for the majority of the time the medium of instruction is the dominant language.

Greymorning describes how bilingualism was created in the USA in 1970s to support Mexicans to learn English upon entering the country. This program worked because the students were learning a dominant language in which they were immersed. However, according to Greymorning, bilingualism does not support endangered languages because students have the ability to leave the bilingual classroom and not be immersed only in the target language. Because of this, learners simply default into the dominant language both in society and in the classroom.

At the same time for our students, there is no risk that they will not learn English. In the context they live, how could they not? Society, television, books, radio, sport, and social media means that they are immersed in it every day. English can be a subject of study at an immersion school, but it should not dictate what happens throughout school day.

Facilitating GGFS as an extension of community

In order to revitalise a language, the approach adopted needs to be community-driven and enveloped. A school program or language school cannot do the job alone, and it would be unfair to place that pressure on the children. These issues should be thoroughly considered when proposing and administering a language program in order to ensure that it's supported by community.

Bularri Muurlay Nyanggan – Two-path strong

In 2010, we voluntarily commenced our work of facilitating after school learning centres for local Goori kids as way to engage them in the idea that learning occurs throughout every facet of life. We thought hard about what we wanted for our children and the best description we could think of was *Bularri Muurlay Nyanggan* – two path strong, meaning strong in culture and strong in education. The thinking was that if we raise our children to be knowledgeable and proud of who they are as Goori people, they'll succeed at school and be equipped with the necessary tools to gain meaningful employment that equates to benefits in happiness and health.

Over the proceeding years, we have continued to grow our programs to include cultural camps, community language lessons, language lessons in partner schools, language lessons at Kulai Aboriginal Preschool, a structured reading acquisition program, sports and social and emotional well-being initiatives, and an in-school tutoring program, *Nyanggan Tutoring Program (NTP)*, delivered in three partner schools. By 2018, our programs were engaging no less than 750 people on a weekly basis, 93% of whom were Goori and all of whom were learning Gumbaynggirr in some capacity.

Tours

In 2015, our attention turned to creating a path toward self-sustainability, and in 2016 we launched a tourism product, the *Giingan Gumbaynggirr Cultural Experience*. In 2017 we opened a cafe, *Nyanggan Gapi Cafe and Catering*. The creation of these enterprises continues to provide young people who engage in our programs with valuable training and employment opportunities in hospitality and cultural tourism.

Cultural tourism provides our communities with a unique opportunity to practice and share culture whilst, at the same time, creating an economy that helps to sustain cultural revitalisation efforts. Our tours are also an important educational tool with which to educate people from all walks of life on the importance of language and cultural revitalisation. Bringing about celebration of language and the understanding that our culture is a strength, not a deficit, has been important in our journey toward opening GGFS.

Community classes

As mentioned above, we commenced our community language classes in 2014 and over time continually improved our teaching, and the drive of our community to engage in language bloomed. Initially these lessons were hosted once per week at the Local Aboriginal Land Council office at Wongala Reserve Aboriginal Estate on a Thursday morning. In 2018, we opened a second class for our advanced students, and in 2019 a third class was opened 80 km north of Coffs Harbour in Grafton. In addition to these classes, we also held numerous gatherings and employed the services of Dr Neyooxet Greymorning to run ASLA workshops to train our advanced speakers to become teachers.

Kulai Aboriginal preschool

In 2015, we commenced teaching both students and staff at Kulai Aboriginal Preschool, which, in 2021, resulted in Kulai becoming a bilingual early childhood education service. Kulai is the main preschool we target for enrolments at GGFS, because we have an existing relationship with the children and know that they have good language ability. Therefore, the opportunity for our children is that they commence learning Gumbaynggirr at the age of 3 and it then remains a journey of life-long learning.

Parents and families

One of the ways in which to ensure GGFS is an extension of community is to make it an enrolment requirement that parents also engage in Gumbaynggirr learning. It is a great way for parents to engage with the development of their children, speak language at home, and engage in school where the community lessons are facilitated. To encourage parents, we offer three lessons at different times during the week, two community classes, and a parent's class during school time.

It is truly humbling that our school has been able to capture the aspirations of so many parents and families. We were able to gain enough trust from parents for them to enrol 14 students in our opening year and 53 in just our second year of operation. This trust, support, and commitment from families inspires us to continually improve and ensure that our children get the best learning outcomes possible. And we have made a promise to all parents that, with their support and commitment, we'll ensure that their children get an education that develops the whole person.

Community investment and engagement in our school is of paramount importance to GGFS and the future of our language and culture. Our children have engaged in this learning and have succeeded. They are able to function in Gumbaynggirr in ways that many of our Elders thought they'd never see again. However, we cannot shift the responsibility of carrying the future of our language solely on our children. They need to know that their parents, families, and community are supporting them to bring language back into everyday use.

A part of our 12 years of *Ngarraanga* was to engage people in the idea that our language and culture is not a deficit, but a strength. Despite our efforts we have still faced resistance. However, at GGFS we have found that even though the opening and continued facilitation of a school is a large, daunting task, and it takes courage to take the 'leap of faith' into actually opening and enrolling students. The size of the task caused some apprehension and fear that we weren't ready and that our school would fail. What we have learned is that 'taking the plunge' is the hardest step. Once this step is taken, the momentum builds and the community benefits.

Re-claiming our birthright and agency

During a very recent conversation with senior Elder, Uncle Gary Williams, I asked him if we should have any fears regarding the apparent cessation of our 'sovereignty' during the failed Voice Referendum. Uncle Gary made the following observation: 'well firstly, sovereignty is a white concept' (Personal communication). In this vein, Moreton-Robinson (2020) highlights that the word 'sovereignty' is not an Indigenous one and, therefore, its meaning is conceptualised differently between Indigenous and western worldviews. She argues that Indigenous sovereignties 'are in and of the earth' (p. 259) and 'as humans we are the embodiment of our lands' (p. 259). Therefore, Indigenous sovereignties cannot be challenged and still operate despite the state's claim to sovereignty.

Given the complex conceptualisation of 'sovereignty', how do we define our birthright to connect with and be custodians of country through the practice of our languages and cultures? How do we define our human right to educate our children in the way we see fit? I don't have the answers to this, but from the experience of helping to grow GGFS, I do see our immersion approach as a way to have agency over our lives and the future of our culture and children.

This is just one of many occasions in which Uncle Gary has guided me through his cultural lens; he constantly reminds me, 'don't complicate things, just continue learning and teaching culture because that is most important'.

Bayi Wajaarr – Love Country

In order for our children to become protectors of Country, they need to connect, know, and fall in love with Country. For 60,000 years Country has been our classroom, we must maintain our connection to the wisdom that country provides. Country is a key component of the GGFS curriculum, which oversees our children connecting through a carefully designed garden at school, and weekly visits to culturally important places in order to learn story and ceremonies. Importantly, ngiindandi Wajaarr ngarraanga, wajaadu ngiina ngarraanga – 'if you respect Country, Country will respect you'.

School registration

In order to open a school that is legally binding, we had to register with the NSW Education Standards Authority (NESA), an onerous process that considered our financial feasibility, premises, and curriculum scope and sequencing.

Due to not having people in our community who speak Gumbaynggirr as their first language, and only a handful of qualified teachers with language ability, maintaining the cultural integrity of our school is also a financial challenge. The government funding provided to schools on a per student basis was not sufficient to cover the staffing requirements in our opening year 2022. It was due to the genuine allyship of the Paul Ramsay Foundation (PRF) and TAFE NSW, plus other partners that enabled us to submit a financial feasibility model that met the requirements of the NSW Education Standards Authority (NESA). Put simply, if not for PRF and TAFE, GGFS wouldn't have opened.

In addition to financial considerations, much hard work and thinking went into creating a curriculum that both educates our children in the way we see important from a cultural lens and that satisfies the requirements of NESA. There was much joy and relief with their positive feedback about our integrated curriculum and the more than 20 policies submitted.

By July 2021, although we had submitted all policies and curriculum to NESA and secured philanthropic partners, it seemed we were 'down and out' due to having no premises. Therefore, we re-planned for a 2023 opening. Thankfully, however, in the same month TAFE NSW surprised us with a gift of premises. Specifically, they gifted us with a decommissioned brick laying facility that required our attention to make school ready. It was an act of allyship that got us started.

Ngilina Jawgarr Biiwayay – Conclusion

As highlighted throughout, our community did not just wake up one day and decide to open a school. It took years of community work to build trusting relationships and prove our capacity to key decision makers in order to achieve registration with NESA. This work culminated in the opening of GGFS in 2022. In total it was 12 years of Ngarraanga – connecting with youth, their families, and community, and establishing enterprises to support our young people that enabled school opening. Through this process, it naturally became a community asset, and we now ensure that our school remains an extension of community.

It is important to continually strive to become a genuine immersion school within the next five years. If we don't strive to this level of fluency among our students, we run the risk that our children only speak their language at school and for cultural ceremonies. It is our goal that our children have the ability and desire to speak Gumbaynggirr in all facets of life as their default language. At this time of climate crisis, there are benefits to the world in the reawakening of Indigenous languages, and many of those benefits are only realised through language. As described by M. K. Turner and Children's Ground (2023, p. 25):

> Language and culture are intimately connected. Languages hold knowledge systems that are unique to the holders of that language. It is widely known that with the loss of languages, we are losing significant and important expertise through 'knowledge erosion'.

Despite the disruption to our culture that occurred because of colonisation, we are lucky to have much of our culture intact. This provides us with the opportunity to ensure that our children are Gumbaynggirr Daari – Gumbaynggirr strong. Our graduates will be *Bularri Muurlay Nyanggan* – two path strong, strong in culture and strong in education. Through their cultural grounding and integrity, our children will change the world, and they will carry their culture with pride, evidenced by speaking their language when they want, where they want, and in all facets of life.

References

Department of Infrastructure, Transport, Regional Development and Communications (DoITRDC), Australian Institute for Aboriginal and Torres Strait Islander Studies (AIATSIS) & Australian National University (ANU). (2020). *National Indigenous Languages Report (NILR)*. Australian Government. https://www.arts.gov.au/sites/default/files/documents/1national-indigenous-languages-report-pdf-introduction.pdf

Dunstan, L., Hewitt, B., & Tomaszewski, W. (2017). Indigenous children's affective engagement with school: The influence of socio-structural, subjective and relational factors. *Australian Journal of Education*, *61*(3), 250–269.

Greymorning, Neyooxet. Neyooxet is an Arapaho Language Teacher and Developer of Accelerated Second Language Acquisition (ASLA). Personal communication.

Moreton-Robinson, A. (2020). Incommensurable sovereignties: Indigenous ontology matters. In B. Hokowhitu (Ed.), *Routledge handbook of critical Indigenous studies* (pp. 257–268). Taylor & Francis Group.

Purdie, N., Boulton-Lewis, G., Fanshawe, J., Tripcony, P., & Gunstone, A. (2000). Positive self-identity for indigenous students and its relationship to school outcomes. Department of Education, Training and Youth Affairs. https://www.researchgate.net/publication/254580491_Positive_self-identity_for_indigenous_students_and_its_relationship_to_school_outcomes.

Turner, M. K. & Children's Ground. (2023). Apmerengentyele. The M.K. Turner Report: A Plan for First Nations-Led and Designed Education Reform in Australia. https://childrensground.org.au/wp-content/uploads/2023/07/The-MK-Turner-Report-Childrens-Ground-2023.pdf

Williams, Uncle Gary. Uncle Gary is a Senior Elder and CEO of Muurrbay Aboriginal Language and Culture Co-operative. Personal communication.

Part III
Aboriginal and Torres Strait Islander Contact Languages in Education

7 The Diverse Indigenous Creole Languages and First Nations Language Repertoires in Queensland, with Information for Educators

Denise Angelo, Carly Steele, Bernadine Yeatman, and Allan Yeatman

Who we are

Denise Angelo is a non-Indigenous researcher and teacher based at the Australian National University. She works with diverse First Nations communities and peoples and with schools on the many facets of contemporary Aboriginal and Torres Strait Islander language contexts, including teaching and learning traditional languages, recognising creole languages and Indigenised Englishes, and supporting English as an Additional Language/Dialect (EAL/D).

Carly Steele is a non-Indigenous academic in the School of Education at Curtin University. Prior to joining academia, she worked as a teacher for 12 years in NSW, WA, NT, and QLD. Much of her teaching experience is in regional and remote parts of Australia serving First Nations communities.

Bernadine Yeatman is a Yidinji woman from the Yarrabah Aboriginal Community in far north Queensland. She is a fully trained and practising teacher and has been working in the field of education for over 20 years. Bernadine also conducts key language research for her community as well as raising awareness and achieving recognition for Yarrie Lingo/Yarrabah Creole – the local creole language of the Yarrabah speech community.

Allan Yeatman is a Yidinji man from the Yarrabah Aboriginal Community in far north Queensland. He also has connections to the Kuku-Njunkul, Kuku-Djangan, and Kuku-Yalanji tribes. Allan has long-term experience working at the local school. He has also been involved in researching the local language situation, especially the local creole language – Yarrie Lingo/Yarrabah Creole, and was part of the team that developed the famous At da Crick community vernacular language poster.

DOI: 10.4324/9781003441021-11

Introduction

Situated in the north-east of the continent, the state of Queensland has a long and complex language story, which differs from the rest of the continent in some important ways. Queensland is home to both Aboriginal peoples and Torres Strait Islander peoples, the two Indigenous cultural groupings of First Nations peoples in Australia (see Figure 7.1). Aboriginal peoples' homelands encompass the mainland and associated waters and islands; Torres Strait Islander peoples' homelands include the islands and waters of the Torres Strait located off the far north tip of Queensland. The brutal legacy of Queensland's colonial history has had enduring effects for First Nations peoples today. Under government legislation and policy, First Nations peoples experienced enforced and severe control over their freedom of movement and other human rights, working for little or no recompense and in many cases with dislocation from their Country and close family. This has also had a profound impact on the languages First Nations peoples here speak. In many parts of Queensland, Indigenous contact languages from the early days have developed into creole languages. Today, these Indigenous creole languages serve as a mark of linguistic resilience and resistance to English and express distinctive First Nations identities (O'Shannessy et al., 2024).

Indigenous creole languages have a considerable footprint in the present-day Indigenous language landscape. On the national level, two creole languages are recognised as having the largest speakership of any Indigenous language in Australia today, Yumplatok (Torres Strait Creole)-Cape York Creole and Kriol. Yumplatok-Cape York Creole (see below for discussion of naming) is spoken primarily in Queensland, while at its easternmost periphery Kriol extends into Queensland. In addition, there are more localised creole languages, such as Yarrie Lingo/Yarrabah Creole and Kowanyama Creole, which are less well-recognised.

Despite their significance, awareness of Indigenous creole languages is not high and support for speakers is inconsistent. To address this, the following chapter has three aims. The first is to describe Indigenous creole languages spoken in Queensland today. We will outline the major groupings of these creole languages, their histories, and their present-day contexts. Second, we describe traditional languages, creoles, and Englishes that are present in contemporary Indigenous language landscapes and compare different common multilingual repertoires involving all these language types. Thirdly, we provide information about approaches that can be used to address the needs of Indigenous creole language speakers.

Overview of different language types

In order to understand the different First Nations languages of Queensland it is first necessary to distinguish the various types that exist. Depending on where in Queensland you are, Indigenous creole languages, traditional languages, and

The Diverse Indigenous Creole and First Nations Languages 111

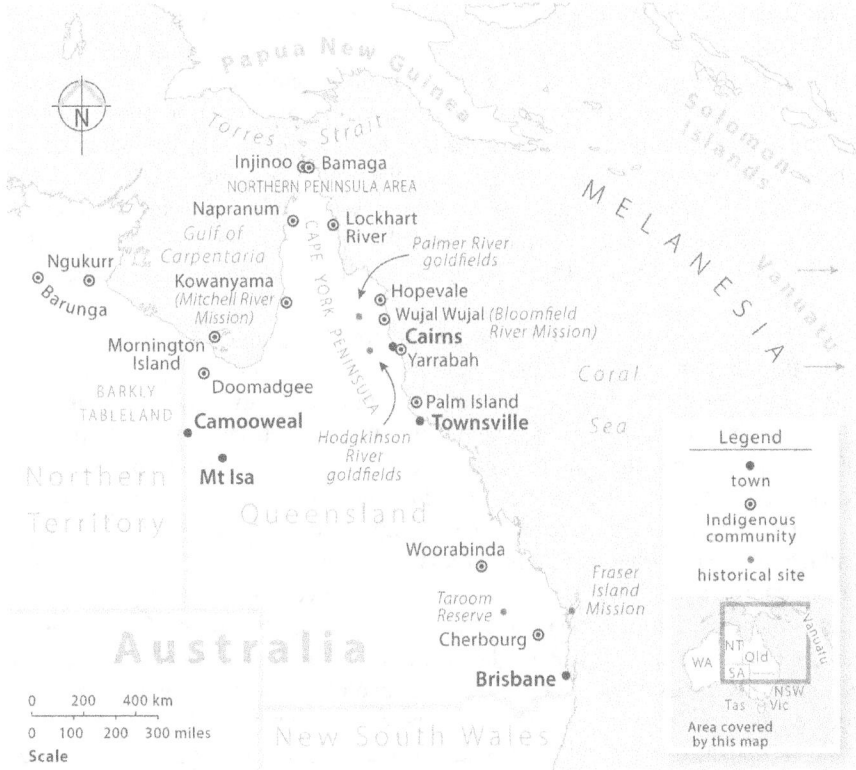

Figure 7.1 Map of locations referred to in this chapter
Cartography © Brenda Thornley 2024

Englishes (as described below) will be present to different extents and so they will play different roles for children, families, and communities.

Indigenous creole languages

Indigenous creole languages are a prominent feature of the contemporary First Nations language landscape in Queensland (see Figure 7.2). Creole languages are full languages that have their origins in language contact between non-Aboriginal and First Nations people and which are now spoken by entire language communities. As Indigenous creole languages are spoken almost exclusively by Aboriginal and Torres Strait Islander people, they are 'Indigenous' languages, even though they have different histories to traditional languages. It should be noted they also attract different attitudes, too.

Creole languages can be categorised as a type of 'contact language', along with their historical precursors, pidgins, and with mixed languages (O'Shannessy et al., 2024). Each Indigenous creole language in Queensland has its own language contact pathway and reflects different language influences, such as the inclusion of local traditional language elements. In Australia, Indigenous creoles are 'English-lexified' because much of their vocabulary is, historically, derived from English. Creoles are not, however, direct descendants from any one language. Hence, speakers of an English-lexified creole do not automatically and fully understand speakers of English – and vice versa – even though there may be some 'overlap' of some words. For this reason, in high stakes English settings the provision of an interpreter is most appropriate, whereas this would not be the case for somebody who speaks a variety of English (e.g., Aboriginal English – see below and Chapter 9 of this volume).

A creole language is historically derived from a 'pidgin' – a language code generated during contact between speakers in multilingual settings, who lack a common language. Therefore, technically, a pidgin is not anybody's first language. However, in some situations, communication may have been dependent upon the use of a pidgin language, for example, where multiple First Nations peoples were forcibly relocated to a mission, government settlement, or labouring situation. Under such circumstances, speakers used a pidgin to communicate with each other and it expanded and became more expressive to meet their communicative needs. Owing to its frequent use, this expanded pidgin evolved to become a creole, being acquired and used as a first language by a younger generation of speakers. Unlike a pidgin, a creole is spoken as a first language and has become the main language of a community. A hallmark of creole language evolution is that words from original source languages often remain somewhat recognisable but not the other language systems: sentence structures, word endings, meanings, and sound patterns are reconfigured, and new systems emerge.

As creole languages are relatively 'new' compared to traditional languages, it typically takes time for their community and wider society to appreciate fully the ramifications of the language situation, and to achieve recognition and establish a naming convention. It should be noted that the 2020 *National Indigenous Languages Report* uses the term 'new languages' to embrace contact languages, including creole languages and mixed languages, to explicitly include them as Indigenous languages and to contrast them with traditional languages. Nowadays, Yumplatok (Torres Strait Creole) is probably the most recognised creole language name in Queensland. Some other creole languages are also gradually gaining recognition, including Yarrie Lingo/Yarrabah Creole. Where speakers of creole languages are not properly recognised, they are often thought, incorrectly, to be speakers of one of their source languages. In Queensland, this 'misrecognition' might involve designating the language (incorrectly) as English. The presence of vocabulary of historical English origin gives rise to the erroneous idea that creole languages are just another dialect of English. This is not correct, but nor is this widely known.

The following provides a brief description of each of the creole language groupings represented in Queensland, in terms of its naming, geographical spread, origins, and current recognition. Locations of Queensland creole languages and historically related Melanesian creole languages are identified in Figure 7.2.

The Diverse Indigenous Creole and First Nations Languages 113

Key to creole languages

Kriol

Yumplatok (Torres Strait Creole) & Cape York Creole

which includes:
1. Lockhart River Creole
2. Napranum Creole

Gulf creole languages
3. Kowanyama Creole
4. Mornington Island Creole

Creole languages & varieties in communities with historical language superdiversity
5. Yarrie Lingo (Yarrabah Creole)
6. Palm Island Talk
7. Woorie Talk
8. Cherbourg Talk

Melanesian creole languages
9. Tok Pisin
10. Solomon Islands Pijin
11. Bislama

Figure 7.2 Map of Queensland creole languages and related Melanesian varieties
Cartography © Brenda Thornley 2024

Torres Strait-Cape York Creole

This creole language is spoken across the Torres Strait and in northern Cape York, northwards from Lockhart River (in the east) and Napranum (in the west), including the Northern Peninsula Area (see Figure 7.2). Aboriginal and Torres Strait Islander people living in these areas understand each other but speak distinct dialects of their creole. In addition, there are large populations of people who come from these areas who now live on the mainland, particularly in Cairns and Townsville.

Over the years, this creole has been known by a number of names, depending on the location. The term 'Yumplatok' has become increasingly common in the Torres Strait, but it is called 'Torres Strait Creole' here, too. More informally, it might also be called 'Broken' (although First Nations people elsewhere in Queensland also commonly use this term to describe any creole or 'heavy' Aboriginal English). In Aboriginal communities on Cape York, the names 'Yumplatok' and 'Torres Strait Creole' have not gained much traction. Here this creole language was first described as 'Cape York Creole' (Crowley & Rigsby, 1979). In Cape York communities, the local creole might simply be called 'Creole', or be accompanied with its local or regional place name, 'Lockhart River Creole', 'Napranum Creole', 'Cape York Creole', etc.

This creole language of the north-east of the state, which could inclusively be called 'Torres Strait-Cape York Creole', developed from a shared history of labouring in the early industries of the region, such as harvesting sandalwood, bêche de mer ('trepang' or 'sea cucumber'), trochus shell, and pearling. Poorly paid, unpaid, indentured, or even kidnapped multilingual workforces came from the Torres Strait and Cape York, as well as from Melanesia and the South Pacific (Tryon, 2009), Malaysia, Indonesia, Japan, and even further afield. This cultivated the use and spread of a 'pidgin' which developed into a creole when taken on by First Nations communities. Related creoles that developed from this context are also spoken in Melanesian countries, such as Bislama in Vanuatu, Tok Pisin in Papua New Guinea, and Pijin in the Solomon Islands.

In the Torres Strait, the spread of this creole is also associated with the spread of Christianity via Pacific Islander missionaries. It is also the language that connected the eastern and western Torres Strait Islands, which were previously separated linguistically. Famously it was the language which was used to help organise the 1936 Maritime Strike in which Torres Strait Islanders came together to fight for equal pay (Sellwood, 2022). Likewise, Cape York Creole has served to enhance communication between members of newly formed communities including government settlements and missions. The shared maritime histories of the Torres Strait and the Cape York Peninsula distinguish this creole-speaking area from some of the other contact languages in Queensland.

The use of Torres Strait-Cape York Creole in schooling has for the most part been informal, with local staff communicating instructions or concepts to students via their shared spoken language. Some decades ago, poor attitudes about creole languages and misunderstandings about multilingualism worked against them having a more formal role in education. Bucking that trend, in the 1990s, the school at Inijinoo in the Northern Peninsula Area implemented a bilingual program with L1 literacy teaching in Injinoo Creole, which is still regarded as successful by the local educators who were involved, and the then students, now adults. In more recent times, beyond that particular program, language awareness initiatives have been used to increase speaker understanding and to assist students with contrasting features of their L1 creole and their L2 Standard Australian English. There is an increasing pride discernible amongst speakers of Torres Strait-Cape York Creole.

Kriol

This creole language extends from western Queensland through the Northern Territory and into the Kimberley region of Western Australia. Across this wide area there are many different local and regional dialects of Kriol, as well as other differences, such as the Kriol spelling systems that have been developed in different jurisdictions. Even the use of the name 'Kriol' – the extent it is recognised and employed to refer to this creole language – differs throughout *Kriol Kantri* 'the Kriol speaking area'. For example, the use of the term 'Kriol' virtually ceases on the Queensland side of the border, even though Aboriginal families from Camooweal or Doomadgee in Queensland can use their varieties with Aboriginal peoples from neighbouring areas of the Barkly Tableland and Gulf of Carpentaria in the Northern Territory.

The history of Kriol is tied to the overland spread of pastoral industries, south to north, through western Queensland. The pidgin that developed on the first site of invasion and colonisation in Sydney in New South Wales travelled with the moving frontier that dispossessed First Nations peoples, occupying their countries and exploiting their labour. The linguistic seeds of this pidgin were used by First Nations people in subsequent multilingual situations, such as on cattle stations, in mining camps, or on missions and government settlements. The best-known instance of Kriol development is associated with the Roper River Mission at Ngukurr, NT. The pastoral industry in particular brought Aboriginal people from Queensland and their pidgin/creole into the Northern Territory and from there into the Kimberley region of Western Australia.

Although Kriol is one of the Indigenous creole languages that has a fair degree of official recognition on the national stage, varieties of Kriol are rather invisible in Queensland, although some church groups in western areas of Queensland, like Mt Isa, utilise liturgical materials produced in Kriol. Currently there are no contexts in which Kriol literacy is formally taught in Queensland schools. In contrast, in the Northern Territory, large amounts of early reading materials were produced by the Literature Production Centre in Barunga (formerly Bamyili), with much of this body of work available online (see Territory Stories section of the NT Libraries and Archives: https://territorystories.nt.gov.au/?query=Kriol). Also in the Northern Territory, the Aboriginal Interpreter Service provides interpreters for Kriol speakers, and there are Kriol Awareness courses for professionals (Ngukurr Language Centre, 2024) and Kriol-based projects for community members (Meigim Kriol Strongbala, 2019).

The Gulf: Mornington Island and Kowanyama

These creole-speaking communities are situated between Torres Strait-Cape York Creole and Kriol, and the local creole spoken in each location suggests influence from both quarters. Angelo (2023) provides linguistic and historical sketches of these creole languages. Neither creole language has gained consistent official recognition, certainly nowhere near the extent of Kriol or the Yumplatok/Torres Strait Creole part of the north-eastern creole. For example, neither are listed on the 2016 Australian Standard Classification of Languages (ASCL) from the Australian Bureau of Statistics, which is how the speakers of different languages are counted in the national Census (Australian Bureau of Statistics [ABS], 2016). However, both Mornington Island and Kowanyama have undertaken Community Vernacular Language Poster projects which illustrate the everyday way these languages are spoken by most community members as their first language. At this stage, there is no standardised way of spelling words in either of these creoles, nor is there a standardised way of naming the actual languages. For example, Mornington Island people might refer to Mornington Island Creole descriptively as a 'slang', 'broken English', or 'pidgin' type of language, referencing its informal sphere of use, its English-related and/or contact language properties.

Mornington Island Creole developed through a complex history of links to the Gulf area and the Queensland mainland. From the 1860s onwards, colonial activities – particularly those associated with the cattle industry – had encroached on nearby Gulf country, an industry that came to involve many Mornington Islanders working across northern Queensland and beyond. A mission, established on Mornington Island in 1914 and running into the 1970s, operated a dormitory system for children, local as well as those from the mainland, separating them from their parents and from opportunities to learn their traditional languages with their families. Mornington Islanders also worked as boat crew, for example on vessels supplying missions around the Gulf and up to the Torres Strait. Their labour in cattle and maritime industries exposed them to pidgin and creole varieties spoken in different places. In its present-day form, Mornington Island Creole includes items and phrases from Lardil, Kayardild, and other traditional languages from the mainland, and in this way it connects people, country, languages, and culture.

Kowanyama Creole developed through early multilingual language contact settings in the local area. By the 1860s, colonial occupation and exploitation of First Nations lands was underway in Cape York, with pastoral leases and the Palmer River gold rush commencing in 1873. The Trubanamen Mission was established in 1905, replaced by the Mitchell River Mission in 1916. Labouring in the cattle industry also brought speakers of different Aboriginal language groups together. With its own large cattle herd, Mitchell River Mission functioned as a training ground for the cattle industry and supplied Aboriginal labour far and wide, enabling the uptake and spread of northern contact languages. Mitchell River Mission's harsh dormitory and language regime doubtless hastened language shift by preventing children from associating with family members and using their traditional language(s). The mission was run by the Anglican Church until 1967, and then the

Queensland government until control was transferred to Kowanyama community in 1987. Nowadays, Kowanyama Creole is recognised as a signature of Kowanyama identity, as the title of Kowanyama's Community Vernacular Language Poster says: 'Kowanyama talkbud - Chay! We all talk like dat ere!'

Yarrie Lingo/Yarrabah Creole, Woorie Talk, and other creoles in former government Settlements

The former government Settlements of Yarrabah, Palm Island, Woorabinda, and Cherbourg were sites of extensive language contact, where over 12,000 Indigenous people were relocated from the 1890s to the 1970s under a draconian piece of Queensland legislation, the Act of 1897 (Mushin et al., 2016). Residents came from a large number of different traditional language groups. Most also brought with them multiple experiences with contact languages, including what was current in their original homelands and what was developing locally in their Settlement, as well as from outside labouring contexts and/or contact with other Settlements. Under the Act, residents were segregated from mainstream English-speaking society, apart from short-term work contracts. Hence there existed a superdiversity of languages (i.e., scores of traditional language backgrounds and a number of contact languages), a continually re-forming speech community with new arrivals and returning labourers, and restricted access to English. These factors, amongst others, shaped the contact languages in the communities. Owing to their shared histories, the contact languages spoken in these Settlements appear to have much in common. The creole languages spoken at Yarrabah and Woorabinda, Yarrie Lingo/Yarrabah Creole and Woorie Talk, have been the focus of recent linguistic studies with community members (Angelo, 2023; Munro & Mushin, 2016; Mushin et al., 2016; Yeatman & Angelo, 2023).

Yarrabah Mission was established in 1892. First Nations peoples in the region had been subjected to encroaching colonisation, first by bêche de mer fishermen in the 1850s, but intensifying with the Palmer and Hodgkinson gold rushes in the hinterlands in the 1870s and the establishment of the nearby township of Cairns in 1876. Language use in Yarrabah was strongly influenced by a variety of contact languages and by fluent speakers of the many (over 40) traditional languages of residents. As labour providers, Yarrabah residents participated in maritime, plantation, cattle, and domestic work, where contact languages were often spoken amongst the multilingual and polyethnic workforces. Most Yarrabah residents came from the north of Queensland, but not exclusively. Yarrabah Mission absorbed a number of other missions, including Fraser Island to the south and Bloomfield River to the north. Further adding to the super-diverse linguistic make-up of residents, Yarrabah also had Industrial School status, housing a high proportion of state-sanctioned Indigenous child removals. Until 1942, Yarrabah Mission ran a dormitory system, effectively promoting language shift by placing children of diverse language backgrounds – local and incoming – together, and away from adults. Nowadays, 'Yarrie Lingo' the local name for 'Yarrabah Creole' has been steadily gaining recognition.

Indeed, following the counting of Yarrie Lingo/Yarrabah Creole speakers in the 2021 Census, Yarrabah became the third largest community of Aboriginal language speakers in Australia, although the actual creole language name does not yet appear in these statistics (ABS, 2022).

In central Queensland where Woorabinda is located, the northwards moving frontier of the pastoral industry began occupying First Nations from the 1850s. Language contact was entrenched by the time the government Settlement of Woorabinda was established in 1927 with the relocation of Aboriginal peoples from the earlier Taroom Reserve established in 1911. Woorabinda also ran a dormitory system where children were separated from their families. Many Woorabinda residents laboured in the pastoral industry before and after entering the Settlement so linguistic seeds from the early pastoral contact language were plentiful. The population at Taroom, and then Woorabinda, primarily represented central and south-western First Nations at first, but the Lutheran Hopevale Mission from the far north was moved to Woorabinda at the start of World War II, and removals of First Nations from the north and north-west to Woorabinda also increased over time. Research suggests that this turbulent linguistic history has given rise to an 'intermediate creole', a creole language with more lexifier language influences – that is, more obvious overlaps with English than some other 'heavier' creoles might have (Munro & Mushin, 2016). Woorabinda residents all recognise their own way of talking, and it signifies their 'Woorie' identity. Nevertheless, although public awareness and acknowledgement of 'Woorie Talk' has been growing slowly over the years, it is still only inconsistently acknowledged by service providers and in the wider community.

Traditional languages

Across Queensland, there are over 100 traditional First Nations languages connected with the mainland and islands, including the Torres Strait (State Library of Queensland [SLQ], 2024). These languages are connected enduringly through the land to Aboriginal and Torres Strait Islander peoples, regardless of the extent to which they are spoken today. Traditional languages are entirely different from English, in terms of their sounds, words, sentence structures, and they are significant for expressing culture and identity. Across much of the continent and in Queensland, invasion and colonisation have disrupted the transmission of First Nations traditional languages. This legacy means that there are only a few areas of Queensland where children may learn a traditional language as their first and main language from birth, such as Wik Mungkan on western Cape York and Kala Kawaw Ya in parts of the top west of the Torres Strait. Elsewhere in the state, Aboriginal and Torres Strait Islander peoples have undergone a shift in their language use. For some language groups, this shift is more recent, and younger generations can still learn their traditional language from older generations who speak their language fluently. However, in much of the state, First Nations people are working to renew their language by learning it from available community remembrances and archival sources.

Englishes

Almost all schools in Queensland deliver the classroom curriculum via Standard Australian English. This is the language of Australian institutions, mainstream media, organisations, and businesses. This variety of Australian English has been standardised through documents such as Australian Government style manuals (Australian Public Service Commission, 2023). Standard Australian English thus serves as a kind of benchmark for English language use in Australia for official and educational functions. It is also the language spoken as a first language by some First Nations people.

In terms of the forms of spoken English employed in everyday communication across Australia, such as between family and friends, Australian Englishes have been classified in different ways for instance, some use the term General Australian English to describe the most common or 'average' variety (contrasting with either Cultivated or Broad varieties). In education circles, 'academic English' may also be used: this refers to a particular selection of English language resources that meet academic expectations.

Many First Nations people in Queensland have their own ways of using English, which reflect their cultural backgrounds. This means they can often tell where each other come from on the basis of a word or other language feature. These Indigenised varieties of English are a powerful resource for Aboriginal and Torres Strait Islander peoples as they convey their identities as First Nations people. In Queensland, these Indigenised varieties have sometimes been called 'Aboriginal English(es)' or 'Torres Strait Island English' (Eades, 2014; Malcolm, 2018; Shnukal, 2001).

There is a wide range of Aboriginal and Torres Strait Islander Englishes in Queensland:

- Some are 'lighter' and comprehensible by those who speak General or Standard Australian English, even though they are different, with some different vocabulary or styles of talking. Just like other dialects of English (e.g., New Zealand English or different dialects in the UK), these differences do not necessarily mean speakers have English language learning needs.
- Some are 'heavier' and very different from General or Standard Australian English – so much so that children who come to school speaking these varieties might not automatically understand their teachers. This is a similar situation to that of speakers of Indigenous creole languages, as previously described. Indeed, in Queensland and elsewhere, research has now shown that a number of varieties once described as 'Aboriginal English(es)' in the 1970s have since been reappraised as creole languages as the field of creolistics developed. Such varieties include Yarrie Lingo/Yarrabah Creole and Woorie Talk/Woorabinda Creole (Angelo, 2023; Munro & Mushin, 2016).

First Nations multilingualism in Queensland

Numerically, most First Nations students in Queensland speak a variety of English as their main language, followed by those who speak an Indigenous creole language, then by those who speak a traditional language (we note that this pattern might be similar or might vary compared to other parts of Australia, as described throughout this volume). However, these proportions of language speakers can be dramatically different at a local level. For example, in many far north Queensland Indigenous communities, community members all speak a creole language with each other as their main language. In addition, and depending on learning opportunities, children, their family members, and other people in their community are also likely to have some knowledge of other languages. In fact, as a cultural orientation, Australian First Nations peoples have been positively disposed toward cultivating multilingualism.

To assist with understanding First Nations students' languages, including the place of creole languages, and how schools can support languages and language learning, some important 'language ecologies' are described in Table 7.1. A language ecology refers to place-based language use. The language spoken by students as their L1 and main language with family is a communication, cognition, and identity strength. Their learning of other languages, in addition, can be supported at school as L2 to become additional language strengths. It is important for school staff to discuss with parents/caregivers and community members which languages are spoken by students so that appropriate language support structures can be implemented. This step is key because every child's language should be respected.

Table 7.1 Indigenous language ecologies.

Spoken by most children, families, and community members as their main language and L1:		
• an English	• a creole language	• a traditional language
Additional languages students can be supported to learn in school as a target L2 are:		
• traditional language(s)	• Standard Australian English • traditional language(s)	• Standard Australian English
Characteristics of these different language ecologies:		
Indigenous community members speak an English largely mutually comprehensible to Standard Australian English speakers. Traditional languages are learned in addition through school and/or community teaching.	Indigenous community members speak a creole, or a 'heavy' Aboriginal English for the most part not mutually comprehensible to Standard Australian English speakers. English is learned in the classroom and is often used only in school and with non-Indigenous people outside of school. Traditional languages are learned through school and/or community teaching.	Indigenous community members speak a traditional language, not mutually comprehensible to Standard Australian English speakers. English is learned in the classroom and is often used only in school and with non-Indigenous people outside of school.

The Diverse Indigenous Creole and First Nations Languages 121

In many locations in Queensland, local First Nations community members will share a similar pattern of multilingualism. However, this is not always so. In larger towns, for example, Aboriginal and Torres Strait Islander people could have very different language backgrounds because their families could be:

- newcomers from other parts of Australia;
- Indigenous community members from surrounding areas which have a different language ecology;
- original traditional owners or long-term residents of several generations.

Hence, while it is a useful head start to be informed about common language ecologies, it is also important not to make assumptions.

On the ground views

To begin, Bernadine Yeatman and Allan Yeatman, the Aboriginal co-authors of this chapter share their observations and advice for educators and policy makers. They are both experienced Aboriginal educators from Yarrabah, who are speakers of Yarrie Lingo, and who have also been involved in researching their creole language.

Getting started

Educators should learn about the community they work in, present day and history. In the case of Yarrabah, for example, it is the largest Indigenous community in Queensland with a population of 2,505 residents (Australian Bureau of Statistics (ABS), 2021). Our community has grown from a mission which was established in 1892 with around 100 residents on the traditional lands of the Gunggandji-Yidinji peoples. The early mission residents were predominantly local Gunggay- and Yidiny-speaking peoples, but Indigenous people from many other First Nations were brought here, too.

Local language situation

It is also important that educators learn about the local language ecology. Today, at Yarrabah, as with many Indigenous communities in Queensland, three kinds of languages are represented:

i Creole is spoken by many students in Queensland. In our community, Yarrie Lingo is the name that we use for Yarrabah Creole. It is an historical fusion of influences of traditional Aboriginal languages and English varieties, but it is not English and it is not a traditional language either. Yarrie Lingo is the language of everyday communication in the Yarrabah community. It is the language that

Yarrabah children speak and understand fully and easily. It is the language that our children start school with.

ii The Traditional Language of this area is Gunggay-Yidiny. This language is being revived in the school in language classes. The fact that it is being revived means that few people know it. It has cultural significance, but it is not the main language of communication for community members.

iii Standard Australian English is not the language of our community and it is not the language that most community members use in everyday conversations. As is the case in many creole-speaking areas, Yarrabah community members' proficiency in Standard Australian English varies widely. However, classroom teachers and other incoming service providers all speak Standard Australian English when communicating with the people of Yarrabah. At school, the curriculum is also delivered in English. Therefore, students are very much dependent on their teachers' know-how with delivering all subjects in a way that responds to the language needs of the students.

Some personal observations

For the school and the Yarrabah community, the production of our *At da Crick* poster, a community vernacular language poster in Yarrie Lingo, has considerably raised the visibility and recognition of the creole spoken here (see Figure 7.3). This poster project has proven to be a major step forward in the school's and community's acknowledgement and understanding of our language situation, past and present. However, awareness of Yarrie Lingo – and actively accommodating Yarrie Lingo speakers – is still quite variable.

The majority of new teachers come to our school not aware that Yarrabah students are speakers of a creole language and not of English. They start with the assumption that students are English speakers which results in Yarrabah students not receiving targeted language support as EAL/D learners in their English-medium classrooms. As a result, the students' educational experiences and learning outcomes are negatively impacted. Many new teachers get noticeably fatigued, from concentrating all day on communicating with students who speak a language different to their own, as this first-year teacher explains:

> At the end of the first day of teaching, I came away feeling overwhelmed and exhausted due to the fact that I found it hard to understand what the children were saying. I had to really listen to what they were saying and then process what they had said and then respond.

On the other hand, local educators, such as ourselves, also feel exhausted at the end of the school day, due to the fact that we have to listen carefully to what English speakers are saying, mentally translate what they say into Yarrie Lingo and then respond back to them in English. This is what our students have to do, too, but usually with fewer English resources.

English speaking teachers do not automatically and fully understand Yarrie Lingo speakers and vice versa. While local teacher aides are fluent speakers of Yarrie Lingo, a language strength, many of them find high levels of English demanding, especially when communicating about the curriculum and other technical matters with their English-speaking teacher colleagues. This can impact on the quality of communication and on the quality of support they offer the students as well as each other.

Guidance for teachers

There is a need for all educators to be made aware of the different types and histories of languages in communities and to understand the different roles that these languages play in students' lives (e.g., in preservice education and in teacher induction programs). Teachers must be provided with a 'languages toolkit' suited to working in the various communities. It would include creole language awareness and recognition activities, English language teaching skills, and material on supporting the revival of traditional languages. Adding English as a second language to Indigenous students' repertoires should be done sensitively and productively, always from the perspective of respecting the students' home language and acknowledging that they are learners of English. Schools should provide encouragement for families and caregivers to actively support their children's language learning journeys at school by encouraging pride in speaking local languages such as Yarrie Lingo.

Schools should assign a bilingual member of staff to work as a 'code conduit', a language, culture, and knowledge broker. There should be allotted planning and conversation times between classroom teacher, 'code conduit' and Indigenous teacher aide to ensure quality communication and partnerships. Schools in Indigenous creole-speaking communities should mandate planning and teaching using an 'EAL/D' approach which supports student learning of an English-medium curriculum. Ideally this would include a designated timeslot in the school's weekly timetable for English language teaching.

More important things to know

The world over, multilingual people outnumber those who are monolingual, and adding languages to our existing language repertoires is entirely natural and feasible. However, as described by Bernadine Yeatman and Allan Yeatman, schools do not always recognise students' creole home language nor support their additional language learning. Yet acknowledging students' creole home language and explicitly and supportively teaching an additional target language in the classroom is known to support academic achievement (Carter et al. 2020). This section outlines more of the important dynamics that impact on Aboriginal and Torres Strait Islander students who speak creole languages.

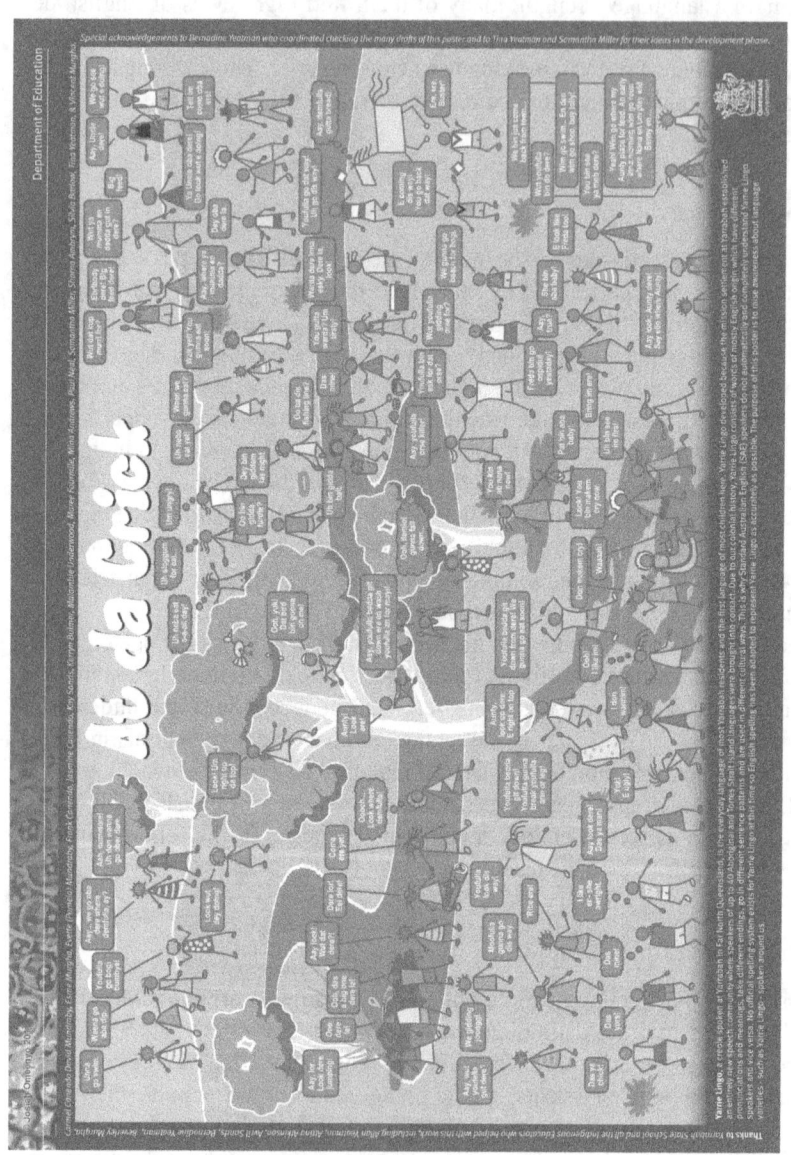

Figure 7.3 At da Crick, a community vernacular language poster in Yarrie Lingo
Reprinted with permission from the Queensland Department of Education and in consultation with members of Yarrabah community.

Misrecognition

Misrecognition is about mistakenly believing one thing to be something else. Speakers of creole languages are often 'misrecognised' and are mistakenly believed to be speakers of their creole's lexifier language. In the first instance this can occur because a lexifier language, such as English, has historically contributed considerable material to a creole, such as Yarrie Lingo/Yarrabah Creole.

Misrecognition also occurs because of entrenched social assumptions and language ideologies. The default language setting in Australia is English. Indigenous Englishes and creole languages can all too easily be assumed (erroneously) to be poorer versions of English. If students are assumed to be English speakers, they will not be supported to learn English as an additional language, nor will their additional language learning achievements be tracked or celebrated.

Noticing and awareness

For speakers of Indigenous creole languages, learning the language which is the national standard, but also the historical lexifier and colonial language, represents a conceptually different task to most other language learning situations. In typical second or foreign language learning situations, the target language is perfectly clear to learners – it is separated. This is not the case for creole-speaking students in English-medium classrooms (Berry & Hudson, 1997). The apparently shared linguistic material can obscure the target language because students are actively drawing on their creole in their efforts to process or guess what is being taught. While drawing on all resources can support comprehension, it also blurs the target language, making it harder to learn it as a separate language system.

For students who are Indigenous creole speakers, 'noticing' the differences between their own language and Standard Australian English as a target language is therefore pivotal. Schmidt's (1990) Noticing Hypothesis states that for language to be acquired, it must first be noticed. Even very young creole-speaking students notice some of the highly salient differences between their home way of talking and school talk (Dixon, 2018) and are able to regulate their use according to home and school contexts (e.g., p. 279; p. 288), and to recognise that (non-Indigenous teachers) do not understand their language (p. 290). However, Siegel (2010) explains that speakers of English-lexified creoles may not necessarily 'notice' all of these differences and so cannot acquire what has not been significant to them. Due to the linguistic overlap between a creole and its lexifier language, speakers may be able to make themselves generally understood as long as contextual enrichment supports meaning-making for those involved in the interaction (Angelo & Hudson, 2018). In successful interactions, some differences can seem somewhat 'communicatively redundant' (Long, 2007, p. 62).

And where linguistic differences do not appear to impede communication, there is also less recognition of the language teaching support required for learning a target language. Hence there is a need for language awareness programs that explicitly compare and contrast students' creole language with Standard Australian English. This helps educators and students to notice the real extent of their additional language learning journey (Angelo & Carter, 2015; Angelo & Hudson, 2020; Berry & Hudson, 1997; Carter et al., 2020)).

Where Indigenous creole-speaking students are not supported by using EAL/D teaching approaches, this can impact their 'motivation' (Berry & Hudson, 1997) and their levels of investment in learning (Nero & Ahmad, 2014). From a sociocultural point of view, if students' language is not intentionally valued, nor recognised as the language of their family and community – that is, part of their cultural and self-identity – then they may feel that learning English is a needless imposition, involving endless correction or even failure (Sellwood & Angelo, 2013).

Language minoritisation

There is a pervasive view that English is the 'natural, neutral, and universal norm' (Zhang-Wu & Tian, 2023, p. 121). This perspective has been labelled the 'monolingual mindset' in Australia (Clyne, 2005, p. 11), where this ideology licences attitudes that do not value languages or language learning. Viewing languages other than English from the monolingual mindset positions them as not worthwhile, irrelevant, and even deviant. In countries like Australia, where English is the dominant and majority language, other languages and their speakers can be minoritised in society. This can happen in official ways, through language policies, for example, and unofficially in the ways that minoritised languages are viewed by people in society. Often these two forms of minoritisation interact. For example, in Australia, speakers of Aboriginal and Torres Strait Islander languages – traditional and creole – have not been consistently and equitably included and serviced in education, and, historically, these languages have even been actively suppressed. While that is no longer the case, the legacy of these language policies continues, and is evident in the small numbers of ongoing Indigenous language programs in schools and universities. It is also evident in the lack of bespoke policy for describing, recognising, naming, and responding to Indigenous creole languages, with ramifications for how speakers of these languages access public services such as education delivered in Standard Australian English (Angelo, 2024; Sellwood & Angelo, 2013). This minoritisation limits the agency of speakers to use their languages in all aspects of their lives, a profound injustice – one that speakers of English in Australian society do not experience. All of this also means that the general public is rarely exposed to Indigenous creole languages, a further limitation on the growth of public language awareness. Therefore, minoritisation significantly impacts the recognition and status of Indigenous contact languages, fuelling a cycle of marginalisation from education and other policy areas and general society.

Status and prestige

Because of some surface similarities that Indigenous creole languages share with their English lexifier, they can be misrecognised as (a kind of) English; but because of the differences, creole languages are also often unfairly evaluated as poorer or lesser versions. In mainstream domains where Standard Australian English is the norm – which is most – creole languages can be highly stigmatised. Creole languages may be unrecognised and unwelcome in the classroom and may be unutilised in school communications with community members (Angelo & Carter, 2015; Carter et al., 2020; Sellwood & Angelo, 2013). These perspectives can be linked to the monolingual mindset (Clyne, 2005) and standard language ideologies (Siegel, 2010) (as described above), which skew thinking about languages other than English, particularly those such as creole languages that are perceived as 'non-standard'. Outside of English-dominated mainstream contexts, however, creole speakers use their language for all their intra-community conversations without issue. In these contexts, Indigenous creole languages are not denigrated; this is the proper way to speak. In fact, the use of Standard Australian English by one community member to another would raise eyebrows.

It is the normative positioning of Standard Australian English in the schooling system, and the lack of education about First Nations language contexts, that unconsciously influence educators who – in lieu of other information – may then view Indigenous contact languages as inferior. Lippi-Green (1997) argues that education systems perpetuate 'the standard language ideology' to reinforce the inferior status of vernacular languages and sustain the power structures that currently exist. However, we argue, like Poetsch et al. (2024), that teachers are change agents. In many creole-speaking communities, it has been teachers who have drawn attention to the mismatch of children's language to the mainstream medium of instruction and have actively worked with community members to build their awareness and that of students and other teachers and of their wider community about the creole language.

There is also the relationship between Indigenous creole languages and traditional languages to consider. Amongst Aboriginal and Torres Strait Islander peoples, traditional languages are automatically accorded very high cultural status, as it is through traditional languages that First Nations peoples are connected to their countries and cultures. Indigenous creole languages, while expressing a contemporary Indigenous identity and community resistance to English, have a different sociocultural niche (Angelo, 2021). Also, unfortunately, in some circles, the role of Indigenous creole languages in language shift has been misconstrued: of course, it is the historical colonial contexts or ongoing present-day minoritisation that have not enabled speakers of traditional languages to speak their languages sufficiently for children of the next generation to learn them and not the allure of speaking a creole or an English. It is also important to note that in creole-speaking communities, it is the local creole language that is the medium which enacts local and contemporary Indigenous identity and the medium that community members use to disseminate their knowledge and culture intergenerationally, including teaching about traditional language and culture.

Language and identity

Languages go to the heart of our identities. This goes for creole languages too. The languages we hear and learn from birth connect us with our families and caregivers. Many young children will have a main language they use every day for expressing themselves at home and for communicating and learning about the world, along with some knowledge of other languages that occur in their environments. This first and main language (L1) does all the heavy lifting in children's emotional and intellectual lives. It is key to their identity – who they are and how they express themselves. When children's L1 differs from the language used to deliver classroom curriculum, this can be very unsettling and can undermine their sense of confidence as learners in the classroom. They deserve to be supported in their main L1 through local staff, and to be respectfully taught the language of schooling. Moreover, like all First Nations children, Indigenous creole L1 speakers will also be connected to their Country through their traditional language affiliations and may also have some opportunities to learn them. This adds another layer of language(s) to First Nations children's identities.

The main message for teachers is to celebrate creole-speaking students as creole speakers, as your interest is profoundly motivating for them. This is a simple, but effective measure which can all too easily be overlooked. Furthermore, the goal is additive bilingualism for students and language maintenance for their communities, so be sure to acknowledge their existing creole language prowess and to encourage their learning of other languages.

What to do in the classroom?

We all know that it is teachers who make a difference, so to support optimal classroom learning for Indigenous creole-speaking students, educators need to make an active personal and professional commitment to growing a 'language perspective'. This is a step that involves you working respectfully with First Nations students, colleagues, and community members to develop shared understandings of their language contexts and to implement language-informed responses in your classroom teaching. In doing so together, you will be change agents, pushing back on the unhelpful legacies of the monolingual mindset in education that have failed to respond to the educational needs of creole-speaking students.

Recognising Indigenous creole languages and their speakers has not been front and centre for policy makers, curriculum writers, preservice training, and so forth. There may have been scant attention to the language situation where you are working, so the creole language may be undocumented, and language awareness programs may not have been consistently implemented, leaving few resources available for you to learn from or work with. First Nations students, colleagues, and community members who speak an Indigenous traditional and creole languages are the primary sources of knowledge and are crucial to engaging with these languages. In Queensland in recent decades, there have been concerted efforts to work with First Nations educators to do just this.

Examples of educational initiatives

As educators, you will be very aware of how education documents change from year to year, and these differ across state, Catholic and independent school sectors too. The information that follows points you toward the type of initiatives and information to be on the lookout for, to build your understandings of First Nations students' language situations and to develop your 'language perspective' teaching toolkit for creole-speaking students.

One set of early initiatives in Queensland was inspired by the *Fostering English Language in Kimberley Schools* (FELIKS) professional learning program and its teacher resource book, *Making the Jump* (Berry & Hudson, 1997), which were originally developed with Kriol-speaking communities in the north of Western Australia. FELIKS informed educators about creole languages, and Kriol specifically, and helped get them started with teaching features of Standard Australian English. Informed by those approaches, the Indigenous Education and Training Alliance (IETA) – a partnership between the Queensland Department of Education and James Cook University – developed a suite of resources with First Nations educators in far north Queensland, such as a DVD of Indigenous speech samples from far north Queensland (Ketchell & Taylor, 2002) and a booklet on distinctive features of Torres Strait Creole (Berry et al., 2003). At that time, the Catholic Education Office (CEO) in Townsville also began to provide professional development to teachers about some Queensland Indigenous creole languages, using localised language information in *Right Talk Right Place* (Knight, 2003). These initiatives reflect understandings of creole language situations in Queensland at that time, and these have continued to expand since (see for instance Yeatman & Angelo, 2023).

Another complementary set of initiatives identifies First Nations students who are learners of English as an Additional Language/Dialect, which also necessarily involves recognising their multilingualism as speakers of languages other than English as their L1, many of whom are creole speakers in Queensland. Between 1997 and 2003, a team of experienced First Nations educators, classroom teachers with EAL/D expertise, and experts in second language assessment developed the *Bandscales for Aboriginal and Torres Strait Islander Learners* ('Indigenous Bandscales') to describe Queensland's Indigenous EAL/D cohort (Hudson & Angelo, 2014). These Indigenous Bandscales mapped out trajectories of second language English proficiency development for students with Indigenous language backgrounds and in Indigenous community contexts. The Indigenous Bandscales are a standalone tool used by Independent Schools Queensland, while elements have since been incorporated into a statewide summary Bandscales tool for classroom teachers in Queensland state schools (Hudson et al., 2023). Collaborations across state and territory jurisdictions have produced the *Capability Framework: Teaching Aboriginal and Torres Strait Islander EAL/D students*. This document guides teacher professional growth in knowledge and practices that optimise First Nations EAL/D learners' engagement and achievement in classroom learning delivered through the English language (Department of Education Training & Employment [DETE QLD], 2013).

In the state schooling system, housed within the Far North Queensland Indigenous Schooling Support Unit (FNQISSU), the Language Perspectives team undertook large-scale professional development and evidence gathering projects, such as *Understanding Children's Language Acquisition Project* and *Bridging the Language Gap* (Angelo & Hudson, 2020). They developed a wide range of teaching resources in collaboration with First Nations community members and some of these are described below.

The Languages Perspective Team worked closely with First Nations communities around Queensland to understand their diverse language contexts. One initiative involved documenting the local way(s) of speaking, or vernacular, via poster projects. A poster was created with First Nations community members that visually represented the community and included figures with speech bubbles of the language they speak when doing everyday activities. The poster projects had several impacts, most importantly building visibility and recognition of the local vernacular spoken by Indigenous community members, and building confidence in discussing language matters. In many cases, the posters gave impetus to communities to name their languages, further assisting recognition. The posters were designed as accessible resources that displayed linguistic differences between English and the Indigenous contact languages spoken. In schools, the posters were visible artefacts and could be used as teaching points. This expanded their purpose from primarily building awareness and recognition, to being used to explicitly teach language differences. The posters—ten so far—have resonance as conversation starters in communities without their own poster, as they illustrate a range of Indigenous creoles and Aboriginal Englishes and this encourages comparisons with other local vernaculars. See Angelo et al. (2019) for a fuller description of the process of developing a community vernacular language poster and Yeatman and Angelo (2023) showing locations of finalised poster projects at that point in time.

First Nations enduring oral cultural practices encompass yarning and storytelling as a way of transmitting knowledge intergenerationally. Personal language stories are integral to building understandings about languages not only as an abstract concept but as a lived experience. The personal language stories of speakers of Indigenous creole languages have featured in academic literature (Angelo & Carter, 2015; Sellwood & Angelo, 2013; Yeatman & Angelo, 2023) and in teacher professional development and initial teacher education (ITE). The Language Perspectives team worked with First Nations community members to share their language stories, including the languages of their families, their observations of their own and other First Nations peoples' everyday language varieties, and their experiences of language attitudes and beliefs, especially about having a first language that is different from Standard Australian English. These are stories of personal language strengths and resilience, personal qualities which are all too often obscured by misunderstandings of creole language situations. The results are sometimes sad, and sometimes funny, but provide very real insights into what it means to speak a (misrecognised) language other than English in an education system designed exclusively for Standard Australian English speakers. These stories have been used in senior years schooling in the English subject, teacher professional development, and form the basis of assessment in an Initial Teacher Education degree subject that focuses on Teaching English as a Second Language to Indigenous Students at James Cook University – the only one of its kind in Australia.

The language awareness continuum (see Figure 7.4) was developed by Angelo (2006) to describe the sociolinguistic and language knowledges that build language awareness along a developmental pathway (Angelo & Hudson, 2020). It is designed to assist teachers and students to develop shared understandings of students' language context. Carter et al. (2020) include a suite of practical activities aligned to the language awareness continuum. The community vernacular language posters and the language stories described above are two resources that can be used as a point of discussion for each step in the language awareness continuum. For example, the community vernacular language posters can support learners to note how different people can have 'different kinds of talk' (step 1). This 'entry level' step can be illustrated in the here and now and so also suits young creole-speaking students who are likely to have early levels of English. Equally, the posters can be used as a springboard to 'compare home language and standard English at all linguistic levels' (step 4) when creole-speaking students' English is more developed for undertaking this. The language stories might be useful to help 'research history of language use in the community' (step 5), 'study historical and present socio-economic factors in language shift' (step 6), and 'explain linguistic, historical, and current relationship between contact and other non-standard varieties to standard languages' (right at the top of the continuum, step 7). For further ideas about language awareness activities and how they can be used in the classroom, see Carter et al. (2020), Steele (2020), and Yeatman & Angelo (2023).

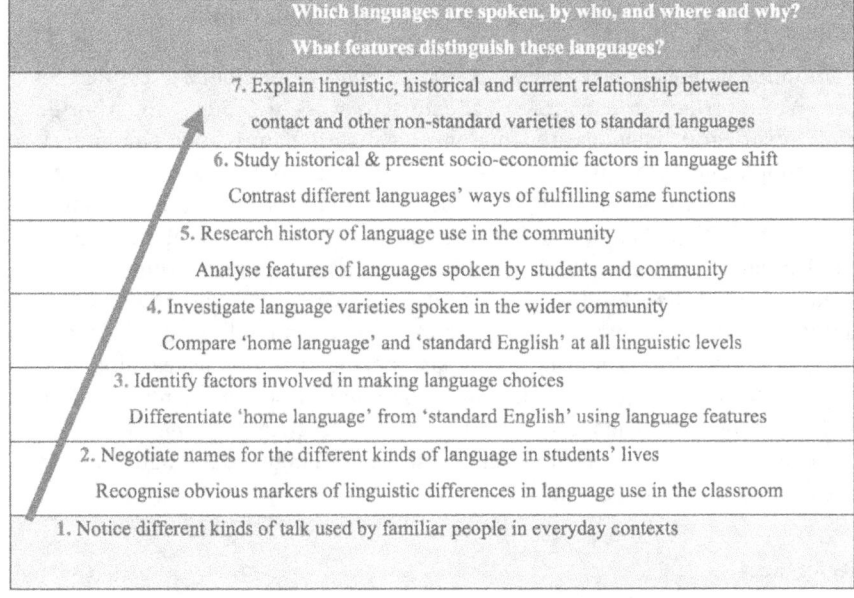

Figure 7.4 Language awareness continuum: Steps to build language awareness

Conclusion

In this chapter we have presented an introductory guide to the Indigenous creole languages spoken in Queensland today by many First Nations students and their families and communities. The guide offers a glimpse into the diversity of creole languages in this state and the complex language contact histories that have shaped them. It clarifies that creole languages are neither an English nor a traditional language, although the influences of both are obvious. This guide hopes to serve as an entry point for educators for growing their awareness of these less recognised languages, and their understandings about the many reasons behind their current invisibility.

We have sought to emphasise that wherever an Indigenous language, including a creole language, is spoken as the first and main language of children and their families then it is this language which is at the heart of family relationships and self-expression, and which supports knowledge and culture transmission from babyhood and onwards throughout life. Indigenous language speakers have a major language strength in their language repertoires: by speaking their language (creole or traditional), First Nations peoples in Queensland can also assert their identity.

Using a language ecologies model, this guide has also explained the common contemporary patterns of multilingualism amongst First Nations peoples and the different ways traditional languages, creole languages, and Englishes might figure in their repertoires. In an Indigenous language ecology where a creole language is spoken as the main language between community members, then First Nations students will acquire this creole as their L1 and over time expand their language repertoires to include Standard Australian English and traditional Aboriginal or Torres Strait Islander languages, given appropriate opportunities.

We acknowledge that educators are often granted little training for working with Indigenous language speaking student cohorts, particularly creole speakers. We nevertheless encourage educators to work together with Aboriginal and Torres Strait Islander students and local staff, family, and community to understand and recognise students' language backgrounds and to respond in your teaching accordingly. Creole-speaking students benefit from language awareness initiatives and first language support as well as recognition of their English language learner status and the intentional and respectful teaching of Standard Australian English, the language in which classroom curriculum is delivered in Queensland. Together we can oust the monolingual mindset from our classrooms. You can bring a language perspective to your teaching, knowing that languages are at the heart of communication and communication is key for students to engage in learning and for teachers to impart knowledge. Together we can celebrate Indigenous students' language strengths and their learning of additional languages.

References

Angelo, D. (2006). *Language Awareness Continuum [Curriculum Resource]*. Far North Queensland Indigenous Schooling Support Unit.

Angelo, D. (2021). Creoles, education and policy. In U. Ansaldo, & M. Meyerhoff (Eds.), *The Routledge handbook of pidgin and creole languages* (pp. 286–301). Routledge.

Angelo, D. (2023). Contact language case studies. In C. Bowern (Ed.), *The Oxford guide to Australian languages* (pp. 765–780). Oxford University Press.

Angelo, D. (2024). Indigenous language ecologies framework. A tool for inserting Indigenous contact languages and their speakers into policy in Australia. *Journal of Pidgin and Creole Languages, 39*(1), 34–70.

Angelo, D., & Carter, N. (2015). Schooling within shifting langscapes: Educational responses within complex Indigenous language ecologies. In A. Yiakoumetti (Ed.), *Multilingualism and language in education: Current sociolinguistic and pedagogical perspectives from Commonwealth countries* (pp. 119–140). Cambridge University Press.

Angelo, D., Fraser, H., & Yeatman, B. (2019). The art of recognition. Visualising contact languages with community vernacular language posters. *Babel, 54*(1–2), 34–40.

Angelo, D., & Hudson, C. (2018). Dangerous conversations: Teacher-student interactions with unidentified English language learners. In G. Wigglesworth, J. Simpson, & J. Vaughan (Eds.), *Language practices of Indigenous youth* (pp. 207–235). Palgrave Macmillan.

Angelo, D., & Hudson, C. (2020). From the periphery to the centre: Securing the place at the heart of the TESOL field for First Nations learners of English as an Additional Language/Dialect. *TESOL in Context, 29*(1), 5–35. https://doi.org/10.21153/tesol2020vol29no1art1421

Australian Bureau of Statistics (ABS). (2016). *Australian Standard Classification of Languages (ASCL) – 1267.0.* https://www.abs.gov.au/AUSSTATS/subscriber.nsf/log?openagent&ASCL_12670DO0001_201703.xls&1267.0&Data%20Cubes&F84620CF6E13F7E8CA257FF1001E68A7&0&2016&28.03.2017&Latest

Australian Bureau of Statistics (ABS). (2021). *Yarrabah 2021 Census all persons Quick-Stats local giovernment area LGA37600.* https://abs.gov.au/census/find-census-data/quickstats/2021/LGA37600

Australian Bureau of Statistics (ABS). (2022). *Language statistics for Aboriginal and Torres Strait Islander peoples.* https://www.abs.gov.au/statistics/people/aboriginal-and-torres-strait-islander-peoples/language-statistics-aboriginal-and-torres-strait-islander-peoples/latest-release

Australian Public Service Commission. (2023). *Australian Government Style Manual [Website].* https://www.stylemanual.gov.au/

Berry, R., & Hudson, J. (1997). *Making the jump: A resource book for teachers of Aboriginal students.* Catholic Education Office.

Berry, R., Hudson, J., Anson, E., & Bani, E. (2003). *Working with making the jump using Torres Strait Creole examples.* Indigenous Education and Training Alliance.

Carter, N., Angelo, D., & Hudson, C. (2020). Translanguaging the curriculum: A critical language awareness curriculum for silenced Indigenous voices. In P. Mickan, & I. Wallace (Eds.), *The Routledge handbook of language education curriculum design* (pp. 144–174). Routledge Taylor & Francis Group.

Clyne, M. (2005). *Australia's language potential.* University of New South Wales Press.

Crowley, T., & Rigsby, B. (1979). Cape York Creole. In T. Shopen (Ed.), *Languages and their status* (pp. 153–207). Winthrop Publishers Inc.

Department of Education Training & Employment (DETE) (QLD). (2013). *Capability framework. Teaching Aboriginal and Torres Strait Islander EAL/D learners.* The State of Queensland (DETE). https://education.qld.gov.au/student/Documents/capability-framework-teaching-aboriginal-torres-strait-islander-eald-learners.pdf

Dixon, S. (2018). Alyawarr children's use of two closely related languages. In G. Wigglesworth, J. Simpson, & J. Vaughan (Eds.), *Language practices of Indigenous children and youth* (pp. 271–299). Palgrave Macmillan.

Eades, D. (2014). Aboriginal English. In H. Koch, & R. Nordlinger (Eds.), *The languages and linguistics of Australia. A comprehensive guide* (pp. 417–447). de Gruter Mouton.

Hudson, C., & Angelo, D. (2014). Concepts underpinning innovations to second language proficiency scales inclusive of Aboriginal and Torres Strait Islander learners: A dynamic process in progress. *Papers in Language Testing and Assessment*, *3*(1), 44–84.

Hudson, C., Angelo, D., & Creagh, S. (2023). Instantiating justice, fairness and inclusiveness in English as an Additional Language/Dialect assessment frameworks: Unpacking the evidence base for the Bandscales State Schools (Queensland). *Studies in Language Assessment*, *12*(2), 235–271. https://doi.org/10.58379/RXAZ8430

Ketchell, J., & Taylor, P. (2002). *The FELIKS approach: Speech samples for north Queensland [DVD]*. Indigenous Education & Training Alliance.

Knight, L. (2003). *Right talk right place: A resource book for teachers of Aboriginal & Torres Strait Islander students in north Queensland schools*. Catholic Education Office.

Lippi-Green, R. (1997). *English with an accent. Language, ideology, and discrimination in the United States*. Routledge.

Long, M. H. (2007). *Problems in SLA*. Lawrence Erlbaum Associates Publishers.

Malcolm, I. (2018). *Australian Aboriginal English. Change and continuity in an adopted language*. de Gruyter Mouton.

Meigim Kriol Strongbala. (2019). Website. https://meigimkriolstrongbala.org.au/rop/

Munro, J. M., & Mushin, I. (2016). Rethinking Australian Aboriginal English-based speech varieties: Evidence from Woorabinda. *Journal of Pidgin and Creole Languages*, *31*(1), 82–112.

Mushin, I., Angelo, D., & Munro, J. M. (2016). Same but different. Understanding language contact in Queensland Indigenous settlements. In J.-C. Verstraete, & D. Hafner (Eds.), *Land and language in Cape York Peninsula and the Gulf country* (pp. 383–407). John Benjamins Publishing Company.

Nero, S., & Ahmad, D. (2014). *Vernaculars in the classroom: Paradoxes, pedagogy, possibilities*. Routledge.

Ngukurr Language Centre. (2024). *Yuma wandi len Kriol?* (Do you want to learn Kriol?) [Website]. https://ngukurrlc.org.au/news/

O'Shannessy, C., Angelo, D., & Simpson, J. (2024). Toward a typology of Australian contact languages. *Journal of Pidgin and Creole Languages*, *39*(1), 1–32. https://doi.org/10.1075/jpcl.00137.osh

Poetsch, S., Angelo, D., & Radley, R. (2024). Aboriginal and Torres Strait Islander students, families, communities and languages. In R. Maloney, L. Harbon, & S. Oguro (Eds.), *Multilingualism for teachers* (pp. 43–66). Cambridge University Press.

Schmidt, R. (1990). The role of consciousness in second language learning. *Applied Linguistics*, *11*(2), 128–158.

Sellwood, J. (2022). Supporting multilingual communities: contact languages and traditional languages [Webinar]. In Australian Institute for Aboriginal and Torres Strait Islander Studies (AIATSIS) (Ed.), *AIATSIS policy symposium*. https://aiatsis.gov.au/publication/118245

Sellwood, J., & Angelo, D. (2013). Everywhere and nowhere: invisibility of Aboriginal and Torres Strait Islander contact languages in education and Indigenous language contexts. *Australian Review of Applied Linguistics*, *36*(3), 250–266.

Shnukal, A. (2001). Torres Strait English. In D. Blair, & P. Collins (Eds.), *English in Australia* (pp. 181–200). John Benjamins.

Siegel, J. (2010). *Second dialect acquisition*. Cambridge University Press.

State Library of Queensland (SLQ). (2024). *Aboriginal and Torres Strait Islander languages* [Website]. https://www.slq.qld.gov.au/discover/first-nations-cultures/aboriginal-and-torres-strait-islander-languages

Steele, C. (2020). *Teaching Standard Australian English as a second dialect to Australian Indigenous children in primary school classrooms* [PhD thesis]. University of Melbourne.

Tryon, D. (2009). Linguistic encounter and responses in the South Pacific. In M. Jolly, S. Tcherkézoff, & D. Tryon (Eds.), *Exchange, desire, violence. Oceanic encounters: Exchange, desire, violence* (pp. 37–56). http://www.jstor.org/stable/j.ctt24h8jn.9.

Yeatman, B., & Angelo, D. (2023). Recognising Yarrie Lingo, the creole language of Yarrabah Community in Far North Queensland Australia. *Journal of Pidgin and Creole Languages*. https://doi.org/10.1075/jpcl.00124.yea

Zhang-Wu, Q., & Tian, Z. (2023). Raising critical language awareness in a translanguaging-infused teacher education course: Opportunities and challenges. *Journal of Language, Identity & Education*, 22(4), 376–395. https://doi.org/10.1080/15348458.2023.2202589

8 Kriol in the Northern Territory

Rikke L. Bundgaard-Nielsen, Brett J. Baker, and Jocelyn E. Uibo

Who we are

Rikke Bundgaard-Nielsen is a Danish psycholinguist and Senior Lecturer at The University of Melbourne. She studies first and second language acquisition and processing and has worked with speakers of a range of traditional and new Indigenous Australian languages. She is interested in how sharing knowledge about the shape, acquisition, and use of Indigenous languages can improve educational outcomes for Indigenous students.

Brett Baker is an Associate Professor in Linguistics at The University of Melbourne, with around 30 years of experience working closely with Indigenous people in the Roper River region and Numbulwar. He has published books and articles on grammatical topics in Australian languages and engaged in grass-roots maintenance and revival efforts in regional Aboriginal language centres.

Jocelyn Uibo is a Nunggubuyu/Estonian early childhood educator who has taught in early primary school and preschools in both remote and urban contexts in the Northern Territory. She grew up in Numbulwar, Batchelor, and Darwin, where she currently lives with her family.

Kriol in the NT

Kriol is an English-lexified creole language spoken in Northern Australia by approximately 20,000 people (AIATSIS/Commonwealth of Australia, 2005; Schultze-Berndt et al., 2013). Note: It is possible, if not likely, that Kriol consists of multiple regional dialects across the continent, and even within the NT, but this is an understudied area (see Dickson & Durantin, 2019; Munro, 2000).

Kriol is what is known as a *contact language*. Contact languages are languages that sometimes result from extensive interaction between language groups that are not mutually bilingual (also see Chapter 7, this volume). In the Northern Territory (NT), Kriol has developed in the past 100–150 years, from contact between

DOI: 10.4324/9781003441021-12

speakers of Australian Indigenous languages and English in areas associated with the pastoral industry in the Northern Territory, Queensland, and Western Australia (Harris, 1986; Munro, 2011; Sandefur, 1979).

Kriol is predominantly a spoken language, acquired as a first language by children in communities where it is the *lingua franca* (community language) as well as an additional language by children in communities where traditional Indigenous languages are still spoken. According to the NT Department of Education, Kriol is the dominant Indigenous language or a major language in the Northern Territory communities of Ngukurr, Numbulwar, Urapunga, Jilkminggan, Minyerri, Borroloola, Barunga, Beswick, Bulman, Binjari, Katherine, Timber Creek, Bulla Camp, Amanbidji, and Manyallaluk (NT Department of Education, 2020). In many of these communities, English is primarily acquired through formal schooling.

Despite Kriol being the largest Indigenous language after Aboriginal English, there are currently no bilingual English-Kriol programs in operation in the NT, even though bilingual programs have positive results: For example, Yirrkala School in Northeastern Arnhem Land teaches students *both ways* in the local Indigenous language Yolngu Matha and English, and in 2020, eight students graduated Year 12, with university entry-level scores. A bilingual program was operating at Barunga in the 1970s, shortly after the NT government instituted bilingual education programs in NT schools, but the bilingual programs in the NT were shut down in 1998 (though a few were later reinstated, none in Kriol). In Ngukurr, teachers decided to teach in Kriol in 1978, though the materials were in English (Angelo, 2021, p. 63).

The origins of Kriol in the NT

Pidgin in the NT

European settlement in the Northern Territory was the catalyst for the introduction and use of English-based pidgins in the NT as it was in the north of Western Australia and Queensland (Simpson, 2024). Pidgins are grammatically simplified languages that combine elements from two or more languages used in language contact settings, where interlocutors do not speak each other's languages. European settlement in the NT, however, happened much later than widespread European settlement along the Eastern seaboard. The first European settlements in the Northern Territory were three military garrisons: one on Melville Island (from 1824 to 1829), one at Raffles Bay (from 1827 to 1829), and one at Port Essington (from 1839 to 1848). This relatively shallow time-depth gives us an unusual opportunity to learn about the context in which the NT pidgin(s) and later Kriol were formed.

The military garrisons induced the first extended contact between European settlers and Indigenous Australians in the NT. And despite reports of hostility between the settlers and Indigenous Australians, an English pidgin emerged from the contact. There is also evidence that the Indigenous population of the area already spoke a *Macassar pidgin* developed because of regular contact with Macassar sailors harvesting trepang (sea slugs) (Harris, 1986; Urry & Walsh, 1981), and some have argued that the first English-based pidgin used the already existing Macassar pidgin as a model or frame. There is substantial evidence that the first English-based pidgin was, at least in part, brought to the NT by the non-Indigenous colonisers from New South Wales, where an English-based pidgin had been used in the Sydney area (Simpson, 1996; 2000; 2024; Troy, 1993; Tryon & Charpentier, 2004). Evidence for this idea is the use of words from nautical jargon such as *pikanini* 'child' and *sabi* 'know' (both derived from Portuguese), as well as words that have been traced to the Aboriginal languages of New South Wales, including *binji* 'belly' and *bogi* 'swim' (Harris, 1986, p. 288). It is also likely that the early pidgins of the NT had Chinese influence (Harris, 1986). A second English-based pidgin reportedly emerged later, on the Adelaide River (1864–1866), and both the garrison pidgins and the Adelaide River pidgin influenced a more enduring pidgin when European settlement became permanent with the establishment of Darwin in 1870 and spread with the establishment of the cattle industry across the Top End (Harris & Sandefur, 1984).

A creative capture of the early NT pidgin (including Chinese elements) has been appreciated for generations by readers of Jeannie Gunn's autobiographical novel *We of the Never Never* (1908). The novel details Gunn's experiences at Elsey Station, located near present-day Mataranka in the westernmost parts of the Roper River drainage basin—precisely where the early NT pidgins eventually creolised and became the primary language of a community at the Roper River Mission.

The two quotes below illustrate several features of the pidgin also found in Kriol today, including the use of the non-subject pronoun form *me* as a subject, the nautical term *savey* (*sabi*, 'to know'), the use of '-*im*' as a transitive verb marker, special uses of vocabulary such as *all day* to mean 'continuously', and the preposition *longa* (see Munro, 2004, for further discussion):

> Our business was yard-inspection [...]. We, of course, had ridden out, but Goggle-Eye had preferred to walk. '*Me all day knock up longa horse*,' he explained striding comfortably along beside us (Gunn, Chapter 10, our italics);

and,

> '*Him Rosy!*' he said, thus introducing his booty and without further ceremony Rosy requested permission to 'sit down' on the staff. Like Cheon she carried her qualifications on the tip of her tongue: '*Me savey scrub 'im, and sweep 'im, and wash 'im, and blue 'im, and starch 'im*,' she said glibly, with a flash of white teeth against a babyish pink tongue (Gunn, Chapter 11, our italics).

Creolisation in the NT

There are different theories about how *creolisation* (the development of a Creole language, often from an expanded pidgin) occurs. Most theories of creolisation, however, point out that children often play a special role in the process, and that it is typically the case that creolisation happens in communities where the people find the (expanded) pidgin *useful* to them. We know this, not from investigations of the acquisition of spoken languages or creoles, but from observations of the birth of a *sign language* in Nicaragua.

In a very famous and well-documented case from Nicaragua, changes to education policies in the 1970s and 1980s led to dramatic changes in the social lives of deaf children (Senghas, 1995). Where deaf children had, until then, spent most of their time at home and used idiosyncratic *home signs*, the new education policies brought together deaf children in a school for the deaf. This provided children with both the *opportunity* and the *need*—the first cohort consisted of 50 children aged four to 14 years—to find a way to communicate with each other. At first, communication was difficult, but as they interacted with each other, the children changed the gestures and home signs they knew and expanded their vocabulary quickly, just like small children do. Importantly, their previously simple signs also became more systematic and regular, and the structure of their sentences became much more complicated.

The story of the formation of Nicaraguan Sign Language (NSL) illustrates the language creation abilities of children very well, but it also illustrates that such creation only occurs if it has the right *conditions*. In the case of NSL, deaf children found themselves needing to communicate with other deaf children, and this need provided the impetus for change and development. Understanding the process of creolisation in the NT also requires knowledge of the *creators* or linguistic innovators, and a clear understanding of the sociolinguistic situation that created sufficient impetus or pressure for it to happen, like in the case of NSL.

There are several suggestions for how Kriol developed in the NT (see Meakins, 2014, for a critical review, as this exceeds the scope of the present chapter), but one prominent theory is that Kriol developed relatively *abruptly*, because of the Roper River Mission dormitory system, in a manner like what was observed for NSL. The Roper River dormitory system was established as a direct consequence of frontier conflict between cattle farmers and corporations, including The Eastern and African Cold Storage Company, and Indigenous people (Roberts, 2005). The Eastern and African Cold Storage Company violently protected its financial interests in the Roper Basin by employing gangs of Indigenous men, led by a non-Indigenous man or men with Indigenous and non-Indigenous ancestry (Harris, 1986, p. 157) to hunt and shoot the 'wild' (Harris, 1986, p. 157) Indigenous population.

This violent treatment of the Indigenous population was viewed with concern by some organisations, and the Church Missionary Society (CMS) in Victoria established a mission on the Roper River in August 1908 as a safe haven. Within a year, the Roper River Mission was home to approximately 200 Indigenous people (Sandefur, 1979, p. 13), and a rudimentary school with a dormitory was in operation, as the missionaries hoped that removing the children from their families and traditional lifestyle would assist the process of *civilising* and educating them in the Western tradition.

By 1913, a total of 53 children (26 girls and 27 boys) between the ages of five and 18 years lived in the mission dormitory. They came from Marra, Warndarrang, Alawa, Ngalkgan, and Ngandi families, as well as the southernmost groups of the

Rembarrnga and Nunggubuyu people. These were not language groups that habitually lived together, though they had, and continue to have, familial and ceremonial ties to each other. The abrupt creolisation hypothesis suggests that this unusual interaction between children from different language groups created an environment like the one that saw the creation of NSL. We emphasise, however, that this is not the only account of creolisation in the NT, and some researchers disagree with this analysis and point out evidence of regional differences in Kriol in the NT and highlight the timing of the development of Kriol as factors inconsistent with abrupt creolisation (see Bundgaard-Nielsen & Baker, 2016; Munro, 2004).

Indigenous attitudes to Kriol

Indigenous (and non-Indigenous) attitudes to Kriol are complex. While it is generally well-known and agreed upon that *traditional languages* are a strong part of Indigenous people's identity, country, and belief systems, and that access to and connection with traditional language and cultural practice is critical to wellbeing (see e.g., AIATSIS/Commonwealth of Australia, 2005, p. 40; Dockery, 2010), this attitude is not always extended to Kriol. Indeed, many speakers of Kriol, and Kriol-speaking communities, have had relatively negative attitudes to Kriol, to the use of Kriol as a community language, and to the support of Kriol in the school system and elsewhere in the public domain. Likewise, many academics have focused their efforts on the study and promotion of traditional Indigenous languages, though there are exceptions to this.

The complex attitudes of many Indigenous people to Kriol are reflected in the way that Kriol is discussed in relation to the traditional Indigenous languages. In many communities, the word *language* is used exclusively to refer to the heritage or traditional Indigenous language(s) of a community, excluding Kriol (Rhydwen, 1995, p. 113). Some people also worry that speaking Kriol will stop children from learning and using their traditional languages, and some worry that support for Kriol will reduce the already limited support for traditional Indigenous languages (Meakins, 2014; Schmidt, 1990). Marmion et al. (2014) also found that many Indigenous people 'feel [that] traditional languages are more important than recently developed Indigenous languages' (p. 38), though they also think that

> [s]peakers of [...] Kriol, Yumplatok and Aboriginal English should be given appropriate support, including interpreter/translator services and first-language education (bilingual education).

Kriol as 'Broken English'

In addition to reservations towards Kriol due to its role in language shift, negative attitudes towards Kriol also sometimes reflect the view that Kriol is not a proper or complete language, but an imperfectly acquired or 'perverted', 'broken', and 'corrupt' version of English (Harris, 1986, p. 5). This position treats differences between English and Kriol as problems or mistakes to be rectified. A stronger position underpins the belief that *English-only* should be taught in schools to facilitate communication and relations with the wider Australian community and increase access to mainstream English-based education and employment.

Another related view has been that Kriol really is a continuum of varieties, some of which are more like English (acrolectal) and some of which are more like Indigenous languages (basilectal). This is an idea borrowed from the study of Caribbean creole languages. Under this view, Kriol speakers control a range of Kriols (language registers) and use versions of Kriol that are similar to English in some situations and other versions in other situations. This view sometimes leads to the problematic assumption that Kriol-speaking children do not have to learn English as a second language—they just have to pick the right register for the educational setting.

Kriol has also sometimes been seen as a dialect of English, and this can lead to similarly problematic assumptions about children's language use and language ability in the classroom. Whatever the *historical* relationship between Kriol and Australian English, NT Kriol is not mutually intelligible with English (barring overlap in the lexicon and some phrases). This means that Kriol-speaking children face a language learning hurdle in the classroom—even though they sometimes use words that are shared with English—and educators need to be mindful of both verbal and non-verbal cues for students who speak Kriol as a primary language and allow for students to have thinking time before they may be able to communicate in their second or third spoken language of Standard Australian English (SAE).

And even though some words may be shared between Kriol and English, this does not mean that Kriol-speaking children have a head start in the learning in English: some researchers have even argued that acquiring a second dialect (or closely related language) can be more difficult than acquiring a different language (Siegel, 2010). This is partly because of *identity* issues: people who use a dialect that is not their L1 may be regarded as *inauthentic* both by their own and their adopted language communities. In other words, Kriol-speaking children may find it hard to speak English in a classroom because they feel like they are pretending or acting in a way that is inconsistent with their identity. If possible, classroom teachers should allow local Aboriginal educators or community elders to help students gain the confidence to speak in both Kriol and SAE in education settings and encourage students to build the skills to learn and communicate in both languages successfully.

Attitudes changing, and changing attitudes

The negative attitudes towards Kriol described above are, however, shifting in some parts of the NT. A recent study in Ngukurr, where 93% of the population speaks Kriol at home (ABS, 2021), revealed largely positive views and pride in Kriol (Hendy & Bow, 2023). The study also shows that support for Kriol is not mutually exclusive with support for traditional Indigenous languages, nor should the opposite be the case; beyond practical and financial constraints, there is no need for first and heritage language education to be limited to just one of the two. Indeed, as Hendy and Bow (2023, p. 79) highlight, 'the high prestige of traditional languages does not necessarily lessen the prestige of Kriol in a given community'. This view is also consistent with the results from a Community Engagement Study in Ngukurr conducted by the Yugul Mangi Development Aboriginal Corporation (2019) which showed that almost all respondents want their children to read and write in Kriol—as well as their traditional languages—at school. Pride in Kriol—and recognition of the usefulness of Kriol—is also indicated by a community desire to share Kriol with people from outside of the community as described by Ngukurr resident Karen Rogers: 'I think [non-Indigenous people learning Kriol] is important because some of our Elders here don't communicate really with English very well' (Hendy & Bow, 2023, p. 86).

Kriol linguistics

Delivering the Australian Curriculum to Aboriginal students in SAE requires teachers to be aware of and acknowledge that the primary language for many students is Kriol. This means that teachers need to tailor their lessons to help bridge the learning gap from the students' primary language of Kriol to allow the children to learn to communicate in SAE in the school setting. It also requires teachers to recognise that, in their communities, many students *only* communicate in their first language of Kriol and do not have conversations in SAE outside of the classroom.

Teaching Kriol-speaking students—and scaffolding their acquisition and development of SAE skills—also requires education staff to have appropriate linguistic understanding, and we discuss some of the characteristics of Kriol below. Linguistic knowledge, however, must be paired with genuine cross-cultural understanding. When education staff members enter communities in which English is an additional language, or meet students from non-English speaking communities, it is crucial that they are aware of the different language groups, cultures, and customs of the communities that they are living and working in. Teachers can gain this type of understanding with the help of the schools' cultural advisors, and through engagement with the key community stakeholders. Gaining this type of knowledge ensures that students develop a sense of belonging in the classroom. It also ensures that students' cultural identities, and community values and expectations, are considered in the teaching practice. This includes a role for the primary languages spoken by the students to be displayed and recognised in the classroom, as well as activities that support the students' cultural identity.

Kriol vocabulary

The contribution of English and several Indigenous languages to Kriol has resulted in a very interesting vocabulary. The exact proportion of Kriol words from each language has not been quantified, although the Kriol dictionary (Lee, 2014) provides an indication for each headword of its use in the four dialect areas recognised. The Indigenous contribution to Kriol differs according to region, and each regional variety uses vocabulary drawn from the local traditional languages. There is no in-depth survey of this question, but Sandefur (1986, p. 55) provides a brief discussion of dialectal variation arising from geographical factors, and the following example:

> For example, *manuga* 'money' (from 'stones') was borrowed from one of the languages around Ngukurr. It is commonly used at Ngukurr and known by

Kriol speakers in the communities immediately surrounding Ngukurr, but it is virtually unknown by Kriol speakers elsewhere.

Kriol words adapted from English differ in how similar they are to their SAE cognates (cognates are words in different languages that have shared origins but somewhat different forms in each language, such as, for example, *stone* in English, *stein* 'stone' in German, and *sten* 'stone' in Danish). This means that some Kriol words are *very similar* to their English counterparts, while other words sound *very different*. These differences may reflect when each word became a part of Kriol or the pidgins that came before. Very old Kriol adaptations of English words tend to differ more from their SAE cognates than newer words, but it is not always possible to predict what an English word might sound like in Kriol. Among typical differences in the *shape* of words sourced from English is changing fricatives to either stops (e.g., /dibidi/ for the English term 'DVD') or affricates, and differences in the voicing specifications of stop consonants (/dalim/ for Eng. 'tell'). The vowels in some words may also have changed (e.g., /baːɖ/ or /beːɖ/ for Eng. 'bird'), and in some words multiple (even all) segments have changed (e.g., /tʃabitʃ/ for Eng. '(church) service', where voiceless fricative /s/ has become voiceless affricate /tʃ/; voiced fricative /v/ has become voiced stop /b/; and vowels /ɜ/ and /ɪ/ have become /a/ and /i/, respectively).

Kriol phonology

The Kriol sound system—the vowels and consonants of Kriol and their pronunciation—is important to understand and be aware of particularly for those involved in education who are working with students from such a background. The sound system of Kriol can best be described as an *amalgamation* of English and Indigenous features of both consonants and vowels. This means that Kriol shares some—*but not all*—of the sounds of English and *add* to this a number of speech sounds that are used in many Indigenous Australian languages—but *not in English*. There are also differences in how some of the sounds shared with English are pronounced, much like we might be able to discern differences between some sounds as they are spoken in Australian English and how they might be spoken in Scottish English, New Zealand English, or US English. These differences are not *mistakes* or *errors*, but reflect the students' first language knowledge, and teachers need to be aware of the language characteristics of Kriol and the pronunciations of the language when beginning to assess students on the Australian Curriculum or the Northern Territory Curriculum for English. This is particularly important when assessing the academic learning, language, and communication skills of Kriol-speaking students when they communicate with teachers and other non-Aboriginal Standard English-speaking people.

Kriol consonants

The Kriol consonant inventory is presented in Table 8.1. As can be seen in this table, Kriol shares many consonants with English (in **bold**), including its stop consonants / p b t d k g/, affricates /tʃ dʒ/ (as in 'church' and 'judge'), nasals /n m ŋ/ (as in 'no', 'moo' and the last sound in the word 'sing'), fricatives /f s ʃ h/ (as in 'foe', 'see', 'shoe' and 'he'), lateral /l/ (as in 'lie'), and approximants /w j/ (as in 'we' and the first sound in 'yes') and also /ɹ/, which is very close to the way that 'r' (as in 'roo') is pronounced in Australian English. For the most part, these sounds are pronounced similarly in Kriol and English, but there are important differences: When the voiceless /p t k/ occur in the middle of the word, they are *long* (the silent period in the middle of the consonant is extended in duration) as well as voiceless. This is a feature shared with some Indigenous languages, and it means that Kriol speakers, including children in the classroom, may hear typical English voiceless stops as their voiced counterparts because they are not *long* (e.g., English 'puppy' might be heard by a Kriol speaker as /pabi/, not /papi/). One way to overcome this challenge might be for teachers to enhance the duration of /p t k/ when teaching phonics, to better scaffold learning, by, for examples, pronouncing a word like 'puppy' almost as 'pup+bee'.

In addition to speech sounds shared with English, Kriol also has several sounds that are shared only with traditional Indigenous languages (in *italics* in Table 8.1). This includes dental stops /t̪ d̪/ made by the tongue forming a *d-* or *t*-like sound at the back of the teeth (such as 'dis' with a dental stop instead of 'this' with a dental fricative), as well as retroflex /ʈ ɖ/ made by the tongue making contact at the back of the alveolar ridge and curling the tongue tip back; this sounds very much as in an American pronunciation of *rd* in words like 'card'. There are also retroflex nasal and lateral sounds /ɳ ɭ/ which similarly sound like American English pronunciations of *rn* in words like '**ba**rn' and *rl* in words like 'cu**rl**'. The alveo-palatal sounds also include a nasal and lateral ('l-sound') /ɲ ʎ/ that sound to English speakers like *ny* and *ly* sequences. So /ɲ/ sounds like the *ny* sequence in '**can**yon' and /ʎ/ sounds like the *ly* sequence in 'bul**li**on'. There is also an additional 'r-sound', written /r/ in linguistics, which is like the trilled or tapped *r*-sound in Scots English, Spanish, or Italian. Because these speech sounds are additional to those used in English, they may not be obviously problematic in the context of learning English orthography.

It is also extremely important to notice what speech sounds are *not* present in Kriol but are present in English, as these may also cause difficulty in teaching literacy in English—and this is another area that may be difficult for Kriol-speaking children in the classroom. Unlike English, Kriol has no dental fricatives /θ/ as in '**th**ink' or /ð/ as in '**th**is'. This leads many speakers of Kriol to substitute dental fricatives with the dental *stops* such as 'd' for 'th' and so saying 'dis' instead of 'this'. Kriol also does not have voiced fricatives: this means that English /s/ and /z/ both count as instances of Kriol /s/, and therefore, differentiating the name '**S**ue' from an amusement park with exotic animals—the '**Z**oo'—can be very difficult. The same is the case for /f/ versus /v/ ('**f**eign' versus '**v**ain'), and for /ʃ/ (as in '**sh**ip') versus /ʒ/ though this is much less of a potential problem for young learners as words with /ʒ/ are rare in English (e.g., 'measure').

Teaching English phonetics to Kriol-speaking children, in this domain, may require explicit teaching approaches also used with other non-native English-speaking children. This includes articulatory and listening practice for students

Table 8.1 The consonant inventory of (Roper) Kriol, adapted from Baker et al. (2014) and Schultze-Berndt et al. (2013).

	Labial	Dental	Alveolar	Retroflex	Alveo-palatal	Velar	Glottal
Stops	**p b**	*t̪ d̪*	**t d**	*(ʈ) ɖ*		**k g**	
Affricates					**tʃ dʒ**		
Fricatives	**f**		**s**		**ʃ**		**h**
Nasals	**m**		**n**	*ɳ*	*ɲ*	**ŋ**	
Laterals			**l**	*ɭ*	*ʎ*		
Approximants	**w**		*r*	*ɻ*	**j**		

Note: Shared sounds are in bold, and sounds found in Kriol but not in Australian English are in italics.

to *tune in* to speech information that is not part of the first language, something perhaps best achieved by highlighting the sounds in context—such as when reading shared *big books* as a whole group or class. Opportunities to copy or practice pronunciation, and even to compare and discuss differences in pronunciation or grammar between Kriol and SAE, may also help both speech production and speech perception in English.

Kriol vowels

Indigenous Australian languages also differ from English in the number of vowels: Most Indigenous Australian languages have just three to five vowels—/i a u/ or /i e a o u/—and sometimes long and short versions, e.g., /i/ versus /iː/, whereas Australian English has 11 *monophthongs* (i.e., a vowel with a single sound) namely /iː ɪ e æ ɐː ɐ ɔ oː ʊ ʉː ɜː/ (as in 'heat', 'hit', 'head', 'had', 'hard', 'hut', 'pod', 'poured', 'could', 'clued', 'heard' (plus the unstressed vowel /ə/) and six diphthongs /æɪ ɑe oɪ æɔ əʉ ɪə/ (as in 'hay', 'high', 'toy', 'how', 'toe', 'hear') (Harrington et al., 1997). This means that Kriol speakers have to use vowels that integrate the different types of vowels from traditional language and from English. In Kriol, this process has resulted in the creation of a five-vowel system in which each vowel comes in a *long* or *doubled* form, and in a 'short' form (see **Table 8.2**), plus *diphthongs* (i.e., a vowel with two sounds): /ei ai ou oi au/(Schultze-Berndt et al., 2013). This system is large enough to maintain many of the vowel contrasts in words that come from English though the vowels sound different to the vowels in SAE words, even when the Kriol word has originally come from English.

Case study of Kriol orthography

When different sound systems amalgamate like they have done in Kriol and many other contact languages, speakers typically do not have a suitable orthography (i.e., written form, spelling system) to support their language. As is clear from Kriol in the NT, neither the orthographies of the contributing Indigenous languages, nor the

Table 8.2 Correspondences between the vowels of Australian English and Kriol, adapted from Bundgaard-Nielsen and Baker (2015).

Keyword	AusE	Kriol
bead	iː	iː
bid	ɪ	i
bed	e	e
bad	æ	
bard	ɐː	aː
bud	ɐ	a
board	oː	oː
pod	ɔ	o
booed	ʉː	uː
good	ʊ	u
bird	ɜː	eː, aː

orthography of English are suitable for the writing of Kriol. So how do communities approach their need for a suitable orthography?

Religious institutions, and in particular missionary activities, have played a major role in the creation of grammars and orthographies for many Indigenous languages in Australia (and elsewhere in colonial settings). A source of pride for many Kriol speakers is the publication of the Holi Baibul (Holy Bible) in Kriol in 2007. This translation is the only complete translation of the Bible in any Australian Indigenous language, and the 27-year-long effort (Angelo, 2021, p. 76) had the important benefit of producing many literate speakers of Kriol, through direct involvement in translation activities, and/or through associated literacy education such as Sunday Schools.

Literacy development does not only centre on religious activities, however, and concerted community-based efforts in Ngukurr, supported by the Yugul Mangi Development Aboriginal Corporation's *Meigim Kriol Strongbala* 'Making Kriol Strong' community education program, has resulted in the development of an orthography for (Roper) Kriol. This orthography has been widely embraced in Ngukurr, where people feel that Kriol literacy is important and should be taught to children in school. Through its literacy advocacy, the development of a community-centred Kriol orthography, and through the production of literacy materials, like the Kriol Elfabet poster (Figure 8.1), translations of children's books and the creation of original literature in Kriol, the Meigim Kriol Strongbala program has made great strides in strengthening Kriol literacy in Ngukurr, both for children in the classrooms and in the wider (adult) community.

Kriol grammar

Kriol grammar shares some characteristics with English, but there are also many differences. These differences mean that Kriol-speaking children in the

Figure 8.1 The Kriol alphabet poster

Reproduced courtesy of Batchelor Institute Press. Published by Batchelor Press in association with Meigim Kriol Stongbala, Yugul Mangi Development Aboriginal Corporation, Ngukurr. Poster design by Sarah Martin.

classroom must acquire a new grammatical system to use SAE. It is not just a question of learning a different vocabulary and a new sound system but keeping sentence structures the same. Hence, allowing students to learn in both Kriol and SAE in the classroom as a bilingual setting is beneficial for all primary Kriol speakers.

Among some of the salient differences between SAE and Kriol is the Kriol use of *-im* to mark transitive verbs; this is not done in English, even when the verbs are otherwise the same, and sound similar in the two languages. Kriol also does not use the suffix '-ed' to signal past tense, nor plural endings '-s' on nouns to indicate more than one (e.g., *papi-dog* can refer to one or more puppies). These differences can result in uncertainty—from the perspective of an English speaker—about whether a child has understood a text or narrative, or even correctly understood classroom instructions, as it can be unclear whether a child is referring to one or more entities of the same kind and, therefore, understanding the content of a narrative. It can also lead to uncertainty about whether or not a child understands basic arithmetic.

Kriol also has a pronoun system that is quite different from English—lacking some distinctions in English and including some not made in English (see Table 8.3). Kriol speakers typically do not make a distinction between subject and object forms (e.g., the use of *we* versus *us*, in English), with some rare—optional—distinctions like *ai* (first person singular *subject*) versus *mi* (either first person singular *subject* or *object*), and *dei* (third person plural *subject*) and *dem* (third person plural *object*). However, Kriol speakers do make distinctions on the basis of *number* in ways that English-speakers do not: Where English speakers talk either of singular entities (I; me; you *singular*) or plural entities (we; us; you *plural*; they; them), Kriol speakers talk in terms of singular (mi; ai; yu; im) and plural (melabat; mibala; yumob; olabat, etc.), but also in terms of a dual category for combinations of two people. The dual system is complex and captures combinations of specific individuals, like *'you and me specifically'* (yunmi), and *'me and someone who is not you'* (mindubala/minbala) (again, see Table 8.3).

To illustrate the differences in the pronoun systems between SAE and Kriol, consider the Kriol utterance *'Dei bin stat lenimbat mi'* reported by Munro (2004, p. 42) and translated as *'They started teaching me'*. We can translate each of the components as follows: *dei* represents the third person pronoun (English 'they'), *bin* marks the past tense, *stat* corresponds to English 'start', and *lenimbat* has three sub-components: *len* means 'learn' or 'teach', *im* makes a verb transitive, and *bat* makes a verb progressive, just like the verb ending '-ing' in English. The Kriol pronoun *mi* corresponds to English 'me'.

Importantly, Kriol also lacks a gender or animacy distinction in the 3rd singular pronoun: the use of *im* can refer to any male, female, or non-human or inanimate referent. This difference between English and Kriol (and between English and many other languages, including Mandarin) might lead educators to think that Kriol-speaking students do not clearly understand the difference between males and females, that they do not understand a narrative in a text or struggle to summarise a text appropriately.

Table 8.3 Kriol subject pronouns, adapted from Schultze-Berndt et al. (2013), Munro (2004), and Sandefur (1979).

	Singular	Dual	Plural
1st exclusive	mi, ai	mindubala ~ minbala	mela(bat), mibala,
1st inclusive		yunmi	(wi)
2nd	yu	yundubala	yumob
3rd	im, i	dubala	olabat, alabat, alaba

However, Kriol speakers also make distinctions in pronouns in ways that are *not* implemented in English. For instance, Kriol makes a distinction between referents that are specifically *two in number* versus *more than two* (see the dual forms in Table 8.3). Kriol also distinguishes between an *inclusive* first person (we, including you) versus *exclusive* (we, not including you) which is an almost universal feature of traditional Australian languages, but not usually implemented in English.

Other features that set Kriol apart from SAE is a greater flexibility in word order, and differences in the way articles are used, as in an example like '*Bat* **thad** *nyuwan Wulis* **im** *gudwan du, ngabi*?' (from Schultze-Berndt et al., 2013). This can be translated as '*But the new Woollies is good too, isn't it?*' Kriol speakers often use the article *thad* (also spelt *det, thet, jat, dat*) to introduce a *topic* in a conversation and then cross-reference with the pronoun *im*, which both occur in this sentence.

Another difference is that the topic marker *thad/det* (from English *that*) can sometimes be used like the English definite article *the*, but unlike the latter can be used with proper names and in other contexts where *the* or *that* would sound strange in English, as with '*det* Mission Gorge' (a placename, cited in Munro, 2004, p 112) or '*det* Birna' (a personal name, cited in Nicholls, 2016, p. 348). Once more, using a bilingual approach and explicitly drawing the students' attention to the differences will help them by building upon their home language, while linking this to their English language learning.

Conclusions

Kriol is a Creole language, which shares elements with both English and its contributing Indigenous languages. Kriol likely evolved from one or more pidgins spoken across the NT and, in fact, in other parts of Australia, particularly in areas associated with the cattle industry. It is still not clear how this process unfolded, and whether Kriol has evolved in multiple locations over time, but children have been argued to have played an important role in the process of creolisation. There is no published, comprehensive Kriol dictionary or grammar available at the present, but existing materials demonstrate that Kriol has a different vocabulary, sound system, and grammar to English. These differences have often been ignored under the assumption that Kriol speakers command different speech styles, and that some of these styles are very similar to SAE. Ignoring differences between the two languages, especially in education settings, can lead to poor learning outcomes for Kriol-speaking children. This is a significant challenge worthy of attention because Kriol speakers make up a large proportion of the NT population and there is a significant number of speakers in the north of Western Australia and Queensland as well. We hope the present chapter will contribute to the improvement of education for Kriol-speaking children as well as contribute to better appreciation for the Kriol language and Kriol-speaking communities in the wider community.

References

Angelo, D. (2021). *Countering misrecognition of Indigenous contact languages and their ecologies in Australia* [Unpublished doctoral thesis]. The Australian National University, Canberra.

Australian Bureau of Statistics. (2021). Mataranka. https://abs.gov.au/census/find-census-data/quickstats/2021/SAL70179

Australian Institute of Aboriginal and Torres Strait Islander Studies (AIATSIS)/ Commonwealth of Australia. (2005). *The National Indigenous Languages Survey (NILS) report*. Department of Communications, Information Technology and the Arts.

Baker, B., Bundgaard-Nielsen, R., & Graetzer, S. (2014). The obstruent inventory of Roper Kriol. *Australian Journal of Linguistics*, 34, 307–344.

Bauer, F. H. (1964). *Historical geography of white settlement in part of Northern Australia. Part 2: The Katherine-Darwin region*. Canberra: CSIRO. Retrieved August 23, 2023, from https://nla.gov.au/nla.obj-2813003998/view?partId=nla.obj-

Bundgaard-Nielsen, R., & Baker, B. (2015). The vowel inventory of Roper Kriol. *Proceedings of the 18th International Congress of Phonetic Sciences*, Glasgow, 2015, 1–5.

Bundgaard-Nielsen, R. L., & Baker, B. J. (2016). Fact or furphy? The continuum in Kriol. In F. Meakins, & C. O'Shannessy (Eds.), *Loss and renewal: Australian Languages since contact* (pp. 177–216). De Gruyter Mouton.

Bundgaard-Nielsen, R. L., Baker, B., Bell, E., & Wang, Y. (2023). Stop contrast acquisition in child Kriol: Evidence of stable transmission of phonology post Creole formation. *Journal of Child Language*, 1–37. https://doi.org/10.1017/S0305000923000430

Department of Education. (2020). Kriol factsheet.

Dickson, G., & Durantin, G. (2019). Variation in the reflexive in Australian Kriol. *Asia-Pacific Language Variation*, 5(2), 171–207. https://doi.org/10.1075/aplv.00005.dic

Dockery, A. M. (2010). Culture and wellbeing: The case of indigenous Australians. *Social Indicators Research*, 99(2), 315–332. https://doi.org/10.1007/s11205-010-9582-y

Harrington, J., Cox, F., & Evans, Z. (1997). An acoustic phonetic study of broad, general and cultivated Australian English vowels. *Australian Journal of Linguistics*, 17, 155–184.

Gunn, J. (1908). *We of the Never Never*. Hutchinson.

Harris, J. W. (1986). *Northern Territory pidgins and the origin of Kriol*. Department. of Linguistics, Research School of Pacific Studies, Australian National University.

Harris, J., & Sandefur, J. (1984). The creole language debate and the use of creoles in Australian schools. *The Australian Journal of Indigenous Education*, 12(1), 8–29. https://doi.org/10.1017/S0310582200013092.

Hendy, C., & Bow, C. (2023). Should Munanga learn Kriol? Exploring attitudes to non-Indigenous acquisition of Kriol language in Ngukurr. *Australian Review of Applied Linguistics*, 46(1), 76–98. https://doi.org/10.1075/aral.20084.hen

Hudson, J. (1985). Grammatical and semantic aspects of Fitzroy Valley Kriol (Series A, Vol. 8). *Summer Institute of Linguistics, Australian Aborigines and Islanders Branch*.

Lee, J. (2014). Kriol-English interactive dictionary. *Australian Society for Indigenous languages*. http://ausil.org.au/Dictionary/Kriol/index-en.htm

Marmion, D., Obata, K., & Troy, J. (2014). *Community, identity, wellbeing: The report of the second National Indigenous Languages survey*. Australian Institute of Aboriginal and Torres Strait Islander Studies.

Meakins, F. (2014). Language contact varieties. In H. Koch, & R. Nordlinger (Eds.), *The languages and linguistics of Australia: A comprehensive guide* (pp. 365–416). Mouton.

Munro, J. (2000). Kriol on the move: A case of language spread and shift in Northern Australia. In J. Siegel (Ed.), *Processes of language contact: Studies from Australia and the South Pacific* (pp. 245–270). Fides.

Munro, J. (2004). *Substrate language influence in Kriol: The application of transfer constraints to language contact in northern Australia* [PhD thesis]. University of New England, Armidale, NSW.

Munro, J. (2011). Roper River Aboriginal language features in Australian Kriol: Considering semantic features. In C. Lefebvre (Ed.), *Creoles, their substrates, and language typology* (pp. 461–487). John Benjamins.

Nicholls, S. (2016). Grammaticalization and interactional pragmatics: A description of the recognitional determiner *det* in Roper River Kriol. In F. Meakins & C. O'Shannessy (Eds.), *Loss and renewal: Australian languages since contact* (pp. 333–364). De Gruyter Mouton. https://doi.org/10.1515/9781614518792-017

Rhydwen, M. (1995). Kriol is the color of Thursday. *International Journal of the Sociology of Language*, *113*, 113–120, https://doi.org/10.1515/ijsl.1995.113.113

Roberts, T. (2005). *Frontier justice: A history of the Gulf country to 1900*. University of Queensland Press.

Sandefur, J. R. (1979). *An Australian creole in the Northern Territory: A description of Ngukurr-Bamyili dialects*. Summer Institute of Linguistics.

Sandefur, J. R. (1986). *Kriol of North Australia: A language coming of Age* (Vol. 10). Summer Institute of Linguistics, Australian Aborigines Branch.

Schmidt, A. (1990). *The loss of Australia's Aboriginal language heritage*. Aboriginal Studies Press.

Schultze-Berndt, E., Meakins, F., & Angelo, D. (2013). Kriol. In S. M. Michaelis, P. Maurer, M. Haspelmath & M. Huber (Eds.), *The survey of pidgin and creole languages, volume 1: English-based and Dutch-based languages*. Oxford University Press. https://apics-online.info/surveys/25

Senghas, A. (1995). The development of Nicaraguan sign language via the language acquisition process. In D. MacLaughlin, & S. McEwen (Eds.), *Proceedings of the Boston University conference on language development 19* (pp. 543–552). Cascadilla Press.

Siegel, J. (2010). *Second dialect acquisition*. Cambridge University Press.

Simpson, J. (1996). Early language contact varieties in South Australia. *Australian Journal of Linguistics*, *16*(2), 169–207.

Simpson, J. (2000). Camels as pidgin-carriers: Afghan cameleers as a vector for the spread of features of Australian Aboriginal pidgins and creoles. In J. Siegel (Ed.), *Processes of language contact: Studies from Australia and the South Pacific* (pp. 195–244). Collections Champs linguistiques. Fides.

Simpson, J. (2024). After 1788: Contact varieties in the first sixty years of Australia's colonisation. *Journal of Pidgin and Creole Languages*, *39*(1), 71–124. https://doi.org/10.1075/jpcl.00130.sim

Troy, J. (1993). Language contact in early colonial New South Wales 1788 to 1791. In M. Walsh, & C. Yallop (Eds.), *Language and culture in Aboriginal Australia* (pp. 33–50). Aboriginal Studies Press.

Tryon, D. T., & Charpentier, J.-M. (2004). *Pacific pidgins and creoles. Origins, growth and development*. Mouton de Gruyter.

Urry, J., & Walsh, M. (1981). The lost 'Macassar' language of northern Australia. *Aboriginal History*, *5*, 91–108.

Yugul Mangi Development Aboriginal Corporation. (2019). *Stronger communities program: Ngukurr progress report*. Stronger Communities for Children, Department of Prime Minister and Cabinet.

9 Aboriginal English in Education

Ian Malcolm, Patricia Königsberg, and Glenys Collard

Who we are

Ian Malcolm is Emeritus Professor of Applied Linguistics at Edith Cowan University, where he served for 38 years following three years as a high school teacher in Collie. His publications include *English and the Aboriginal Child* (co-authored, 1982), *Linguistics in the Service of Society* (editor and co-author, 1991), *Towards More User-Friendly Education for Speakers of Aboriginal English* (co-author, 1999), *The Habitat of Australia's Aboriginal Languages* (co-editor, 2007), and *Australian Aboriginal English: Change and Continuity in an Adopted Language* (author, 2018). For more than 30 years he has been working together with Patricia Königsberg, Glenys Collard, and others in bicultural teams to develop a more inclusive approach to education for Aboriginal students.

Patricia is a linguist and educational leader who works in the Department of Education of Western Australia. With extensive experience teaching students of all ages across metropolitan, regional and remote areas of Western Australia, Patricia has dedicated many years working collaboratively with Glenys Collard, Ian Malcolm, and others to co-design and deliver multiple research projects and educational publications on Aboriginal English. Patricia is passionate about empowering Aboriginal and non-Aboriginal students and teachers to value and recognise Aboriginal English as an essential linguistic resource to educational success through two-way learning.

Glenys Collard is a Nyungar matriarch within her nuclear family of over 400 people. Glenys has pioneered the original Nyungar Language Project and played a key part, with Ian Malcolm, in developing understandings in Aboriginal English through the West Australian linguistic research. She has held a range of government positions, including in the Aboriginal Legal Service and co-managed the West Australian Department of Education's ABC of Two-Way Literacy and Learning and Tracks to Two-Way Learning projects alongside Patricia Konigsberg. Glenys holds an Honorary Research Fellowship at the University of Western Australia where she continues to be actively engaged in linguistic research on Aboriginal English.

DOI: 10.4324/9781003441021-13

Introduction

Aboriginal English is a form of English with which many Aboriginal and Torres Strait Islander speakers identify. Although it includes some regional variation, and exists in heavier and lighter varieties, it can be appropriately seen (as by its speakers) as a variety held in common by people from a similar cultural heritage across the continent. Linguists may write about the dialect's linguistic features, its sociolinguistic rules and the ways in which it conforms, or fails to conform, to the patterns of other Englishes, but to the speakers of this dialect it is a part of their lived experience. As such, Aboriginal English embodies a shared perception of the world which is distinctive to Aboriginal and Torres Strait Islander speakers and inseparable from the world they know. It is how life is conceived. Its conceptualisations make sense of life.

In Western Australia, English language samples from Aboriginal school communities have been collected and analysed jointly by Aboriginal and non-Aboriginal researchers and educators. This research, carried out through a range of collaborative projects between linguists and educators (Eagleson et al., 1982; Hodge & Courts, 1981; Malcolm, 1995, 2018a; Malcolm & Grote, 2007; Malcolm et al., 1999), has significant implications. Findings have also been compared and documented with similar linguistic data and research conducted over some 50 years around the Australian continent (Malcolm, 2018b).

Recent studies have found that

> In many parts of Australia, for example remote Aboriginal communities, very little SAE (Standard Australian English) may be spoken, and it may be limited to school settings (Poetsch, 2020; Angelo & Hudson, 2020; Wigglesworth et al., 2018) (as cited by Steele et al., 2023).

Similarly, work carried out by Konigsberg, Collard, and Malcolm with Aboriginal educators throughout Western Australia over a period of some 30 years has found that Aboriginal English is far more prevalent among Aboriginal students than previously thought. Moreover, Aboriginal students' work-samples collected from all phases of learning through the four Western Australian programs (i.e., the ABC of Two-Way Literacy and Learning, Tracks to Two-Way Learning, Aboriginal Literacy Strategy, and more recently EALD Hub Champions Program) show that Aboriginal English not only occurs in remote areas, but is also strong in regional and metropolitan areas, including the South-West regions of Western Australia. (See for example Department of Education of Western Australia, 2016; Education Department of Western Australia, Association of Independent Schools of Western Australia and Catholic Education Office of Western, 2000; Disbray & Loakes, 2013; Konigsberg, 2013; Konigsberg & Collard, 2007; Konigsberg et al., 2012; Malcolm, 1995, 2002; Malcolm et al., 1999; Purdie et al., 2010; Rochecouste & Malcolm, 2003.)

The need for recognition of the use of Aboriginal English among the current generation of Aboriginal English speakers has been evidenced in the Western Australian Department of Education's 2023 Student Census which indicates that

Aboriginal English is the most common language spoken by students from language backgrounds other than Standard Australian English. In this census, 6,781 students were identified as speakers of Aboriginal English (Department of Education of Western Australia, 2023). The existence of such data serves to illustrate the social impact of Aboriginal English among today's Aboriginal youth. Any lack of recognition of the extent to which this dialect is used risks social division, exclusion and, in educational contexts, disengagement.

To ignore Aboriginal English in education, or to override it with Standard Australian English, is to ignore the means by which Aboriginal speakers have come to understand and relate to their shared life as a cultural group. When education is delivered without due regard to Aboriginal English, it becomes irrelevant to their lives. At the same time, educators have a moral obligation to equip speakers of Aboriginal English for life in a world which involves communication both with Aboriginal English speakers and with members of the wider population who have access to Standard Australian English.

To meet this need, the education of speakers of Aboriginal English (especially in school contexts where they will be learning alongside non-Aboriginal learners) needs to perform four essential functions, namely to:

1. embrace the lived experience expressed in Aboriginal English, giving due recognition to the linguistic and conceptual life which Aboriginal English speakers bring to school;
2. facilitate interchange of knowledge and experience both between speakers of Aboriginal background and across the two groups – Aboriginal English speakers and speakers of non-Aboriginal backgrounds;
3. enhance awareness of the relationship between language and life, both within the Aboriginal community and in the non-Aboriginal community;
4. provide all students with evidence of tangible benefits for the life their school is preparing them for, both through the maintenance of Aboriginal English and through the acquisition of Standard Australian English, and associated cultures.

An education that serves these functions presupposes:

- improved cultural inclusion, entailing the recognition of the conceptualisations underlying the use of Aboriginal English;
- the provision of support to Aboriginal speakers in recognition of the conceptualisations underlying Standard Australian English;
- Aboriginal and non-Aboriginal participants in the education (both educators and students) learning from one another;
- a clearer focus on the benefits of learning for all students involved.

Attitudes to Aboriginal English

It is clear that Aboriginal English speakers value the distinctiveness of their dialect, in that they have maintained it over an extended time in the face of opposition from educators and from the community generally, sometimes expressed by derogative labelling of its speakers as 'uneducated' or 'uncivilised'. For example, some years ago in response to an interviewer asking if they have ever tried to change their English, a group of Aboriginal teacher assistants responded that the change that was expected of them was 'what we call *flash* or putting it on'. They went on to say: 'I think that's why a lot of blacks don't try to speak better because…sometimes other blacks'll laugh at them' (Eagleson et al., 1982, p. 155). Recently, there has been some shift in language attitudes towards Aboriginal English and creoles (see for example, Sellwood & Angelo, 2013, and also Rodríguez Louro & Collard, 2020). The pressure for the maintenance of Aboriginal English comes from the community of its speakers, for whom its distinctive forms of expression imply authenticity and resistance to being 'flash'. Derived from the various forms of English which were brought to their shores, as well as from the experience of responding to colonisation, it constitutes an English which Aboriginal speakers have culturally embraced to make it their own.

Recent work by Dovchin (2020) introduces the term 'linguistic racism', that is 'racism based on an individual's use of language, accent, dialect, repertoire and speech' (p. 2, after Alim et al., 2016). Linguistic racism is experienced in many contexts where a standard language variety is privileged. In the Australian context, Oliver and Exell (2020) report feelings of shame among Aboriginal people when unable to speak proficiently in Australian English, not to mention the risk of being labelled as 'linguistically deficient [and] lacking full aptitude' (Dovchin, 2020, p. 2).

In a classroom context, unconscious bias attributed to Aboriginal English will, by extension, negatively affect Aboriginal learners. They may feel misunderstood or even mis-judged as being less knowledgeable or incapable of achieving success. Such misunderstandings can lead to detrimental outcomes for both Aboriginal English-speaking learners and educators and can result in Aboriginal English-speaking learners being labelled as having a 'language deficiency' or 'language disorder'. Educators may then resort to the wrong support mechanisms with negative consequences such as learners becoming uncommunicative and reserved, or even unruly and disruptive (Malcolm, 1982). Learners' social and emotional well-being may also be affected leading to further disengagement (Cheshire & Edwards, 1998; Heit & Blair, 1993; Smitherman, 1977; Esch, 2011).

Form and formation of Aboriginal English

As has been noted (Malcolm, 2018a, 2018b), there were processes of retention, elimination, modification, and extension involved in the generation of a form of English that met the needs of Aboriginal speakers. The selectiveness by which Aboriginal speakers adopted some features and not others from the dialects they heard, and also drew upon their traditional languages, reflects what they wanted to make their own. Some of the processes, which come from various data sets, have been summarised (from Malcolm, 2018b) as follows. (It should be noted that samples cannot always be attributed to specific locations as many Aboriginal and Torres Strait Islander people will have lived in different areas of the country.)

1   Retention

- Non-standard morphological features retained from English dialects

    e.g., *yous* (Scottish and Irish) [adding the plural]; *hisself, theirselves* (Scottish and SW English) [adding the possessive]

- Non-standard syntactic features retained from English dialects

    We was going 'we were going' (Scottish, Irish, and North-eastern)
    She never died 'she didn't die' (Scottish, North-eastern, and South-eastern)
    I didn't know nothing 'I didn't know anything' (British English generally)
    We went for walk 'We went for a walk' (Northern English)
    Nother woman e got 'He got another woman' (Northern and Welsh English)
    What she said? 'What did she say?' (Northern English)
    You'll get shame, eh? 'You'll be embarrassed, won't you?' (Scottish and Channel Island English)
    One got sick, init? 'One got sick, isn't that right/what do you think?' (Welsh, South-east, and South-west English)
    This man what walk round 'The man who walks around' (South-east and South-west English)

- Lexis:

    gammon 'nonsense' (18th century English)
    humbug 'annoy'

- Discourse:

    Cos she lives with her Nan and Pop (Scottish English) [explanatory follow-up].

2   Elimination

- Phonology:

    My boss's a elder 'My boss is an elder' [deletion of /-n/]
    th'other fella 'the other fellow' [deletion of /i:/]
    onna, inna 'on the/a' 'in the/a' [deletion of /ə/]
    alla 'all the' (or plural of 'the') [deletion of /ə/]
    wanna 'want to' [deletion of /t/]
    jes, jis, 'just' [deletion of /t/]

- Morphology:

    turtle 'some turtles' [unmarked plural]
    That man car 'that man's car' [unmarked possessive]

- Syntax:

    That a pretty snake 'that's a pretty snake' [zero *be*]
    They green 'they're green' [zero *be*]
    You whitefella? 'Are you a non-Aboriginal person?' [zero *be* and *a*]

- Lexis:
    avoiding the name of a deceased person

- Discourse:
    non-use of politeness forms (e.g., *May I...; Excuse me...*)

3 Modification

- Phonology:

    Interchange of front vowel (from Kriol) e.g.,/gɪt/and/gɛt/
    Replacing/ə/with/a/, as in *fella*
    Monophthongisation of diphthongs, e.g.,/*de:*/'there'
    Plosive substitutes for fricative consonants, e.g., *tink* 'think'
    Epenthesis, e.g.,/ʌgəli/'ugly' (inserting a vowel)

- Morphology:

    We goin along a road 'We were going...' (zero *be*)
    I bin light a fire 'I lit a fire' (past tense derived from 'been')
    gonna 'will' (more embodied future marking)
    bendy-one (adding a nominalising suffix to an adjective)
    shy-way (adding a nominalising suffix to an adverb)
    belong, or *bong* (more embodied marking of possessive)

- Syntax:

    Me an Jody bin go and getting grapes (innovative combination of definite and continuous forms of past tense)

- Lexis:

    sister girl, waterflood, shame job, coldsick (innovative compounds)
    schooling 'going to school' (conversion from noun)
    borrow 'lend' (semantic shift)
    revision mirror 'rear vision mirror' (modified lexical adoption)

4 Extension

- Metaphor, e.g., *smash* 'fight'
- Lexical transfer from Aboriginal languages, e.g., *bogey* 'swim'; *yorgas* 'girls'

It is important for teachers of Aboriginal students to understand why people of Aboriginal culture have selectively adopted English. To regard their departures from standard English forms as errors, or inaccuracies, would be to seriously mis-judge them. The fact is that, in order to make English their own, they have needed to give it cultural endorsement, enabling it to reflect their own conceptualisations and perspectives (Malcolm & Rochecouste, 2000).

There are many principles underlying the modification of English by Aboriginal speakers. Some are listed Table 9.1 before we consider their implications for pedagogy.

Table 9.1 Principles underlying the modification of English by Aboriginal speakers.

Relevance to travel/ movement	Rather than assuming that those spoken to are of a settled dwelling-place, Aboriginal speakers may relate them to ongoing movement, as is traditional in Aboriginal society (e.g., *sit down, stop* meaning live or reside [Malcolm, 2018b, p. 102]; Matthew was campin at my house [Malcolm, 2018b, p. 140]).
Relevance to participants and their participation	Aboriginal discourse incorporates frequent reference to the participants, their relation to the speaker, and their understanding of what has been said (e.g., *you know, sistergirl*).
Recognition of interconnections – human/non-human	For example, *He's horse* [terrific guy] (Douglas, 1976, p. 18); *this kangaroo big bloke* (Malcolm, 2018b, p. 72); *cheeky animal* – meaning dangerous animal (Malcolm, 2018b, p. 152).
Levelling of animate/ inanimate distinction	For example, *'But he still there, that bone'* (Malcolm, 2018b, p. 92); *hurt that motor car* 'drove really fast' (Collard, 2011, p. 31); *heal the wound of the earth* (Malcolm, 2018b, p. 141); *a proper feed* 'a desirable girl' (Malcolm, 2018b, p. 141).
Levelling of gender distinction	Affiliation: use of Aboriginal English implies a sense of affiliation among the speakers, entailing a 'flexibility' with reference to genders and kinship. *When e little girl* may mean 'When she was a little girl'. The term *mate,* from Australian English may be used with male or female reference (Malcolm, 2018b, p. 111).
Intention of an action may be identified with the means of achieving it	For example, *kill* may be used to mean 'hit, or kill' (Malcolm, 2002, p. 63; 2018b, p. 108); *learn* 'teach or learn' (Malcolm, 2018b, p. 101, 142), as in *I learnt him a lot of things...* Also *drop* may be used to refer to the intended result of a hit, as in *Karl dropped im in the head and that bird never die* (Michael, aged 11, Leonora); *Go away two pigs before I'll drop you* (Eagleson et al., 1982, p. 235).
Thought and speech interrelation may be emphasised	*He reckon, oh I'm sorry* (Malcolm et al., 2002, p. 64) and *reckon,* may apply to either thought or speech.
Physical/spiritual interrelationships may be assumed	For example, *clever* 'exercising spiritual powers' (Malcolm, 2018b, p. 102); present/past, e.g., *they left the windows open so the spirit goes out* (Malcolm, 2018b, p. 139).

(*Continued*)

Aboriginal English in Education 159

Table 9.1 (Continued)

Embodiment of meaning	Aboriginal English speakers will often embody the meaning of what they are expressing by means of modifying pronunciation (i.e., physical), morphology (i.e., linguistic), or expanding through use of metaphor (i.e., metaphorical). For example: • Physical: (e.g., *loooong*). Note: This option is also open to any English speakers but is more commonly taken by Aboriginal English speakers. • Linguistic: (e.g., *yous, hisself, slow-way* 'slowly' (Malcolm, 2018b, p. 69); *rain time* 'when it rains' (Malcolm, 2018b, p. 69; *most rottenest* 'worst', *waterflood* 'flood', *sandbeach* 'shore' (Schnukal, 1988:83); *schooling* 'going to school', *shellin* 'gathering shells' (Malcolm, 2018b, p. 100); *mum's mum* 'grandmother' (Malcolm, 2018b, p. 124). Also pronunciation of *his* as /hi:z/, implying possessive (Malcolm, 2018b, p. 124). • Metaphorical: (e.g., *clean water mob* 'a lot of clean water' (Malcolm, 2018b, p. 72); *smash* 'fight', *Dreaming* 'creation time' (Malcolm, 2018b, p. 102); *deadly* 'very good' (Malcolm, 2018b, p. 103); *stranger* 'non-Aboriginal', etc.), *old boy* as a term of respect (Malcolm, 2018b, p. 110).
Assumption of situationally relevant meaning	For example, *what you bloke comin for?* (implies the plurality of *bloke*, without marking it) (Malcolm, 2018b, p. 131); use of location markers, e.g., *...near Miller's Pool **there*** (Malcolm, 2018b, p. 131); *Last week our family...we **go** rabbiting* (implies past tense of 'go', without marking it) (Malcolm, 2018b, p. 133); *Well, 'e seen **this** dingo* (demonstrative implies shared conception) (Malcolm, 2018b, p. 134).
Cultural transfer of meaning	For example, *grannies* meaning grandchildren or grandparents (Malcolm, 2018b, p. 101); *little mummy, little daddy* (terms of address by parent to child) (Malcolm, 2018b, p. 146); *auntie, uncle* (may be extended to cover niece and nephew); *shame* 'transgressing cultural norms' (Malcolm, 2018b, p. 102); *country* 'traditional land' (Koch & Koch 1993:46); distinguishing *boomers* 'large male kangaroos' from other kangaroos (Malcolm, 2018b, p. 108); *hand* 'hand/arm' (Malcolm, 2018b, p. 110); *roast* 'outdoor event involving cooking meat in fire'; *supper* 'evening meal at home', also known as *feed* (Malcolm, 2018b, p. 127);

(*Continued*)

Table 9.1 (Continued)

	home 'with family', rather than a place of residence (Malcolm, 2018b, p. 128); *long* may entail a vertical dimension (Malcolm, 2018b, p. 128); *family* may refer to extended family (Malcolm, 2018b, p. 147).
Modified transfer	For example, *remote controlled community* 'remote community'; *earsdropping* 'eavesdropping'; *revision mirror* 'rear vision mirror' (Malcolm, 2018b, p. 103); *ownlation* '[own] relation' (Malcolm, 2018b, p. 104).
Elision of syllables	For example, *cross* 'across', *leven* 'eleven', *splain* 'explain', *cos* 'because', *drecly* 'directly', *I'na* 'I want to', etc.
Elision of phonemes	For example, *alla* 'all the', *onna* 'on the', *inna* 'in the', *ere* 'here', etc.

The distinctiveness of Aboriginal English may be related to its sensitivity to the interrelationships between the speakers and the contexts seen to relate to them. The features we have isolated highlight, particularly, four related aspects:

- Language and the physical context: the situation and setting which the speaker assumes (and expects the listeners to assume);
- Language and the human context: the receivers of the language, and the way in which they relate to the speaker and what he/she has to say;
- Language and the cultural context: the cultural conceptualisations which are assumed to underlie what is being put into language;
- Language and the spiritual context: the potential spiritual significance of what is being said.

The ever-presence of these interrelated dimensions is constantly informing what the users of Aboriginal English are saying.

Aboriginal English and the implication for teachers

Teachers of Aboriginal English-speaking students need to have a raised awareness of the meaning of their communication on all these levels and need to apply this awareness both in their own communication and in their interpretation of the students' responses. It is also necessary to take account of the fact that Aboriginal students in classrooms will vary in their degree of exposure to both Aboriginal English and Standard Australian English. The following is an extract from a discussion of this and its implications by our Aboriginal author Glenys Collard:

> There are many layers of knowledge and understanding that only time has enabled us to build into our speech so... we are able to use and adapt the ways that Aboriginal English continues to survive today. However, not all Aboriginal people speak Aboriginal English or even understand what Aboriginal English is.

As one of my twenty year old great-grand-daughters has said to us: 'Aboriginal English is really a whole lifestyle, if you are living as an Aboriginal family or group, then the chances are that you would be speaking Aboriginal English'. Her little brother-boy spent eleven years in care with non-Aboriginal people, when he came back to live with her, everything Aboriginal seemed foreign to him – he still has a difficult time adjusting back into family life [with those] who are all Aboriginal English speakers.

There is evidence of miscommunication happening all the time. There is a huge disservice done to Aboriginal people, children and adults when you don't have the knowledge of how Aboriginal English works and how to use it appropriately in the many different situations. This is the part that comes into Cultural Safety.

If you grew up living away from, or outside of, your Aboriginal family home or family group environment, then you would be living in a non-Aboriginal-English speaking world. There could be many reasons for this. One could be that your parents chose to change their ways of life by adapting to another lifestyle, one that required changes to match their and their children's own lifestyle.

Just imagine an onion and all of its different layers. The core of the onion represents most speakers of Aboriginal English. We share through our speech patterns cultural conceptualisations from our Aboriginal ways of speaking. Just like the very middle of an onion, we as Aboriginal English speakers can access the knowledge being shared by making meaning from one another as Aboriginal people just as our old people did. Aboriginal English allows us as Aboriginal people to do this at the deepest levels.

There are some things that just can't be accessed or understood even by our own Aboriginal people who are not speakers of Aboriginal English themselves. An example that comes to mind is the difference between these two statements:

'Tell the mob about it' versus 'All us mob got to know about this… We have to tell all our own mob about it …'

Both these statements are in Aboriginal English but only the second statement is from the core of the onion. Words can't stand alone. They are intrinsic to the culture and the very essence of our being and identity.

Towards a more two-way approach in teaching Aboriginal students

To encompass the complexity of the hidden understandings in communication in Aboriginal English, as described above by Malcolm and Collard, a two-way approach, as introduced by the Western Australian Department of Education is, therefore, not just about learning Standard Australian English. It is a philosophy that underpins cross-cultural collaboration (see for example, Rodriguez Louro & Collard, 2021). Working two-way requires the flow of information to be reciprocal. It requires Aboriginal English speakers to develop the understandings transmitted through a Western cultural lens, and at the same time, it requires non-Aboriginal people to develop a respect for, and an appreciation of, the deep-level cultural conceptualisations that are embedded in Aboriginal English communication. In this case, teachers position themselves as co-learners.

As a teaching and learning strategy, the two-way approach accords to some extent with the concept of translanguaging by taking into account the existing language repertoires of learners and, in doing so, promoting greater fairness in the classroom (Garcia & Kleyn, 2016). Translanguaging is a pedagogical approach that aims to create additional opportunities for learners 'to use their varied linguistic and multimodal repertoires to express themselves and enhance learning in actual classroom practice' (Xu & Fang, 2024). As such, like the two-way approach, it protects speakers of minoritised languages who might otherwise be marginalised in a dominant language society. Accepting and respecting both languages as legitimate entities also underlies the two-way approach which focuses specifically on the acceptance of the minority dialect, Aboriginal English, in the classroom.

As with translanguaging, the two-way approach seeks to eliminate linguistic boundaries by allowing space for learners to express themselves using whatever linguistic resources they have at their disposal. This can incorporate borrowing words/phrases from one dialect to use in another to enhance production at the surface level (i.e., utterance or sentence). In a classroom context, what was frequently called code-switching not only provides the framework through which linguistic boundaries can be made visible to the learner (Grote et al., 2014), but also supports the development of a clear understanding of the differences between Aboriginal English and Standard Australian English.

Importantly, the situation of Aboriginal English differs markedly from other English language learning contexts. Unlike immigrant students, many Aboriginal students have no other key source of knowledge about their cultural traditions. They have no other home country to keep their history and culture strong, so for many, Aboriginal English provides the only conduit to understanding the fundamental conceptualisations of their society. This need is stipulated in the Australian Curriculum:

- that Aboriginal and Torres Strait Islander students are able to see themselves, their identities, and their cultures reflected in the curriculum of each of the learning areas, can fully participate in the curriculum, and can build their self-esteem,
- that the Aboriginal and Torres Strait Islander Histories and Cultures cross-curriculum priority is designed for all students to engage in reconciliation, respect, and recognition of the world's oldest continuous living cultures (ACARA, n.d.-b).

Past government policies have attempted to override the culture held by Indigenous Australians. As shown through the above examples, much of that traditional cultural knowledge and conceptualisation is now preserved through Aboriginal English. This important fact needs to be recognised in all three broad categories: revitalisation, renewal, and reclamation of the Language Revitalisation Pathway (ACARA, n.d.-c), as well as the need to approach language education with an 'intentionally decolonising stance' (Seymour & Angelo, 2023, p. 174).

In the context of the above Garcia and Kleyn state that

> The language practices of minoritized people must be sustained and developed within the communicative context in which they are used by bilingual speakers and not as isolated museum pieces.
>
> (Garcia & Kleyn, 2019, p. 19)

Numerous studies in second (additional) language acquisition report the many benefits of being able to learn using one's own home language when learning an additional language (Cummins, 2006). In addition to an increased sense of being valued and subsequent increased motivation, these benefits include better self-expression and increased lateral thinking abilities. This evidence is supported by Siegel (2010) who maintains that allowing Aboriginal learners to talk in ways that are familiar, that is, to use their home dialect/language in the classroom, extends their cognitive abilities (Siegel, 2010).

Considerable research also supports the maintenance of first language or dialect skills in other mainstream educational contexts (Cummins, 2006). Peltier (2010) reiterates earlier work published by Leap (1993) about American (USA) Indian English, in that one's own dialect is central to an individual's identity and ties to community, and without the security of the familiar, learners are unable to venture into the unfamiliar (Lindfors, 1991). Therefore, students need to feel safe in the knowledge that they will be fully supported in understanding and applying new concepts.

As shown with the selection of examples provided earlier, Aboriginal English not only reveals a clear set of systemic linguistic features and sociolinguistic rules (Eades, 2013; Malcolm, 2018b). It also entails certain environmental, human, conceptual, and spiritual assumptions which influence communication. The importance of cultural conceptualisations in the process of communicating needs to be understood by non-Aboriginal teachers and peers alike. Aboriginal learners need to be given frequent opportunities to articulate their understandings and their real-life experiences as part of their education. These understandings are summarised below.

- Their shared perception of human events in a context of ongoing motion, interrupted by temporary stopping. This implies a more environmentally determined perspective, rather than one which is controlled (and limited) by the ever-presence of the built environment. The teacher needs to recognise the relevance to students of ongoing human movement through the environment, and the limitations of a geographically constrained perspective. This recognition is necessary to enable the teacher to understand and accept the students' references to one another as being *camped* or *sat down* at a given location. It will also be relevant

to understanding the students' references to their movements as *footfalcon* (going on foot), going along a road and *go and getting grapes*. It also implies their shared perception of the inclusivity of the human context in which linguistic communication takes place, whereby the communicator and the receivers are fully aware of one another.
- The teacher needs to recognise that Aboriginal students are heedful of the need to be shown the relevance to them of what is being communicated. This is reflected, for example, by the use of tags, as in *You'll get shame, eh?* and *One got sick, init?* It further implies awareness of the cultural conceptualisations which are assumed to underlie what is being put into language.
- The teacher is dependent on cultural conceptualisations which embrace not only the meanings s/he wishes to express but also those the Aboriginal students can be expected to share and receive. The conceptualisations, for example, of *cheeky* 'dangerous', *borrow* 'lend', *drop* 'knock out', *country* 'traditional land', *blue* 'drunk', *niddy* 'the last one in the family', *horse* 'terrific guy', and many others would be inaccessible to speakers without the assistance of Aboriginal English speakers.
- In addition to the physical, human, and conceptual contexts of the communication, a potential spiritual context needs to be allowed for. To communicate meaningfully with Aboriginal students, the teacher needs to know when they may be drawing on a culturally specific spiritual level of interpretation. This may apply to such expressions as *finding our door open at night time, One devil came to me, wudarchi* 'mischievous little man' and *smoke* as 'ritually cleanse us'.

The importance of Aboriginal English

Aboriginal English is important at all levels of education:

> At the federal level, the Australian government's 'Empowered Communities' initiative seeks to 'involve First Nations communities and governments working together to set priorities, improve services and apply funding effectively at a regional level. It aims to increase First Nations' ownership and give First Nations people greater influence over decisions that affect them'.
> (National Indigenous Australian Agency, n.d.).

Within schools, much emphasis has been placed on how curriculum materials tend to employ a Western middle-class viewpoint and how this can exclude learners whose cultural and linguistic backgrounds have, historically, been marginalised (Hammond, 2015). Instead, there is a need to develop a 'strength-based' education whereby Aboriginal learners are given a voice (Lopez & Lois, 2009), and where Aboriginal students are able to 'succeed as Aboriginal people' (Department of Education of Western Australia, 2023). These important educational initiatives rely on communication between speakers of Aboriginal English and non-Aboriginal people. Unless communicative exchange can occur, giving Aboriginal English speakers true cultural endorsement, any related initiatives are little more than tokenism.

Co-design at all levels is essential for these initiatives to work (also see Chapters 2 and 11 of this volume). Originally framed in the field of science to learn from Indigenous knowledge frameworks to combat climatic and environmental changes, the notion of co-design has become another important concept (Parsons et al., 2016). In educational contexts, co-design needs to operate at all three levels: the classroom, the staffroom, and the community. Here again, Aboriginal English plays a key role in negotiating curriculum design with community and Aboriginal staff and clearly requires mutual comprehensibility through a shared understanding of the miscommunication that can occur between speakers of Aboriginal English and Standard Australian English.

The recognition and accommodation of Aboriginal English appears in the *Australian Curriculum* (ACARA, n.d.-a), the *National Capability Framework - Teaching Aboriginal and Torres Strait Islander EALD Learners* (Departments of Education: Queensland, Western Australia, Northern Territory and New South Wales, 2013), and teacher support materials developed by the relevant Australian state government departments of education. In Western Australia, the *Teaching for Impact* resources form part of the recently released Western Australian Department of *Education's Quality Teaching Strategy* (2022). This strategy emphasises the need to recognise and value the knowledge that Aboriginal children bring with them to school and acknowledges the role of the home language, i.e., Aboriginal English, as having a significant impact on student outcomes.

Barriers to success: Aboriginal English-speaking students need to have the same opportunities to excel in Standard Australian English as non-Aboriginal learners. One of the key issues faced by many teachers is a lack of understanding of their students' existing language knowledge and meta-linguistic awareness. This can only be overcome in an environment that offers cultural and linguistic safety where Aboriginal English speakers feel valued and supported in who they are and how they speak. As noted above, when Aboriginal English-speaking students express themselves freely, the educators can learn the intricacies of their dialect. They can become aware of the linguistic features and cultural conceptualisations used and predict which features of Aboriginal English are particularly distinct from Standard Australian English and will be difficult for their students.

A second major issue is that Aboriginal English-speaking learners may be unaware of the existence of Standard Australian English – very often they see themselves as already speaking English. For them, Aboriginal English **is** English. Consequently, both teachers and learners need to be able to identify what distinguishes the two dialects: to have observed the differences, to have foregrounded them in lesson design, and to have created a time and place for students to use them. This needs to be done with a clear understanding and acknowledgement of the cultural influences underlying learners' oral and written performances.

Finally, here is the last word from Glenys Collard:

Aboriginal English is an important part of Australia's history, not only is it our Aboriginal history, it's also part of non-Aboriginal people's history.

Understanding what Aboriginal English is, how and why it exists and how it continues to evolve is very relevant today.

All Australian citizens should have some knowledge of the role Aboriginal English plays. The more conversations we have, the more we will want to know about it. Yarning and hearing how our descendants overcame obstacles, and how our own Elders tackled the Englishes that were forced upon them, will teach us all about the deeper layers of understanding the world.

Our Aboriginal people were able to hang onto language and culture that was forbidden through government policies of the day. However, they were able to carry a lot of our Aboriginal history and culture by using our own way of talking, using their own English words with our own Aboriginal meanings for words.

We acknowledge the traditional custodians of the lands throughout Australia. We acknowledge parents, families, and communities as the first educators of their children. Aboriginal people have a long tradition of teaching and learning through sharing their connections with the land and sea, and through their stories and lived experiences that are passed from generation to generation. We recognise and value the learning that Aboriginal learners bring with them from their homes and communities.

The authors also would like to acknowledge Dr Judith Rochecouste for her editorial support.

References

Alim, S. A., Rickford, J. R., & Ball, A. F. (Eds.) (2016). *Raciolinguistics: How language shapes our ideas about race*. Oxford.

Angelo, D., & Hudson, C. (2020). From the periphery to the centre: Securing the place at the heart of the TESOL field for First Nations learners of English as an Additional Language/Dialect. *TESOL in Context, 29*(1), 5–35. https://doi.org/10.21153/tesol2020vol29no1art1421

Australian Curriculum, Assessment and Reporting Authority [ACARA] (n.d.-a). Curriculum: Student diversity—Teaching students with English as an Additional Language or Dialect (EAL/D): English as an Additional Language or Dialect Teacher Resource: EALD Overview and Advice in Student Diversity, *V9.0 Australian Curriculum*. https://docs.acara.edu.au/resources/EALD_Overview_and_Advice_revised_February_2014.pdf

Australian Curriculum, Assessment and Reporting Authority [ACARA] (n.d.-b). Curriculum: Aboriginal and Torres Strait histories and cultures, V8.4, in *V9.0 Australian Curriculum*. https://www.australiancurriculum.edu.au/f-10-curriculum/cross-curriculum-priorities/aboriginal-and-torres-strait-islander-histories-and-cultures/

Australian Curriculum Assessment and Reporting Authority [ACARA] (n.d.-c). Framework for Aboriginal Languages and Torres Strait Islander languages, V8.4, in *V9.0 Australian Curriculum*. Language Revival Learner Pathway (LR) structure pathway. https://www.australiancurriculum.edu.au/f-10-curriculum/languages/framework-for-aboriginal-languages-and-torres-strait-islander-languages/structure/

Cheshire, J., & Edwards, V. (1998). Knowledge about language in British classrooms: Children as researchers. In A. Egan-Roberson, & D. Bloome (Eds.), *Students as researchers of culture and language in their own communities* (pp. 191–214). Hampton Press.

Collard, G. D. (2011), *A Day in the Park*. Western Australian Department of Training and Workforce Development.

Cummins, J. (2006). *Language, power and pedagogy – Bilingual children in the crossfire*. Multilingual Matters.

Department of Education of Western Australia. (2016). *Aboriginal English storybooks*. https://myresources.education.wa.edu.au/programs/story-books-in-aboriginal-english. Videos accessible through YouTube. https://www.youtube.com/watch?v=2a2E695JTe8; https://www.youtube.com/watch?v=8VbZw21v0Tk; https://www.youtube.com/watch?v=nqT-J3nslRE

Department of Education of Western Australia. (2021). *Focus 2924*. education.wa.edu.au

Department of Education of Western Australia. (2022). *Quality teaching strategy and associated teaching for impact resources*. Department of Education, Western Australia, Perth. https://www.education.wa.edu.au/web/annual-report/teaching-learning-excellence and https://ecm.det.wa.edu.au/connect/resolver/view/TFIK12T000/latest/index.html

Department of Education of Western Australia. (2023). *Department of education annual report 2022-23*. Department of Education, Western Australia, Perth. https://www.education.wa.edu.au/web/annual-report/download

Departments of Education: Queensland, Western Australia, Northern Territory and New South Wales. (2013). *Capability Framework – Teaching Aboriginal and Torres Strait Islander EALD Learners*. A project initiated by the Senior Officers National Network of Indigenous Education (SONNIE), Queensland Department of Education, Training and Employment. https://education.qld.gov.au/student/Documents/capability-framework-teaching-aboriginal-torres-strait-islander-eald-learners.pdf

Disbray, S., & Loakes, D. (2013). Writing Aboriginal English & Creoles: Five case studies in Australian education contexts. *Australian Review of Applied Linguistics, 27*(3), 285–301. https://doi.org/10.1075/aral.36.3.04dis

Dovchin, S. (2020). Introduction to special issue: Linguistic racism. *International Journal of Bilingual Education and Bilingualism, 23*(7), 773–777. https://doi.org/10.1080/13670050.2020.1778630

Douglas, W. H. (1976). *The Aboriginal Languages of the South-West of Australia* (2nd ed.). Australian Institute of Aboriginal Studies.

Eades, D. (2013*). Aboriginal ways of using English*. Aboriginal Studies Press.

Eagleson, R. D., Kaldor, S., & Malcolm, I. G. (1982). *English and the Aboriginal child*. Curriculum Development Centre.

Education Department of Western Australia, Association of Independent Schools of Western Australia and Catholic Education Office of Western. (2000). *Deadly ways to learn package*. Australia Education Department of Western Australia.

Esch, E. (2011). Recognition in the context of educational diversity. In C. N. Candlin, & J. Crichton (Eds.), *Discourses of deficit*. Palgrave Macmillan.

Garcia, O., & Kleyn, K. (2016). Translanguaging theory in education. In O. Garcia, & K. Kleyn (Eds.), *Translanguaging with multilingual students: Learning from classroom moments* (pp. 10–54). Routledge.

Garcia, O., & Kleyn, K. (2019). *Translanguaging as an act of transformation in The Handbook of TESOL in K-12* (p 19). Wiley Online Books, John Wiley & Sons Ltd.

Grote, E., Oliver, R., & Rochecouste, J. (2014). Code-switching and Indigenous workplace learning: Cross-cultural competence training or cultural assimilation? In K. Dunworth, & G. Zhang (Eds.), *Critical perspectives on language education* (pp. 101–117). Springer.

Hammond, Z. (2015). *Culturally responsive teaching and the brain: Promoting authentic engagement and rigor among culturally and linguistically diverse students*. Corwin/Sage.

Heit, M., & Blair, H. (1993). Language needs and characteristics of Saskatchewan Indian and Metis students: Implications for educators. In S. Morris, K. McLeod, & M. Danesi (Eds.), *Aboriginal languages and education: The Canadian experience* (pp. 103–128). Mosaic Press.

Hodge, R., & Courts, D. C. (1981). Communication and the Teacher. Longman Cheshire.
Koch, G., & Koch, H. (1993). *Kaytetye Country, Alice Springs*. Institute for Aboriginal Development.
Konigsberg, P. (2013). Two-way bi-dialectal education in Western Australia. *Journal of International Education, 19*, 136–140.
Konigsberg, P., & Collard, G. (Eds.) (2007). *Ways of being, ways of talk*. Department of Education and Training. http://sway.office.com/d1UCdeMlRI0LCHQ1?ref=Link
Konigsberg, P., Collard, G., & McHugh, M. (Eds.) (2012). *Tracks to two-way learning*. Department of Education and Department of Training and Workforce Development, Western Australia. https://education-resources-prod.equ.com.au/programs/tracks-to-two-way-learning.
Leap, W. L. (1993). *American Indian English*. University of Utah Press.
Lindfors, J. W. (1991). *Children's language and learning* (2nd ed.). Ally and Bacon.
Lopez, S. J., & Louis, M. C. (2009). The principles of strengths-based education, *Journal of College and Character, 10*(4), 1–8. https://doi.org/10.2202/1940-1639.1041
Malcolm, I. G. (1982). Verbal interaction in the classroom. In R. D. Eagleson, S. Kaldor, & I. Malcolm (Eds.), *English and the Aboriginal child* (pp. 165–192). Curriculum Development Centre.
Malcolm, I. G. (1995). *Language and communication enhancement for two-way education*. Centre for Applied Language Research, Edith Cowan University. https://ro.ecu.edu.au/cgi/viewcontent.cgi?article=8175&context=ecuworks
Malcolm, I. G. (2002). *Aboriginal English genres in Perth*. Centre for Applied Language and Literacy Research and Institute for the Service Professions, Edith Cowan University.
Malcolm, I. G. (2018a). The representation of Aboriginal cultural conceptualisations in an adopted English. *International Journal of Language and Culture, 5*(1), 66–93.
Malcolm, I. G. (2018b). *Australian Aboriginal English: Change and continuity in an adopted language*. Mouton De Gruyter.
Malcolm, I. G., & Grote, E. (2007). Aboriginal English: Restructured variety for cultural maintenance. In G. Leitner, & I. G. Malcolm (Eds.), *The habitat of Australia's Aboriginal languages, past present and future* (pp. 153–179). Mouton de Gruyter.
Malcolm, I. G., Haig, Y., Königsberg, P., Rochecouste, J., Collard, G., Hill, A., & Cahill, R. (1999). *Towards more user-friendly education for speakers of Aboriginal English*. Centre for Applied Language and Literacy Research, Edith Cowan University.
Malcolm, I. G., Konigsberg, P., & Collard, G. (2021). Aboriginal English and responsive pedagogy in Australian education. *TESOL in Context, 29*(1), 61–93.
Malcolm, I. G., Konigsberg, P., Collard, G., Hill, A., Grote, E., Sharifian, F., Kickett, A., & Sahana, E. (2002). *Umob deadly: Recognized and unrecognized literacy skills of Aboriginal youth*. Centre for Applied Language and Literacy Research, Edith Cowan University.
Malcolm, I. G., & Rochecouste, J. (2000). Event and story schemas in Australian Aboriginal English discourse. *English World-Wide, 21*, 261–289.
National Indigenous Australian Agency. (n.d.). *Empowered communities*, Australian Government, Canberra. https://www.niaa.gov.au/indigenous-affairs/empowered-communities
Oliver, R., & Exell, M. (2020). Identity, translanguaging, linguicism and racism: The experience of Australia Aboriginal people living in a remote community. *International Journal of Bilingual Education and Bilingualism, 23*(7), 819–832. https://doi.org/10.1080/13670050.2020.1713722.
Parsons, M., Fisher, K., & Nolan, J. (2016). Alternative approaches to co-design: Insights from indigenous/academic research collaborations. *Current Opinion in Environmental Sustainability, 20*, 99–105. https://doi.org/10.1016/j.cosust.2016.07.001
Peltier, S. (2010). Facilitating language and literacy learning for students with Aboriginal English dialects. *Canadian Journal of Native Education, 32*, 114–142.
Poetsch, S. (2020). Unrecognised language teaching: Teaching Australian curriculum content in remote Aboriginal community schools. *TESOL in Context, 29*(1), 37–58. https://doi.org/10.21153/tesol2020vol29no1art1423

Purdie, N., Meiers, M., Cook, J., & Ozolins, C. (2010). *Evaluation of the Western Australian Aboriginal literacy strategy: Report to the department of education, Western Australia.* Australian Council for Educational Research [ACER]. ISBN: 978-0-86431-949 4.

Rochecouste, J., & Malcolm, I. G. (2003). *Aboriginal English genres in the Yamatji Lands of Western Australia.* Centre for Applied Language and Literacy Research, Edith Cowan University.

Rodríguez Louro, C., & Collard, G. D. (2020, June 16). 10 ways Aboriginal Australians made English their own. *The Conversation.* https://theconversation.com/10-ways-aboriginal-australians-made-english-their-own-128219

Rodriguez Louro, C., & Collard, G. (2021). Working together: Sociolinguistic research in urban Aboriginal Australia. *Journal of Sociolinguistics, 25*(5), 785–807.

Schnukal, A. (1988), *Broken: An Introduction to the creole language of Torres Strait.* Research School of Pacific & Asian Studies. Australian National University.

Sellwood, J., & Angelo, D. (2013). Everywhere and nowhere: Invisibility of Aboriginal and Torres Strait Islander contact languages in education and Indigenous language contexts. *Australian Review of Applied Linguistics, 34*(3), 250–266.

Seymour, J., & Angelo, D. (2023). Seeing the positives in assessment. Contributing to a 'literature of doing' school-based Aboriginal language revival programs. *Studies in Language Assessment, 12*(2), 168–204.

Sharifian, F., Truscott, A., Königsberg, P., Malcolm, I. G., & Collard, G. (2012). *Understanding stories my way: Aboriginal-English speaking students' (mis)understanding of school literacy materials in Australian English.* Institute for Professional Learning, Department of Education.

Siegel, J. (2010). *Second dialect acquisition.* Cambridge University Press.

Smitherman, G. (1977). *Talkin and testifying: The language of black America.* Wayne State University Press.

Steele, C., Dobinson, T., & Winkler, G. (2023). Using teacher-researcher collaborations to respond to the demands of 'real-world' EAL/D learning contexts across the curriculum. *TESOL in Context, 32*(1), 109–129.

Wigglesworth, G., Simpson, J., & Vaughan, J. (Eds.). (2018). *Language practices of Indigenous children and youth, the transition from home to school.* Palgrave MacMillan.

Xu, Y., & Fang, F. (2024). Promoting educational equity: The implementation of translanguaging pedagogy in English language education. *Educational Journal of Language Studies, 18*(1), 53.

Part IV

Learning and Teaching the Curriculum through Aboriginal and Torres Strait Islander Languages

10 Gija Curriculum at Purnululu School

*Sophia Mung, Libby Lee-Hammond,
and Rhonda Oliver*

Who we are and where we come from

Sophia Mung is a Jarlaloo woman from Gija Country where Boornoolooloo school is located. In close collaboration with Libby, she is part of the leadership team at the school and, in particular, she leads the Gija language and culture program. Libby Lee-Hammond has been principal of Boornoolooloo (Purnululu) Aboriginal Independent Community School for four years. She has worked closely with Sophia, Gija Educators – sometimes called Aboriginal Teaching Assistants (ATAs), curriculum consultants, linguists, and teachers at the school, as well as the local community to develop a curriculum and pedagogy that is most appropriate for the students at this school. Rhonda Oliver is a research academic at Curtin University where she has undertaken a number of studies about Aboriginal speakers' language use and the development of learning and teaching approaches that cater best for Aboriginal learners. She worked alongside Sophia and Libby to tell the story of Boornoolooloo School.

Introduction

Boornoolooloo (Purnululu) Aboriginal Independent Community School (PAICS) is located on Gija Country in the East Kimberley region. The small community the school is located in is Woorrerranginy, also known as Frog Hollow. The school is close to Purnululu National Park, referred to in English as the Bungle Bungles, a heritage listed tourist destination. The change in spelling from Purnululu to Boornoolooloo is a result of time spent with linguist Frances Kofod who, with others, has recently published a Gija Dictionary.

The school is owned and governed by a school board that is made up entirely of Gija people. It was founded in 1991 when it was determined that families wanted their children to learn 'both ways'. Both ways or two ways learning, as the name implies, describes a philosophical approach to learning whereby traditional, Indigenous

Australian knowledges and understandings are combined in respectful ways with those emanating from Western academic contexts (Ober, 2009). Sophia describes it as following both 'Gardiya ways' (non-Aboriginal ways) and 'our (Gija) ways'.

The motto of the school is Land, Law, Family and these three principles underpin all aspects of the school's vision, strategic plan, and day-to-day operations. This motto was developed by the Manambarram (Elders) of the community when the school first started. They wanted the children to learn and understand the strong connection between these three aspects of their culture. Firstly, they wanted their children to learn that this is the land of their ancestors, and their community has a spiritual connection to Boornoolooloo. The Elders wanted the children to learn to respect their land and to care for it. Second, they wanted the children to understand the strict kinship laws that must be adhered to and, again, the Elders wanted the children of the community to learn and follow these laws at school. This is especially important in a community made up of just seven families – albeit large and extended families. Sophia provides an example of how this is enacted: At the school, rather than calling her 'Miss' or 'Ms Mung' as would occur in many schools, she makes sure the students call her in a way that reflects their relationship with her. This depends on how they are connected via the Jarlaloo part of her family tree and so the term they use are the Gija words for 'grandmother', 'aunty', 'sister' or 'daughter' accordingly. In doing so, the importance of rich kinship connections is continually reinforced to the students. Finally, family is all important – not just because of these kinship laws, but also because of the connection and care that Gija people have for each other, and because family is the cornerstone of Gija culture. Aligning with this, and because of the interconnected relationship between language and culture, the promotion and revitalisation of their traditional language, Gija, is a fundamental starting point for teaching and learning at the school.

Although the school is small, with an enrolment of just 38 students, there are five teachers employed at the school along with a large number of local staff, including six Gija educators (ATAs). The students are grouped into three class cohorts. The *wanyanyagam* (youngest children) attend a multi-age class catering for K–2, the *welyenggem* (older children) attend a class catering for years 3–6, whilst the *nawarraram* (teenagers) attend a class catering for years 7–10. Unfortunately, and as is the case in many remote locations, those wishing to finish high school have to relocate to boarding schools in the state capital of Perth or move to other locations and board there or live with extended family members.

Contesting the curriculum

Based mostly on the results of national standardised testing (Australian Curriculum Assessment and Reporting Authority, 2017), there have been ongoing calls to address the poor educational outcomes of Australian Aboriginal students, especially for those living in regional and remote areas. At the same time, however, many have questioned the validity of using such instruments – because they are neither culturally nor linguistically appropriate (e.g., Guenther et al., 2015; Hall, 2018; Shay & Wickes, 2017; Simpson & Wigglesworth, 2018). In fact, many argue that such testing regimes only serve to perpetuate 'othering' and deficit views of Aboriginal students (Malcolm, 2001; Simpson & Wigglesworth, 2018).

Along with a number of other positive initiatives and formal declarations, at PAICS there is acknowledgement of the important and valuable inclusion of the Framework for Aboriginal Languages and Torres Strait Islander Languages in the Australian Curriculum (ACARA, 2015). Indeed, the staff at Boornoolooloo have been able to build upon this Framework to support their students. However, for those working at the coalface at PAICS it is clear that the current national curriculum does not serve Aboriginal students well. This is because it is based on a 'Western-centric' view of knowledge itself and about Australia and Australian school students. Even new policy and curricular continue to be developed in a similar way to those that preceded them (Moodie, 2018). Students who speak a language or dialect other than Standard Australian English (SAE) within their homes and community are at best marginalised and, in practice, many of those who speak English lexified creoles and dialects are often not identified as English as an Additional Language or Dialect (EAL/D) learners. Furthermore, the curriculum appears to be based on the erroneous assumption that EAL/D learners share the same cultural understandings and experiences as the 'mainstream' population. For instance, this is reflected in NAPLAN testing where authors such as Simpson and Wigglesworth (2018) show that the test measures cultural knowledge, rather than simply literacy and numeracy skills.

As the United Nations Declaration on the Rights of Indigenous Peoples (UNDRIP, 2007) states in Article 14:

Indigenous peoples have the right to establish and control their educational systems and institutions providing education in their own languages, in a manner appropriate to their cultural methods of teaching and learning.

States shall, in conjunction with indigenous peoples, take effective measures, in order for indigenous individuals, particularly children, including those living outside their communities, to have access, when possible, to an education in their own culture and provided in their own language.

Therefore, in the minds of many, including those teaching at Boornoolooloo, the National Australian curriculum and the assessment protocols that align with this are not fit for purpose for Indigenous children in remote schools. In fact, when working within the confines of the mainstream curriculum, staff at this school have found it necessary to have individual education plans for every student. This means that all children at the school are on a modified curriculum program. Whilst this is vital for meeting the needs of students, it places heavy demands on the teaching staff. To address this and to make the teaching program at Boornoolooloo not only feasible, but appropriate and relevant to who the students are and where they live, the school has embarked on an ambitious plan and program of work to reconfigure the curriculum at the school. And it is an iterative process with the teachers and leadership at the school continually seeking ways to decolonise the programs and processes that have been imposed on Gija people through the institution of schooling. By doing so, the school envisions promoting and supporting the rights of Gija children enshrined in Article 14 of UNDRIP (2007).

In the following we describe the context of this curriculum development and the practices that have been incorporated within the school.

The school context

The students at the school range in age from 4 to 16 years. They are all EAL/D learners, speaking Kriol – a variety called Gija Kriol – as their home language and as the lingua franca at school. Students are also learning to speak the traditional language Gija. Their proficiency in and exposure to SAE (outside of school) is limited.

At school the children are taught by the non-local teachers using SAE, but due to the impact of colonisation, many Gija people do not speak their traditional language and so their first language is instead Kriol. Because of this, in each classroom there is a local Kriol speaking educator working to support the students. Importantly, all the students are also taught Gija following a specific and purposefully developed curriculum that has been accepted and formally approved by Western Australia's School Curriculum and Standards Authority (SCSA) – a process that took 18 months to complete. Short lessons are conducted in Gija in every class, every day. It was decided that regular short lessons were a better approach than longer once or twice weekly lessons. The analogy for this is music practice – anyone who has learnt a musical instrument knows that frequent repeated practice is better than less regular longer practice sessions. In addition to these daily Gija lessons, each morning school starts with a whole school meeting involving staff and students which is conducted mostly in Gija language, as a language that is being revived, these daily sessions help reinforce vocabulary. These meetings have been running for some time and now the students take responsibility for leading them. At this meeting the events of the day are outlined, what the weather is like that day and other important events are discussed – as noted predominantly using the Gija language. The students are encouraged to engage in whole body listening and there is invoking of ancestors to help them during the day. As they stand up to leave and walk out, they are all farewelled in Gija with all saying *Jirrayam*.

To develop the necessary resources so that the teachers can follow the Gija language curriculum, staff at the school have worked with a teacher linguist consultant and two Gija linguists. As noted above, a Gija dictionary has recently been published, which required careful documentation of the language and related orthography. Other resources also have been developed including a Kriol alphabet that has been a collaboration with Miriwoong Language Centre. The school also hopes to develop a set of early readers in Kriol. The aim of these projects is to enhance children's early reading and to support their early acquisition of reading fluency through having texts that are written in their first language or mother tongue. This approach is supported by a vast body of literature, for example Cummins (2021) and Lo Bianco (2019) who argue that children's ability in English, mathematics, numeracy, and literacy is stronger if we also support their mother tongue.

In addition to developing a dedicated Gija language curriculum, to address the cultural needs and understanding of the students, the school also has developed and had approved a specifically developed Humanities and Social Sciences (HASS) curriculum, Arts curriculum and Science curriculum (a long process that took 12 months). These learning areas are taught in place of the usual Western Australian HASS, Science and Arts curriculum and have as their focus a Gija-centred world view. This means that some of the process strands, for example, that are followed look a little different from a Gija perspective rather than a Western/English-centric world view. An additional strand *Ngoongoo* has been added to reflect uniquely Gija knowledge and ways of learning. At the time of writing, submissions for the remaining learning areas (Health and Physical Education, Technology, English, Mathematics) are in the process of review and/or development.

All these measures have been undertaken at Boornoolooloo to reclaim culture and language by placing them at the centre of learning. In conjunction with this, the pedagogy employed at the school is integrated, multilingual, and multimodal. It is also a strength-based approach – founded on skills and knowledge that the students bring to school and then building upon this to target their needs. For example, students are regularly taken out 'on Country' – but these are not just a bush trips to have fun, rather they are excursions that involve learning about Gija ways – looking after 'Country' and each other, learning about the environment and culture and then demonstrating knowledge in a variety of ways (e.g., using artwork and writing to make books or developing bilingual videos and posters about what they know and have learnt). This also includes cultural practices embedded within the experience: One example Libby and Sophia provided was describing the cultural practice that occurs when they take all the students to the nearby water way (Frog Hollow Creek). Before new people enter the water, they must be given a *mantha* (a welcome). Even the very young students now take responsibility for this, knowing that this *mantha* must occur for everyone, including visitors. The children will take new people to the water and conduct this important welcome ceremony, speaking in Gija language to introduce the visitor to the ancestors and ask them to watch over the visitors and keep them safe in that location.

These integrated learning experiences are designed to develop student skills and understanding across the whole curriculum – in Gija, Kriol, and English, with the teaching and learning experiences bringing together learning in literacy, science, mathematics, HASS, and the arts. For instance, one project which was based on a significant local place and a Dreaming story, had the children at the school involved in learning about two species of birds (note: the program development is provided in more detail below). The story of *Thirringgenji* (Owlet Nightjar) and *Joowijgarneny* (Bowerbird) involves understanding habitats, bird behaviour in the daytime and nighttime, and ultimately the value of trust and honesty. As the whole school focus for two terms, the project was supported through a collaboration with Sharing Stories Foundation to create a digital animation of the Dreaming story and a performance related to this (see Figure 10.1).

For the performance, the students were involved in making props (costumes of birds, a bower, spears, and spearpoints) and drawing background scenes. For the documentary, the students created the sound effects, including the imagined sounds of twinkling stars and beetles crawling on the ground.

178 *Celebrating First Nations Languages and Language Learning*

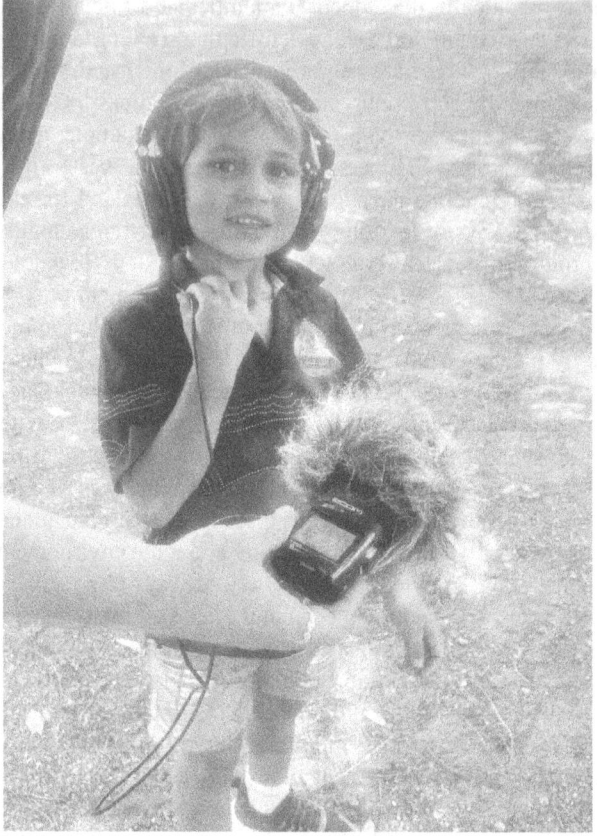

Figure 10.1 A kindy student is recording sound for the animation of the Thirringgenji doo Joowijgarneny story. Photograph by the author.

In this program and, in fact, all programs of work at the school, Gija language is always at the centre of the teaching planning process, how the assessments are set and how these are reported. The way this is approached and undertaken is illustrated in the following section using two examples of whole school programs that were based on Dreaming stories.

Dreaming stories as a foundation for learning

Dreaming stories, or stories passed down through the generations of Aboriginal peoples from the Dreaming, serve to connect people from today with their origins from the past. They are the stories explaining creation and historical events representing the spiritual and philosophical understandings of the people who hold and then tell these stories. They can be told orally, but also shared through painting, dance, and song. They are an integral part of Gija culture and language and, therefore, the passing on of these stories is an imperative for cultural and linguistic survival. Hence, at Boornoolooloo School, Dreaming stories are the foundation of the whole school curriculum, although as Libby acknowledges, it an evolving process—one they have been supported in its development by Dr Greg Vass (from Griffith University) who is part of the 'Culturally Nourishing Schools Project'. Greg has acted as a 'critical friend' to the school, offering to assist in developing processes that prioritise Gija voices in the curriculum.

As a first step in this process, the community and linguists work with school leadership and staff to determine which stories are most appropriate for children and what might be rich stories for making curriculum connections. Gija Elders are invited to share the Dreaming stories. Sophia describes how it is important to get the right people, the Traditional Owners 'who that story belongs to' to tell the story. If the story has not yet been recorded, members of the school and linguists work with these Elders, and with appropriate permission, record their stories. The school also has access, through recordings by linguists, to stories told by people who are 'no longer with us'. The next step involves having Gija staff members look at and listen to the story together. They consider what students need to know – linguistically, culturally, and also in terms of the whole curriculum. They also consider how the assessment will be undertaken. This is then shared with the non-local staff and together the curriculum connections are further refined and a plan developed that integrates all the relevant facets of the curriculum across all subject areas and at all phases of schooling. As noted above, this is an evolving process and the staff have been working to map out a cycle of Dreaming stories so that the curriculum is comprehensive and addresses all the requisite learning outcomes. In terms of delivery, short stories constitute the teaching and learning focus for a term, and longer stories continue for a semester. The following provides a description of two programs of work that have been undertaken in this way:

Thirringgenji doo Joowijgarneny: **The Owlet Nightjar and the Bower Bird story**

As noted above, this program of learning was based on this Dreaming story. In this story, *Thirrenggenji* (the Owlet Nightjar) makes *jimbarlim* (spearpoints) from *yarlgal* (white quartz). *Joowijgarneny* (the Bower Bird) sees the opportunity to steal these shiny points for decorating its bower to attract a mate. To do this, he tricks his friend into telling him when he sleeps (during the day), *Joowigarneny* sneaks up to *Thirrenggenji's* home when *Thirrenggenji* is asleep and steals the *jimbarlim*. When *Thirrenggenji* wakes to find his *jimbarlim* missing, he asks *Joowijgarneny* if he knows what happened, but his friend tells him he does not know where the *jimbarlim* has gone. The *Joowijgarneny* and *Thirrenggenji*, who were once brothers sharing the same skin, are forever estranged by this betrayal. The children at the school heard the story told to them in Gija language, they spent the semester learning the language related to the story. They wrote the story bilingually, drew and painted representations of the story. In fact, many cross-curricular aspects emerged from this story. For example, there were mathematics and science lessons related to the birds and the making of the bower and spearheads. With one of the teachers who has a music background, songs were also co-written about the story. These catchy tunes meant that children were heard singing their language throughout the day.

An organisation called the 'Sharing Stories Foundation' worked with the school to produce a very high-quality film and multitouch book about this story. A team of professional creatives worked with the school to bring the story to life through digital animation, a dramatic re-creation of the story using a green screen as well as professional recording of the songs (see Figure 10.2). The book can be found at: https://sharingstoriesfoundation.org/resource/thirringgenji-doo-joowijgarneny-the-owlet-nightjar-and-the-bowerbird/

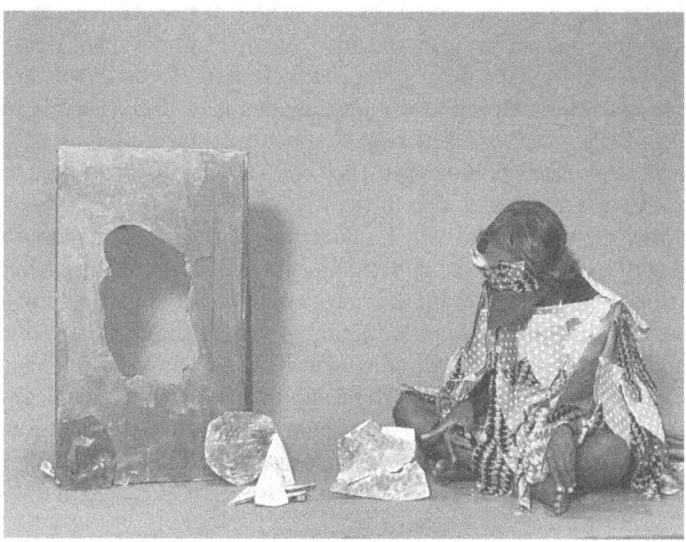

Figure 10.2 A student dramatises the Thirringgenji doo Joowijgarneny story on a green screen to create an animation. Photograph by the author.

Woorra Wooral Moonga

On the occasion of the school's 30th Anniversary, local Gija community members decided that it was an appropriate occasion to re-awaken a particular *Moonga Moonga* (women's corroboree) which had not been performed since the matriarch of the community had passed away. *Badigal 'Buttercup' Mung Mung* is the ancestor who dreamt this *Moonga Moonga*, she is also the great grandmother of many of the children who are currently attending the school. Buttercup taught other women of her generation the *Woorra Wooral* dance which consisted of eight sections or 'legs'. In this ceremony, only women and girls dance and men and boys sing. The school decided to adopt the waking up of this *Moonga Moonga* as a whole school project for a term. The school had access to film footage from the 1980s of women (including Buttercup) dancing this *Moonga Moonga* and with that as a starting point, the children began to learn the story and all the various elements it encompasses. This included language, dance, and songs related to particular locations 'on Country', and various individuals and creatures were depicted in the performance. The songs were transcribed and the children began to learn them at school. However, when it came to singing publicly, the children demonstrated a lack of confidence. The school engaged a musician from a large Kimberley town to come and do singing workshops with all the children. An Elder (Buttercup's son) also came into the school regularly and taught the children to sing the songs in the correct way. Two of Buttercup's daughters, now in their seventies, came to teach the girls the dances. The students helped make the traditional garments for the women and girls in the performance, and community artists provided artwork (known as 'boards') to accompany the dance. The garments worn by the women and girls consisted of three parts and were assembled by the girls who were engaged in some integrated mathematics learning to measure each performer and the fabric accordingly. They also had to ensure that each performer had a complete set of garments that were the right size on the day of the performance and they used various technologies to assemble the garments.

Together these different elements culminated in a cultural performance for the whole community (see Figure 10.3). The older students had to learn organisational skills for this performance – making lists, organising time schedules, and so on. It brought the community into the school, but also the school into the community, and it was a celebration of learning about culture and language.

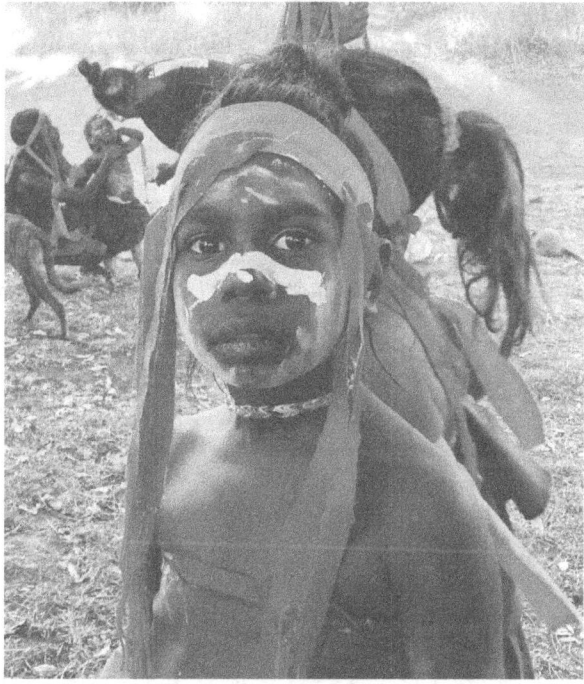

Figure 10.3 One of the Purnululu school students ready to participate in the performance of the Woora Woorral Moonga Moonga. Photograph by the author.

As a result of the success of these projects, the school decided to identify a series of stories to focus on over the next seven years and to repeat this in a seven-year cycle. These whole school projects will be the focus of the curriculum each term or semester.

Conclusion

This chapter has described an evolving approach of teaching and learning at a remote school – one based on significant input from *Manambarram* (Elders) – including their telling of traditional stories. Whilst some schools use themes for a term or project-based learning, at PAICS, Dreaming stories from Gija Country are the central organisers for curriculum from Kindergarten to Year 10. Using the processes described in this chapter, the school continues to seek ways to include Gija voices, knowledges, stories, language, and law into every aspect of its operations. It is a pedagogy that builds upon students' strengths and interests, and with the learning of Gija language and culture at the centre of all that is done. Local and non-local staff work together collaboratively to plan, teach, and assess in ways that are culturally appropriate. Its success, demonstrated by the engagement of the students, also reflects the strong involvement of the community and especially the Elders. With this approach, the school expects to see a shift in student learning outcomes in the long term. We know that students who are strong in culture are more resilient and this is a protective factor in the lives of children whose right to an education in their own language and culture is a step closer to reality in this school.

References

ACARA. (2015). Framework for Aboriginal languages and Torres Strait Islander languages. https://www.australiancurriculum.edu.au/f-10-curriculum/languages/framework-for-aboriginal-languages-and-torres-strait-islander-languages/

Cummins, J. (2021). *Rethinking the education of multilingual learners: A critical analysis of theoretical concepts*. Multilingual Matters. https://doi.org/10.21832/9781800413597

Guenther, J., Disbray, S., & Osborne, S. (2015). Building on 'Red dirt' perspectives: What counts as important for remote education? *The Australian Journal of Indigenous Education, 44*(2), 194–206.

Hall, L. (2018). 'Not looking at us level': Systemic barriers faced by Aboriginal teachers in remote communities in Central Australia. *Journal of Critical Race Inquiry, 5*(1), 74–101.

Lo Bianco, J. (2019, April). *Remarks to the Aboriginal independent community schools conference*. AISWA.

Malcolm, I. (2001). Aboriginal English: Adopted code of a surviving culture. In D. Blair, & P. Collins (Eds.), *English in Australia* (pp. 201–222). John Benjamins.

Moodie, N. (2018). Decolonising race theory: Place, survivance and sovereignty. In K. Gulson, J. Maxwell, S. Rudolph, & G. Vass (Eds.), *The relationality of race in education research* (pp. 33–46). Routledge.

Ober, R. (2009). Learning from yesterday, celebrating today, strengthening tomorrow. *The Australian Journal of Indigenous Education, 38*, 34–39.

Shay, M., & Wickes, J. (2017). 'Aboriginal identity in education settings: Privileging our stories as a way of deconstructing the past and re-imagining the future. *The Australian Educational Researcher, 44*(1), 107–122. https://doi.org/10.1007/s13384-017-0232-0.

Simpson, J., & Wigglesworth, G. (2018). Language diversity in Indigenous Australia in the 21st century. *Current Issues in Language Planning, 20*, 67–80.

United Nations (General Assembly; UNDRIP). (2007). Declaration on the Rights of Indigenous People. https://social.desa.un.org/issues/indigenous-peoples/united-nations-declaration-on-the-rights-of-indigenous-peoples

11 Content Language Integrated Learning (CLIL) for Learning Aboriginal and Torres Strait Islander Languages

Helen CD McCarthy, Jacqueline Hunter, Russell Cross, and Rhonda Oliver

---

Who we are

Helen CD McCarthy has worked with and learned from the Warnindilyakwa, Yolngu, Nyungar (Wudjari and Ngadju) First Nations peoples of Australia across primary, secondary, and tertiary settings. For over 40 years, her interest has been in bidialectal approaches for the development of holistic, emergent curriculum frameworks that venerate Indigenous epistemological traditions and ways of knowing.

Jacqueline Hunter is a proud Bardi woman. She lives in the community of Ardiyooloon (One Arm Point) in the far north of Western Australia (WA). She has worked at the local school in her community for many years and is currently completing her Bachelor of Education.

Russell Cross is based in the Faculty of Education at the University of Melbourne and is the coordinator of their CLIL Teacher Education Lab. His background is in bilingual education and immersion, with his research focusing on the social, cultural, historical, and political nature of the knowledge base that informs second language teacher education.

Rhonda Oliver's family has been in Australia since at least colonisation. She originally trained as a primary school teacher and then quickly moved into ESL teaching and worked in schools for more than a decade before becoming an academic. She now works at Curtin University in the School of Education as a research professor.

Introduction

In a curriculum that is already crowded, it can be hard for schools and individual teachers to provide sufficient space to address the needs of their students adequately. Explicit opportunities for language learning are often limited, be these foreign languages or English in contexts where students come to school with non-English language backgrounds or, of particular relevance to this chapter, the traditional languages of Aboriginal and Torres Strait Islander students. Instead, what is common is for languages targeted for teaching to be shoehorned into restricted periods within the timetable, resulting in a limited language program often positioned as an 'add-on' to other school priorities. Such an approach means that language learning is often isolated and disconnected from the rest of the curriculum, making it difficult for students to develop their understanding of new content while also restricting their meaning-making in the target language (i.e., the language being taught at school). In this case, the target language is Bardi which is the traditional language of the Ardiyooloon community, although at present, mostly only Elders speak it.

This seems to be a lost opportunity: Learning language while learning content can provide teachers with an efficient and flexible way to achieve two tasks simultaneously with one single action. Furthermore, teaching traditional Aboriginal and Torres Strait Islander languages (which can be some students' home languages) and bringing the related cultural knowledge into the classroom has enormous academic, social, and emotional benefits, especially for students from these backgrounds (Angelo & Carter, 2015; Oliver et al., 2021). It signals explicit support for their language and culture, strengthening their identity. The importance of this lies in the association between a strong sense of identity and academic success (Purdie et al., 2011). When learners feel their language and culture are supported and valued (and, where possible, incorporated into the curriculum), their attitude to learning and schooling is generally positive. Similarly, in some countries, the language of instruction is foreign to most learners. For example, in Mozambique, which has 20 distinct first languages, Portuguese is adopted as the official language in schools (Coyle et al., 2010). As the language of instruction is far removed from the students' lived life experiences, it is estimated that 75 per cent of children fail school (Heugh, 2000). As a result, content and language-integrated approaches have become an instrumental paradigm 'providing a pragmatic response towards overcoming linguistic shortcomings and in promoting equal access to education' (Coyle et al., 2010, p. 7). Wilson et al. (2019) suggest that supporting language and cultural identity encourages the development of positive self-efficacy and resilience, and together, these promote positive educational and later employment outcomes.

Incorporating traditional languages into classroom teaching is particularly important for those students who may speak a traditional language at home or who may not speak it but are exposed to it through their cultural background and extended family. It has long been known that strength in the first language (and dialect) enhances success in second language achievement. As early as 1976 (and again in 2000), Cummins described the interrelationship between language learners' first or home language and their second language learning, and in particular, how the strength in the former supports success in the latter. This is particularly important in the Australian context where, for example, Aboriginal and Torres Strait Islander students come to school speaking a dialect (e.g., Aboriginal English) or language (e.g., Kriol or a traditional language) that is not Standard Australian English, and yet for academic success, they need to learn and then operate in this 'new' language. Therefore, providing opportunities to strengthen home language at school is advantageous not only because of affective factors (identity, self-efficacy, and attitudes as described above) but also because it can have a direct impact on the learning and use of English.

However, to date, it seems that many schools do not regularly engage as well as they could in identity-affirming approaches for Aboriginal and Torres Strait Islander students (Shay & Sarra, 2021), such as teaching traditional/home languages. What is more common within the Indigenous education space is for deficit discourses to be predominant (Patrick & Moodie, 2016), with the focus being on what students cannot do rather than what they can, particularly with respect to language and literacy. This is exacerbated by a curriculum that privileges Standard Australian English over other languages and dialects and where bilingualism/bidialectalism and plurilingualism are constructed as the exceptions and monolingualism as the norm (Nguyen et al., 2014). There is a need to counter how these attitudes manifest in education, and we suggest that Content Integrated Language Learning (CLIL) might provide a way forward. Not only does it allow for the inclusion and support of home language and cultural teaching, but it also enables teachers to simultaneously teach curriculum content.

What is CLIL?

Although the term Content and Language Integrated Learning (CLIL) emerged in the mid-1990s (Marsh & Frigols Martín, 2013), Coyle et al. (2013) reason, 'CLIL is not a new form of language education. It is not a new form of subject education. It is an innovative fusion of both' (p. 10). CLIL is an approach that simultaneously teaches a 'new' language alongside the teaching of new knowledge and skills drawn from other content-based areas of the curriculum. In Australia, for example, CLIL is most often used for teaching foreign languages, such as in Oliver et al. (2019), where Mandarin is used as the language of instruction for teaching science and mathematics to mostly English-speaking background students. Their study found that not only did students acquire Mandarin with greater success than in traditional foreign language classes, but their mathematics and science learning and even their English literacy achievements were enhanced (as demonstrated in the school's National Assessment Program in Literacy and Numeracy [NAPLAN] results).

Although CLIL shares much in common with the Canadian immersion approach and dual language schooling in the United States of America, a key point of difference is that CLIL is less about how bilingual provision is organised at a *structural* or programmatic level (i.e., how much of the curriculum is delivered in the target language, or how language use is distributed by curriculum area, teacher, schedule, or even physical spaces within the school (e.g., Muñoz-Muñoz & Briceño, 2021), than the *pedagogic practices* that occur within such settings. This has enabled CLIL to be taken up across a wide range of contexts as it is less about structural needs at a whole-of-school or even program level than decisions made at the level of instructional practice between teacher and students. Similarly, in effective immersion classrooms, many (if not all) of the aspects that comprise what can be understood as 'CLIL pedagogy' are often present, arising from the need to meet the academic demands of the curriculum while using a language that is not the student's first language.

This understanding of CLIL as a pedagogic model is informed by Coyle et al. (2010): Coyle's (2006) 4C's framework comprising content, communication, culture, and cognition to identify 'what' specific learning demands emerge when content and language are brought together as a dual instructional focus since both are new for the learner. Content is subject matter derived from non-language areas of the curriculum—such as concepts and skills from science, history, or music—which drives decisions about the language needed to access and express knowledge that it relates to (i.e., the communication element of the 4Cs framework; Llinares et al., 2012), the kinds of thinking that demonstrate an ability to internalise and use the knowledge gained (cognition; Dalton-Puffer, 2013), and the assumptions at work in how both the language and content are mobilised appropriately to the norms of the language users, the discipline, and the classroom community (culture) (Cross, 2023).

While the 4Cs help determine 'what' needs to be planned for, scaffolded, and assessed to support and evidence learners' development of both language and content, a related set of pedagogic principles (Coyle et al., 2010) provide guidance for 'how' these demands can be met in practice, and the kinds of quality teaching and learning experiences that support dual-instructional goals. Although somewhat abstract (see Coyle et al., 2010, p. 42 for full discussion), the essence of the principles is teaching focused on providing interaction between teachers and other peers through tasks that are *thinking-based,* with support to then express the knowledge being constructed together—learning—through explicitly modelled language. While communicative language teaching focuses on learning how to read, write, listen, and speak in the target language, this focus on 'knowledge building through talk' (Coyle & Meyer, 2021) means CLIL is perhaps better understood as '*concept-driven* language instruction' (Cross, 2021), with the primary instructional focus being to develop the learners' skills to *think* in the new language.

The unique demands of working with new knowledge in a new language lead to final tools helpful for specifically unpacking the *communication* dimension of the 4Cs further—the 'language triptych' (Figure 11.1).

Language *of* learning is language that expresses the content being studied (e.g., 'subtraction', 'fraction', or 'x groups of y make z' in mathematics; or 'bunsen burner', 'taxonomy', or 'a is caused by b' in science), while language *for* learning is the language needed to engage in classroom activities as learners. Although the

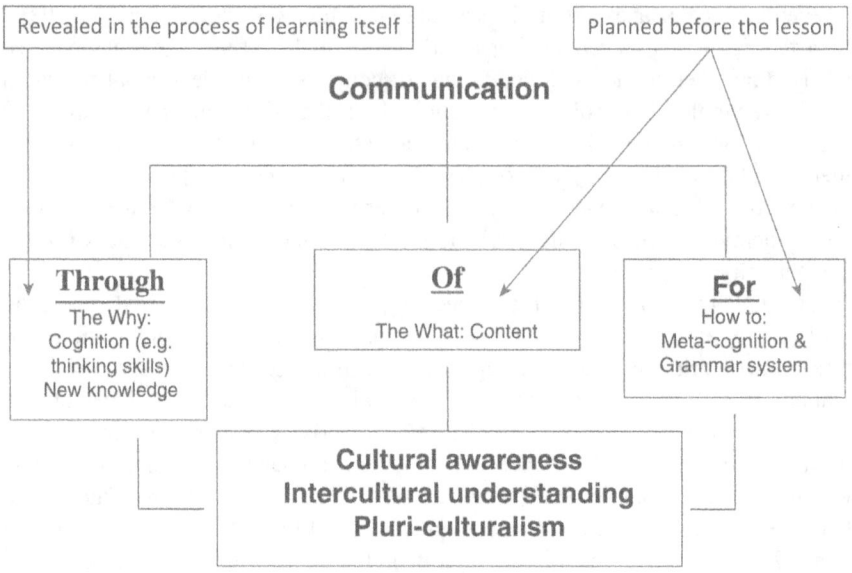

Figure 11.1 CLIL language triptych (adapted from Coyle, 2007).

latter tends to be more generic as it can apply across content areas (e.g., 'Can I check what you mean?', 'Let's think of x options', etc.), it may also have content-specific characteristics, such as 'What do you estimate the total will be close to?' for a task in mathematics, or 'Label the diagram' in science. Both language of and for learning can—and should—be planned before the lesson as they help identify language to be scaffolded and assessed to support and show evidence of learning. In contrast, language *through* learning is not identified before the lesson but is revealed in the process of learning itself. It is language that emerges as students grapple with engaging in the content and couched in terms such as 'How do I say…?', 'Does this mean…?', and 'What do you call …?'. Although it cannot be planned for as an intentional instructional intervention, being aware of this language is significant as it points to 'what to teach next'. Language through learning is an indication of where students are at in relation to their current limits of learning, or zone of proximal development, as suggested by the Vygotskian (Vygotsky, 1978) understandings of learning that underpin CLIL's core pedagogic principles discussed above.

To summarise, the power of CLIL is its flexibility as a bilingual instructional approach that is highly adaptable to different settings, reliant on not having to establish structural conditions at a whole-of-school level but on how teaching and learning are approached at the level of instructional practice. Therefore, the framework and tools offer significant potential, in theory, for working with any language in any context where learning and teaching are at play. Research has demonstrated its success in Australian schools across different settings and world languages (Cross, 2013, 2015). However, the question remains as to what extent these same ideas help understand ways of working with curriculum content and Australian Indigenous languages. This is particularly the case given the need for instructional models that successfully engage Aboriginal learners in using their languages—this is vital for their long-term revitalisation. In the remainder of this chapter, we explore this question.

CLIL as a theoretical and pedagogical approach for language learning and teaching Aboriginal and Torres Strait Islander languages

In this next section, we use a case study as an illustrative example of how CLIL is being used in a remote Aboriginal community in Western Australia. We show how it can be used to facilitate students' learning of the Bardi language, Bardi Jawi culture, and science through a two-way approach to learning.

Case study

Bardi Jawi—Saltwater People of Ardiyooloon

One Arm Point Community or Ardiyooloon (pronounced AR-dee-yoo-loon) is on the Dampier Peninsula in the Kimberley Region of Western Australia. The Bardi Jawi people (also known as the 'Saltwater people') have lived there for millenniums, and they remain deeply connected to their land, sky, and sea country, nourished by their cultural and language traditions learned from their ancestors. Living in harmony with the cyclic six seasons, daily life continues to be governed by changes in the weather. In turn the seasons influence what is happening in the life cycle of the endemic plants and animals. Together, this environmental and ecological information lets the local people know such things as when certain plants flower, the fish are fat and ready to eat. Sharing this knowledge by reading their Country's meteorological, marine, and terrestrial signs (noting some seasons last only a few weeks), family groups have thrived for thousands of years living on and by the azure waters of the peninsula.

In 1899, a mission was established on Sunday Island (Iwanyi)—approximately seven kilometres east of One Arm Point, later affiliated with the United Aborigines Mission (UAM). With the arrival of the missionaries, life changed. When the mission was closed in 1960, many Bardi Jawi people moved between Sunday Island and the mainland, with families living between Derby and Lombadina. By the late 1960s, people began to move back to One Arm Point, and by the early 1970s, a small school under a bough shelter was erected on Middle Beach. These days, Bardi Jawi people's culture and language are embedded in the school curriculum, which integrates Aboriginal ways of being, doing, and knowing.

Aboriginal ways of being, doing, and knowing

Kickett-Tucker (1999) describes Aboriginal ways of being, doing, and knowing as '…working in groups, cooperation, sharing common group goals and learning by observation, an understanding of the real-life significance of school-based learning, and jovial social interactions in the learning environment' (as cited in Gray & Partington, 2003, p. 147). Amagula and McCarthy (2021, p. 204) describe it this way:

> By living in the community and knowing the backgrounds and real-life experiences children brought with them to the learning environments, meant that teachers can build on this richness and upon the students' passions, interests and ways they like to learn.

For students, school attendance is desirable when it means being 'with your mob' in intergenerational family groups, participating in collaborative, practical 'hands-on' learning, speaking, co-constructing, and sharing knowledge in a familiar language, which provides '… a communal and non-hierarchical place where learning occurs within an appropriate negotiated space and within realistic timeframes in ways that are attentive to cyclical and/or seasonal variations' (McCarthy, 2019, p. 93). Today, the ease of this style of engagement is strongly reflected in the relationship between the local Bardi Jawi teachers and the students, where the learning milieu is personal and egalitarian. Furthermore, the school embraces 'two-way learning' in both the Bardi language/Bardi Jawi culture and English. This is reflected in the school's vision statement:

> …to facilitate a welcoming, safe and stimulating inclusive environment where Aboriginal culture is embraced, celebrated and embedded into the school curriculum. Students are supported and encouraged to reach their academic potential and staff are committed to helping students become strong, proud and resilient members of society.
> (One Arm Point Remote Community School Plan, 2019, p. 1)

This statement has been used to inform the Community School Plan supported by the school's Aboriginal Education Manager, Jacqueline Hunter. In addition to this role, Jacqueline also teaches Bardi Language. Aligned with the Bardi Language Program is a two-way science program that she, Elders, and Bardi Jawi Rangers work together to deliver. The Rangers help by delivering cultural activities, including art, spear making and throwing, hunting and cooking, as well as participating in excursions around the community and to local beaches and reefs. Regular cultural days are also facilitated by local Aboriginal staff and local community members. The success of these learning opportunities is founded upon the whole-school collaborative processes of developing school plans and policies that, in turn, facilitate the capacity building of developing a working School and Community Partnership Agreement.

Bardi language and two-way science classes

As indicated above, Jacqueline has integrated the Bardi Language Program with a two-way science program. The foundation of these programs is the teaching of language, kinship systems, culture, and ecological knowledge by local Aboriginal people (i.e., Elders and Rangers) to the students 'On Country' (i.e., on their traditional lands). This has resulted in integrated, culturally responsive learning that connects the *Western Australian Curriculum: Science* to Aboriginal language and knowledges.

As part of the two-way science program, the students explore the interdependence of sea birds, sea creatures, and marine and terrestrial ecosystems, with most of the learning occurring in and through the Bardi language. With the other local people, Jacqueline works to encourage lots of talking, which is important for the students as they learn about these science topics but also as they learn Bardi. They are encouraged to spend a lot of time observing, recording, measuring or counting, and discussing what they see in their environment. Jacqueline and Bardi Jawi Rangers make sure to highlight the language most useful to the content they are teaching (e.g., the names of the seasons, plants, and animals; words used to describe changes that occur in these and in their environments). In doing so, they draw the student's attention to the language needed to discuss the content of the different science topics.

Within the Bardi Language Program, speaking also has real-life communicative purposes. Again, this is facilitated by the children participating in 'hands-on' science activities. These activities help to make language learning interactive and cooperative, with the learning occurring in pairs or small groups and with the students supporting each other. At the same time, as they share their language and cultural knowledge, Elders from the community and the Rangers are also able to assist the students. For instance, they may do such things as demonstrating the different parts of the land, sky, and sea country, showing what plants, animals, and insects may look like or what they may be doing. They also model key skills such as 'close' listening to and observations of the environment, but at the same time, they also highlight key science terms and language. For example, they may point out to the students changes in the wind direction, the different amount and type of rain that comes, what grasses are growing, and what different insects and animals have appeared. They will also do things such as peeling off the bark of certain trees to show what is happening underneath. When they do these types of things, they encourage the students to 'hypothesise' about why these changes might occur and then, based on their observations, make recordings of what they see and hear and then provide possible explanations for why these changes might happen.

Technologies play an important role in this program, too. In conjunction with the Bardi Jawi Rangers as future custodians, the young people learn to use equipment to record and explore elements of their environments. As a first step, they may use Google Maps to pinpoint the places they are going with the Rangers and then check this against tidal information to make sure it is a safe time to go (e.g., because of the expansive tidal movements and speed of currents, etc.). They use cameras to take still and video recordings of what they see, including underwater cameras to record their observations. They incrementally progress to using sophisticated marine and terrestrial-monitoring equipment such as secchi discs to measure ocean turbidity and Baited Remote Underwater Video Systems (BRUVS) to measure fish stocks. All this information is combined so that digital technologies can be used to keep a record of longitudinal changes. Together, the digital data collected by the students is being used to help protect and maintain the sustainability of their land and sea country.

This real-life and contextual meaningful learning (that is done using Bardi) also aligns closely to the mathematics and particularly the science curriculum. For instance, after making recordings using different technologies, when the students are back at school, they translate this information into such things as bar graphs to show the results, and they draw detailed images and pictures to further illustrate what they saw using the underwater cameras. Again, using Bardi language as the language of instruction, they then discuss the outcomes and what this may mean to their environments in the future and what can be planned now to help protect their Country. Building upon this, they undertake research online and use their iPads to explore what is happening in other communities so that they may utilise these ideas in their own communities.

While these learning activities occur as part of science and the Bardi Language Program, the students often demonstrate a transfer of these skills into other subject areas. For example, in literacy lessons, when writing their own stories, they will often insert Bardi words, especially about local plants and animals. In this way, they can build upon their deep cultural knowledge and what they have learned in the Bardi Language/two-way science program to enhance their literacy learning. Similarly, they bring their observations from their science learning into their artwork—representing their heightened environmental and cultural awareness as part of their art—both in their drawings and paintings. Jacqueline described a specific example of how a recent class experience demonstrated the transference of learning across the curriculum: The students had read a book about turtles written by an Aboriginal author from another community. The students followed the model of this book to write their own class book, bringing to the task abundant knowledge they had learnt about their environment and about their Bardi Jawi culture. During the writing of this text, many of the students moved fluidly between Bardi and English because they could draw on their deep-level understanding both about the content and the language associated with it. Furthermore, when illustrating their book, they were able to apply their observational skills and knowledge about their environment to provide detailed accounts of the turtles' habitat.

In the following, Jacqueline provides a detailed account of one unit of work that forms part of the Bardi Language/two-way science program around the six seasons to show how these two programs provide strong and integrated learning opportunities.

Bringing in local content and language integrated learning: How it is done

Learning the Bardi Jawi six seasons

At the beginning of this unit of work, the children listened to the story of the six seasons, told by the Elders. The story about the six seasons was embedded in ancestorial contexts, an explanation passed down from the Dreaming about why creation has occurred in the way that it has. Culturally, this is a very important story because daily community life and its activities in Ardiyooloon (e.g., hunting and gathering actions) differ according to the seasons.

Students were then given the Bardi Six Seasons Chart. This is a local resource designed specifically for oral and written Bardi language revival. When the students used this chart, they were encouraged to remember the six seasons: Ngaladany, Irralboo, Barrgana, Jalalay, Lalin, and Mankal.

These seasons are described and discussed, particularly in relation to community life. For example, Ngaladany is the hot and humid season that comes at the end of the Wet Season, where there is no wind and no fruit, and it is a time when nature moves very little. Jalalay is the short warming-up season with prevailing West winds. With the low tides comes a good feed of oysters, clam shells, and mussels on the reefs.

They then watched a documentary showing the Bardi/Jawi Rangers 'On Country' walking and talking their way through the different seasons. The students then came together, sharing their ideas with partners, choosing one of the six seasons to illustrate what was happening across the marine and terrestrial ecosystems, and reporting on all the food and animal cycles using Bardi. Elders and Rangers then worked alongside the students to demonstrate the different indicators of each season (plants, animals, and insects). This is also supported by other local resources.

The students recorded what they found using their own words, drawings, and/or photographs. Next, they shared the season they documented with others in the class, describing what they found out about it and what it means to live so interconnected to their community, creating an understanding of the real-life significance of school-based learning.

This was followed by other field trips to land and sea country to provide further opportunities for students to hear and use the Bardi language introduced by the Elder and Rangers and by their teacher, Jacqueline. When they went out 'On Country', the students were encouraged to listen and observe carefully. For instance, they were asked to focus on the changes in the winds, and the rain, what grasses are growing (or not), what stage of change (metamorphosis) insects like dragonflies are in and how these all differ according to the season. On returning to class, the students shared what they learnt, both orally and in writing.

In this unit, as in others, Jacqueline used a mix of formative and summative assessments. For instance, she used task-based assessment (Were the students able to find a community with similar seasons to Ardiyooloon?) and assignment-based (Were the students able to make a collage poster/digital infographic about a chosen season?). She also observed their contributions during 'On Country' lessons to see if they demonstrated learning. Jacqueline also collected anecdotal records, made observations about students' engagement, and encouraged student self-evaluations. She has also experimented with peer assessments (e.g., at the end of the presentations about the different seasons, students gave feedback about how informative it had been). Finally, she has also undertaken oral interviews in real-life contexts in a culturally appropriate, student-friendly manner to ascertain individual student achievement in Bardi.

Conclusion

The depth of understanding and depth of local knowledge gained from being taught in two or more languages cannot be understated. It is also the reason why many disenfranchised Indigenous communities are taking ownership of two-way learning as a decolonising strategy to establish culturally safe places for their children to learn and for their Indigenous knowledge systems to be given parity of esteem. Doing it this way, students can demonstrate the success of the language program by using their full linguistic repertoire. They are able to think about culture and use language through social interaction, which is integral to deep, rich, real-life learning, and CLIL provides a framework for this to occur.

Using a Bardi Language/two-way science program, Jacqueline has implemented a program that closely aligns with the 4C's framework of CLIL: content, communication, culture, and cognition. She has been able to engage members of the community in its delivery and have the students learn about their environment, culture, and language both in the classroom and, importantly, 'On Country'. This has resulted in integrated and culturally responsive learning. Finally, by taking this approach, she is able to foster not only her students' active engagement with meaningful learning experiences but also be able to bring back the traditional ways of integrating the community's profound kinship systems connection to Country with the school and its learning programs.

References

Amagula, J., & McCarthy, H. C. D. (2021). Red ochre women: sisters in the struggle for educational reform. In M. Shay & R. Oliver (Eds.), *Indigenous Education in Australia* (pp. 202–214). Routledge.

Angelo, D., & Carter, N. (2015). Schooling within shifting landscapes: Educational responses in complex Indigenous language contact ecologies. In A. Yiakoumetti (Ed.), *Multilingualism and language education. Sociolinguistic and pedagogical perspectives from Commonwealth countries* (pp. 119–140). Cambridge University Press.

Coyle, D. (2006). Developing CLIL: Towards a theory of practice. In N. Figueras (Ed.), *CLIL in Catalonia: From theory to practice* (pp. 5–29). APAC.

Coyle, D. (2007). Content and language integrated learning: Towards a connected research agenda for CLIL pedagogies. *International Journal of Bilingual Education and Bilingualism, 10*(5), 543–562.

Coyle, D., Hood, P., & Marsh, D. (2010). *CLIL*. Cambridge University Press.

Coyle, D., Hood, P., & Marsh, D. (2013). *CLIL: Content and language integrated learning*. Cambridge University Press.

Coyle, D., & Meyer, O. (2021). *Beyond CLIL*. Cambridge University Press.

Cross, R. (2013). Research and evaluation of the content and language integrated learning (CLIL) approach to teaching and learning languages in Victorian schools. Victorian Department of Education and Early Childhood Development. https://minerva-access.unimelb.edu.au/items/0047a915-237d-5502-9bd4-3846d2a0074c

Cross, R. (2015). Defining content and language integrated learning for languages education in Australia. *Babel, 49*(2), 4–15.

Cross, R. (2021, August 18). *Travelling pedagogies: Resituating the knowledge base for CLIL professional learning across contexts* [Featured presentation, Virtual Symposium 170 Part 1, The dynamics and challenges of teacher education for immersion and CLIL contexts: Preparing teachers to integrate language and content]. World Congress for Applied Linguistics, AILA 2021, Groningen, The Netherlands. Retrieved from https://aila2021.dryfta.com/component/dryfta/program/detail/155/s170-1-2-the-dynamics-and-challenges-of-teacher-education-for-immersion-and-clil-contexts-preparing-teachers-to-integrate-language-and-content

Cross, R. (2023). Addressing social equity by making explicit the implicit value systems within content and language learning: A pedagogical framework for culture within CLIL. *AILA Review, 35(2)*, 180–202.

Cummins, J. (1976). The influence of bilingualism on cognitive growth: A synthesis of research findings and explanatory hypotheses. *Working Papers on Bilingualism, 9*, 1–43.

Cummins, J. (2000). *Language, power, and pedagogy: Bilingual children in the crossfire: Volume 23.* Multilingual Matters.

Dalton-Puffer, C. (2013). A construct of cognitive discourse functions for conceptualising content-language integration in CLIL and multilingual education. *European Journal of Applied Linguistics, 1*(2), 1–38.

Gray, J., & Partington, G. (2003). Attendance and non-attendance at school. In Q. Beresford & G. Partington (Eds.), *Reform and resistance in Aboriginal education: The Australian experience.* University of Western Australia.

Heugh, K. (2000). *The case against bilingual education and multilingual education in South Africa.* PRAESA.

Kickett-Tucker, C. (1999). School sport self-concept of urban Aboriginal school children: teacher influences, AARE – NZARE National Conference, Melbourne, 29 November– 2 December 1999.

Llinares, A., Morton, T., & Whittaker, R. (2012). *The roles of language in CLIL.* Cambridge University Press.

Marsh, D., & Frigols Martín, M. J. (2013). Content and Language Integrated Learning. In *The Encyclopedia of Applied Linguistics.* https://doi.org/10.1002/9781405198431.wbeal0190

McCarthy, H. C. D. (2019). Learning by design: Crafting the knowledge processes to enable pre-service secondary teachers to design authentic learning. In T. Dobinson & K. Dunworth (Eds.), *Literacy unbound: Multiliterate, multilingual, multimodal* (pp. 87–111). Springer.

Muñoz-Muñoz, E. R., & Briceño, A. (2021). It is not if, but when: Organizational and leadership recommendations for the upcoming demand for expanded DL programs and their articulation. *Journal of Leadership, Equity, and Research, 7*(3), 1–15.

Nguyen, B., Oliver, R., & Rochecouste, J. (2014). Embracing plurality through oral language. *Language and Education, 29*(2), 97–111. https://doi.org/10.1080/09500782.2014.977294

Oliver, R., Angelo, D., Steele, C., & Wigglesworth, J. (2021). Translanguaging possibilities and pitfalls for language teaching. *Language Teaching Research, 25*(1), 134–150. https://doi.org/10.1177/1362168820938822

Oliver, R., Sato, M., Ballinger, S., & Pan, L. (2019). Content and Language Integrated Learning classes for child Mandarin L2 learners: A longitudinal observational study. In M. Sato & S. Loewen (Eds.), *Evidence-based Second Language pedagogy: A collection of Instructed Second Language Acquisition studies* (pp. 81–102). Routledge.

One Arm Point Remote Community School Plan. (2019). Western Australian Department of Education Schools Online. https://www.det.wa.edu.au/schoolsonline/school_planning.do?schoolID=5583&pageID=AD25

Patrick, R., & Moodie, N. (2016). Indigenous education policy discourses in Australia: Rethinking the 'problem'. In T. Barkatsas & A. Betrtem (Eds.), *Global learning in the 21st century* (pp. 163–184). Brill.

Purdie, N., Milgate, G., & Bell, H. R. (2011). *Two way teaching and learning: Toward culturally reflective and relevant education*. ACER Press. https://research.acer.edu.au/indigenous_education/38

Shay, M., & Sarra, G. (2021). Locating the voices of Indigenous young people on identity in Australia: An Indigenist analysis. *Diaspora, Indigenous and Minority Education, 15*(3), 166–179. https://doi.org/10.1080/15595692.2021.1907330

Vygotsky, L. S. (1978). *Mind in society*. Harvard University Press.

Wilson, B., Abbott, T., Quinn, S. J., Guenther, J., McRae-Williams, E., & Cairney, S. (2019). Empowerment is the basis for improving education and employment outcomes for Aboriginal people in remote Australia. *Australian Journal of Indigenous Education, 48*(2), 153–161. https://doi.org/10.1017/jie.2018.2.

Part V

Learning, Teaching, and Assessing Learning in Standard Australian English for Speakers of Aboriginal and Torres Strait Islander Languages

12 Aboriginal and Torres Strait Islander Students' Language and Learning through a Both Ways Approach

Robyn Ober

Who I am and where I come from

I am Dr. Robyn Ober, a Mamu/Djirribal woman from North Queensland and a Lead Researcher at Batchelor Institute, Northern Territory. My association with Batchelor Institute spans over three decades. I have been at the front line of the development of both-ways pedagogy, working to combine Indigenous and non-Indigenous ways of knowing, being, and learning in teaching practice and in research. I work in the fields of Indigenous educational leadership and both-ways teaching and learning, and my work has appeared in journals, and national reports and has been presented at conferences. I have been called upon numerous times to consult about education delivery, both-ways education, and Indigenous research methodologies in national and international Indigenous educational contexts.

In 1983, I began my teacher education training at Batchelor College (former name of Batchelor Institute), where I was introduced to the philosophy and practice of both-ways education. This approach helped me to reflect on my own language story, which contrasted with most students who fluently spoke their traditional languages and variations of Aboriginal Kriol/s. I was the total opposite, speaking English as my first language, and coming from an urban, North Queensland township with very little knowledge of my people and our traditional practices and languages. I felt I was a minority in the large student cohort and would often fall silent when asked about my language and cultural background during classes. I eventually learnt about Australian Aboriginal English (AAE) and how it is the first language for the majority of Aboriginal people because of horrific historical government policies that prevented and penalised the speaking of traditional Aboriginal languages. Jagera and Dulingbara linguist, the late Dr. Jeanie Bell, wrote extensively on the emergence and evolvement of Aboriginal English especially in south-east Queensland. Dr. Bell states that, 'because of the devasting effects of colonisation on blackfellas in this

> country – through disease, murder and other forms of attempted genocide over the past 200 years – our language and culture has taken on a different shape and form' (Bell, 2002, p. 43). Today I proudly state that AAE is my first language with strong linguistic influences from Far North Queensland and Top End Darwin Aboriginal English varieties.

Introduction

As with many children from diverse cultural societies, Aboriginal children have a rich and varied linguistic repertoire, with language skills they have developed from interacting within their communities. Aboriginal and Torres Strait Islander children enter the Australian school system strong in these first languages that they learn from their parents, family, and community members. The children develop their first languages by observing, mimicking, listening to, and interacting with family members through baby and toddler speech before moving onto pre-schooler talk. Prior to entering an early childhood classroom environment, they may have learnt to speak traditional Aboriginal or Torres Strait Islander languages, creoles (e.g., Kimberley Kriol) and/or diverse varieties of AAE. They may draw on several languages and dialects to communicate in appropriate ways and in various contexts, for different audiences and purposes. That is, their language use will vary depending on who they are communicating with at home, in their community, and later at school. When they enter the school system, these are the languages they are comfortable with, and strong and confident to use when speaking.

AAE is the most common dialect used by Australian Aboriginal people (also see Chapter 9, this volume). In fact, it is the first language used by most Aboriginal people living in urban Australia, but also others living in regional areas. Ober and Bell (2012) state that 'this form of communication is rich, highly structured and a complex form of the English language and it is widely appropriated in the social and cultural domains of Aboriginal people' (p. 60). In addition to AAE, there are Aboriginal people, especially those living in remote communities who speak a traditional language. They are called traditional languages because these were some of approximately 250 languages spoken 'in this country (Australia) before the British invasion' (Eades, 1993, p. 2). Sadly, there are not many (approximately 12) still being learnt as a first language. Horrific historical encounters have meant that most Indigenous Australian languages have been intentionally silenced. However, Bell (2002) points out that whilst Aboriginal languages have not survived intact, some have survived but in 'varying degrees of healthiness' (p. 43).

Aboriginal and Torres Strait Islander creole languages developed from early contact languages in Australia. 'A creole is generally said to be a pidgin which has become the mother-tongue of a speech community' (O'Donnell & Todd, 1980, p. 44) (see Chapters 7 and 8, this volume for discussion of creoles). Pidgin English emerged as a contact language for Aboriginal people and other social groups such as Chinese miners, Japanese divers in the Torres Strait, white pastoralists, missionaries, settlers, and migrants who because of life's circumstances lived and work together. Although Aboriginal people were competent in multiple traditional languages, because of colonisation, they had to develop a common language to communicate with non-Aboriginal people. Therefore, pidgin English or what some still refer to as 'broken English' emerged as the *lingua franca* for Aboriginal and non-Aboriginal people. Pidgin English then developed into varieties of Aboriginal creoles, which are now recognised as the first languages for many Aboriginal people especially those who reside in northern Australia. Creoles are not specific to Australia, but are spoken world-wide, and depending on the speech and linguistic communities, are often English or French based due to the former colonial expansion of these countries. The spelling of Kriol is different from the general term creole, and is used to identify a specific Northern Australian Aboriginal creole. There are regional varieties that range from heavy to light Kriol, with inclusion of traditional language words, terms, and jargons that align to specific speech communities located within particular regions.

Today, along with Aboriginal English and traditional languages, Kriol is recognised as the first language for many young Aboriginal children entering school from remote, regional, and rural areas across Australia. There are also many children who are multilingual with varying degrees of competency in their various languages and dialects. It is important to note that when Aboriginal children enter school, the language that is predominately spoken and used for teaching and learning is SAE, which is often a new language for many young Aboriginal and Torres Strait Islander children, especially those living in regional and remote areas. Understandably this can impact their learning and their self-identity and well-being.

Language and learning

Language, culture, identity, and learning go hand in hand in an integrated and interrelated way. 'Aboriginal English is no exception, one cannot do one without the other, these cultural traits are tightly embedded and intertwined to express meaning in a particular social and cultural context' (Ober, 2009, p. 38). Therefore, it is imperative that educators seriously consider the social, cultural, and linguistic repertoires of their students across all levels of education – from young children, to secondary and even, tertiary students.

One way to incorporate students' backgrounds in teaching is through a 'strengths-based approach' (Lopez & Louis, 2009). This is achieved by recognising the capability of students and by drawing on and building upon their own cultural perspectives, positionings, and intellectual capital in the classroom. Such an approach also considers the students' rich, cultural, and linguistic heritage and knowledge systems. It is important that educators recognise these aspects as their students' foundational knowledge base, weaving in relevant cultural content when planning and delivering the curriculum. This way of teaching not only enables students to draw on their own social, cultural, and linguistic repertoires, but it also helps them to develop a sense of pride and confidence in what they already know and can do.

The use of Indigenous students' first languages, such as AAE, Kriol, or traditional languages, is instrumental for teaching in a meaningful and accessible strength-based approach. It ensures Indigenous students receive the same quality education enjoyed by all Australian students – providing them the opportunity to not only understand and unpack the educational content, but also to challenge, speak back, and call out western standpoints and disturb the space of the educational norms, processes, and practices. As such it is about empowering and equipping Aboriginal and Torres Strait Islander students with the knowledge, skills, and conceptual understandings that are critical for them to 'slip and slide' into the multiple worlds of Aboriginal and mainstream Australian and global community spaces.

'Slipping and sliding' is a term that has emerged from a conversation that occurred during my PhD research study (see Ober, 2019), which focused on the topic, AAE as a social, cultural, and linguistic marker in Indigenous Tertiary Education. The term was coined by an experienced Aboriginal lecturer as she reflected on her extensive teaching experience in the common units – 'Public Communication' and 'Telling Histories', which were both compulsory higher education units previously offered at Batchelor Institute as part of students' first year of studies across all disciplines.

The term 'slipping and sliding' was used by Ober (2019) to capture, and represent, the continuous fluidity and flexibility of movement between languages and cultures that often come into play when Aboriginal and Torres Strait Islander people come together, be it in school, a tertiary setting, or even in everyday social life. One could argue that this moving to and fro between linguistic codes, cultural perspectives, and social domains happens in all socio-cultural contexts; however, the difference here is that it is less common in mainstream educational learning environments. As Malcolm (2014) states, 'when AE speakers enter an education system based on SAE there is an assumed priority given to the dialect which does not have their primary identification' (p. 2). In other words, SAE and the world view it represents is usually given priority with a higher status and greater levels of recognition than AAE (or other Aboriginal and Torres Strait languages) even though AE is 'spoken throughout Australia, as either the first or second language of the great majority of Aboriginal people' (Eades, 1993, p. 2). Therefore, the concept of 'slipping and sliding' is an important one for educators to understand, as this phenomenon represents learners going beyond the spoken language and understanding to how language is used as a vehicle to move in and out of diverse social, cultural, and linguistic spaces.

In many ways, the concept of slipping and sliding is similar to the sociolinguistic concept of 'translanguaging'. Introduced by Garcia and Wei (2014), translanguaging represents how multilingual speakers move in and out of their different language and/or dialectal varieties that exist within their different intercultural spaces and how they draw on their own socio-linguistic and cultural repertoires to achieve this. Previously, the movement between different languages (and dialects) was called codeswitching, but Garcia and Wei (2014) argue why this label is no longer sufficient stating that:

> … translanguaging differs from the notion of code-switching in that it refers not simply to a shift or a shuttle between two languages, but to the speakers' construction and use of original and complex interrelated discursive practices

that cannot be easily assigned to one or another traditional definition of a language, but that make up the speakers' complete language repertoire.
(Garcia & Wei, 2014, p. 22).

Regardless of whether the term used is slipping and sliding or translanguaging, this concept of fluid movement in linguistic and conceptual understanding reflects the way many Indigenous Australians use language, including when they are learning. Despite this, at present it is not something adequately reflected (some might argue even included) in the Australian curriculum.

Language use and the Australian curriculum

Although the Australian curriculum acknowledges that Australia is a multicultural and multilingual country, there is still a strong preference given to SAE in the school system. For example, it is noted in the curriculum that, 'Australia is a linguistically and culturally diverse country, with participation in many aspects of Australian life dependent on effective communication in Standard Australian English' (ACARA, n.d., a). Although there is recognition that Aboriginal and Torres Strait Islander people have their own ways of representing and communicating knowledge, traditions, and experiences, and that they have 'contributed to Australian society and to its contemporary literature and its literary heritage through their distinctive ways of representing and communicating knowledge, traditions and experience' (ACARA, n.d., a), there is little acknowledgement of the strong and diverse first languages that young Indigenous children bring with them when entering school. Consequently, there is insufficient inclusion within current pedagogy about the ways these students use their languages and dialects.

Language and literacy

Despite the inclusions in the curriculum as outlined above, in terms of literacy progression, ACARA (n.d., b, p. 3) makes it clear that SAE is the language of instruction, especially in terms of literacy learning:

> The literacy progression describes the observable indicators of increasing complexity in the use of SAE language. The literacy progression includes the elements of Speaking and listening, Reading, and viewing and writing.

By implication, and in practice (especially in terms of assessment), those who speak another language or dialect as their first are disadvantaged, and consciously or unconsciously viewed as 'deficit'. The narrative around language diversity, particularly for AAE, Kriol, and other language speakers is that they have a 'problem' that needs to be 'fixed'. This sentiment is one often reflected by politicians and the media (see Steele & Oliver, 2024).

It is important to note here that many Aboriginal parents want their children to learn English and to learn in both ways. This is because they recognise building on 'home talk' strengthens their cultural identity, but they also recognise that SAE is the language of power and governance, and necessary for school learning. Yet, the main way it has been taught means that SAE is perceived by Aboriginal people as a 'secret language' and one that can heavily impact on their lives. According to the late Dr. M. Yunupingu (1993), language is the most important thing in Yolŋu (Aboriginal) children's life. He states that, 'Our children (need to) study their clan languages in school. They (need to) learn to understand the deep meanings and to read and write in their mother's and father's languages' (p. 3). At the same time, SAE also holds an important place for Yolŋu people. Therefore, children should be taught in a way which prioritises Yolŋu culture, knowledge, and language, but also balances this foundational knowledge with SAE. To achieve this, a both-ways (a balanced curriculum) and a strength-based approach is needed to ensure children are 'active Aboriginal members of our contemporary Australia' (Yunupingu, 1993, p. 9).

Learning SAE is required for survival within Australian society, but it also empowers Aboriginal people to talk back, call out, debate, discuss, and argue about critical issues that impact Indigenous Australians. That is, SAE is an important language that empowers Aboriginal children to interact and function in Australian society. As stated by ACARA (n.d. a), 'proficiency in English is invaluable globally and contributes to nation-building and to internationalisation'. In most schools across the nation, it is the language that underpins literacy skill development. Further, English helps students to 'engage imaginatively and critically with literature to expand the scope of their experience' (ACARA, n.d. a). However, there is also a need to recognise that Indigenous children come to school with established first languages and rather than being viewed as deficit, it should be acknowledged that they are equipped to learn already. Therefore, the question to be asked by educators is:

> How can young Aboriginal children's languages be recognised, acknowledged, strengthened, and developed through the Australian school system?

I suggest a first step is to recognise that Aboriginal children have a culturally rich, linguistic heritage and a knowledge system that they bring with them when entering the school gates. What is needed is an understanding of how this linguistic and cultural knowledge can be further strengthened through the school curriculum and its implementation, embedding Aboriginal peoples' intricate cultural knowledge into thematic content in a both-ways and strength-based approach to learning.

Recognition of children's home languages

As noted, AAE is the first language for most Aboriginal people in urban Australia. It is often used by those living in regional and remote areas who may have a traditional language(s) and/or Kriol as their first language as the *lingua franca* (i.e., common language) by Aboriginal people from different language backgrounds. It is not surprising, therefore, that children often communicate and engage with others using this variety when they are in a school context, including in the classroom and playground. Other research has also found that it will be used by Aboriginal secondary and tertiary students – for social purposes, but also to understand and make meaning (Ober, 2019; Malcolm, 2014). I illustrate how this occurs in the following transcripts that are extracts taken from previous research (Ober, 2019). In this study, I explored the role and function of AAE in education. I used a narrative and theoretical approach I call 'Kapati' (cup of tea). I yarned with the study participants, often over a cup of tea, to explore their perception, ideas, and opinions. I was able to capture significant stories related to teaching and learning experiences in diverse educational contexts. Here a student teacher is explaining her experience of using AAE to communicate with several children who come from remote communities who are now attending school in Darwin. The student teacher explains the importance of AAE as well as the use of body/hand/facial gestures for communicating effectively with these children. According to her, the children responded positively when she used AAE (a dialect she shares and speaks proficiently); however, she was often reprimanded by the classroom teacher for using such 'home talk' as a language of instruction, even though it was very effective for providing explanations about new content and conceptual understandings to the children.

Transcript 1 (15-05-14)

S1, S2: Student Teachers
IS1: Indigenous Staff Member

IS1:   How do the kids respond to that when you use it (AAE).
S1:   Oh, the kids respond perfectly fine, it's the teachers that I get pulled up
IS1:   So, the kids are comfortable and they understand you
S1:   Yeah, the kids are comfortable, and it's the same like what you said, I've had kids from Tiwi, Port Keats, you name it, and I don't speak (their) language but I can talk in a, y'know, in a creole, broken, whatever they wanna call it nowadays. So, I'll cut my English down a bit 'whichway you mob, you mob sabbi what we doin?' and (use) the hands, body language.
S2:   we all speak heaps with our hands don't we.
S1:   and if I see like y'know little one doin the wrong thing, it's like (whisper) which way? And it'll be like that thing y'know 'whichway?' Or I'm on the wrong way, yeah well come this way.

By using a dialect known by the student teacher and the students, the Indigenous staff member was able to support the inclusion and recognition of children's home language in the teaching and learning context. Furthermore, by hearing their home language used in the classroom, she was able to engender a sense of cultural safety. It also provided an opportunity for them to respond to and engage in discussions with ease, confidence, and pride. I want to point out here that although teachers from an SAE background are not able to use this language, even simply asking students and having them share how things are said at home or things they know about beyond the classroom, signals recognition and acceptance of the legitimacy of the students' 'home talk'. Furthermore, by explicitly demonstrating acceptance and recognition of the students' background, teachers will develop positive and strong relationships with their students.

Positive relationships, particularly between teachers and students are vital for good educational outcomes (Exell & Gower, 2021). Through a strength-based approach which draws upon children's social, cultural, and linguistic repertoires, strong relationships between Aboriginal students and teachers can be established. When teachers demonstrate their awareness of the language skills, knowledge, and conceptual understandings that young Aboriginal children bring with them into the school and classroom context, there is potential for rich learning to occur. Hence it provides a window of opportunity for classroom teachers as they navigate teaching the curriculum content and the learning space, they are working in.

It is interesting that in Transcript 1 above, the use of AAE was frowned upon by the classroom teacher. What triggers such feelings of disapproval? Would the reaction be the same if a teacher was able to use the home language of a newly arrived migrant child? Undoubtedly, SAE is the language of instruction in schools and it is also perceived as the language of power (e.g., for governance, business, and finance). However, as a formal written and oral language, it is often perceived as superior to other minority languages and dialects, such as AAE. Yet the term 'standard' is not used because it is a benchmark, rather it is the form of a language (be this English, Italian, German) – one that is codified and so closest to the written form.

In fact, the idea that students must be taught only through the 'standard' has been contested. For example, Oliver et al. (2021) describe the importance for learning by embracing students' 'home talk' and supporting learning through translanguaging. Researchers Van Gelderen and Guthadjaka (2019) describe the importance of such inclusion at Gawa Christian School on Elcho Island, stating 'Gäwa Elders expect the school to embrace the teaching of Warramiri "language and culture", in order to cover the full spectrum of an appropriate Yolŋu education'. The students enter school with a strong social, cultural and language foundation, which is then built upon, through a strength-based approach to teaching and learning in the school.

Strength-based and two-way approaches

The following transcripts provide examples of the both-ways or two-way teaching and learning approach. In Transcript 2, the classroom teacher (CT in transcript) is asking the Year 5 class to share stories about their dad or another male relative. The student (S) has mentioned his Jawiji which in many Aboriginal Kriol languages means grandfather, but the teacher has misinterpreted this name for George. In this transcript, it is evident that the young students slip and slide between AAE, Kriol, and Australian English to make meaning (noting Kimberley Kriol is the main language of the cohort).

Transcript 2

CT:	Um… S, what does who who's YOUR special person? Is it your…
S:	Jawiji.
CT:	Your George. So what do you like about him? ((The teacher has misunderstood what S has said))
S:	Because he buy me icy pole an'… e m buy me a… Xbox an' e m… e buy me Legos, an' toys.
CT:	Ah, so he buys you lots of stuff, fantastic…
S:	<CLICK> <CLICK> ((meaning yes))

You can see in this transcript terminology such as 'la', 'langa' (there or location), 'bin' (past tense), 'e' for 'he' 'em' for them, or 'em'. The student has also used the 'click, click' sound with his teeth and tongue to communicate agreement to the question asked by the teacher. Young Aboriginal people often use this clicking sound to communicate with their peers their agreement or satisfaction with the outcome of a situation. Whilst it was good that the teacher could scaffold the meaning, it clearly would have been helpful if she was also aware of kinship terms, such as Jawaji for grandfather. Generally, it is important for classroom teachers to be aware of children's linguistic repertoire and to expand their knowledge of the rich and diverse languages, which can be drawn upon for teaching and learning purposes. Being willing to be a continual learner is the first step towards establishing and building relationships with the children, families, and community members. It is also the route for building good rapport and respectful relationships with key stakeholders, fostering honest engagement and conversations between teachers and community members.

In Transcript 3, the student has informed the teacher he has made a mistake by writing Dear Dad instead of Jawiji, but the teacher still is not aware of the difference between Dad and Jawiji:

Transcript 3

S:	Excuse me Miss.
CT:	Yeah.
S:	I–
CT:	You're writing a letter to your, who are you writing to?
S:	Jawij, but, but I bin say Dad. ((meaning I wrote Dad))
CT:	Do you wanna rub it out?

This student has mistakenly written Dad instead of 'jawaji' and wants to correct it in the written text. As with many Indigenous students, relationship and kinship terms are important and so he wants to ensure that the right terminology is used in the letter. This would have been an opportunity for the teacher to draw on the student's social and linguistic repertoire and to bring this into his schoolwork. However, the teacher is unaware of such kinship terms, and so she misses the opportunity to enquire about their meaning and advance her own understanding, and to help develop a greater understanding through both-ways learning for the student.

Strategies to draw on students' social, cultural, and linguistic repertoires

The following section provides further practical ideas and strategies for classroom teachers to use, with a particular focus on Aboriginal and Torres Strait Islander students' social, cultural, and linguistic repertoires. Note, especially in remote communities, there may be several languages spoken in the community, with one dominant Aboriginal language as the lingua franca, or alternatively, regional varieties of AAE or Kriol may be spoken as the first language by children, with adults speaking traditional languages. So as a first step, it is important to observe and listen to the language(s) being spoken by students in the classroom. Familiarise yourself with the types of talks and the language groups that are established and emerging within the student cohort. As a teacher, this will give you an indication of the social, kinship, cultural, and linguistic varieties, and groups in your classroom. This may not be immediately apparent, so be patient; the language groups will become evident the longer you interact and engage with the students, families, and community. Having this awareness will not only allow you to understand your students better, but it will enable you to bring cultural and linguistic understanding into your teaching and then to scaffold the students' learning. For example, in the following transcript, the young students (S1and S2) share lots of information based on their cultural knowledge and language about bush food.

Transcript 4 – Bush Walk

S1: Yeah look Miss, Miss (name), Miss (name)
Dis something on now, a womma
S2: E know aboudit, e know aboudit
S1: You know....
But you need to clap it on your hand hard a'
S1: Yeah, you have to wait till it's kin' of yellow or something ... Yeah really really yellow and big. Den you can bang it ting, slap it on your hand an you can lick it or som... it tastes ... yeah um sweet. anything inna ah womma. Our nanna told us dis. E tell us everything.

The young student (S1) is initially speaking in Aboriginal English; however, he easily slips into – Martu Wangka, when he identifies the bush food 'womma' during the bush walk. He explains the process of eating the food to ensure the sweetness of the plant is extracted in the correct way, including how the colour of the plant indicates whether the plant is ready or not to eat. The bush food is 'womma' and this cultural knowledge was taught to him by his 'nanna', who taught him about his country. He proudly states that, 'E tell us everything', meaning 'she taught him everything'. It is interesting, student (S2) states, 'e, know boudit' – meaning he knows about it. By being able to slip and slide, the young boy (S1) is able to demonstrate in-depth knowledge about his local country and in a language which he learnt from his grandmother – and do so with enthusiasm and pride, which may not have been possible if he had tried to do so in SAE.

As teachers, not only is it important to connect with the local Aboriginal educators, community, parents, and elders to establish positive relationship and develop understanding, it is also important to remember, 'one size does not fit all'. As a teacher, do some research before you enter a community school to ensure you are abreast of the languages/dialects that are prominent in the region. In these intercultural teaching contexts, it is also important for to adapt teaching pedagogies to suit the language and linguistic capabilities and strengths of their students – in this case, taking students on a bush walk so they have the opportunity to demonstrate their knowledge.

Indigenous ways of knowing, being, doing, and making meaning are tightly embedded and intertwined with different languages. Languages are more than oral communication, there are cultural rules, boundaries, protocols, tone, and relationship that come into play when conversations and speech events are initiated. These ways differ from non-Indigenous ways of doing things, so again an awareness is needed about such differences. For instance, in the next scenario a student teacher (ST1) is explaining how she smoothly incorporated 'the look' as one of her classroom management strategies. In Transcript 5, this student teacher explains to another (ST2) how using 'the look' is a way to remind, guide, and lead the child to behave according to the school's values and philosophy. 'The look' is a social and disciplining gesture that young Aboriginal children are familiar with, and in this specific context, social connections between the adult and child are already established.

Transcript 5 – Classroom Observation

ST1: yeah, I just put it back on the...and sometimes I didn't have to speak, I just gave them *that look* to let them know they were doing the wrong thing and I kinda stopped and looked and (pause)
ST2: hesitated
ST1: hesitated for a little while, then I looked at them to – they knew straight away to come back.

Here the student teacher is mindful of the school's philosophy and quickly acts to remind this child about these values as the need arises. This is a good teaching strategy and one that I expect most experienced teachers would use; however, in this case the student teacher would most certainly be related to and, therefore, connected socially with the children. With that relationship comes certain obligations, such as respect, trust, and authority. Mr. Dana Ober warned Batchelor Institute students, 'not to drift unwittingly or unthinkingly into white mind' (McCormack, 2004). This is an example of how the student teacher has drawn on her ways of communicating by using 'the look', from the home environment, and smoothly incorporated it into classroom management strategies from an Indigenous cultural practice. Whilst non-Indigenous teachers might not be able to use a culturally aligned gesture with the same effectiveness, it clearly illustrates that there are different ways of knowing, being, doing, and making meaning, and that these all vary according to people's cultural and language background. Furthermore, instances such as 'the look' provide opportunities to teachers to explicitly ask about and help students to recognise different ways the same message can be conveyed in different languages and contexts.

Conclusion

Indigenous Australians have a wide and varied linguistic repertoire, which embraces their cultural knowledge, conceptual understandings, values, beliefs, processes, and protocols which is intrinsically embedded into their cultural identity. There is value in classroom teachers working from a pedagogical strength-based and both-ways approach to ensure students' knowledge and languages are recognised and respected within the classroom context. There are potential opportunities for teachers to draw on to students rich and diverse knowledge as a pathway to teaching curriculum content in a culturally appropriate, safe, and meaningful way. This approach would open opportunities for local community members to be involved in the teaching and learning process by drawing on their own traditional knowledges and languages.

References

ACARA. (n.d., a). *English rationale.* https://www.australiancurriculum.edu.au/f-10-curriculum/english/rationale/
ACARA. (n.d., b). *National literacy learning progression.* national-literacy-learning-progression.pdf; australiancurriculum.edu.au
Bell, J. (2002). Linguistic continuity in colonized county. In J. Henderson & D. Nash (Eds.), *Language and native title* (pp. 43–52). Aboriginal Studies Press.
Eades, D. (1993). Aboriginal English, PEN 93, Newtown, NS.W. PETA Primary English Teaching Association, Australia, 1–4.
Exell, M., & Gower, G. (2021). Developing strong relationships with Aboriginal students, families, and communities. In M. Shay & R. Oliver (Eds.), *Learning and teaching for deadly futures: Aboriginal and Torres Strait Islander students in Australian classrooms* (pp. 86–97). Routledge.
Garcia, O., & Wei, L. (2014). *Translanguaging: Language, bilingualism and education.* Palgrave McMillan UK.
Lopez, S. J., & Louis, M. C. (2009, April) The principles of strength-based education. *Journal of College & Character*, X(4).
Malcolm, I. (2014, October). Education in Australian English: The challenge for Aboriginal English speakers. Paper presented at Australian Council of TESOL Association (ACTA) International Conference 'Meeting the Challenge', Melbourne.
McCormack, R. (2004). Common units: Politics and rhetoric. Ngoonjook, (25), July 2004, 25–33. https://search.informit.org/doi/10.3316/ielapa.969729651119986
Ober, R. (2009). Both-ways: Learning from yesterday, celebrating today, strengthening tomorrow. *The Australian Journal of Indigenous Education*, 38, 34–39.

Ober, R. (2019). Aboriginal English as a social, cultural and identity marker in Indigenous Tertiary Educational Contexts (Unpublished doctoral dissertation). Batchelor Institute of Indigenous Tertiary Education.

Ober, R., & Bell, J. (2012). English language as juggernaut – Aboriginal English and Indigenous languages in Australia. In V. Rapatahana & P. Bunce (Eds.), *English language as hydra – Its impact on non-English language cultures* (pp. 60–75). Multilingual Matters. https://doi.org/10.21832/9781847697516-010

O'Donnell, W. R., & Todd, L. (1980). *Varieties in contemporary English*. George Allen & Unwin.

Oliver, R., Angelo, D., Steele, C., & Wigglesworth, J. (2021). Translanguaging possibilities and pitfalls for language teaching. *Language Teaching Research, 25*(1), 134–150. https://doi.org/10.1177/1362168820938822

Steele, C., & Oliver, R. (2024). Distraction in Australian language education policy: A call to re-centre language rights. *Current issues in Language Planning*, 1–26. https://doi.org/10.1080/14664208.2024.2358273

van Gelderen, B., & Guthadjaka, K. (2019). Renewing the Yolŋu 'Bothways' philosophy: Warramiri transculturation education at Gäwa. *The Australian Journal of Indigenous Education, 50*(1), 147–157. https://doi.org/10.1017/jie.2019.2

Yunupingu, M. (1993) Voices from the land. *Yothu Yindi: Finding balance*. 1993 Boyer Lectures. Published by ABC Books Sydney NSW.

13 Aboriginal and Torres Strait Islander Students' Language Learning for Literacy Development

Debra Hannagan and Grace Lewis

Introduction

We acknowledge the Bardi, Djugun, Yawuru, Gija, and Whajuk Nyoongar traditional custodians of the lands on which this chapter was written and pay respect to elders past and present. Additionally, we acknowledge and pay respect to the Jabirr Jabirr and Ngumbarl people, without whom Waardi Limited and the work discussed in this chapter would not exist. We would also like to recognise and thank the staff and families of Christ the King Catholic School, Djarindjin Lombadina who were involved in the learning experiences we describe in this chapter.

This chapter explores the topic of teaching language and literacy to First Nations students who are speakers of traditional or contact languages and are learning Standard Australian English (SAE). We would like to position ourselves, the authors, in relation to this topic. Debra is a non-Indigenous educator and applied linguist who lives on Djugun and Yawuru Country in Rubibi (Broome). Grace is a Bardi woman and educator, currently living on Whadjuk Nyoongar Country (Perth). Grace and Debra worked together from 2021 to 2022 when Grace was teaching on Bardi Country at Christ the King Catholic School, Djarindjin Lombadina and Debra was a visiting literacy consultant for the Literacy Acquisition for Pre-primary Students (LAPS) program run by Waardi Limited. This partnership facilitated the development, implementation, and sharing of strategies to support the language and literacy learning of Aboriginal students. In this chapter, Debra shares linguistic and educational theories and strategies, and Grace shares her perspective as a First Nations person and her experience implementing translanguaging strategies in her teaching.

We begin this chapter by discussing the linguistic diversity of Indigenous Australian contexts with a particular focus on the Kimberley region where our pedagogical examples are based. We describe linguistic features and educational practices and perspectives in relation to language and literacy development for Indigenous students. Next, we examine contemporary perspectives on language and literacy learning with a focus on translanguaging pedagogy. We explore how these approaches can be adapted to Indigenous Australian educational contexts, sharing examples from our own practice. We conclude with recommendations for educators of First Nations students in Australia.

DOI: 10.4324/9781003441021-19

Aboriginal and Torres Strait Islander Languages and Education in Australia

Australia boasts a rich diversity of Indigenous languages and cultures, a wealth which has been widely undervalued since colonisation (Simpson et al., 2009, in Salmon et al., 2019). The devaluing and stigmatisation of people's language, culture, and identity can significantly impact wellbeing (Dovchin, 2020). Institutions such as education systems have a pivotal role in either perpetuating or challenging these patterns and power structures (Fairclough, 2013). Educators must teach SAE literacy, the currency of power in Australia, in a way that supports First Nations learners' identity and wellbeing. Educational institutions have a responsibility to implement pedagogical practices that achieve both outcomes. An important consideration in the evaluation of such outcomes is their alignment with communities' own wishes about their children's education (Guenther et al., 2019).

Aboriginal languages in the Kimberley

The 'Kimberley' region, in which our pedagogical examples are based, spans 400,000 square kilometres in the north of Western Australia (Regional Development Australia Kimberley, 2025). Its sparse population of 35,000 people is over 40% Indigenous (Australian Bureau of Statistics, 2021). It is home to 40 traditional Aboriginal languages, standing as the most linguistically diverse region in Australia, both historically and in current times in terms of Aboriginal languages (Kimberley Language Resource Centre, 2018) (Figure 13.1).

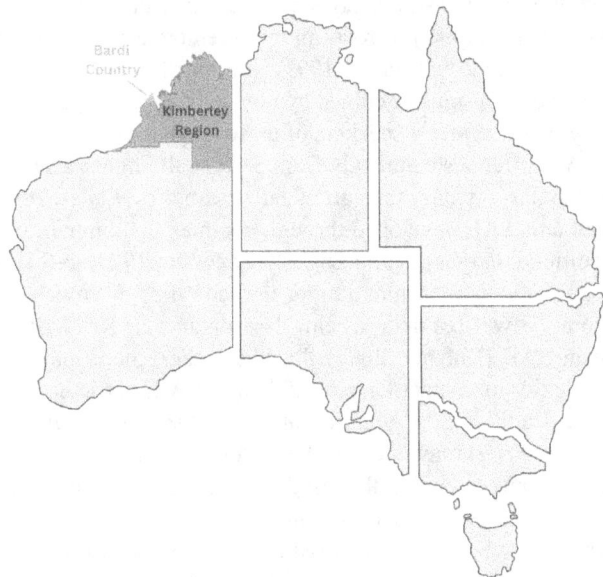

Figure 13.1 Location of Bardi Country in the Kimberley Region, Western Australia (map is approximate, stylised and not to scale). Sources: AIATSIS (1996); Canva; Kimberley-WA-2017 by Canley CC BY 4.0.

The vitality of traditional languages in the region varies widely. The strongest of these languages, Kukatja, is spoken in very remote communities in the southeast Kimberley by people of all ages as a dominant lingua franca across different heritage language groups (Bamford, 2019, p. 29, December; Guardian News and Media Limited, 2011, April). The increasing influence of English on the language of younger people has led to much generational language variation: Kukatja is considered vulnerable to endangerment, other languages like Bardi are already endangered, and some languages are no longer in use (Guardian News and Media Limited, 2011, April). Endangered languages may be spoken by older generations but no longer learned as a first language by children. Senior interpreter and translator for Aboriginal Interpreting Western Australia and member of the Kimberley Language Resource Centre, Annette Kogolo, describes the situation for her language, Walmajarri: 'Children learn and listen to language at home but do not speak it… They may speak bits and pieces of it when they are older' (A. Kogolo, personal communication, 11th March 2024). An impact on language endangerment is whether people have opportunities to use the language in all domains of life, such as at home, work, and school.

The main first languages of Aboriginal children in the Kimberley are Australian Aboriginal English (AAE) and Kriol (an English-lexified creole language), with much regional variation noted due to the diversity of First Nations languages across this vast area (McGregor, 2004). These contact languages – Kriol and Aboriginal English – exist on a continuum, with acrolectal varieties of AAE (i.e., varieties closer to English – as a language that carries prestige) more common in larger towns with higher non-Indigenous populations, and basilectal varieties (i.e., varieties further from English) of Kriol in more remote areas where the influence of SAE is less (Butcher, 2008; Eades, 1993). It is worth noting here that the terms 'Kriol' and 'Aboriginal English', coined by non-Indigenous linguists, may be used interchangeably or not at all by speakers of these languages.

Kriol and AAE differ systematically from SAE at all linguistic levels, including phonology, vocabulary, syntax, semantics, and pragmatics (Eades, 1993). The phonology of Kriol and AAE developed through complex combinations of the sound systems of traditional languages and English (Sandefur, 1979, in Sandefur, 1981). Many traditional languages feature a more limited range of vowels than English, resulting in some vowel phonemes being less distinct in Kriol or heavier AAE varieties than in SAE (Butcher, 2008). In other cases, there may be more phonological complexity in contact languages than in SAE, particularly when words are derived from traditional languages (Butcher, 2008). For example, the voiced velar nasal phoneme (ng) may occur at the start of words in many traditional languages, whereas it only occurs in the middle or end of words in SAE. In terms of vocabulary, English words can have meanings in contact language varieties that are distinct from their SAE meanings (Butcher, 2008; Eades, 1993). These may be shaped by deeper language features such as the semantics, schemas, values, and world views embodied within traditional languages. For example, the word mum, with the narrower meaning of birth mother in SAE can have a broader meaning in Kriol and AAE to include a birth mother's sisters (Eades, 1993). Contact languages have their own distinct syntax, influencing the ways plurals, possessives, and many other grammatical features are used (Butcher, 2008; Eades, 1993). They also include unique text structures. For example, AAE has been identified as having distinct narrative genres, including hunting stories and warning stories (Sharifian & The Department of Education WA, 2012). At the level of discourse, contact languages can differ greatly from SAE, underpinned by differences in culture, values, attitudes, and world view. Because SAE and contact language varieties all use an English-based lexicon, it can be harder to distinguish differences in deeper language features, making miscommunication and misunderstanding more difficult to identify.

Language and education in the Kimberley

Over the years, various educational practices have been implemented in the Kimberley region, influenced by evolving perspectives on language and learning. As occurred elsewhere in Australia, First Nations children were historically prevented from speaking their mother-tongue traditional languages in English-dominated educational environments. Shaped by a monolingual perspective and assimilationist policies, such subtractive approaches to multilingualism resulted in home language loss and have had an enduring negative impact on First Nations people's identity and wellbeing (Dockery, 2010; Roberts, 1995, in Verdon & McLeod, 2015). This is underscored by Grace's reflections as an educator and Aboriginal person: 'As a teacher who returned to Bardi Country, I have had to learn my mother's language to teach the baawa [Bardi word for 'children'] the importance of our language'. The contact languages that have allowed Indigenous people to maintain cultural meanings have also been subject to linguistic discrimination, often perceived as deficit versions of English and rendered invisible in educational contexts (Angelo & Sellwood, 2013). There is a need for an alternative additive view of bilingualism that fosters continued development of the learner's first language alongside learning of second language/s. This view supports the maintenance of identity and is aligned with effective language instruction (Murphy & Evangelou, 2016). For educators of First Nations students, language awareness is a crucial skill to overcome dominant perspectives which perpetuate inequity, and to recognise and value the linguistic resources learners bring to the classroom (Angelo & Carter, 2015).

In the Kimberley region, previous system-wide initiatives aimed to promote language awareness through two-way learning and code-switching approaches, acknowledging children's first languages alongside the teaching of SAE literacy (e.g., Berry & Hudson, 1997; Department of Education, Western Australia & Department of Training and Workforce Development, 2012). At an international level, research has led to a perspective shift away from codeswitching and towards code-meshing or translanguaging as being more aligned with natural multilingual language use and equitable instruction (e.g., García, 2017; Young et al., 2013). Locally, recent trends in education, influenced by a focus on measurable data (e.g., Hattie, 2012), have led to a shift towards explicit and Direct Instruction in SAE and less attention to valuing children's linguistic resources. At the same time, however, many schools and communities are making efforts to revitalise traditional languages and empower local language groups. On a smaller scale, some schools, communities, and systems are working to also utilise and build upon children's existing linguistic resources through translanguaging pedagogy. Despite this, dominant monolingual, SAE-centric ideologies and educational practices prevail. There is a need for renewed attention to the linguistic needs of Indigenous students, integrating current perspectives on language and literacy acquisition.

Second language literacy acquisition

Second language literacy acquisition involves complex, dynamic interactions of developing knowledge and skills across languages (Genesee et al., 2006). Different aspects of literacy development are variously impacted by emerging multilingualism (Bialystok, 2007; Bialystok et al., 2005). Phonological awareness, an important skill for literacy learning, is a general cognitive ability that can transfer across languages (Bialystok, 2007; Bialystok et al., 2005). This is not necessarily the case for vocabulary, though higher order vocabulary skills and overlapping cognates may transfer across languages (Genesee et al., 2006) (an example of a cognate is the word 'modern' in English and 'moderne' in French). For speakers of contact languages, overlapping vocabulary may support SAE literacy acquisition, though there is also room for confusion where words have different meanings (e.g., English deadly meaning fatal in English, but good in AAE). Differences between dialects may be less noticeable and, therefore, more challenging to acquire (Steele, 2020). This is particularly true for culturally embedded aspects of language, such as semantics, pragmatics, and world view. There is currently little conclusive research about the development of grammar and discourse skills across languages (Genesee et al., 2006). A study analysing how AAE-speaking students retold SAE narratives identified their varying reinterpretations of texts (Sharifian & The Department of Education WA, 2012). A useful way to conceptualise the transfer of linguistic knowledge and skills across languages is to see the first language as a resource for learning (Bransford & Schwartz, 1999 in Genesee et al., 2006). This perspective aligns with translanguaging pedagogy that capitalises on emergent multilingual learners' strengths of natural, dynamic language use (García, 2017). The following section, drawing on contemporary literature, outlines ways in which this approach can be integrated into reading and writing instruction for First Nations learners, drawing on examples from Grace's early years class on Bardi Country.

Linguistically inclusive literacy learning environments

Establishing a linguistically inclusive literacy learning environment for emergent multilingual First Nations students involves creating a 'translanguaging space', a safe atmosphere in which all learners' language skills and practices are welcomed (Wei, 2011). Every learner should have the opportunity to draw upon prior knowledge, which is recognised as an important resource for learning (e.g., Hattie, 2012). Teachers need to know about children's skills, motivation, and knowledge, including their language and culture (Hattie, 2023). In Grace's class, language and literacy profiles were developed for each child to identify and track their needs, strengths, and interests through assessment and collaboration with local staff and families. Such collaborations are a vital aspect of creating an inclusive environment.

The learning environment plays an important role in legitimising First Nations learners' linguistic and cultural knowledge and practices. Learners' languages should be valued and visible. For example, Grace's learning environment included English and Bardi word walls and three-way charts featuring Bardi, SAE, and children's home language of AAE. Grace created a translanguaging space by modelling and encouraging the fluid use of linguistic resources from different codes to optimise meaning making. Students' prior knowledge in their home language of Aboriginal English was seen as a starting point for learning of both SAE and Bardi. This is an important consideration for educators of First Nations learners whose first language is a contact language, as represented in Figure 13.2.

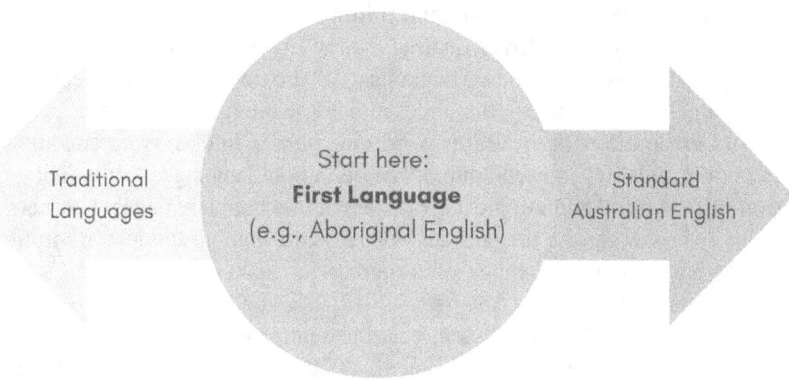

Figure 13.2 Contact Languages as a Starting Point for Learning

Linguistically inclusive learning environments include multimodal opportunities for learners to build on prior knowledge. Decolonising the learning environment includes recognising that semiotic resources can extend beyond environmental print to include cultural artefacts (Kroik, 2023). For example, including artefacts that children encountered during family hunting trips in the outdoor learning environment allowed Grace's students to demonstrate their rich cultural and linguistic knowledge through play. Learners were also encouraged to draw upon this knowledge through oral language experiences in reading and writing lessons. Following this approach children should be invited to share their experiences and perspectives in the language they feel most comfortable communicating in. Inviting learners to use their first language to share and respond may help them overcome the 'silent period' experienced by some second language learners (Harris, 2019). We now outline ways in which a translanguaging space can be embedded in reading and writing instruction.

Translanguaging reading instruction

Translanguaging pedagogy can be integrated into a range of teaching strategies before, during, and after reading experiences. Before reading, text introductions provide opportunities to explicitly label the language/s a text is written in, activate learners' prior knowledge, and create a space for translanguaging. Students can be invited to make predictions using their existing linguistic and cultural knowledge with a picture walk through the text (Espinosa & Lehner-Quam, 2019). These predictions, being derived from students' own cultural backgrounds, may differ from the meanings presented in the text. Using prediction is a useful way to explore these differences prior to reading to facilitate text comprehension during reading. This strategy was used in Grace's early years class before reading the story *From Head to Toe* by Eric Carle (1997) to her emergent multilingual students. Discussing and introducing the names of the animals in the story provided an opportunity for children to draw on and make connections to their prior knowledge, sharing their experiences in their first language of AAE. Learners' knowledge was built upon by labelling languages and introducing new vocabulary. Where appropriate, connections were made with Bardi vocabulary the children were learning, for example, comparing the word crocodile with the Bardi word *linggoord*. Children were encouraged to clap out the syllables in each animal's name in both languages, capitalising on an opportunity to build phonological awareness across both languages. Learners were also invited to dramatise the animals' movements, making the lesson multimodal and drawing on their full range of resources for making meaning, an important aspect of translanguaging (Andersen, 2017; Bengochea et al., 2020). Children were highly engaged in the lesson, echoing sentiments expressed about such an approach used elsewhere (e.g., Seals et al., 2020; Yuille & Marshark, 1983 in Yang et al., 2021).

During reading, opportunities can be created for extensive dialogue, enabling learners to draw on their own experiences and develop, strengthen, and experiment with linguistic resources (Worthy et al., 2013). Learners should be encouraged to utilise their entire linguistic repertoire when discussing texts (Osorio, 2020). For example, they can use multiple languages to confirm and adjust predictions (Espinosa & Lehner-Quam, 2019). In Grace's class, during the reading of a story about farm animals, children were again invited to draw on and make connections to their prior knowledge. When they predicted that a 'bullock' was in the story, drawing upon their AAE vocabulary, this language was valued and used as a foundation for new learning of the SAE word 'cow'. They were able to discuss that if the story was written in AAE, the word 'bullock' would be used, but as this story was written in SAE, the word 'cow' was used instead. Using learner's first language as a resource during reading experiences can help to refine their mental imagery, supporting comprehension (Yang et al., 2021). This strategy can also support metalinguistic awareness, helping learners make connections between languages and tune into linguistic similarities and differences (Naqvi et al., 2013; Worthy et al., 2013; Yang et al., 2021).

Through text-based experiences, multilingual adults can model translanguaging using the breadth of their knowledge, experience, and multimodal resources (Han et al., 2021). Translanguaging can be used to respond to children, ask questions, and direct their attention to new vocabulary (Moody et al., 2021). A less intimidating way for teachers to support translanguaging may be using a 'repeat and affirm' strategy to validate students' language use and build upon their linguistic resources, such as the way Grace repeated and affirmed children's use of the word 'bullock' in the example above (Moody et al., 2021). Grace advises, 'teachers should position themselves as learners, both of children's first language, and the language of the Country they are teaching on'. She recommends looking for opportunities to use texts as a springboard for learning about Indigenous languages and cultures. For example, stories about families can be opportunities to learn local language words for family members, while other texts may provide opportunities to learn the names of local animals, seasons, etc. This can model valuing of Indigenous knowledge and open up spaces for First Nations learners to share their own cultural and linguistic knowledge. Teachers may also collaborate with other educators to coordinate multilingual strategies, building upon each other's contributions by translating, summarising, explaining, defining, repeating, and rephrasing (Pontier & Gort, 2016). Educators' use of translanguaging in reading instruction has been associated with creating rapport with students, increasing talk time in the target language, and increasing the enjoyment, engagement, and participation of multilingual students in reading experiences (Seals et al., 2020; Yuille & Marshark, 1983 in Yang et al., 2021).

An important strategy for integrating translanguaging during reading is the use of multilingual texts. Translanguaging Read Alouds (TRA) are described in a range of studies from educational contexts, homes, libraries, and online communities. TRAs are seen as beneficial for all students: as 'mirrors' offering emergent multilingual learners a reflection of their own language practices, and as 'windows' and 'sliding doors' granting monolingual students access to other worlds (Bishop, 1990 in Espinosa & Lehner-Quam, 2019; Moody et al., 2021). Learners have equal opportunities to use their knowledge and be their authentic selves, promoting agency and cultivating inclusive and accessible learning environments (Espinosa & Lehner-Quam, 2019; Han et al., 2021; Worthy et al., 2013). While teachers need not be multilingual to facilitate TRAs, the availability of multilingual texts is essential (Han et al., 2021; Moody et al., 2021; Osorio, 2020). Given the limited resources for TRAs, collaborative efforts to create such texts with families and communities are encouraged (Han et al., 2021; Naqvi et al., 2013; Osorio, 2020; Seals et al., 2020). In Grace's teaching context, a multilingual Read Aloud text was developed through a collaborative process. A local Bardi educator had created a skipping song using AAE, SAE, and Bardi which was recited during outside play time. Recognising the potential of this text for Read Aloud, it was transformed into a class book for choral reading. Such collaborative projects offer opportunities to prioritise, value, and validate the knowledge of local Indigenous staff, families, and children themselves.

Translanguaging practices can also be integrated into opportunities to expand upon understandings of texts, share responses, and generate new ideas and texts. Through rich discussion of texts, teachers can foster and develop students' linguistic and semiotic (i.e., symbolic communication including gestures) resources as they share their understandings and responses using their own language, knowledge, and experiences (Worthy et al., 2013). Students may retell and innovate on stories read (Espinosa & Lehner-Quam, 2019). Text innovation is a strategy which was used often in Grace's class. For example, a collaborative text was generated with students innovating on the story *We're Going on a Bear Hunt*, to create the more locally contextualised *We're Going on a Mayal Hunt* (Mayal is the Bardi word for goanna). This text integrated SAE and Bardi language through translanguaging. Grace reflected that next time she would look to create a text which used children's first language of AAE to further support building upon their existing linguistic resources. Such innovations provide opportunities for texts to be compared with children's own lives to identify similarities and differences, and to collaboratively generate texts for future reading experiences. One limitation of using SAE texts for the creation of texts is that the deeper layers of language such as text structure, schemas, attitudes, values, and world view may be difficult to translate and remain shaped by dominant SAE norms. Existing translanguaging texts written by First Nations authors from different contexts can provide a starting point for text innovations which may be more aligned with Indigenous students' perspectives. Additionally, this emphasises the importance of writing opportunities to generate new texts sharing learners' own perceptions and world views.

Translanguaging writing instruction

Various approaches from translanguaging pedagogy can be applied to writing instruction for multilingual First Nations students. Learners can use translanguaging to support each other throughout the writing process. This may be facilitated by strategically pairing writing buddies or by providing time and space for collaborative learning in an environment in which translanguaging is valued. Partnerships may involve learners who share a first language, or who have different proficiencies (Celic & Seltzer, 2013). They can create an environment for risk-taking and provide support to students as they write (Bauer et al., 2017). By interactively planning their writing through drawing and talking, students may use the breadth of their linguistic repertoires to elaborate ideas and experiment with vocabulary (Bauer et al., 2017). A translanguaging writing partnership evolved organically in Grace's class when, inspired by learning about the digraph 'oo', two Pre-primary students pooled their linguistic resources to brainstorm and write words they knew. While both students were AAE speakers, one child spoke heavier AAE with more elements of Bardi, and the other spoke lighter AAE with more features of SAE. The list they generated included the Bardi and AAE words goowid (moon in Bardi) and oolaman (old woman in AAE). The children's work was shared with their families and the Bardi language teacher and celebrated with pride. Grace reflected, 'Neither of them could have achieved this on their own, and it wouldn't have worked if I had intervened. I had to let them negotiate between themselves'. Providing space for children to pool their linguistic resources in writing experiences can assist problem solving and self-regulation and allow for more richness, complexity, and depth in thinking and learning (Ollerhead et al., 2020; Velasco & García, 2014).

A useful strategy for writing instruction is Interactive Writing, which offers rich opportunities for integrating translanguaging practices and privileging learners' knowledge (Celic & Seltzer, 2013). Grace used this approach to regularly co-construct translanguaging texts with her class, demonstrating conventions and creating space for learners to negotiate the writing process. Following discussion with the children about what had happened one morning, Grace wrote, 'Miss E said, 'Big Rain Coming". The children corrected her, 'No, "Bigges mob rain comin"'. The students' feedback was used to refine the text. Grace reflected: 'Teachers need to be open to learning alongside students and to using the advice of local language speakers'. Her reflections echo the literature about the importance of seeking acceptability judgements from members of local speech communities when creating translanguaging texts (Seals et al., 2020). Interactive Writing lessons that incorporate learner input can generate writing models that reflect and legitimise learners' knowledge and perspectives.

Interactive Writing lessons can also serve as a platform for explicit teaching of linguistic differences (Celic & Seltzer, 2013). For example, Grace used Interactive Writing to co-construct a recount with her students, demonstrating versions of the text in AAE and SAE, below.

AAE: 'On da weeken we bin go Penda Bay. We'm catch bigges mob fish'.
SAE: 'On the weekend we went to Pender Bay. We caught a lot of fish'.

This side-by-side comparison provided an opportunity to explicitly teach language differences at the word and sentence level, for instance highlighting the way past tense can be marked. A limitation of direct translation is that it can neglect linguistic differences at the discourse level and may not acknowledge the rich narrative genres learners bring to the classroom. To promote learners' agency and allow their voices, genres, and perspectives to be heard and valued, teachers should also create space for free expression (Andersen, 2017; Flynn et al., 2021). For example, in the composition phase of the writing process, Story Circles or Yarning Circles can encourage learners to draw upon their full linguistic repertoire (Flynn et al., 2021). Creating space for multilingual genres, voices, and discourse is an important aspect of translanguaging pedagogy (Kiramba, 2017).

Multilingual texts that privilege First Nations perspectives may be generated through integrated learning experiences in partnership with community members. Stories from other First Nations peoples may serve as a springboard for learning, drawing on cultural similarities and shared songlines. For example, after she shared a rainbow serpent story with her class, Grace's students expressed an interest in learning about the story's connection to Bardi Country. Using the children's interest and prior knowledge as a starting point, Grace invited the Bardi language teacher, Mr V, to answer the children's questions. This began a journey of learning involving oral storytelling, visual mapping, and an on-Country visit to the site linked to this story. Students later drew and wrote about the experience and created a book together, each contributing at their own ability level with their choice of linguistic resources. Integrating Humanities and Social Sciences, this learning journey yielded work samples for assessment developed through the process, and the final product of a multilingual translanguaging text as a resource for future learning. This example illustrates how strong partnerships with communities can facilitate rich learning experiences which allow first Nations discourse into educational spaces (Pietikäinen & Pitkänen-Huhta, 2013) (Figure 13.3).

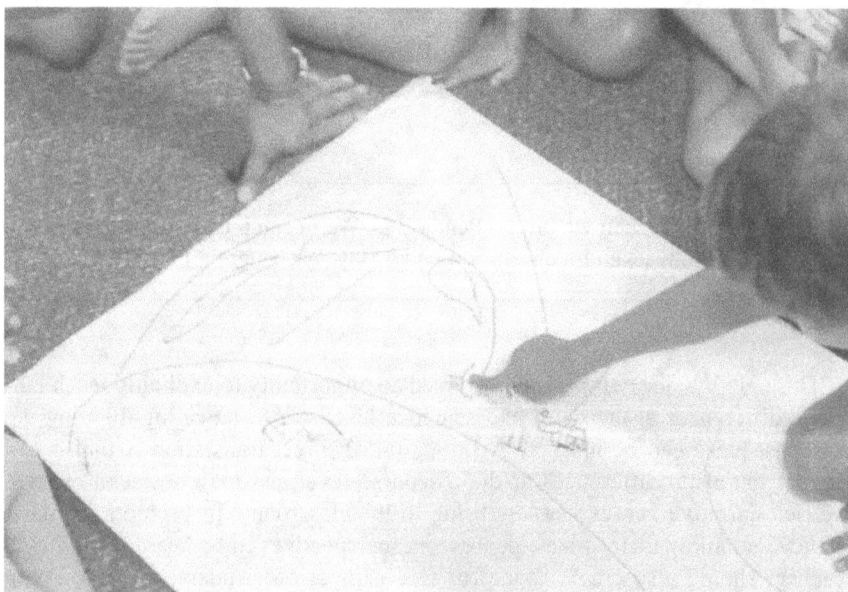

Figure 13.3(a–c) Developing a multilingual text *(Continued)*

Aboriginal and Torres Strait Islander Students' Language Learning 223

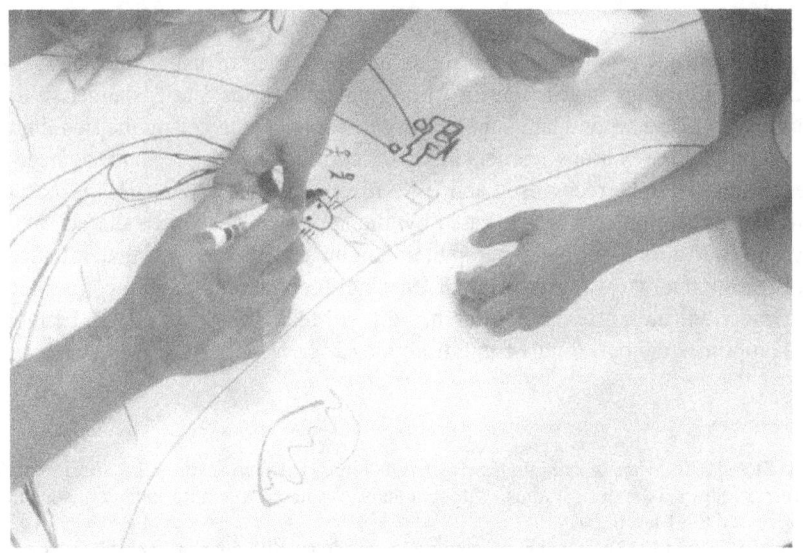

Figure 13.3(a–c) (Continued)

Conclusion

In this chapter, we have shared insights and examples of using translanguaging pedagogy in literacy instruction for Aboriginal and Torres Strait Islander students learning SAE as a second language or dialect. We have touched on the rich linguistic strengths First Nations learners bring to learning experiences and the need for these strengths to be recognised and legitimised. Language awareness is a crucial skill that underpins, and is facilitated by, the approaches we have shared. We encourage educators to further develop their language awareness and that of their students through a two-way exchange of learning in collaboration with communities. As Grace indicates: 'Be open to learn. You will make mistakes. It will be messy, but sometimes the best things come from mess'.

References

AIATSIS (1996). *Map of Indigenous Australia*. The Australian Institute of Aboriginal and Torres Strait Islander Studies. https://aiatsis.gov.au/explore/map-indigenous-australia Accessed 8th March, 2024.

Andersen, K. N. (2017). Translanguaging pedagogy in multilingual early childhood classes: A video ethnography in Luxembourg. *Translation and Translanguaging in Multilingual Contexts, 3*(2), 167–183. https://doi.org/10.1075/ttmc.3.2.02and

Angelo, D., & Carter, N. (2015). Schooling within shifting langscapes: Educational responses in complex Indigenous language contact ecologies. In A. Yiakoumetti (Ed.), *Multilingualism and language education. Sociolinguistic and pedagogical perspectives from Commonwealth countries* (pp. 119–140). Cambridge University Press.

Angelo, D., & Sellwood, J. (2013). Everywhere and nowhere: Invisibility of Aboriginal and Torres Strait Islander contact languages in education and Indigenous language contexts. *Australian Review of Applied Linguistics, 36*, 250–266, https://doi.org/10.1075/aral.36.3.02sel

Australian Bureau of Statistics. (2021). *Kimberley 2021 census all persons quickstats*. Australian Bureau of Statistics. https://www.abs.gov.au/census/find-census-data/quickstats/2021/51001

Bamford, M. (2019, December 29). *Researchers map ancient language in West Australian outback*. ABC News, Australian Broadcasting Corporation. https://www.abc.net.au/news/2019-12-29/researchers-map-ancient-languages-in-west-australian-outback/11760406

Bauer, E. B., Presiado, V., & Colomer, S. (2017). Writing through partnership: Fostering translanguaging in children who are emergent bilinguals. *Journal of Literacy Research, 49*(1), 10–37. https://doi.org/10.1177/1086296X16683417

Bengochea, A., Sembiante, S. F., & Gort, M. (2020). Exploring the object-sourced transmodal practices of an emergent bilingual child in sociodramatic play. *Journal of Early Childhood Research, 18*(4), 371–386. https://doi.org/10.1177/1476718X20938078

Berry, R., & Hudson, J. (1997). *Making the jump: A resource book for teachers of Aboriginal students*. Catholic Education Commission of Western Australia.

Bialystok, E. (2007). Acquisition of literacy in bilingual children: A framework for research. *Language Learning, 57*(s1), 45–77. https://doi.org/10.1111/j.1467-9922.2007.00412.x

Bialystok, E., Luk, G., & Kwan, E. (2005). Bilingualism, biliteracy, and learning to read: Interactions among languages and writing systems. *Scientific Studies of Reading, 9*(1), 43–61. https://doi.org/10.1207/s1532799xssr0901_4

Bishop, R. S. (1990). Mirrors, windows, and sliding glass doors. *Perspectives: Choosing and Using Books for the Classroom, 6*(3), ix–xi.

Bransford, J. D., & Schwartz, D. L. (1999). Rethinking transfer: A simple proposal with multiple implications. *Review of Research in Education, 24*(1), 61–100.

Butcher, A. (2008). Linguistic aspects of Australian Aboriginal English. *Cultural Linguistics & Phonetics, 22*(8), 625–642.
Carle, E. (1997). *From head to toe.* Penguin.
Celic, C., & Seltzer, K. (2013). *Translanguaging: A CUNY-NYSIEB guide for educators.* https://www.cuny-nysieb.org/wp-content/uploads/2016/04/Translanguaging-Guide-March-2013.pdf
Department of Education, Western Australia & Department of Training and Workforce Development. (2012). *Tracks to two-way learning.* West One Services.
Dockery, A. M. (2010). Culture and wellbeing: The case of Indigenous Australians. *Social Indicators Research, 99*(2), 315–332. https://doi.org/10.1007/s11205-010-9582-y
Dovchin, S. (2020). The psychological damages of linguistic racism and international students in Australia. *International Journal of Bilingual Education and Bilingualism, 23*(7), 804–818. https://doi.org/10.1080/13670050.2020.1759504
Eades, D. (1993). *Aboriginal English. PEN 93.* Primary English Teaching Association.
Espinosa, C. M., & Lehner-Quam, A. (2019). Sustaining bilingualism: Multimodal arts experiences for young readers and writers. *Language Arts, 96*(4), 5.
Fairclough, N. (2013). *Critical discourse analysis: The critical study of language.* Routledge.
Flynn, E. E., Hoy, S. L., Lea, J. L., & García, M. A. (2021). Translanguaging through story: Empowering children to use their full language repertoire. *Journal of Early Childhood Literacy, 21*(2), 283–309. https://doi.org/10.1177/1468798419838569
García, O. (2017). Translanguaging in schools: Subiendo y Bajando, Bajando y Subiendo as afterword. *Journal of Language, Identity & Education, 16*(4), 256–263. https://doi.org/10.1080/15348458.2017.1329657
Genesee, F., Geva, E., Dressler, C., & Kamil, M. (2006). Chapter 6 Synthesis: Cross-linguistic relationships. In D. August & D. Shanahan (Eds.), *Developing literacy in second-language learners: Report of the National Literacy Panel on Language-Minority Children and Youth.* Lawrence Erlbaum Associates Publishers, 153–174.
Guardian News and Media Limited. (2011, April). Endangered languages: The full list. *The Guardian Datablog.* https://www.theguardian.com/news/datablog/2011/apr/15/language-extinct-endangered Accessed 8 March 2024.
Guenther, J., Lowe, K., Burgess, C., Vass, G., & Moodie, N. (2019). Factors contributing to educational outcomes for First Nations students from remote communities: A systematic review. *The Australian Educational Researcher, 46*(2), 319–340. https://doi.org/10.1007/s13384-019-00308-4
Han, M., Duinen, D. V. V., & Weng, A. (2021). Interactive read-alouds as translanguaging spaces. *The Reading Teacher.* https://doi.org/10.1002/trtr.2059
Harris, R. (2019). Re-assessing the place of the "silent period" in the development of English as an additional language among children in early years settings. *TEANGA, the Journal of the Irish Association for Applied Linguistics, 10*, 77–93. https://doi.org/10.35903/teanga.v10i0.71
Hattie, J. (2012). *Visible learning for teachers: Maximizing impact on learning.* Routledge.
Hattie, J. (2023). *Visible learning: The sequel.* Routledge.
Kimberley Language Resource Centre. (2018). *KLRC strategic plan: 2020 consultation draft.* https://klrc.org.au/wp-content/uploads/2020/10/KLRC-Strategic-Plan-August-2020-consultation-draft.pdf
Kiramba, L. K. (2017). Translanguaging in the writing of emergent multilinguals. *International Multilingual Research Journal, 11*(2), Article 2. https://doi.org/10.1080/19313152.2016.1239457
Kroik, D. (2023). *The construction of spaces for Saami language use: Language revitalisation in educational contexts.* https://urn.kb.se/resolve?urn=urn:nbn:se:umu:diva-205392
McGregor, W. B. (2004). *The languages of the Kimberley, Western Australia.* Taylor & Francis Group.
Moody, S. M., Matthews, S. D., & Eslami, Z. R. (2021). Translanguaging during shared read alouds: A case study. *Literacy Research and Instruction,* 1–24. https://doi.org/10.1080/19388071.2021.1889724

Murphy, V., & Evangelou, M. (Eds.). (2016). *Early childhood education in English for speakers of other languages.* British Council.

Naqvi, R., McKeough, A., Thorne, K., & Pfitscher, C. (2013). Dual-language books as an emergent-literacy resource: Culturally and linguistically responsive teaching and learning. *Journal of Early Childhood Literacy, 13*(4), 501–528. https://doi.org/10.1177/1468798412442886

Ollerhead, S., Crealy, I., & Kirk, R. (2020). 'Writing like a health scientist': A translingual approach to teaching text structure in a diverse Australian classroom. *Australian Journal of Applied Linguistics, 3*(1). https://doi.org/10.29140/ajal.v3n1.301

Osorio, S. L. (2020). Building culturally and linguistically sustaining spaces for emergent bilinguals: Using read-alouds to promote translanguaging. *The Reading Teacher, 74*(2), 127–135. https://doi.org/10.1002/trtr.1919

Pietikäinen, S., & Pitkänen-Huhta, A. (2013). Multimodal literacy practices in the Indigenous Sámi classroom: Children navigating in a complex multilingual setting. *Journal of Language, Identity & Education, 12*(4), Article 4. https://doi.org/10.1080/15348458.2013.818471

Pontier, R., & Gort, M. (2016). Coordinated translanguaging pedagogy as distributed cognition: A case study of two dual language bilingual education preschool coteachers' languaging practices during shared book readings. *International Multilingual Research Journal, 10*(2), 89–106. https://doi.org/10.1080/19313152.2016.1150732

Regional Development Australia Kimberley (2025). *About the Kimberley.* Regional Development Australia Kimberley. https://www.rdakimberley.com.au/about/about-the-kimberley/ Accessed 19 January 2025.

Roberts, C. A. (1995). Bilingual education program models: A framework for understanding. *Bilingual Research Journal: The Journal of the National Association for Bilingual Education, 19*(3–4), 369–378. https://doi.org/10.1080/15235882.1995.10162679.

Salmon, M., Doery, K., Dance, P., Chapman, J., Gilbert, R., Williams, R., & Lovett, R. (2019). *Defining the indefinable: Descriptors of Aboriginal and Torres Strait Islander Peoples' cultures and their links to health and wellbeing.* Aboriginal and Torres Strait Islander Health Team, Research School of Population Health, The Australian National University.

Sandefur, J. (1981). A new Aboriginal language? *The Australian Journal of Indigenous Education, 9*(1), 52–60.

Sandefur, J. R. (1979). *An Australian creole in the northern territory: A description of Ngukurr-Bamyili dialects.* Summer Institute of Linguistics.

Seals, C. A., Olsen-Reeder, V., Pine, R., Ash, M., & Wallace, C. (2020). Creating translingual teaching resources based on translanguaging grammar rules and pedagogical practices. *Australian Journal of Applied Linguistics, 3*(1), 115–132. https://doi.org/10.29140/ajal.v3n1.303

Sharifian, F. & The Department of Education WA. (2012). *Understanding stories my way: Aboriginal-English speaking students' (mis)understanding of school literacy materials in Australian English.* Department of Education WA.

Simpson, J., Caffery, J., & McConvell, P. (2009). *Gaps in Australia's Indigenous Language Policy: Dismantling Bilingual Education in the Northern Territory.* Australian Institute of Aboriginal and Torres Strait Islander Studies.

Steele, C. (2020). *Teaching Standard Australian English as a second dialect to Australian Indigenous children in primary school classrooms.* [Doctoral Dissertation]. University of Melbourne. https://rest.neptune-prod.its.unimelb.edu.au/server/api/core/bitstreams/9381369c-d887-5b4f-a9ef-cb71ee3b5ce6/content

Velasco, P., & García, O. (2014). Translanguaging and the writing of bilingual learners. *Bilingual Research Journal, 37*(1). https://doi.org/10.1080/15235882.2014.893270

Verdon, S., & McLeod, S. (2015). Indigenous language learning and maintenance among young Australian Aboriginal and Torres Strait Islander children. *International Journal of Early Childhood, 47*(1), 153–170. https://doi.org/10.1007/s13158-015-0131-3

Wei, L. (2011). Moment analysis and translanguaging space: Discursive construction of identities by multilingual Chinese youth in Britain. *Journal of Pragmatics*, *43*(5), 1222–1235. https://doi.org/10.1016/j.pragma.2010.07.035

Worthy, J., Durán, L., Hikida, M., Pruitt, A., & Peterson, K. (2013). Spaces for dynamic bilingualism in read-aloud discussions: Developing and strengthening bilingual and academic skills. *Bilingual Research Journal*, *36*(3), 311–328. https://doi.org/10.1080/15235882.2013.845622

Yang, S., Kiramba, L. K., & Wessels, S. (2021). Translanguaging for biliteracy: Book reading practices in a Chinese bilingual family. *Bilingual Research Journal*, *44*(1), 39–55. https://doi.org/10.1080/15235882.2021.1907486

Young, V. A., Barrett, R., Young-Rivera, Y., & Lovejoy, K. B. (2013). *Other People's English: Code-meshing, code-switching, and African American literacy*. Teachers College Press. http://ebookcentral.proquest.com/lib/curtin/detail.action?docID=3544837

Yuille, J. C., & Marshark, M. (1983). Imagery effects on memory: Theoretical interpretations. In A. A. Sheikh (Ed.), *Imagery: Current theory, research and application* (pp. 131–155). Wiley.

14 Understanding the EAL/D Extra

Assessing English as an Additional Language or Dialect in First Nations Contexts

Denise Angelo, Catherine Hudson, and Suberia Bowie

Who we are

Denise Angelo is a non-Indigenous languages researcher and teacher based at the Australian National University. She works with diverse First Nations communities and peoples and with schools on the many facets of Aboriginal and Torres Strait Islander language contexts: traditional languages, creole languages, and Englishes, including EAL/D.

Catherine Hudson is a non-Indigenous researcher and EAL/D specialist teacher based at the Australian National University. She researches EAL/D proficiency assessment which is inclusive of the language and learning needs of the full cohort of EAL/D learners, inclusive of Aboriginal and Torres Strait Islander EAL/D learners in their diverse language learning contexts.

Suberia Bowie is a Maluilgal, Badhu women from the Torres Strait Region in far north Queensland. She also has connections to the Wuthathi tribe on Cape York Peninsula area. Suberia has worked in schools as a teacher and in leadership positions for over 20 years mainly in the Torres Strait and Cairns region. Her key current role is to lead the Traditional Language and Culture curriculum and Cultural Capability within Tagai State College. Suberia has always been very passionate about improving teaching and learning within schools through utilising English as an Additional Language practices so students can access the curriculum.

Introduction

There should be nothing more natural in Australia than assessing English as an Additional Language/Dialect (EAL/D) learning for those First Nations students who are EAL/D learners. After all, in any educational context where instruction is given through the medium of the English language, the most vital learning characteristic is whether students are fully proficient in the English language, or whether they are in the process of learning it. If students are EAL/D learners, then EAL/D assessment tools can tell us how much of the English language they have acquired so far and what level of English language support they require in order to engage with curriculum content taught via the English language. Where First Nations EAL/D learners go unrecognised, however, they are not granted this extra EAL/D teaching. When EAL/D support is not provided it impacts on First Nations EAL/D learners' achievement throughout their schooling and on their post-school opportunities.

Research in Australia (Creagh, 2014) as well as internationally (Strand & Hessel, 2018) certainly shows the strong link between students' educational achievement in mainstream assessment and their proficiency in English. And yet assessment of English language proficiency is not consistently in the core suite of typical school assessments, nor does it appear in mandated national assessments, or through peak policies, such as the national First Nations policy, Closing the Gap. This is likely due to a lack of overall national EAL/D policy leadership, as jurisdictions utilise diverse EAL/D assessment tools and have documentation advising on their use. At the time of writing, state and territory tools include Bandscales State Schools (Queensland), the EAL/D Progress Map (Western Australia), NT EAL/D Learning Progression (Northern Territory), EAL/D Learning Progression (NSW, ACT, and Tasmania), Learning English: Achievement & Proficiency (LEAP) levels (SA) and English as an Additional Language (EAL) Victorian Curriculum Reporting Resource (Victoria).

In fact, there is currently no national policy in Australia for supporting EAL/D learners, First Nations, and/or overseas backgrounds, and English language proficiency assessment is also not an obligatory accountability required of jurisdictions by the federal government. In this policy environment, EAL/D assessment and reporting for First Nations EAL/D learners is often not consistent, both in terms of assessment implementation and in relation to teaching frameworks and responses. As a result, curriculum teaching and assessment may be unguided for First Nations EAL/D cohorts (Poetsch, 2020, 2023). This troubling state of affairs might possibly change if EAL/D learners do eventually become an identified equity cohort as has been recently recommended (Department of Education (DoE) (Australian), 2023; Productivity Commission, 2022). Despite this, since 2008, First Nations EAL/D learners in years 3, 5, 7, and 9 have been assessed for their achievement via the English language in the National Assessment Program – Literacy and Numeracy (NAPLAN), with their disaggregated results reported (the only group to be singled out in such a manner). This is also done without any guidelines for interpreting their scores according to their EAL/D proficiency levels (Angelo, 2013b; Lingard et al., 2012; Macqueen et al., 2019; Simpson et al., 2011). Similarly, young First Nations students in their first year of school are assessed triennially on the Australian Early Development Census (AEDC), without guidelines for interpreting the resulting early childhood educational picture for EAL/D learner cohorts (Angelo & Hudson, 2023).

This chapter seeks to address this inequity and imbalance. First Nations students who are EAL/D learners deserve fair treatment, and nothing could be fairer than acknowledging an English language learning need and responding to it appropriately in classrooms where the delivery of curriculum content is done via English. The authors use the terms 'First Nations' or 'Indigenous' with respectful intent to refer to Aboriginal and Torres Strait Islander peoples collectively. Torres Strait Islanders' homeland islands and seas are located in the Torres Strait between Cape York and Papua New Guinea, while Aboriginal peoples' countries embrace the mainland, Tasmania, and other islands and surrounding seas.

Our audience for this chapter is classroom teachers and their co-workers, aides, and tutors, including Aboriginal and Torres Strait Islander education workers, and advisers who assist with curriculum and literacy programs in schools. So, to begin, co-author Suberia Bowie, a Torres Strait Islander educator, and school leader, shares her personal experiences as a First Nations EAL/D learner to help us understand the importance of EAL/D assessment. Together, we then explain some of the dynamics that have influenced the too frequent omission of EAL/D assessment for First Nations students from education data, but why this information is pivotal for differentiating students who are learning English. Then we look at the practicalities of undertaking EAL/D assessment and how this assists teachers to provide the 'EAL/D extra' necessary for classroom learning. Finally, Suberia Bowie has the last word, entreating policy makers to back EAL/D assessment for First Nations EAL/D learners. We hope you find useful information here, with practical ideas for your classrooms and your students.

Orientation to the issues: First Nations educator on EAL/D and assessment

From the perspective of an EAL/D learner herself and as an educator who works with EAL/D learners, Suberia Bowie describes her position on the importance of EAL/D assessment for recognising EAL/D learning needs in the classroom as follows:

In my experience, from being a Torres Strait Islander raised in the Torres Strait on a small remote island, I think it's very important to recognise and support Indigenous EAL/D learners. My home languages are Yumplatok (Torres Strait Creole) and a bit of traditional language, Kala Lagaw Ya, the Mabuiag dialect. I understand what it's like to be a student who is multilingual and going through the challenges of trying to understand English at school, and all through university, too. The challenges you face are immense, especially where teachers don't have the training to explain things properly for EAL/D learners and don't know how to support you. You feel incompetent. Your confidence goes down. I have lived through that experience. I know what it's like to be that student. Whole classes of students can fail, all depending on a teacher's ability to break down the English language and explain it. We've also had teachers who have believed in us and have worked through the language with us so we could be successful in education.

I've experienced the challenges of not having that right EAL/D support throughout my education. I know there are so many ways that English language is an issue when education is delivered via that language when we're just learning it. So from my perspective it's very important that educators know how to teach and assess Indigenous EAL/D learners. Teachers should have English language teaching know how: they should build up learners' confidence and have expectations that they can and will achieve. Most teachers need to learn the EAL/D teaching skillset on purpose, seek it out and add it to what they already know. It's debilitating for EAL/D learners whose teachers don't have this EAL/D skillset.

EAL/D assessment – the Bandscales in Queensland, but other jurisdictions have other tools – shows teachers the differences for EAL/D learners. It gives teachers the capacity to identify the English language skills of the student and what English language skills they need to develop and what language support they need to do it. Assessment tools that don't factor in the English language are only looking at the mainstream curriculum side, the academic side, not at the basic, how English language works side. Mainstream assessment goes straight to the curriculum subjects, assuming that students are automatically able to apply the full English language, from the very start. In my experience, in 20 years of teaching, I'd say a lot of Indigenous students in remote communities and in nearby towns – like in the Torres Strait or Cairns in far north Queensland– are not confident in the basics of the English language. So I've seen the benefits of EAL/D assessment – 'bandscaling' as we call it – for alerting teachers to this learning need.

The case for EAL/D assessment for First Nations EAL/D learners

In seeking to gain consistent traction for recognising First Nations EAL/D learners and assessing and providing for their English learning needs, there are many issues at play. The most basic is that First Nations students are linguistically diverse. This means that the First Nations cohort includes children who speak English from birth as their main language and children who do not. So some children are speakers of English as a first language (L1), while some are learning English, adding it as an additional language (L2). For those who are L2 English language learners, they are often at beginning levels on school entry because English is not the main language of their family or community, who instead speak an Indigenous language, a traditional language or a new contact language, like a creole. The linguistic diversity within the First Nations language landscapes is often overlooked at a policy, but also a practice level. One reason for this may be that First Nations EAL/D learners and their traditional or contact language backgrounds are not a big presence in most of the capital cities where governments are based and where policies are generated. Is this perhaps a case of out of sight, out of mind?

Another reason may be that First Nations students are the sole ethno-cultural group to be disaggregated in Australian educational data, such as NAPLAN and the AEDC. This visibility as a single student cohort unfortunately encourages a one-size-fits-all construct that drives undifferentiated education targets and assessments for all First Nations students, as if they all have one and the same language background of full English language proficiency. The well-worn phrase of Australia's 'monolingual mindset' (Clyne, 2005) comes to mind, whereby speakers of languages other than English are blithely ignored. In any case, it is just not good enough to treat First Nations students as if they all speak English as their first and main language.

Another factor that has unfairly worked against the consistent use of EAL/D teaching and assessment approaches for First Nations EAL/D learners is the historically inconsistent recognition and support offered by education providers to the First Nations contingent of EAL/D learners compared to students with overseas language backgrounds. True, there have been targeted funding programs that have come and gone, such as the national English as a Second Language – Indigenous Language Speaking Students (ESL-ILSS) for First Nations EAL/D learners assessed at a beginner level in speaking in their first year of schooling, which ran from 1998 to 2009. However, any comparison between EAL/D learners with First Nations backgrounds and those with overseas backgrounds quickly reveals a disparity with more targeted EAL/D funding and specialist EAL/D support provisions for the latter cohort (Angelo & Hudson, 2020). The lack of consistently visible, nationally led EAL/D programs that intentionally include First Nations EAL/D learners has the effect of deprioritising EAL/D assessment tools and teaching support for this cohort. We argue that a national EAL/D policy would assist jurisdictions in prioritising EAL/D data collection by classroom educators or EAL/D specialists. Importantly, such evidence would acknowledge the presence of First Nations EAL/D learners and keep a focus on their English language learning needs.

Given the absence of national EAL/D policy and data collection, it is not surprising that EAL/D assessment has a low status on the assessment power hierarchy on the ground in schools. EAL/D assessment often loses out to mainstream literacy and numeracy assessment products and processes – those that are actually designed for students who are already full English speakers – a situation not only evidenced in Australia, but in many other English-dominant countries too (see Morita-Mullaney, 2017; Wheeler, 2016). The problem with mainstream assessments applied to EAL/D learners is that they give erroneous impressions about key indicators of progress and barriers for student learning, because no account is taken of students' proficiency in English, the medium of instruction and assessment. As a result, it wrongly seems all that is required is just more (and more) mainstream teaching, for example more literacy, which never addresses the underlying English language learning needs of the students. Furthermore, when mainstream assessments displace EAL/D assessments, this serves to prevent the collection of the type of evidence showing the need for EAL/D language support, in turn, 'invisibilising' EAL/D as a key teaching and learning consideration. As a result, EAL/D assessment can then seem optional rather than a core component for addressing the needs of this distinct cohort of learners.

In addition, and perhaps because of the multiple assessment and teaching burdens carried by educators, some teachers might feel it is simply too time consuming to also engage in EAL/D assessment given all the other assessment tasks they have to get through and report on. Or perhaps they may feel it is too hard, because of it being an unfamiliar assessment tool. However, none of this is necessarily the case. As with using any unfamiliar assessment tool, mainstream or EAL/D, teachers will naturally require some training and opportunity to learn to use it, but teachers will get quicker and more adept at using it with practice. This will be enhanced with systematic professional learning opportunities to develop their knowledge and understanding of EAL/D assessment and how it informs their teaching in ways that lift their EAL/D learners.

Assessment is an expected important part of teaching. We know that keeping track of student learning benefits students' learning. In English language medium classrooms, it is through the English language that students will engage with concepts and will demonstrate their learning. Therefore, EAL/D assessment is vital because it makes English language learning visible. Further, the real power of EAL/D assessment is that it recognises the English language as a factor, and this leads to the understanding that all learning is not housed exclusively with the student but depends on how as teachers we make it linguistically accessible.

Identifying First Nations students who are EAL/D learners

Identifying First Nations EAL/D learners (i.e. recognising that they are indeed EAL/D learners) is a key first step in recognising and responding to their English language learning needs. The next step involves assessing their level of English language learning needs. These steps provide the evidence that teaching approaches will need to be differentiated to include the 'EAL/D extra', the English language teaching and assessment that intentionally supports EAL/D learners.

Barriers to identifying First Nations EAL/D learners

Educators and policy makers might imagine that recognising First Nations EAL/D learners is easy. In actual fact, it turns out that identification has proven somewhat of a barrier to recognising some First Nations EAL/D learners because the right systems have not been put in place. As noted, one important issue is that EAL/D processes and services across Australia have historically been oriented towards students of overseas language backgrounds, often newly arrived and in urban areas, while First Nations EAL/D learners and their contexts have at times been entirely overlooked. Consequently, processes developed for identifying EAL/D learners have been tailored more towards overseas language and education backgrounds, such as questionnaires that ask for students' date of arrival in Australia, their visa category, their country of origin, their literacy and education backgrounds in their own language(s), and so on (Angelo, 2013a; Hudson et al., 2023). Education systems are now playing catch up on this equity issue and are at different stages in the endeavour of including First Nations EAL/D learners.

In addition to the historical legacy of omitting First Nations EAL/D learners, the nature of First Nations language situations can also cause some confusion. As described in chapters throughout this volume, colonisation has led to a diverse contemporary language landscape that includes original traditional Indigenous languages, Indigenous contact languages, such as creoles and mixed languages, and Indigenised Englishes. Generally, there has been a policy vacuum around awareness and recognition of the newer language varieties (Angelo, 2024) which has added further to the confusion. While in some Indigenous communities all local children share a well-recognised language background and are predictably EAL/D learners, in other places, for example in some regional towns, such as Broome WA, Alice Springs NT, or Cairns QLD, Indigenous students' family language backgrounds can vary extensively. Where a newer language is spoken, such as a creole or a heavy Aboriginal English, a standard name for it might not yet be current (Angelo, 2013a).

Practical steps towards identifying First Nations EAL/D learners

For their part, the role of classroom teachers is pivotal in recognising 'invisible' First Nations EAL/D learners. These EAL/D learners are not identified through simple 'on enrolment' processes, but rather through an 'in the classroom' pathway.

Teachers can learn about students' language backgrounds and whether they are potentially EAL/D learners. They do this through their classroom interactions and observations of students and their discussions with First Nations people. The examples in Figure 14.1 serve as 'conversation starters'. These prompts help teachers think about whether a First Nations student is an EAL/D learner.

What have you noticed about the student's way of talking?
Examples:

- When the student sees older siblings during lunch they seem to talk very fast together and I can hardly pick up anything they are saying.
- The student seems to drop a lot of little words, like a, the, is, are, of; and endings too e.g. walk (not walked), dog (not dogs).
- Some things the student says have different meanings: e means he/she/it, ahm means I did something. Pronunciations of words are different too.

How do you think the student's language impacts on classroom learning?
Examples:

- In whole-class situations, the student says very little. With me, one on one, the student says a bit more, with encouragement, usually single words or short phrases.
- The student doesn't understand me easily (so I don't like asking questions in front of the whole class).
- The student actively looks for extra support to confirm meaning, like looking for extra clues when I give instructions (e.g. watches what other students do).
- Student needs more than what I say to engage with lessons – 'visuals' or 'hands on' really support this student to engage.
- When we do a class topic and come back to it again and again so it's familiar, then the student can participate a bit more, otherwise it's much more limited.

What do First Nations staff and/or family say about the student's language/way of speaking?
Examples:

- The student talks the same as everyone in the family and from that community.
- We call it a 'heavy way' of speaking.
- You have to break English down for students from that community, so they can understand it.
- I'm family for the student – I can come and check in with the student and let you know how things are going.

Figure 14.1 Prompts for teachers considering the language background and potential EAL/D status of a First Nation's student

Recognising that an 'on enrolment' pathway does not always work for First Nations students and their families, teachers' observations should also be undertaken of their students' language learning behaviours, the language features they use in their interactions and classroom responses, discussions of their language background, and so forth. An educator's growing hypothesis that a student is an EAL/D learner would then be corroborated through EAL/D assessment such as the Bandscales (see Figure 14.2) used in Queensland, but teachers elsewhere would implement the tool current for their jurisdiction and schooling sector.

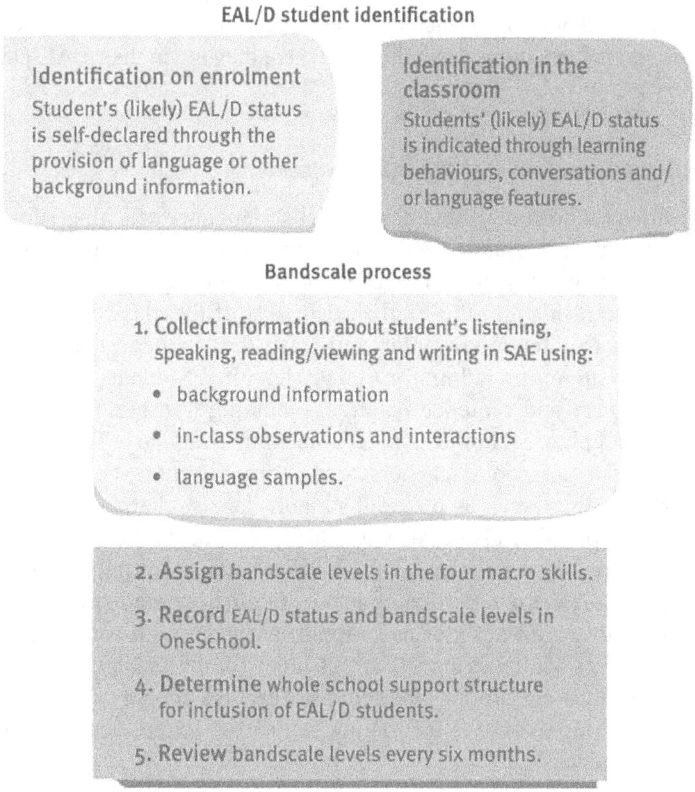

EAL/D student identification

Identification on enrolment
Student's (likely) EAL/D status is self-declared through the provision of language or other background information.

Identification in the classroom
Students' (likely) EAL/D status is indicated through learning behaviours, conversations and/or language features.

Bandscale process

1. Collect information about student's listening, speaking, reading/viewing and writing in SAE using:
   - background information
   - in-class observations and interactions
   - language samples.

2. Assign bandscale levels in the four macro skills.

3. Record EAL/D status and bandscale levels in OneSchool.

4. Determine whole school support structure for inclusion of EAL/D students.

5. Review bandscale levels every six months.

Figure 14.2 Identifying EAL/D students (Department of Education (DoE) (QLD) (2018, p. 9)
© State of Queensland (Department of Education) 2018 CC BY 4.0 creativecommons.org/licenses/by/4.0/

Assessed level of English language proficiency aligns with language teaching support

Regardless of the EAL/D proficiency tool in use in their jurisdiction and sector of schooling, all teachers need to respond to the differential needs of all their students. There is a general range of differentiation that applies to what we do for every student, typically accommodating their learning styles, their interests and aptitudes in different curriculum areas, as well as their social and emotional well-being and personal circumstances. In addition, students' specific learning needs require different kinds and levels of teaching differentiation. EAL/D learners require the 'EAL/D extra', namely English language teaching support: EAL/D assessment indicates how much.

To illustrate, we describe three very broad categories of EAL/D teaching support here. Note that these broad EAL/D support categories do not map exactly onto the levels/stages described in the many different EAL/D assessment tools currently used across Australian state and territory schools. Rather, these are illustrative of the extent and kind of EAL/D teaching support that is critical for EAL/D learners to access classroom curriculum depending on where they are in their EAL/D learning journey.

Intensive and differentiated EAL/D teaching support

EAL/D learners who require intensive English language teaching support may be beginner or post-beginner EAL/D learners. Teachers need to be aware that these learners have full proficiency of their first language(s) and need to work to bridge between this and the English demands of the classroom curriculum. They will need to intentionally plan and teach the language that underlies all classroom curriculum, including for literacy learning. Students will be learning everyday language and sentence patterns, including transactional and instructional words and phrases, not just subject-specific vocabulary. To support meaning making in the classroom, teachers need to provide context-enriched English language scaffolding (such as pictorial support, labels, charts, hands-on activities) and where possible also assistance through students' first languages. Students will require language to be highly familiarised (i.e. initially predominantly formulaic) to enable their participation via English in mainstream classroom learning. With this kind of extensive support around lesson content and taught language, students with beginner EAL/D levels could engage in predictable, routine face-to-face classroom interactions. Teachers support students' continued EAL/D development by encouraging students to extend on their formulaic and learned sentences.

Ongoing and targeted EAL/D teaching support

EAL/D learners who require substantial ongoing and targeted English language teaching support are pre-intermediate and intermediate language learners who need language scaffolding across all subject areas of the mainstream curriculum. Teachers need to know that these learners have full proficiency in their first language(s) – but literacy and education opportunities in their first language(s) vary widely – and teachers will need to work with them to bridge between this and their growing English language proficiency for classroom curriculum learning. Teachers can achieve this by analysing activities and tasks for their language demands and explicitly teaching these. The language of the topic, the background information, the key concepts, and the assessment task, are pre-taught to support maximal meaning making. Deeper understanding of taught curriculum is promoted cumulatively through a variety of meaning and language enhancing materials, such as illustrated resources, summaries of target content in PowerPoints, tables, displays, and where possible also opportunities for explanations/discussions in students' first languages. Key language patterns and the structuring of target text types on specific subjects are intentionally taught and students are given ample opportunities to practise, internalise, and extend on these. Revisiting and recycling taught language assists students to engage with classroom topics and enables students to develop independence in constructing their written texts, drawing on modelled text structures and language features. Teachers should encourage students' attempts to become more independent in their expression of complex ideas (rather than focusing on loss of accuracy) so that their language continues to develop.

Additional EAL/D teaching support

EAL/D learners who require additional English teaching support have levels of English language proficiency that enable them to access classroom curriculum with the teaching that is provided to all students. Students at this level can be missed as EAL/D learners, even though they can benefit a lot from the 'EAL/D extra', so teachers need to look beyond their general spoken and written proficiency (which for example may contain few overt EAL/D features) by identifying their EAL/D proficiency levels. Teachers support their students to value their additive multilingualism, by encouraging use and maintenance of their first language(s). Teachers should continue to break down tasks, with a focus on modelling and scaffolding the expected language components such as complex and varied sentence structures, cohesion, range and depth of vocabulary, text types, etc. Tasks are clarified through pre-teaching and post-teaching of language during reading and drafting processes, to address demonstrated language gaps, unfamiliar material, including cultural, subtleties, details, and so forth. At this level, EAL/D learners still require grammatical teaching and assistance with expressing complex thoughts, and expressing themselves in their own words, e.g. when summarising what they have read or watched.

Assessment and needs beyond EAL/D

If EAL/D learners in need of intensive or substantial ongoing targeted EAL/D support are placed in mainstream curriculum settings with insufficient English language teaching, it is highly likely that they will encounter difficulties accessing and engaging with the curriculum. For such reasons, concerns are sometimes raised about individual EAL/D learners and whether or not they might have additional learning needs beyond their EAL/D status. While in some cases this might be the situation, it is important to recognise that when EAL/D proficiency levels are not taken into account,

EAL/D learner characteristics can be misdiagnosed as their failing to learn rather than their showing progress on the lengthy journey of acquiring English as an L2. This also highlights how problematic it is to use mainstream curriculum and literacy assessment tools and standardised tests which are all designed for L1 English speakers.

Like any other student, any EAL/D learner could, of course, have a specific impairment that should receive specialist assistance. But how are EAL/D learning needs to be teased out from other potential needs when most assessment processes rely on English? A useful procedure developed for this purpose is outlined by Barker (2023) (see Figure 14.3). Should educators be concerned about the progress of an EAL/D learner, then a cycle of learning, teaching, and assessment needs to be planned that focuses on English language growth. This procedure ensures that the classroom educator gets assistance from educators with EAL/D expertise to put into practice EAL/D teaching approaches. Recording how the learner responds is key. If the learner makes progress, then this is evidence that an additional learning need is unlikely, and so the planned EAL/D approaches are continued to support their learning. If, however, there are still doubts, then a more comprehensive Personalised Learning Program (sometimes described as Individual Education Plan) is developed that focuses more intensively on supporting the classroom teacher with delivering effective EAL/D language support for the EAL/D learner's level of proficiency. An EAL/D assessment framework (the NLLIA Bandscales in this instance) can be used for this purpose. If after a period of 1–2 terms, there are still concerns then the student is referred for further assessment of other learning needs.

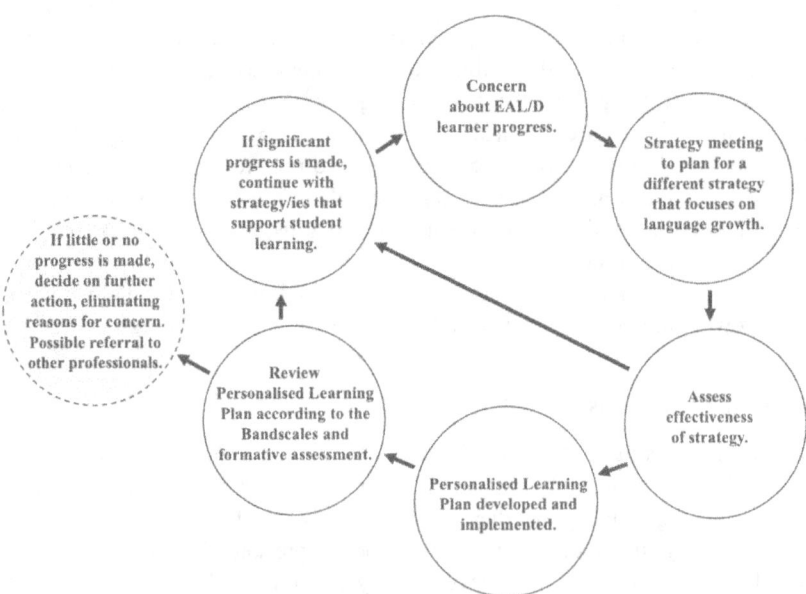

Figure 14.3 Process for distinguishing EAL/D versus an additional need *(Barker, 2023, p. 280)*

EAL/D Assessment and classroom support

Teachers need to assess and support the students' levels of English language development in Listening, Speaking, Reading/Viewing, and Writing using strategies from EAL/D pedagogy. In the following sections we outline assessment and support considerations in each of these four areas. Note: The Listening, Speaking, Reading, and Writing assessment observations draw on those in Department of Education (QLD) (2018 [2013], pp. 15–19).

EAL/D Listening assessment and support

EAL/D Listening tends to be the forgotten skill. It often gets overlooked entirely in literacy improvement agendas. Yet for EAL/D learners in classrooms where English is the medium of instruction, comprehension through listening is critical for engaging in classroom learning and accessing the curriculum.

Very often it is only when we come to assess a written piece of work at the end of a unit of work that we realise we were not aware of the extent of the listening comprehension needs of our students at early EAL/D levels. On the positive side, because listening for all learners tends to be sidelined, there is not a plethora of L1 English-based packages for listening that further marginalise EAL/D learning needs. Instead, teachers can develop targeted awareness of their students' EAL/D listening proficiency assessment in ways that support listening development, which can be transformative.

One cautionary note in this area, however, is that EAL/D listening assessment can be misdirected if the focus is on 'appropriate' behaviours, such as being quiet and paying attention. Indeed, nodding, smiling, or sitting quietly in the early EAL/D proficiency levels can be a strategy used by EAL/D learners to show their goodwill and efforts, but it can misleadingly give the impression that comprehension has taken place when this may not be the case at all (see Hudson et al., 2023). Indeed, descriptions of listening encountered in L1 English-based literacy-oriented progressions can give teachers a quite mistaken impression about the level of listening difficulty for an English language learner. For example, a text read aloud by a teacher that is 'simple' for L1 English speakers to comprehend is extremely unlikely to be 'simple' for an EAL/D learner in the early EAL/D proficiency levels. Listening comprehension for all learners may not be easy in certain contexts, for example with background noise or other distractions, but for EAL/D learners the degree of difficulty will be much greater, because of the added burden of actually understanding the target language. For example, processing specific information from a school assembly announcement will require advanced listening ability for an EAL/D learner, given that it will be announced with normal speed, no preparatory language teaching, no contextual support for meaning making, as well as with the likely distractions of other students and noise. Apart from the effort and concentration that will be needed, the interaction is not face-to-face so there is no chance that the speaker can accommodate to the listening needs of the EAL/D learner.

For teachers to assess the listening levels of their EAL/D learners, insight can be gained from matching classroom observations to the level descriptors on an EAL/D tool. Some of the questions a teacher may consider in assessing *early* EAL/D Listening levels are:

- To comprehend and participate, does the learner depend on familiarity of the topic, or familiarisation through the teaching and recycling of language and concepts?
- Does the learner need extra support, visuals, concrete experiences/materials to develop understandings of the topic (i.e. cannot rely solely on language for comprehension)?
- Does the learner rely on the teacher re-phrasing, attending to speed and/or providing extra wait-time to respond?
- Does the learner respond with rehearsed, high-frequency language, like short, high-frequency phrases drawn from the classroom learning context? Or is the learner able to self-formulate responses?
- Does the learner require one-to-one assistance after teacher instructions to clarify tasks?

Reflection on these observations, and the use of the EAL/D assessment tool, should lead to teachers putting the 'EAL/D extra' teaching and learning focus into their planning to enable better access to the curriculum for EAL/D learners.

EAL/D Speaking assessment and support

EAL/D Speaking can also suffer a lack of emphasis, as mainstream education has a strong focus on literacy, while oracy is often assumed. If speaking is included in mainstream developmental and curriculum frameworks, then it carries the assumption that students are already full L1 speakers of English. With L1 tools, therefore, the performances of EAL/D learners can look inadequate, especially those students in early levels of EAL/D proficiency. This mismatch of assessment for EAL/D learners can lead to misunderstandings about the challenges impeding EAL/D learners' performance. Such misunderstandings may take teachers in the direction of mistakenly referring their students to speech pathologists or towards potentially ineffectual, generic (as opposed to EAL/D) learning support.

To state again, it is in EAL/D proficiency frameworks that the EAL/D perspective is visible. EAL/D frameworks account for the L2 oral language development of students who are in the process of acquiring the English language. Use of an EAL/D framework will direct teachers to observe their interactions with students, and those between students, on the learning at hand (e.g. in a science unit, or a book read in class): how much language can students produce? Language assessment of this kind directs our attention to how classroom learning can be managed optimally. By adding the 'EAL/D extra' to their good teaching, teachers will be able to observe interactions that show students can more readily take up their classroom learning. This 'uptake' demonstrates to teachers that they are catering to the level of support necessary for their EAL/D learners.

Oral language is particularly crucial when very young learners are beginning their literacy learning. For example, predicting the language of a basic reader booklet involves knowing the language in it, distinguishing the sounds that letters represent involves knowing the language, understanding the language of a written text involves knowing the language, as does understanding any questions about it. Students with English as their first language bring at least four or five years' development in speaking English to learning and applying these literacy skills. First Nations EAL/D students bring the same oral development in their own languages but have the challenge of beginning literacy in the additional language that they are just learning (unless they go to one of the few bilingual schools and gain L1 literacy first). EAL/D assessment frameworks give teachers the extra guidance they need in supporting EAL/D learners to develop the oral proficiency in English that will support their classroom learning, including their literacy learning.

Teachers can gather evidence about their students' EAL/D speaking proficiency levels relatively easily from classroom-based interactions. Training will assist in developing these skills but, as with anything, teachers will get more efficient with experience. A point to note in terms of teacher time management is that the technical ease of recording speech nowadays is one thing, but transcribing for accuracy, and even choosing indicative interactions, can be time consuming (for examples of transcriptions of some young First Nations EAL/D learners speaking about a mainstream curriculum topic to demonstrate their classroom learning see Angelo and Hudson, 2018 and Poetsch, 2023). Also note that auto-transcription tends to work poorly with EAL/D learners' approximations.

Transcription is probably best saved for one-off teacher training sessions, working with the guidance of an experienced mentor. For example, the mentor can provide alerts about students' use of language and what this indicates in terms of EAL/D oral language development. In contrast, classroom teachers are constantly making observations about their students. So, putting a language perspective on these observations and noting them down creates the evidence on which teachers can assess learners' levels of speaking proficiency using their EAL/D assessment tool.

For assessing EAL/D Speaking, teachers could keep these questions in mind:

- Does the student rely on the teacher to work with them to co-construct responses to a familiar class topic (e.g. by careful listening, encouragingly re-stating what the student says, etc.)? Or can the student participate in a one-on-one conversation when the teacher adjusts the pace and allows more pausing?
- How much does the student say? Does the student mostly produce very short utterances (i.e. single words, short phrases)? Or can the student assemble their own sentences relatively independently? Could the student express their own ideas over a few sentences?
- How does the familiarity of the language and topic affect what the student can say?

- Does the student's language use mostly reflect rote (pre-assembled) language, highly familiarised from the classroom? Or does the student approximate English by 'having a go'? How close are these approximations – are they a barrier to meaning?
- For speakers of creoles and Indigenised Englishes: Do the student's utterances differ intentionally and significantly from home language?

EAL/D Reading assessment and support

Mainstream reading programmes and their assessments are not designed to support EAL/D learners develop their English language proficiency for the classroom purposes of learning to read nor of reading to learn. Rather, mainstream reading products cater for fully proficient speakers of English. For example, the subject matter of early reader booklets can be on any topic, which does not allow for the prior building of language required by EAL/D learners to optimise comprehension. Again, with mainstream reading products, there is no guide for interpreting or addressing the nature of EAL/D errors in reading texts out loud: for example, non-standard pronunciations, or omitting function words like *is, a, to,* etc. or dropping endings, like the *-ed* on *looked*. English speakers can produce accurate pronunciations and generate correct English sentences without effort so mainstream reading programs do not have anything to say on such matters. EAL/D learners may look like they have 'stalled' on mainstream reading assessments, whereas in actual fact they are internalising a whole additional language. This daunting task requires an EAL/D pedagogical reading approach. General reading interventions will not fulfil this purpose, since they assume that the readers are already speakers of English. In sum, in contrast to mainstream reading programs, EAL/D reading assessment tools account for the language factor, guiding mainstream teachers on how to interpret the performance of their EAL/D students so they will provide the 'EALD extra' for reading support.

Reading assessment using an EAL/D proficiency tool indicates the need for the 'EAL/D extra', so that EAL/D learners who are learning the English language, as well as developing early literacy, will not plateau at the decoding level in reading. EAL/D learners need explicit language teaching such as unfamiliar vocabulary and grammar, as well as literacy teaching such as phonemic awareness, phonics, word attack skills, and so forth. Unlike mainstream reading programs, EAL/D proficiency tools focus more on students' ability to use reading to access classroom learning. They are *not* constructed to show the rapid uptake of a single spelling pattern (like a phonics-based reader booklet) nor to measure the learning of countable, taught pieces of English (such as items in a sight words list or a few vocabulary words in a vocabulary program). EAL/D assessment tools *do* inform teachers, broadly, about EAL/D needs: about the accessibility of written materials for EAL/D learners and how to maximise this. They are tools that will make EAL/D reading needs visible and justify language-oriented approaches for these students.

EAL/D Reading assessment should lead teachers to reflect on the extent to which their teaching choices and actions have responded to EAL/D learners' levels of proficiency, and how we can improve our support. Classroom observations can be used to give teachers the information required to place learners on the levels of their EAL/D assessment tool. Example observations include:

- Can the learner locate written information in the classroom (e.g. words on the board, from displays, etc.)?
- Can the learner decode (read out loud)?
- Can the learner comprehend texts if the topic is well-familiarised and the language has been taught and recycled? Or can the learner extract meaning from a text on an unfamiliar topic?
- To what degree does the learner comprehend age-appropriate texts? Does the learner typically need extra information, such as illustrations, gestures, and re-phrasing, to assist with making meaning of the language in print?
- Does the learner require support to understand comprehension questions successfully? How much information can the learner provide?

Because mainstream reading packages are generally available and used in schools, classroom teachers should try to find creative ways to make them more productive and less unfair for EAL/D learners. For example, the language of a reader booklet can be pre-taught or revisited, with a view to teaching unfamiliar vocabulary and structures and giving EAL/D learners ample opportunity to 'get the hang of' the language and so build up confidence with reading it. Teachers can also make notes of language-based errors or questions which throw students off and plan focused language teaching in response. At best, mainstream reading packages provide us with observations of how our EAL/D learners manage untaught and unpractised language in texts that might also represent unfamiliar experiences and contexts.

EAL/D Writing assessment and support

The use of an EAL/D assessment tool brings understandings of EAL/D students' writing that ensures their progress. Again, mentoring or training assists teachers to develop additional EAL/D teaching and assessment skills. This augments the usual teacher skillsets required for mainstream writing approaches which assume L1 English proficiency. Genre-based approaches to writing, for example, tend to emphasise the end point product, and student writing is assessed according to a genre type framework. This does not guide teachers on how to build the language required to 'fill up' the target genre structure (cf. Angelo, 2012). Nor does this assess and evaluate students' writing for its EAL/D quotient, so it does not provide an evidence base for teachers that ensures and informs EAL/D differentiation. For example, in mainstream genre-based rubrics, there is no category monitoring production of ungrammatical learner approximations of English of various kinds, or the non-production of what for L1 English speakers would be the usual sentence patterns. Mainstream writing rubrics lack this language dimension. Thus, mainstream orientations to writing assessment mean that in the cycle of teaching, assessing and feedback, EAL/D learners will not be ensured of the language assistance they need – the 'EAL/D extra'.

Furthermore, when EAL/D learners progress to attempting to write complex thoughts – and their language errors consequently typically increase– this sign of progress will not necessarily be acknowledged. From a mainstream standpoint, it is likely to be appraised (erroneously) as a lack of achievement. From an EAL/D language perspective, however, an increase in complexity and expressiveness in writing needs encouragement. At this juncture in their development, EAL/D learners are moving from the safety at beginner levels of using formulaic language, to attempting to express complex thoughts, as they do in the intermediate levels. EAL/D assessment tools include this learner behaviour as a sign of progress. The increase in 'errors' requires a learning context supportive of risk-taking to enable ongoing EAL/D development. Use of an EAL/D assessment tool brings language learning and teaching into focus and makes the writing needs of EAL/D students visible.

How can teachers get information about the EAL/D writing levels their students are at and the degree of their needs for EAL/D support? A fruitful way of obtaining writing assessment information involves collecting small draft samples of student writing 'along the way', over the course of a unit of work. Such writing samples give us a window into what students can produce in written English (and into what they are picking up from classroom listening, speaking, and reading). Since these 'along the way samples' are not so crafted, they inform us about how students would express themselves, before scaffolding of the final genre 'product'. Likewise, drafts can help us reflect and improve on how we teach: the uptake of learning, the eventual familiarity of the topic, the words, sentences and connectors produced by students, including those that are generally expected but are not present or that prove troublesome.

EAL/D writing assessment is based on the ongoing observation of EAL/D learners writing outputs in the classroom. Through using EAL/D assessment frameworks for Writing, classroom teachers learn about how EAL/D learners develop their writing skills and the necessary degree of EAL/D support required to support their progress. Teachers can observe for example:

- How much writing does the learner generally produce? Is this an age-appropriate amount? Does the learner's writing reflect their EAL/D level of Speaking and Listening?
- What differences are apparent when the learner writes on the current class unit of work, where relevant language has been unpacked and recycled, versus a one-off writing task?
- Is the learner formulating their own sentences in English? Or are they reproducing formulaic language? Does the writing contain EAL/D learner features such as non-standard word forms?
- Does the writing contain signs of complex language and concepts? What resources does the learner employ to express events at different times, different tenses, temporal words or clauses, etc. How does the learner manage logical connections between clauses and sentences?

Concluding words

To conclude, First Nations educator and co-author, Suberia Bowie, from Tagai College in the Torres Strait, emphasises the pivotal role of EAL/D assessment for First Nations EAL/D learners and urges policy reform on their part.

There's a big push for equity and excellence in Indigenous education, but whether we achieve this depends on what guidance is given. Policy leaders in education need to ensure that policies are written to support English language development to achieve improved educational outcomes for Indigenous students who are EAL/D. If lessons are in English, how much English students have really matters. This is a really important fact. Assessing EAL/D for Indigenous students and teaching according to their EAL/D learning needs to be a core and consistent message, from the top. Too often, it appears that it's optional if and how schools recognise and teach their Indigenous students as EAL/D learners and then if they assess them appropriately, as EAL/D learners. It often comes down to individuals, like the principal, or an educator, to push it. This is not good enough.

There should be constant and consistent national policy direction from above to look after Indigenous EAL/D learners. But EAL/D assessment – together with the teaching responses it indicates – just gets forgotten. It's not in Closing the Gap at the national level. The Australian Curriculum doesn't emphasise it. NAPLAN data doesn't show it. There's always an emphasis on literacy assessments, which must come from people not understanding Indigenous students' language situations and where they are at with English language. Everybody just jumps on literacy as a one-size-fits-all solution for Indigenous students. They don't see the importance of English language in literacy or for student achievement across the whole curriculum (despite being taught in English).

From my point of view, language diversity amongst Aboriginal and Torres Strait Islander people is not factored enough into education, but it should be. Where is the research that looks at Indigenous students who have been brought up speaking English, versus those who have spoken a different language all their lives? We can't put all the Indigenous students in the one box. Even from my experience on various Indigenous education committees, I know that we might all be Indigenous and educators, but this does not mean that we share the same language backgrounds or same education experiences.

So it all comes back to data, languages, and EAL/D data. When it's not understood at the highest national policy levels how important EAL/D is for Indigenous students, then it's not pushed. If there is no national push, then there is no requirement for EAL/D data collection. If there is no solid national EAL/D data, there is no EAL/D evidence base showing how important it is. EAL/D assessment is the answer. The system should demand it and so should we.

References

Angelo, D. (2012). Sad stories. A preliminary study of NAPLAN practice texts analysing students' second language linguistic resources and the effects of these on their written narratives. In M. Ponsonnet, L. Dao, & M. Bowler (Eds.), *Proceedings of the 42nd Australian Linguistics Society conference - 2011*. http://hdl.handle.net/1885/9313

Angelo, D. (2013a). Identification and assessment contexts of Aboriginal and Torres Strait Islander learners of Standard Australian English: Challenges for the language testing community. *Papers in Language Testing and Assessment*, *2*(2), 67–102. https://doi.org/10.58379/XANY2922

Angelo, D. (2013b). NAPLAN implementation: Implications for classroom learning and teaching, with recommendations for improvement. *TESOL in Context*, *23*(1 & 2), 53–73.

Angelo, D. (2024). Indigenous language ecologies framework. A tool for inserting Indigenous contact languages and their speakers into policy in Australia. *Journal of Pidgin and Creole Languages*, *39*(1), 34–70. https://doi.org/10.1075/jpcl.00138.ang

Angelo, D., & Hudson, C. (2018). Dangerous conversations: Teacher-student interactions with unidentified English language learners. In G. Wigglesworth, J. Simpson, & J. Vaughan (Eds.), *Language practices of Indigenous youth* (pp. 207–235). Palgrave Macmillan.

Angelo, D., & Hudson, C. (2020). From the periphery to the centre: Securing the place at the heart of the TESOL field for First Nations learners of English as an Additional Language/Dialect. *TESOL in Context*, *29*(1), 5–35. https://doi.org/10.21153/tesol2020vol29no1art1421

Angelo, D., & Hudson, C. (2023). Phantom young English language learners: The shadowy presence of second language proficiency in (English medium) early childhood assessment. *Studies in Language Assessment*, *12*(2), 1–26. https://doi.org/10.58379/KCDT5699

Barker, B. (2023). EAL/D or an additional need? A cycle of learning, teaching and assessment to discern if an EAL/D student has additional needs to learning English. *Studies in Language Assessment*, *12*(2), 272–285. https://doi.org/10.58379/XSLO8306

Clyne, M. (2005). *Australia's language potential*. University of New South Wales Press.

Creagh, S. (2014). NAPLaN test data, ESL Bandscales and the validity of EAL/D teacher judgement of student performance. *TESOL in Context*, *24*(2), 30–50.

Department of Education (DoE) (Australian). (2023). *Improving outcomes for all: The report of the independent expert panel's review to inform a better and fairer education system*. https://www.education.gov.au/review-inform-better-and-fairer-education-system/resources/expert-panels-report

Department of Education (QLD). (2018 [2013]). *An introductory guide to the Bandscales State Schools (Queensland) for English as an additional language or dialect (EAL/D) learners*. https://education.qld.gov.au/student/Documents/intro-guide-bandscales-state-schools-qld.pdf

Hudson, C., Angelo, D., & Creagh, S. (2023). Instantiating justice, fairness and inclusiveness in English as an additional language/dialect assessment frameworks: Unpacking the evidence base for the Bandscales State Schools (Queensland). *Studies in Language Assessment*, *12*(2), 235–271.

Lingard, B., Creagh, S., & Vass, G. (2012). Education policy as numbers: Data categories and two Australian cases of misrecognition. *Journal of Education Policy*, *27*(3), 315–333. https://doi.org/10.1080/02680939.2011.605476

Macqueen, S., Knoch, U., Wigglesworth, G., Nordlinger, R., Singer, R., McNamara, T., & Brickle, R. (2019). The impact of national standardized literacy and numeracy testing on children and teaching staff in remote Australian Indigenous communities. *Language Testing*, *36*(2), 265–287. https://doi.org/10.1177/0265532218775758

Morita-Mullaney, P. (2017). Borrowing legitimacy as English learner (EL) leaders: Indiana's 14-year history with English language proficiency standards. *Language Testing*, *34*(2), 241–270. https://doi.org/10.1177/0265532216653430

Poetsch, S. (2020). Unrecognised language teaching: Teaching Australian curriculum content in remote Aboriginal community schools. *TESOL in Context*, *29*(1), 37–58. https://doi.org/10.21153/tesol2020vol29no1art1423

Poetsch, S. (2023). Unguided. Assessing young EAL/D learners' achievements in mainstream curriculum areas. *Studies in Language Assessment*, *12*(2), 28–58. https://doi.org/10.58379/ZROG5633.

Productivity Commission. (2022). *Review of the National School Reform Agreement* [Study Report]. https://www.pc.gov.au/inquiries/completed/school-agreement/report/school-agreement.pdf

Simpson, J., Wigglesworth, G., & Loakes, D. (2011). NAPLAN language assessments for Indigenous children in remote communities: Issues and problems. *Australian Review of Applied Linguistics*, *34*(3), 320–343.

Strand, S., & Hessel, A. (2018). English as an Additional Language, Proficiency in English and pupils' educational achievement: An analysis of Local Authority data. https://www.bell-foundation.org.uk/app/uploads/2018/10/EAL-PIE-and-Educational-Achievement-Report-2018-FV.pdf

Wheeler, R. (2016). 'So much research, so little change': Teaching standard English in African American classrooms. *The Annual Review of Linguistics*, *2*, 367–390, https://doi.org/10.1146/annurev-linguistics-011415-040434.

Conclusion

Carly Steele, Robyn Ober, and Rhonda Oliver

This book celebrates First Nations languages, the learning and teaching of these languages, and the important role that languages play in all facets of education. It gives due recognition to the resilience of Australia's First Nations peoples in being able to preserve and revitalise their traditional languages, but also their ability and adaptability to develop and use new languages. In fact, despite a history of oppression and overt policies and practices to suppress, even actively eradicate these languages from our linguistic landscape, First Nations languages not only continue to exist, but in some cases, flourish. This is heartening given that these languages are integral to the cultural and identity of Aboriginal and Torres Strait Islander peoples, and as a way for all Australians to connect with the Country to which they now belong.

The chapters in this book show how the authors have been able to challenge the monolingual mindset (Clyne, 2005) and the pervasive view that English is the "natural, neutral, and universal norm" (Zhang-Wu & Tian, 2023, p. 121). It is a view that has given licence to attitudes that do not value other languages nor the learning of them, rather it positions them on the periphery. In countries like Australia, where English is the dominant and majority language, other languages and their speakers can be marginalised in society. This can happen in official ways, through language policies for example, and unofficially, in the ways that minoritised languages are viewed by people in society. In Australia, speakers of Aboriginal and Torres Strait Islander languages – traditional, creole, and Aboriginal Englishes – have not been consistently and equitably included and serviced in education.

However, as we have seen in this book, educators are change agents. They are language activists, advocates, and allies. In many communities, it has been teachers and educators who have drawn attention to the mismatch between the language children bring to school and the mainstream medium of instruction (see Chapter 7). Chapter 7 describes a large body of work that educators and researchers have collectively produced to build the language awareness of students, other teachers, and the wider community about First Nations peoples' languages.

Such awareness includes recognition of the incredible linguistic diversity that existed before the colonisation of this country, and that continues to exist due to a diversity of factors. Some of this diversity has been captured in the chapters about the learning and teaching of traditional languages (see Chapters 3, 4, 5, 6). These traditional languages are being taught in the classroom through a variety of learner pathways. For example, in L1 learning contexts (Chapter 3), and language revival contexts in Chapters 4, 5, and 6.

Language awareness also involves developing and expanding our knowledge of new Indigenous contact languages such as creole languages, mixed languages, and Aboriginal Englishes, and the implications for speakers of these languages in the SAE-based education system. Chapters 7, 8, and 9 describe the evolution of these languages making clear the need for EAL/D approaches to be used with these First Nations learner cohorts. The chapters in section 5 expand on learning, teaching, and assessment approaches that educators can use in the classroom to respond in culturally and linguistically proactive ways.

Alongside the advocacy evident within this book, the chapters in this volume tell the stories of language activism taking place across the country. Activism extends beyond advocacy to include clear actions that redress past inequalities. This activism is seen at all levels. Chapters 1, 8, 11, 13, and 14 describe the individual efforts of First Nations educators in the schooling system and how through their teaching, they have been able to make a difference. Likewise, Chapter 3 describes the tireless work of Elizabeth, Barbara, Merrkiyawuy, and Fiona over many decades, as well as how they have worked collectively and with support from the Department of Education to deliver bilingual learning in their schools. This is mirrored in Chapter 4 through the work of Des and Larena.

Other chapters demonstrate community-driven language activism. For example, in Chapter 6 there is a description of the grassroots movement to establish the first Aboriginal bilingual school in NSW, the Gumbaynggirr Giingana Freedom School. Chapter 7 describes the community language projects undertaken in Far North Queensland to raise educators' awareness of First Nations children's language ecologies. In Chapter 10, we learn of the collective efforts of school leadership, educators, and the local community to transform the curriculum offered to embrace Gija ways of knowing, doing, and being.

There are also examples of system level responses. In chapter 5, there is an outline of the Aboriginal Languages Teacher Training Course that has been provided in WA since 1998. This unique support structure and learning opportunity has qualified many Aboriginal teachers and is responsible for the dramatic increase in teaching Aboriginal languages across the state with 160 graduates and 24 languages being taught to approximately 15,000 students. Chapter 9 is an introduction to Aboriginal English in education offered by Ian, Patricia, and Glenys, representing the collective efforts of university research with the Department of Education since the late 1970s. Such longevity in educational research and funded programs is exceedingly rare and speaks to incredible drive of both individuals and systems working together to improve teaching and learning.

What is common to all is that this work is not done overnight and instead represents decades of work, if not more. As Clark (Chapter 6) makes clear, their language learning and teaching has relied on the work of the generations prior.

Many of the educators in this book, both First Nations and non-Indigenous, have dedicated their whole professional lives to First Nations languages and language learning. This tireless activism and allyship needs to be recognised, but also better supported now and into the future.

Across Australia, there is a need for improved learning pathways for current and future First Nations language teachers, alongside appropriate recognition of their cultural and linguistic knowledge. This recognition also needs to be reflected in their employment conditions and salaries. Greater support for the development of resources is also required. Such work takes time, and appropriate levels of staffing with the requisite skills and knowledge base are required. States like WA have led change in this area, effectively supporting the training of Aboriginal language teachers and the resourcing of language learning and teaching materials. However, as made clear in Chapter 5, the demand for Aboriginal language programs is greater than they can currently support. Becoming an Aboriginal language teacher is highly skilled work. Moreover, the process of implementing programs requires extensive consultation as described in Chapter 2. Consequently, in this regard, there are no "quick fixes". As the educators in this book have demonstrated, it takes lifetimes or even generations to redress past injustices through establishing First Nations languages programs in schools. Further funding and systemic support is, of course, necessary and welcome in this area.

First Languages Australia is currently doing some important work in this area:

- *Yalbilinya: National First Languages Education Workforce Strategy* (First Languages Australia, 2023) *https://www.firstlanguages.org.au/yalbilinya-strategy*
- *Industrial Guidelines for Employees Delivering First Nations Language and Cultural Education Programs* (First Languages Australia, 2024) *https://www.firstlanguages.org.au/employment-guidelines*

Additionally, further research and educational responses are needed for teaching First Nations speakers of Indigenous creoles and Aboriginal Englishes, which represent a large learner cohort across Australia and especially in WA, NT, and Qld. There is also a continued need for further documentation of and knowledge about new Indigenous languages. This is essential to inform educational practice. As made clear in Chapter 7, our knowledge of *post-colonial Indigenous language is still evolving.*

The chapters in this book illustrate the range of language teaching methods and approaches that are being used across Australia including bilingual programs (Chapters 3 and 6), CLIL (Chapter 11), and translanguaging pedagogies (Chapters 12 and 13), with hopes for the further development of immersion programs (Chapter 6). These approaches offer educators exciting opportunities for language learning and teaching appropriate to their context that will provide solid groundwork for further future innovations in this field.

Universities and education systems also need to play a role in supporting the growth of knowledge and innovation as outlined above. Universities (for example, Batchelor Institute, UNSW, UniSA, ANU, Curtin, and more recently UQ) have played a strong role in supporting the growth of knowledge in this field through the provision of short-course learning, MOOCs (Massive Open Online Courses), graduate certificates, and even master's degrees in Indigenous Language Education (UNSW). However, there is certainly room for more growth. Of particular importance and as noted by Guenther et al. (2023), it is vital for universities to help graduate more local First Nations teachers because of their cultural and linguistic knowledge. Crucially, universities that offer Initial Teacher Education (ITE) degrees should provide the language knowledge and skills to all teacher graduates to enable them to understand the language landscape of Australia and the language ecologies of their students. This will help them in their teaching of First Nations students for both language learning and in all learning areas. It will also support teachers to act as advocates for First Nations languages and language learners in their contexts.

Finally, although there is still a long way to go in this area, there is real cause for celebration for what is being achieved, but also for the aspirations of those involved in this educational space.

References

Clyne, M. (2005). *Australia's language potential*. University of New South Wales Press.

First Languages Australia. (2023). *Yalbilinya: National First Languages Education Workforce Strategy 2023*. https://www.firstlanguages.org.au/yalbilinya-strategy

First Languages Australia. (2024). *Industrial Guidelines for Employees Delivering First Nations Language and Cultural Education Programs 2024*. https://www.firstlanguages.org.au/employment-guidelines

Guenther, J., Oliver, R., Holmes, C., Ober, R., Thorburn, K., Ridley, Dryden, S., & McCarthy, H. (2023). *Final report: Researching school engagement of Aboriginal students and their families from regional and remote areas project*. Emerging Priorities Program (EPP).

Zhang-Wu, Q., & Tian, Z. (2023). Raising critical language awareness in a translanguaging-infused teacher education course: Opportunities and challenges. *Journal of Language, Identity & Education, 22*(4), 376–395. https://doi.org/10.1080/15348458.2023.2202589

Index

Note: *Italicized* and **bold** page numbers refer to figures and tables.

4C's framework 187, 194

AAE *see* Australian Aboriginal English (AAE)
Aboriginal and Islander Education Officer (AIEO) 82, 93
Aboriginal and Torres Strait Islander Corporation of Languages: five C protocols for community language projects 28–34
Aboriginal and Torres Strait Islander Partnerships 71
Aboriginal Land Trust 31
Aboriginal languages 1–3; *see also individual entries*
Aboriginal Languages Teacher Training (ALTT) 84–86, 89, 90, 92, 249
Aboriginal Ranger Program 33
Aboriginal students, two-way approach in teaching 161–164
Aboriginal Teaching Assistants (ATAs) 174
ABS *see* Australian Bureau of Statistics (ABS)
ACARA *see* Australian Curriculum, Assessment and Reporting Authority (ACARA)
Accelerated Second Language Acquisition (ASLA) 100–102
accreditation 44, 90
ACT *see* Australian Capital Territory (ACT)
AEDC *see* Australian Early Development Census (AEDC)
AIATSIS *see* Australian Institute of Aboriginal and Torres Strait Islander Studies (AIATSIS)

AIEO *see* Aboriginal and Islander Education Officer (AIEO)
ALTT In-school Practicum Logbook 87
Amagula, J. 190
Anangu 33, 34
Angelo, D. 116, 130, 131
Anmatyerr 44
Appo, C. 70
Arapaho 100
Archibold, F. 99
Arrernte Curriculum Intelyape-lyape Akaltye 45
ASCL *see* Australian Standard Classification of Languages (ASCL)
ASLA *see* Accelerated Second Language Acquisition (ASLA)
Associate Diploma of Teaching (Aboriginal Schools) 45
ATAs *see* Aboriginal Teaching Assistants (ATAs)
At da Crick 122, *124*
Australian Aboriginal English (AAE) 12, 14, 16, 18, 20, 186, 199–208, 214–221; attitudes to 154–155; in education 152–166; form and formation of 155–160; implication for teachers 160–161; importance of 164–166; modification of **158–160**
Australian Bureau of Statistics (ABS) 116
Australian Capital Territory (ACT): EAL/D Learning Progression 229
Australian Copyright Act 1968 30
Australian Curriculum 69, 162, 165; Version 9.0 3

Australian Curriculum, Assessment and Reporting Authority (ACARA) 15, 203, 204; Framework for Aboriginal Languages and Torres Strait Islander Languages 2, 3, 13, 46, 68, 69, 82, 175
Australian Early Development Census (AEDC) 229, 231
Australian Institute of Aboriginal and Torres Strait Islander Studies (AIATSIS) 34, 74
Australian Languages Policy 2
Australian Standard Classification of Languages (ASCL) 116
awareness 125–126

Bachelor of Education Conversation Course (BECC) 93
Baited Remote Underwater Video Systems (BRUVS) 191
Baker, B. **145**
Balanda 52, 54, 59, 60
Ballangarry, G. F. 99
Bandscales for Aboriginal and Torres Strait Islander Learners ('Indigenous Bandscales') 129
Bandscales State Schools 229, 231
Bardi Jawi six seasons, learning 192–193
Bardi Language/two-way science program 190–192
Barker, B. 238
Batchelor College (later Batchelor Institute of Indigenous Tertiary Education) 57; Remote Area Teacher Education (RATE) program 45
BECC *see* Bachelor of Education Conversation Course (BECC)
Bell, J. 200
Bennett, L. 46
bilingual education 2, 20, 44, 137, 140
bilingualism: dangers of 101–102
bilingual programs 20, 44, 46, 48, 58, 115, 137
Bilingual Resource Development Unit (BRDU) 57–58
BMNAC *see* Bularri Muurlay Nyanggan Aboriginal Corporation (BMNAC)
Boornoolooloo (Purnululu) Aboriginal Independent Community School (PAICS) 173, 175, 179, 182
both-ways teaching 199–210, 215; children's home languages, recognition of 204–205; language and learning 201–203; language and literacy 203–204; language use and curriculum 203; strategies for 208–210; strengths-based approach 206–208; student teachers 205–206
Bow, C. 141–142
BRDU *see* Bilingual Resource Development Unit (BRDU)
Breen, G. 72
Bridging the Language Gap 130
Brisbane 73
BRUVS *see* Baited Remote Underwater Video Systems (BRUVS)
Buchanan, H. 'Tiger' 99
Bularri Muurlay Nyanggan Aboriginal Corporation (BMNAC) 100–101, 106
Bundgaard-Nielsen, R. **145**

Carle, E.: *From Head to Toe* 218
Carter, N. 131
CDU *see* Charles Darwin University (CDU)
Centring Anangu Voices project 33
Charles Darwin University (CDU) 57
Children's Ground 98, 101, 106
children's home languages, recognition of 204–205
CLIL *see* Content Language Integrated Learning (CLIL)
co-design 33–36
code-switching 162, 202, 215
collaboration 32–33; across and within schools 58–60
communicative competence 17
Communities and the Arts 71
Community Engagement Study, Ngukurr 141–142
Community School Plan 190
consent 28–30, 32, 37
contact language 136, 214–215, *217*
Content Language Integrated Learning (CLIL) 19, 184–194, 250; Aboriginal ways of being, doing, and knowing 189–190; Bardi Jawi six seasons, learning 192–193; Bardi Language/two-way science program 190–192; definition of 186–189, *188*; as theoretical and pedagogical approach 189
copyright 30–31
Coyle, D. 186, 187
creolisation 138–140
cultural tourism 102
Cummins, J. 176, 185

254 Index

D-BATE *see* Deakin-Batchelor-Aboriginal Teacher-Education (D-BATE)
Deakin-Batchelor-Aboriginal Teacher-Education (D-BATE) 45
Deakin University 45
Department of Treaty 71
De Silva, L. 99
Dhärratharra 54
Dhiṉ'thun Wayawu 59
Dhuwal 44
Dhuwaya 44
Djambarrpuyŋu 44
Dovchin, S. 155
dreaming stories 178–179
DSDATSIP 71, 73, 74

Eastern and African Cold Storage Company 139
Elders: community 51–57, 68; Gija 179; Gumbaynggirr 99, 100; Manambarram 174, 182
Elders Advisory Council 100
English as an Additional Language and/or Dialect (EAL/D) 5, 14–16, 18, 19, 67, 122, 123, 129, 174, 228–245, 249; additional EAL/D teaching support 237; approaches 20–21; assessment, for First Nations EAL/D learners 231–233; First Nations educator on 230–231; intensive and differentiated EAL/D teaching support 236; listening assessment and support 239–240; needs of 239–240, *240*; ongoing and targeted EAL/D teaching support 236–237; proficiency 235–236; reading assessment and support 242–243; speaking assessment and support 240–242; students, identifying *235*; writing assessment and support 243–244
Exell, M. 155

Far North Queensland Indigenous Schooling Support Unit (FNQISSU) 129
FELIKS *see* Fostering English Language in Kimberley Schools (FELIKS)
First Language Learner Pathway (L1) 13
First Languages Australia (FLA) 73, 85
first language teachers, training 57
First Nations EAL/D learners: barriers to identifying 233–234, *234*; EAL/D assessment for 231–233
First Nations Education System 101

FNQISSU *see* Far North Queensland Indigenous Schooling Support Unit (FNQISSU)
Fostering English Language in Kimberley Schools (FELIKS) 129
Framework for Aboriginal Languages and Torres Strait Islander Languages 2, 3, 13, 46, 68, 69, 82, 91, 175
French 19

Garcia, O. 163, 202–203
Garla-Daarimba Gumbaynggirr 98–99
Gaṯjirrk cycle 51–52, *53*
Gaṯjirrk Program 52
Gäwa Christian School 206
German 18
GGFS *see* Gumbaynggirr Giingana Freedom School (GGFS)
Giingan Gumbaynggirr Cultural Experience 102
Gija curriculum, Purnululu School 173–182; contesting 174–176; context 176–178, *178*; dreaming stories 178–179; Woorra Wooral Moonga 180–182, *181*
Gija Kriol 176
GNTPBC *see* Gunggari Native Title Prescribed Body Corporate (GNTPBC)
Gooniyandi 13, 15; in remote school, teaching 21–24, *23*
Goori 102
Graduate Certificate in Indigenous Language Revitalisation 70
Greymorning, N. 103
Gumbaynggirr Giingana Freedom School (GGFS) 96–106; birthright and agency, re-claiming 104; community classes 103; as extension of community, facilitating 102; parents and families 103–104; registration 105; tours 102–103
Gunggari 68; in Queensland 72–74; revitalisation 72, 74
Gunggari Learner's Guide 73
Gunggari Native Title Prescribed Body Corporate (GNTPBC) 72, 74
Gunggay-Yidiny 122
Gunn, J.: *We of the Never Never* 138
Guthadjaka, K. 206

Harris, F. *88*, 89
Hendy, C. 141–142
Holmer, N. 72
Hunter, J. 190

Index 255

ICIP *see* Indigenous Cultural and Intellectual Property (ICIP)
identity, language and 128
IETA *see* Indigenous Education and Training Alliance (IETA)
ILC *see* Indigenous Languages and Cultures (ILC)
immersion programs 19–20
Indigenous creole languages 111–112, *113*, 128
Indigenous Cultural and Intellectual Property (ICIP) 30–31, 71
Indigenous Education and Training Alliance (IETA) 129
Indigenous Elders 46
Indigenous language ecologies 120–122, **120**
Indigenous Languages and Cultures (ILC) 46, 56
Indigenous Registered Training Organisation 70
Indigenous Teacher Upgrade Program (ITUP) 57
Individual Education Plan 238
initial teacher education (ITE) 130, 251
Institute Public Administration Australia: Best Practice in Corporate Social Values 85
intellectual property rights 30
International Decade of Indigenous Languages (IDIL) 2
ITE *see* initial teacher education (ITE)
ITUP *see* Indigenous Teacher Upgrade Program (ITUP)

Jalumgal Girrwaadu Maaning 99–100
James Cook University: Teaching English as a Second Language to Indigenous Students 130
Janke, T. 71
Jaru 21
Joowijgarneny (Bowerbird) 177, 179–180

Kala Kawaw Ya 118
Kala Lagaw Ya 230
Kawa Kawaw Ya 66
Kickett-Tucker, C. 189–190
Kija 21
Kimberley: Aboriginal languages in 213–215, *213*; language and education in 215–216
Kimberley Kriol 200, 206
kirda 60
Kleyn, K. 163

Kogolo, A. 214
Kowanyama Creole 110, 116–117
Kriol 12, 14, 66, 110, 201, 204, 214; as 'broken English' 140–141; changing attitudes towards 141–142; consonants 143–145, **145**; Gija Kriol 176; grammar 148–149, **149**; Indigenous attitudes to 140; Kimberley Kriol 200, 206; linguistics 142; in Northern Territory 136–150; orthography 146–148, *147*; phonology 143; in Queensland 115; vocabulary 142–143; vowels 145, **145–146**
Kuku Yalanji language program 34
Kulai Aboriginal Preschool 103
kurdungurlu 60

Lajamanu 44
language, as stand-alone subjects 19
language awareness continuum 131, *131*
language deficiency 155
language disorders 155
language for learning 187
language learning, in schools 11–24; approaches 18–19; bilingual programs 20; case study 21–24; challenges 15–16; Content Language Integrated Learning 19; contexts 12–15; EAL/D approaches 20–21; immersion programs 19–20; opportunities 15–16
language minoritisation 126
language of learning 187
Language Policy and Planning (LPP) 67
language reclamation 14, 66, 70, 74, 90
language renewal (LRN) 13–14, 47
language revitalisation (LRV) 13, 47, 68, 70, 72, 74, 84, 86, **86–87**, 87, 100, 163
Language Revival Learner Pathway (LR) 13–14, 19
Languages Other Than English (LOTE) 82
LAPS *see* Literacy Acquisition for Pre-primary Students (LAPS)
Laurie, C. 'Bing' 99
Laves, G. 99
Laynhapuy Homelands School 49
LEAP *see* Learning English: Achievement & Proficiency (LEAP)
Leap, W. L. 163
Learning English: Achievement & Proficiency (LEAP) 229
lingua franca 137, 201
linguistically inclusive literacy learning environments 216–218

256 *Index*

linguistic racism 155
Lippi-Green, R. 127
literacy: development 212–224; language and 203–204
Literacy Acquisition for Pre-primary Students (LAPS) 212
Literature Production Centre, Yuendumu 57–58
Literature Production Centres 45
Lo Bianco, J. 176
local knowledge systems 51–57
local pedagogy 60–62
Logan 73
LOTE *see* Languages Other Than English (LOTE)
LPP *see* Language Policy and Planning (LPP)
LRN *see* language renewal (LRN)
LRV *see* language revitalisation (LRV)
Lutheran Hopevale Mission 118

Macassar pidgin 137–138
Making the Jump (Berry & Hudson) 129
Malcolm, I. 202
Manambarram Elders 174, 182
Mandarin 18
Marmion, D. 140
McCarthy, H. C. D. 190
Melanesian creole languages 112, *113*
Meriam 13
metalinguistic awareness 17, 219
metalinguistics 15
Miriwoong Language Centre 176
misrecognition 125
Mitchell River Mission 116
M. K. Turner Report 101
Moreton-Robinson, A. 5, 104
Mornington Island Creole 116
multilingualism 42–43, 67, 114, 119–121, 129, 132, 215, 216, 237
Munro, J. 149, **149**
Muurrbay Aboriginal Language and Culture Centre 99

NAIDOC (2024) 2, 3, 75, 82
NAPLAN *see* National Assessment Program in Literacy and Numeracy (NAPLAN)
National Assessment Program in Literacy and Numeracy (NAPLAN) 175, 186, 229, 231
National Capability Framework - Teaching Aboriginal and Torres Strait Islander EALD Learners 165

National Indigenous Languages Report (2020) 112
National Policy on Languages 2
NESA *see* NSW Education Standards Authority (NESA)
New South Wales (NSW) 138; EAL/D Learning Progression 229
Ngarrindjeri 14
Nicaraguan Sign Language (NSL) 139, 140
Nixon, L. 99
NLLIA Bandscales 238
Noongar 14
Noongar language curriculum 91
Northern Territory (NT) 2; bilingual programs 19; creolisation in 138–140; Department of Education 45, 137; Kriol 136–150; language ecology 42; NT EAL/D Learning Progression 229; pidgins in 137–138; teaching Aboriginal languages as first languages in 41–62
Northern Territory Curriculum Framework (NTCF) 45, 46
Northern Territory Indigenous Languages and Cultures (NTILC) 46, 47, *47*, 56, 57
noticing 125–126
NSL *see* Nicaraguan Sign Language (NSL)
NSW *see* New South Wales (NSW)
NSW Education Standards Authority (NESA) 105
NT *see* Northern Territory (NT)
NTCF *see* Northern Territory Curriculum Framework (NTCF)
NTILC *see* Northern Territory Indigenous Languages and Cultures (NTILC)
NTP *see* Nyanggan Tutoring Program (NTP)
Nyanggan Gapi Cafe and Catering 102
Nyanggan Tutoring Program (NTP) 102
Nyirrpi *43*, 48; in Warlpiri Triangle 44

O&EECs *see* Outdoor and Environmental Education Centres (O&EECs)
Oliver, R. 155, 186
orthography 16, 84, 144, 176; Kriol 146–148, *147*
Outdoor and Environmental Education Centres (O&EECs) 67
ownership 29, 31, 46, 78, 164, 194

PAICS *see* Boornoolooloo (Purnululu) Aboriginal Independent Community School (PAICS)
Papunya School Curriculum 45

Paul Ramsay Foundation (PRF) 105
Personalised Learning Program 238
Pintupi-Luritja 44
Poetsch, S. 127
prestige 127
PRF *see* Paul Ramsay Foundation (PRF)
Purnululu School: Gija curriculum 173–182

Qld *see* Queensland (Qld)
Queensland (Qld): Act of 1897 117; Bandscales State Schools 229, 231; Department of Education 123, 129, 239; educational initiatives 129–131; Englishes 119; First Nations language repertoires in 109–132, *111*; guidance for teachers 123; Gunggari in 72–74; Independent Schools Queensland 129; Indigenous creole languages 111–112, *113*; Kowanyama Creole 116–117; Kriol 115; Language Policy and Planning 67; 'Many Voices: Indigenous Languages Policy' 69; Mornington Island Creole 116; multilingualism 119–121; Outdoor and Environmental Education Centres 67; P-10 Aboriginal and Torres Strait Islander Languages Syllabus 68; schools, teaching First Nations languages in 66–78; State Library of Queensland 74; Torres Strait-Cape York Creole 114–115; traditional languages 118; Yagara in 75–77; Yarrie Lingo/Yarrabah Creole 117–118, 121–123

Right Talk Right Place (Knight) 129
Roper River Mission dormitory system 139

SA *see* South Australia (SA)
SAE *see* Standardised Australian English (SAE)
SAL *see* School of Australian Languages (SAL); School of Australian Linguistics (SAL)
Sandefur, J. R. 142–143, **149**
Sarra, C. 89
scaffolding 98, 142, 236, 237, 244
Schmidt, R. 125
School Curriculum and Standards Authority (SCSA) 176
School of Australian Languages (SAL) 45
School of Australian Linguistics (SAL) 44
School of Isolated and Distance Education (SIDE): Registered Training Organisation 90

Schultze-Berndt, E. **145, 149**
SCSA *see* School Curriculum and Standards Authority (SCSA)
second language/dialect acquisition 17–18
Second Language Learner Pathway (L2) 14, 19
second language literacy acquisition 216
Settlement of Woorabinda 118
Shannon, P. 99
Sharing Stories Foundation 180
Shepherdson College 58
SIDE *see* School of Isolated and Distance Education (SIDE)
Siegel, J. 163
Skinner, P. C. 99
slipping and sliding 202–203
SLSO *see* Student Learning Support Officer (SLSO)
South Australia (SA): Learning English: Achievement & Proficiency 229
sovereignty 104
SSL *see* Stronger Smarter Leadership (SSL) program
Standardised Australian English (SAE) 4, 5, 12, 14–16, 18, 20, 21, 66, 67, 122, 126, 127, 130, 132, 141–143, 145, 148, 149, 153, 154, 162, 175, 176, 186, 201–206, 209, 212–221, 224
status 127
Story Circles 221
strengths-based approach 201, 202, 204, 206–208
Stronger Smarter Leadership (SSL) program 89
Student Learning Support Officer (SLSO) 99
student teachers 205–206

TAFE NSW 105
Tasmania: EAL/D Learning Progression 229
Teacher Registration Board (TRB) 57
Teaching for Impact 165
teaching resources, in Aboriginal languages 57–58
Thirringgenji (Owlet Nightjar) 177, 179–180, *180*
Tiwi Language Curriculum 45
Toowoomba 73
Torres Strait-Cape York Creole 110, 114–115
Torres Strait Islander languages 1, 2
Townsville 74; Catholic Education Office (CEO) 129

TRA *see* Translanguaging Read Alouds (TRA)
Tracks to Two-Way Learning 152, 153
translanguaging 162, 202–203, 206, 212, 215–218; pedagogy 218; reading instruction 218–220; writing instruction 220–223, *222–223*
Translanguaging Read Alouds (TRA) 219
TRB *see* Teacher Registration Board (TRB)
Turner, M. K. 106
two-way teaching *see* both-ways teaching

UAM *see* United Aborigines Mission (UAM)
Understanding Children's Language Acquisition Project 130
UN International Year of Indigenous Languages 2
United Aborigines Mission (UAM) 189
United Nations Declaration on the Rights of Indigenous Peoples 2–3; Article 14 3, 175, 176
United Nations International Decade of Indigenous Languages 1
University of Queensland 70, 74; Indigenous Language Revitalisation Summer Intensive program 77
University of Sydney: MILE program 70, 72
University of Western Australia 83

van Gelderen, B. 206
Vass, G. 179
Victoria: Church Missionary Society (CMS) 139; English as an Additional Language (EAL) Victorian Curriculum Reporting Resource 229

WA *see* Western Australia (WA)
Wajarri languages curriculum 91
Walmajarri 13
Warlpiri Curriculum Framework (aka Warlpiri Theme Cycle) 45, 56, 61
Warlpiri Triangle: Nyirrpi in 44; teaching Aboriginal languages as first languages in **41–62**; Yuendumu in 44
Wei, L. 202–203
We're Going on a Bear Hunt 220
Western Australia (WA): 2023 Student Census 153–154; Aboriginal language program in schools, establishment of 85–86; Aboriginal Languages Resources File 83, *83*; Aboriginal Languages Teacher Training (ALTT) 84–86, 89, 90, 92; Aboriginal Teacher Training course 86–91, **86–87**, *88*; Department of Education 22, 82, 83, 85, 90, 153–154, 161–162; EAL/D Progress Map 229; Equal Employment Opportunity Diversity Award 85; Framework for Teaching Aboriginal Languages 83; LOTE 2000 strategy 82; Noongar language curriculum 91; School Curriculum and Standards Authority (SCSA) 176; strategic directions 2020–2024 85; Teachers Registration Board 88; teaching Aboriginal languages as first languages in 81–94, **82**; *Teaching for Impact* 165; Wajarri languages curriculum 91; West Australian Outcomes and Standards Framework 83; Yikan Noongar (awakening Noongar) 91–93
Western Australian Curriculum: Science 191
Western Australian Department of *Education's Quality Teaching Strategy* 165
Whitlam, G. 2
Wik Mungkan 66, 118
Williams, G. 104
Willowra 44
Wilson, B. 185
Wolfe, P. 1
Woorabinda 73
Woorie Talk 118
Woorra Wooral Moonga 180–182, *181*
Wubuy Curriculum 45

Yagara: in Queensland 75–77
Yambirrpa Schools: teaching Aboriginal languages as first languages in 49; vision statement *50*
yarning 32
Yarning Circles 221
Yarrabah Mission 117
Yarrie Lingo/Yarrabah Creole 66, 110, 112, 117–118, 121–123
Yikan Noongar (awakening Noongar) 91–93
Yirrkala *43*, 44, 48
Yirrkala School 137; Garma Maths and Galtha Rom 45; teaching Aboriginal languages as first languages in 51

Yolŋu 204; in north-east Arnhem Land 44; teaching Aboriginal languages as first languages in 41–62
Yolŋu Matha 137
Yuendumu *43*, 48; in Warlpiri Triangle 44
Yuendumu School Language Policy 60
Yugambeh 66

Yugul Mangi Development Aboriginal Corporation 142; *Meigim Kriol Strongbala* 'Making Kriol Strong' community education program 146
Yumplatok (Torres Strait Creole) 66, 110, 112, 114–115, 129
Yunupingu, M. 204

For Product Safety Concerns and Information please contact our EU representative GPSR@taylorandfrancis.com
Taylor & Francis Verlag GmbH, Kaufingerstraße 24, 80331 München, Germany

www.ingramcontent.com/pod-product-compliance
Lightning Source LLC
Chambersburg PA
CBHW050530300426
44113CB00012B/2035